D1447722

A LABOUR HISTORY OF IRELAND

A LABOUR HISTORY
OF IRELAND
1824–2000

EMMET O'CONNOR

UNIVERSITY COLLEGE DUBLIN PRESS
PREAS CHOLÁISTE OLLSCOILE BHAILE ÁTHA CLIATH

First published 2011
by University College Dublin Press
Newman House
86 St Stephen's Green
Dublin 2
Ireland
www.ucdpress.ie

ISBN 978-1-906359-56-0

CIP data available from the British Library

*The right of Emmet O'Connor to be identified as the
author of this work has been asserted by him*

Typeset in Scotland in Adobe Caslon
and Bodoni Oldstyle by Ryan Shiels
Printed in England on acid-free paper by
CPI Antony Rowe, Chippenham, Wilts.

Contents

—

Illustrations

—

Preface to the Second Edition

—

The first book on labour by an Irish based academic appeared in 1920. The second appeared in 1977. That says a lot about Irish academics.

The period between 1909 and 1923 was something of a false dawn. These heroic years, of James Connolly and Big Jim Larkin, of syndicalism and soviets, saw the publication of histories of the 1913 lockout and the Citizen Army, the first general history of Labour, and numerous labour-related pamphlets. By the mid 1920s, trade unions had lost a series of big strikes in the post-war slump, which left them divided and in decline. The expectation that Labour would be politically important in independent Ireland turned out to be mistaken. That industrial Labour recovered some importance from the 1930s was small beer to historians preoccupied with politics. In the half century after independence, radicals sustained a pamphleteering tradition, but academic publications on Labour tended to come at lengthy intervals, from writers based abroad.

Change came in the 1970s, as Ireland connected with the so-called new labour history. The first wave of written labour history, in the late nineteenth century, was penned by Marxists, social reformers, or anti-socialists. The best remembered Irish example is Connolly's work, especially his *Labour in Irish History*. The second wave, in the 1920s and 1930s, was dominated by partisan, organisational histories, written by party soldiers in the social democratic or communist traditions. New labour history was a third wave, led by academics from 1945. Its development in Ireland was underpinned by the formation of the Irish Labour History Society in 1973, and the Society's annual journal, *Saothar*. Irish labour history seemed to be an idea whose time had come. The 1960s had seen a new wave of industrialisation, a big growth in union membership, and the issues which had divided unions since the 1920s were finally being left behind. In some quarters it was believed that with industrialisation and urbanisation, Labour must inevitably come into its own. The bibliography now includes an extensive corpus of monographs, and the heightened awareness of the subject is evident in the increased output of commissioned trade union and trades council histories. The chief disappointment has been its limited impact on public history – the view of the past generated by museums, libraries, the media, local societies and so on – which remains inordinately engrossed with nationalism.

As with the earlier version, this edition is intended as an introduction for the general reader and a synopsis for the specialist. The basic aim has been to outline the course of labour history, to set out the different phases of its chronology, and to determine the forces behind its development. While the text has been heavily revised, the two central themes remain. The first of these, unsurprisingly, is the evolution and efficiency of structures, policies, leaderships, and politics. The second theme, the impact of colonisation, may require an explanation. From the 1830s onwards, the trajectory and mentality of trade unions were dictated by economic and political colonisation. During the 1890s, a more complex factor was added to the equation as trade unionism itself was colonised. Attempts to deal with this legacy became intertwined with the class theme in the twentieth century.

Public history needs to move on. In the 1960s, nationalism became displaced by liberalism as the dominant ideology in Irish life. Labour historians too have much catching up to do. As we connected with the third wave, colleagues elsewhere were surfing a fourth wave, distinguished by a rejection of teleology, a challenge to traditional definitions of work by including non-waged labour; and a desire to go beyond the workshop to consider workers in leisure, family, and social relations, and to explore gender, sexual orientations, identities, and mentalities. The 'fall of the wall' in 1989 generated a fifth wave, characterised by an ambition to integrate labour with kindred studies, in gender, race, and culture; and by a greater emphasis on transnational comparison, and on labour as a globalised concept. In Ireland, debate on these topics has hardly begun, and one can only hope that they will shape historiography in the decades ahead.

Acknowledgements

Again I am obliged to Fergal Tobin and Gill and Macmillan for publishing, and to those who assisted with the writing of, the 1992 edition: Professor Fergus D'Arcy, colleagues in the Irish Labour History Society, Nóirín Greene for advice on trade union records, Donal Nevin for details on the origin of *Trade Union Information*, Jim Mullen and Charlie Spillane for technical assistance, and the staffs of the National Archives of Ireland, the National Library, the National Archives of the UK, the British Library, the Public Record Office of Northern Ireland, the University of Ulster libraries in Coleraine and Derry, and Waterford Muncipal Library.

For the second addition I am indebted to the readers for suggestions, and for information and help with sources to John Black, the indomitable Andy Boyd, Martin Cowley, Ciarán Crossey, Adrian Grant, John Halstead, John Martin Hearne, Seán Kelly, Fintan Lane, Edward Longwill, Conor McCabe, Christiane McGuffin, Barry McLoughlin, Eunan O'Halpin, and Michael Taft; the staffs of the Belfast Newspaper Library, the Imperial War Museum, London, the International Labour Organization, Geneva, and the Russian State Archive for Social and Political History, Moscow; and colleagues in the English Society for the Study of Labour History and the International Association of Labour History Institutes. Assistance with illustrations was given by Michelle Ashmore, National Museums, Northern Ireland Picture Library; Frank Boyd, Belfast; John Cunningham, Galway; Jim Collins and Adrian Kerr, Derry; Glenn Dunne, National Library of Ireland; the Irish Labour History Society; Susan Kennedy, Lensmen; Commandant Victor Laing, Military Archives; Joe McLaughlin, University of Ulster Library; Trevor Parkhill, Ulster Museum; Charlie Spillane and Donal Moore, Waterford; and Eamonn Thornton, Drogheda. As ever, the staff of Magee College library persevered in searching for publications through that wonderful relic of free education, the inter-library loan service, and I am grateful to other staff and students at Magee for inspiration and encouragement. Once again it has been a pleasure to collaborate with UCD Press and Barbara Mennell and Noelle Moran, who work with such an endearing minimum of fuss.

Finally, a special thanks is due to Collette, Laura, Deaglán and his Staffordshire Bull Terrier (it's hard to know where the boy ends and the dog begins), and Teena, to whom this edition is dedicated.

All errors are my own responsibility.

EMMET O'CONNOR
University of Ulster
Magee College
July, 2011

Abbreviations and Notes on Terms

—

ORGANISATIONS, NAMES, PLACES AND TITLES

ASE	Amalgamated Society of Engineers
ASRS	Amalgamated Society of Railway Servants
ATGWU	Amalgamated Transport and General Workers' Union
BTUC	British Trades Union Congress
CBI-NI	Confederation of British Industry, Northern Ireland
CDU	Campaign for Democracy in Ulster
CIU	Congress of Irish Unions
CoIU	Council of Irish Unions
CPGB	Communist Party of Great Britain
CPI	Communist Party of Ireland
DL	Democratic Left
ECCI	Executive Committee of the Communist International
EEC	European Economic Community
EU	European Union
FUE	Federated Union of Employers
FWUI	Federated Workers' Union of Ireland
GPO	General Post Office
ICTU	Irish Congress of Trade Unions
IDA	Industrial Development Authority
ILLA	Irish Land and Labour Association
ILO	International Labour Organization
ILP	Independent Labour Party
ILPTUC	Irish Labour Party and Trade Union Congress
INTO	Irish National Teachers' Organisation
IPP	Irish Parliamentary Party
IRA	Irish Republican Army
IRB	Irish Republican Brotherhood
IrLP	Irish Labour Party
ISRP	Irish Socialist Republican Party
ITGWU	Irish Transport and General Workers' Union
ITUC	Irish Trade(s) Union Congress
ITUCLP	Irish Trade Union Congress and Labour Party

IWL	Irish Worker League
IWW	The Industrial Workers of the World ['The Wobblies']
LAW	Loyalist Association of Workers
LRA	Labour Relations Agency
LRC	Labour Representative Committee
LSE	London School of Economics
MEP	Member of the European Parliament
MP	Member of Parliament
NAUL	National Amalgamated Union of Labour
NESC	National Economic and Social Council
NIC	Northern Ireland Committee
NICRA	Northern Ireland Civil Rights Association
NILP	Northern Ireland Labour Party
NIO	Northern Ireland Office
NUDL	National Union of Dock Labourers
NUGGL	National Union of Gasworkers and General Labourers
NUR	National Union of Railwaymen
NWA	National Wage Agreement
OBU	One Big Union
PAYE	Pay As You Earn
PD	People's Democracy
PDs	Progressive Democrats
PESP	Programme for Economic and Social Progress
PNR	Programme for National Recovery
POUM	Partido Obrero de Unificación Marxista
PUO	Provisional United Organisation
PUP	Progressive Unionist Party
RIC	Royal Irish Constabulary
RTE	Radio Telefís Éireann
RUC	Royal Ulster Constabulary
RWG	Revolutionary Workers' Groups
SDF	Social Democratic Federation
SDLP	Social Democratic and Labour Party
SFWP	Sinn Féin/the Workers' Party
SIPTU	Services, Industrial, Professional, and Technical Union
SPI	Socialist Party of Ireland
TD	Teachta Dála
UDP	Ulster Defence Association
UK	United Kingdom
UTA	United Trades Association
UULA	Ulster Unionist Labour Association

UWC	Ulster Workers' Council
WP	Workers' Party
WUI	Workers' Union of Ireland

SOURCES, ARCHIVES AND LIBRARIES

BPP	British Parliamentary Papers
NAI	National Archives of Ireland
NAUK	National Archives of the United Kingdom
NLI	National Library of Ireland
QUB	The Queen's University, Belfast
RGASPI	Rossiiskii Gosudartsvennyi Arkhiv Sotsial'no-Politischeskoi Istorii (Russian State Archive for Social and Political History)
TCD	Trinity College, Dublin
UCC	University College, Cork
UCD	University College, Dublin
UCDA	University College, Dublin Archives
UUMC	University of Ulster, Magee College

NOTES ON TERMS AND MONEY VALUES

By 'Labour' is meant trade union bodies or related political groups, or officials of these organisations. Workers otherwise are referred to as 'labour'.

To distinguish them from trade unionists, the usual convention is adopted of referring to supporters of the Act of Union between Britain and Ireland as 'Unionists', whether members of the Unionist Party or not.

The Irish Trades Union Congress was founded in 1894, added 'and Labour Party' to its name in 1914, changed the title to the Irish Labour Party and Trade Union Congress in 1918, and to the Irish Trade Union Congress in 1930. Throughout this period it was also known simply as Congress.

Following the conventional usage, the Irish Labour Party is referred to as the IrLP in the context of Northern Ireland and the Labour Party in the context of the south.

In 1826 the Irish pound was abolished and replaced with sterling. An Irish pound was reintroduced in 1928, but was pegged with sterling, divided into similar units, and used interchangeably with sterling throughout Ireland up to 1979, when it broke parity and ceased to be accepted in Northern Ireland. In 2002 the Irish pound was replaced in circulation with the Euro. Before decimalisation in 1971, the pound was composed of 20 shillings, and the shilling was composed of 12 pennies. Wage rates between one and two pounds were conventionally expressed in shillings, so that it was more usual to write 25s than £1 5s od, or 26s 9d instead of £1 6s 9d. This practice is followed in the text when noting rates of pay. In other cases, however, monetary amounts are set out in the more usual way for pre-decimal currency, using the £ s d symbols in full. After decimalisation, the pound was divided into 100 pence.

Prologue

—

Following the partial conquest of Ireland in the late twelfth century, the royal charters granted to Anglo-Norman towns provided for trade representation in companies of gilds, which brought journeymen and masters together for the good of their common calling.[1] The gilds were built into the political system. After serving seven years indenture to a member of the gild, a journeyman would be made free on payment of levies to the gild and the Corporation. He might then petition for the freedom of the city and the right to vote. In their economic role, the gilds enjoyed powerful privileges. They could regulate working practices and apprenticeships. Through the Corporations and the assizes they could set wages and prices. Gilds also had a benefit function, and from their sundry incomes could assist needy brethren in distress. In theory, the arrangement offered a mutual accommodation to masters and men, while subordinating both to the common welfare. The gild protected the masters by controlling wages; it protected the employment and wages of journeymen by restricting apprentice-ships and fixing prices; and it protected the consumer by maintaining standards of workmanship. Similarly, the Corporation and the courts could prevent a gild from abusing its privileges, while gildsmen collectively as enfranchised citizens could ensure that municipal government served the interests of commerce. In practice, the system depended on a careful management of the labour supply to restrain either masters or men, on the journeymen's prospects of becoming masters, on medieval social values, and on an economy based on trade rather than industry, and geared to a sheltered local market.

During the seventeenth century, control of the gilds passed back and forth between Catholics and Protestants. Protestants introduced the status of lay, or quarter brother – so called because their membership had to be renewed each quarter – for Catholic gildsmen, permitting them to carry on their trade under

---

1   On the gilds see J. J. Webb, *The Guilds of Dublin* (Dublin, 1929); Seán Daly, *Cork, A City in Crisis: A History of Labour Conflict and Social Misery, 1870–1872, Vol. 1* (Cork, 1978), pp. 253–81; Séamus Pender, 'The gilds of Waterford, 1650–1700, parts I–V', *Journal of the Cork Historical and Archaeological Society* (1953–7), pp. 58–62; and John Cunningham, *'A Town Tormented by the Sea': Galway, 1790–1914* (Dublin, 2004), pp. 74–5, 108–9.

certain disadvantages. Catholics restored their liberties under the brief tenure
of the Jacobite Corporations. The Williamite settlement finally secured a
Protestant ascendancy. As sectarianism intensified under the Penal Laws, the
gilds became instruments of Protestant privilege and levied quarterage
payments on Catholic merchants, shopkeepers, and artisans. Their lingering
claim to serve the common good of the trade was compromised too by the
increasing exclusion of Protestant journeymen from gild membership and the
municipal franchise. The gilds' purpose was in any case in decline. With the
emergence of capitalism, liberalism, mechanisation, and specialisation, parliament began to dismantle or appropriate historic gild functions. Faced with the
collapse of old mechanisms of trade regulation and the alienation of the
masters, journeymen combined in defence of their working interests.

The process of combination was under way from the 1670s in Dublin, and
the early eighteenth century in the provinces.[2] Normally, combinations were
formed for specific purposes such as the defence of wages, hours, and conditions, the regulation of apprenticeships, or the exclusion of 'colts' – men who
had not served a proper apprenticeship – or strangers, and disbanded if the
demands were met; though in Dublin, Belfast, and Cork some combinations
evolved into societies. As traditional forms of control corroded, employers
turned to parliament for help. From 1729 onwards, a series of acts was passed
making combinations of masters or men illegal. In practice, the masters had
little fear of prosecution. For the most part, the acts had no greater effect than
the battery of local statutory restrictions governing industrial relations, and
depended in any case on local law enforcement. Demands for tougher acts
mounted regardless. An economic boom from the 1780s to the end of the
Napoleonic wars, big increases in wages and bigger increases in the cost of
living, brought intense industrial stress. In 1780, the Irish Grand Committee
for Trade concluded that combinations were becoming a threat to prosperity,
and noted that 'committees of trade' among weavers, butchers, coopers, tailors,
and shoemakers were spreading throughout Ireland. Parliament responded
with three combination acts, one applying to the silk trade, another to the
butter and provisions trades, and the third applying generally. A further six

2   Eighteenth-century labour is still in the realm of proto-history, but see John W. Boyle, *The Irish
Labor Movement in the Nineteenth Century* (Washington DC, 1989), pp. 7–25; Andrew Boyd, *The Rise
of the Irish Trade Unions* (Tralee, 1985), pp. 11–30; Fergus A. D'Arcy and Ken Hannigan (eds), *Workers
in Union: Documents and Commentaries on the History of Irish Labour* (Dublin, 1988), pp. 2–3; M. G.
Doyle, 'The development of industrial organisation amongst skilled artisans in Ireland, 1780–1838' (M.
Phil, Southampton, 1973); Brian Henry, 'Combinations, the law, and industrial violence in late
eighteenth-century Dublin', *Saothar* 18 (1993), pp. 19–33; John Swift, *A History of the Dublin Bakers and
Others* (Dublin 1948); and Daly, *Cork, A City in Crisis*, pp. 253–81.

acts were passed by 1789. The general act of 1780 was particularly draconian. It allowed masters to employ as many apprentices as they wished, made it illegal to belong to a journeymen's association, possess membership cards, make wage demands, or hold a meeting of more than seven journeymen, and extended the death penalty to those convicted of attacks on workshops, tools or materials. Twenty thousand artisans paraded in the Phoenix Park in protest, public meetings being lawful for the purpose of petitioning parliament.

By the 1780s, regular combinations of Dublin artisans were functioning under the guise of friendly societies. At least three aggregate assemblies of the Dublin trades were held, in 1789, 1814, and 1824.[3] Dublin societies were certainly the best organised in Ireland and evidently secured a degree of toleration from the masters and magistrates. In Belfast, combination was most advanced among cotton weavers, who were able to negotiate wages with their masters in 1792, 1810, and 1818.[4] Cork's Common Council had an act passed through parliament in 1764 'to prevent unlawful assemblies and combinations of artificers, journeymen, apprentices, labourers, and manufacturers [which] have of late greatly increased in the said city. . .'.[5] Waterford coopers were active in combination from the 1770s, though there is no evidence of a regular society behind them.[6] Generally speaking, provincial combinators were more likely to operate in clandestine conditions and face blacklisting, imprisonment, or fines. Records of strikes, or 'turn outs', appear with increasing frequency from the 1760s, and there were general turn outs in the early 1800s, when wartime inflation spurred unskilled operatives into combination. Unable to enforce a scarcity of labour by regulating apprenticeships, these men processed wage claims through anonymous, threatening letters. Aside from employer hostility, use of the law, and social inequality, the routine brutality of living conditions gave industrial relations an aggressive edge. Violence to property, and sometimes to masters or scabs – as strike-breakers came to be called – made turn outs notorious up to the 1840s.

Genealogically, it is valid to trace the origins of modern trade unionism in the continuum of gilds, combinations, journeymen's associations, and craft unions. Yet trade unionism is not a tradition, but an idea: one which requires no antiquity or arcane ritual to be adopted at any time by any group of persons. The importance of craftsmen lay not in devising, or even sustaining the concept, but in creating its most elaborate expression before the 1890s. The core

---

3 Boyle, *The Irish Labor Movement in the Nineteenth Century*, p. 16.

4 Henry Patterson, 'Industrial labour and the labour movement, 1820–1914', in Liam Kennedy and Philip Ollerenshaw (eds), *An Economic History of Ulster, 1820–1939* (Manchester, 1985), p. 173.

5 Daly, *Cork, A City in Crisis*, p. 264.

6 Emmet O'Connor, *A Labour History of Waterford* (Waterford, 1989), pp. 11–21.

tenet of its creed – collective action for the defence of common interests – was familiar to peasants as much as to artisans. Tensions caused by economic growth and massive demographic pressure on the land holding system produced various regional peasant movements between 1761 and the Great Famine of 1845–50, with discontent most persistent in the west midlands, the south, and the south east. Some groups lasted for months, others for years, and the first such – the Whiteboys – gave its name as a generic term for subsequent agitations. Described by one contemporary as 'a vast trades union for the protection of the Irish peasantry', Whiteboyism usually sprang up to challenge a specific grievance; it offered no programme of general reform.[7] But once in being, Whiteboys often addressed a wider range of issues, such as: tithes, tolls, taxes, rent increases, the price of conacre, renewal of leases, land division, wages, and the employment of strangers. Their support was equally eclectic and extended from small farmers, cottiers, and labourers to urban artisans. Operating in oath-bound secret gangs led by 'captains' with ominous pseudonyms like Slasher, Cutter, or Burnstack, Whiteboys sometimes acted openly to turn land from pasture to tillage, or make plots available for potato cultivation. More usually they sought redress or protected their people through measured terror. Despite the 'Whiteboy Acts' and clerical condemnation, a new and quasi-political version of Whiteboyism – the Defenders – spread from Armagh after 1785. During the 1790s, as war with the French heightened political and economic unrest, popular protest erupted with greater frequency. The Defenders' vague political creed blurred into Catholic sectarianism in Ulster and republicanism in the south. To the extent that the 1798 Rising constituted a culmination of Defenderism, it was in part a trade union revolt.

Whiteboy movements retained a broad social composition, but organised class conflict within the peasantry was not unknown. Faction fighting assumed an increasingly social dimension during the early nineteenth century. Competition for access to land and agricultural employment during the Napoleonic wars produced exceptionally class-based forms of Whiteboyism in the rival Caravats and Shanavests; the Caravats being

> a kind of primitive syndicalist movement whose aim was apparently to absorb as many of the poor as possible into a network of autonomous local gangs, each exercising thoroughgoing control over the local economy

---

7   George Cornewall Lewis, *Local Disturbances in Ireland* (London, 1836), a classic on the topic. See also M. R. Beames, *Peasants and Power: The Whiteboy Movements and their Control in Pre-Famine Ireland* (Brighton, 1983).

and the Shanavests comprising counter-gangs of strong farmers, merchants, publicans, and migrant spalpeens who sought their protection.[8] Both factions operated in east Munster from 1806 until their suppression by the military in 1811.

The dispute between the Caravats and Shanavests is interesting too for its ideological content. Whereas the former defined their message as the unity of the poor against the 'middle class', the latter invoked the vestiges of '98 nationalism to legitimate their counter-terror. And so the story might have gone in Ireland generally, with politics evolving along the lines of contending appeals to class and nation, had it not been for the Act of Union and the economic decline that followed.

8   Paul E. W. Roberts, 'Caravats and Shanavests: Whiteboyism and faction fighting in east Munster, 1802–11', in Samuel Clark and James S. Donnelly Jr (eds), *Irish Peasants: Violence and Political Unrest, 1780–1914* (Dublin, 1983), p. 66.

ONE

FOR TRADE AND PARLIAMENT
1824–48

Our trade and parliament,
Will be to us restored.
O'Connellite song.

—

Trade unions were decriminalised in June 1824 when Westminster revoked all Combination acts.[1] Initially, the post-war recession had raised a clamour for more draconian laws. However legislators, if not employers, could see that the acts were less than effectual. Trade unionists said they encouraged violence. With the tide of history moving towards laissez faire in political economy, a radical utilitarian and master tailor, Francis Place, deftly manoeuvred a parliamentary select committee on deregulation into slipping a repeal bill quietly through parliament. An immediate outbreak of strikes in Britain, due mainly to price rises in a time of good trade, led to another act being introduced in July 1825 which laid down more stringent penalties for violence and intimidation. Legal combination was restricted to matters of wages and hours, but the act confirmed implicitly that trade unions were no longer unlawful. This was of immediate advantage to artisans. It offered nothing to labourers who continued to seek redress through secret societies.

THE WORLD OF LABOUR

In Ireland, the economic world of labour was governed by de-industrialisation and a continuing crisis in agriculture. Being based on the traditional trades, craft unions were the first to suffer the economic palpitations caused by free trade with 'the workshop of the world'. A recession in manufacture followed the removal of the last tariff barriers between Ireland and Britain in 1824.[2] The

1   For an introduction to events in Britain see Henry Pelling, *A History of British Trade Unionism* (London, 1974).
2   For an overview of economic developments see L. M. Cullen, *An Economic History of Ireland since 1660* (London, 1987).

recession had a ruinous impact on many branches of textile production, a sector which still engaged one in five employees in 1841. Though a few ventures of imperial stature – cotton spinning at Portlaw or iron shipbuilding at Cork and Waterford – were launched after 1824, exporters generally lost out to the more rapidly developing British manufactures, while the introduction of steamships and railways increased British penetration of Irish markets. The food processing and packing industries also contracted as better transport allowed safe, fast access to English abattoirs and bacon cellars, creating that cliché of Irish undevelopment, the shipment of cattle on the hoof. Agriculture remained dangerously dependent on British demand, with disastrous consequences after 1845.

The north coped more successfully with external competition. Domestic linen production enjoyed a large export trade by the late eighteenth century.[3] Mechanised cotton production, for the home market mainly, was also carried on in Ulster from the 1770s, and cotton remained the chief textile sector in Belfast until about 1825. When duty free competition from Lancashire drove the industry into terminal decline, the cotton factors switched to flax processing, using the new technique of wet-spinning to make a quantum leap to the forefront of the more promising linen trade. By 1850, there were 26 flax mills in Belfast alone, and linen weaving too would soon become mechanised. Mechanisation in turn encouraged an engineering industry to supply machines. In the short term, the north's first wave of industrialisation brought little benefit to the masses. It destroyed the home-based linen industry across Ulster, and the workshop freedom that went with it, relocating employment in regimented factories to the east of the province. It broke the power of craft unionism in textiles and created a largely unskilled, low waged, labour force. And Protestant dominance of the process at management and shop-floor levels marginalised the Catholic workforce, fostering a sectarian division of labour.

Production of food and clothing engaged the bulk of wage earners before the Great Famine. The first detailed census, in 1841, enumerated 2.2 million occupied males aged 15 and upwards. Almost half that number were farm labourers. The clothing trades employed 212,500 men, nearly half of them weavers, and there were 158,000 men engaged with lodging, furniture, and machinery. The range of female employment was more restricted again. Of just over 1 million working women aged 15 or over, nearly two thirds were in clothing, and two thirds of these, 485,000, were spinners. A further 236,00 were in domestic service. Aside from some rare cases of widows being admitted to craft unions to allow them to earn a livelihood at their late husband's trade,

---

3   Aspects of northern industrialisation are discussed in Liam Kennedy and Philip Ollerenshaw (eds), *An Economic History of Ulster, 1820–1939* (Manchester, 1985).

women lay beyond the ambit of labour organisation. Whiteboy gangs remained active among urban and rural labourers, but craft unions were the only formally organised voice of the working class at this time, and out of 3.2 million waged workers only 240,000 were craftsmen. Furthermore, Dublin was the only city where craft unions could claim an abiding strength. Dublin's 10,000 or so unionised craftsmen should not be confused with the working class as a whole, but on the Repeal question, the craft unions did reflect popular feeling.

In the short term, undevelopment benefited the craft elite by reproducing a scarcity of skilled and an abundance of unskilled men. Wage differentials between skilled and unskilled were greater in Ireland than in Britain. Economic weakness also made industry vulnerable to protracted strikes. Employers occasionally imported British artisans to break strikes, but it was an expensive option which usually provoked an aggressive reaction. That combinations could operate at all indicates the relatively strong bargaining position of craftsmen vis à vis labourers. The craft unions profited from, rather than created, this situation. The employers' claim that combinations were pricing them out of the market was based on highly selective evidence. One case in point, commonly cited, was the decline of Dublin's shipbuilding industry, choked to death by restrictive practices.[4] Generally speaking, trade union attempts to restore the wage cuts introduced in the post-war recession met with fierce and successful resistance.

Average weekly wage levels in the Dublin building trades rose from 25s in the 1810s to a little over 26s for the next three decades. Dublin printers and shipwrights maintained even better wage levels over this period. Most were less fortunate. Average skilled rates in textiles rates fell from 26s 9d per week in the 1810s to 21s 6d in the 1820s and then continued falling, to 11s 8d by the 1840s. Outside Dublin, many textile operatives were reduced to penury after the 1820s. In the leather trades, a Dublin craftsman earned about 19s 10d in the 1820s, and 14s by the 1840s. Average rates for other Dublin trades declined from 30s 2d in the 1820s to 24s 6d in the 1840s. Provincial wage levels were generally lower. Waterford artisans in good trades earned about 20s per week in the 1830s. Weekly rates for carpenters in Derry fell from 20s in 1821–2 to 16s in 1831–4. In Galway in 1845, daily wages for artisans ranged from 2s for wheelwrights to 4s 6d for bakers; labourers earned 10d to 1s per day. The majority of urban general workers received 7s to 8s weekly, while a prized job in Guinness's paid about 12s per week in 1824. Apart from domestic servants,

---

4 Robert Kane, *The Industrial Resources of Ireland* (Shannon, 1971; first edn Dublin, 1844), pp. 391–427 discusses trade unionism and wage rates as deterrents to capital investment.

the lowest paid male workers were agricultural labourers. Before the Great Famine, they formed three sub-classes: indoor servants receiving bed and board in return for a yearly wage; cottiers holding a cabin and an acre or so of land at fixed rent, payable in labour; and landless outdoor labourers, some of whom cultivated a plot on conacre. Most outdoor labourers and men engaged on public works schemes subsisted on 8d to 10d per day in the 1830s. If dieted, the labourer received 4d to 6d per day. During these decades, urban employees were compensated by the falling cost of bread and clothes. In Dublin, bread prices dropped by 44 per cent between 1816–20 and 1840–4, artisans wages fell by 27 per cent between the same periods. Although the wage decline was fairly steady, bread prices fluctuated. In some trades the wage decline was even steeper.[5]

Health services were rudimentary, and welfare provision relied largely on charity. Trade slumped after a bad harvest, so that every decade had one or two years of economic recession. The craftsman could afford to put money aside for rainy days; the labourer could not. Imports of meal, flour, and grain usually mitigated the periodic harvest failures, but famine struck in 1728–9, 1740–1, and 1822, while near famine conditions obtained in 1742, 1756–7, 1799–1800, 1812, 1817, and 1819.[6] In these afflictions, the desperate could do little other than form a menacing crowd. There were numerous examples of food riots in urban Ireland at this time, especially during the subsistence crises of 1812 and 1817. The riots presumed a pre-capitalist notion of 'moral economy', that the rich had a duty to relieve the starving poor in times of food shortages, and that people were entitled to protest, even violently, against profiteering or the hoarding or export of food. The widespread acceptance of 'moral economy' is reflected in the *Waterford Mirror* of 14 June 1817, after a pattern of food rioting spread across towns from Tralee to Kilkenny: 'The narrative of the week is pretty much the same for all the scenes of disturbance. Riot, danger, subscription [for relief] and tranquility have everywhere followed in regular succession'. It was a precarious system of welfare, and the social elites were gradually abandoning the tradition

---

5   For Dublin craft rates and bread prices see Fergus A. D'Arcy, 'Skilled tradesmen in Dublin, 1800–50: a study of their opinions, activities, and organisations' (MA, UCD, 1968), pp. 168–76, appendix VII, pp. xliii–li; For other wage rates see British Parliamentary Papers (BPP), *Third Report from the Commissioners for Inquiry into the Condition of the Poorer Classes in Ireland* (1836) XXX, pp. 100–4; *First Report from the Select Committee to Inquire into the State of the Law regarding Artisans and Machinery* (1824) V, pp. 189–90; on Galway see John Cunningham, *'A Town Tormented by the Sea': Galway, 1790–1914* (Dublin, 2004), p. 75. For conditions of agricultural labourers on the eve of the Famine see John W. Boyle, 'A marginal figure: the Irish rural labourer', in Samuel Clark and James S. Donnelly Jr (eds), *Irish Peasants: Violence and Political Unrest, 1780–1914* (Dublin, 1983), pp. 311–38.

6   Emmet O'Connor, *A Labour History of Waterford* (Waterford, 1989), pp. 8, 18.

of 'moral economy' for the new theory of 'political economy' and its arguments for the sanctity of the market.[7]

EARLY LABOUR ORGANISATION

Craft unions understood their function to be benefit and protection. Depending on the peculiar requirements of the trade, the wealthier societies might provide benefit for unemployment, victimisation, sickness, tramping, or emigration. But most unions maintained funds for mortality only, relying on loans in cases of emergency.[8] Friendly societies were more important with regard to benefit. Under the Friendly Societies Act (1829), which updated an original act of 1797, 281 such societies were registered; 119 of them in Dublin. The remainder were spread throughout the anglophone east of the country from Derry to Cork.[9] Other sources of help for thrifty artisans were the savings banks and loan companies which developed after 1815 to provide credit for small depositors. Protection meant the defence of wages, jobs, and working practices. In the canon of craft unionism, there were three 'acts of tyranny' committed by masters: the employment of too many apprentices or boys, the employment of cheap or non-union labour, and wage reductions. Ideally, craftsmen hoped to deal with the three by regulation, protection, and arbitration, respectively. Their method in struggle was to be the public appeal or, failing all else, the turn out. In reality, the difficulties in winning effective public support and the prohibitive cost of strikes led unions frequently to resort to violence. With a few exceptions, craftsmen alone had the bargaining strength to combine openly. That strength, they believed, rested ultimately on their ability to maintain a scarcity of labour; without it, the artisan would sink into the poverty that engulfed the labourer. Therefore, controlling entry to the trade was vital, and more useful than strikes.

Societies were mostly small, local, and based on a trade recognised traditionally by a gild. Nonetheless, many unions maintained contact with

---

7   This concept of 'moral economy' was pioneered by E. P. Thompson in 'The moral economy of the English crowd in the eighteenth century', *Past and Present*, 50 (1971). On its relevance to Ireland, see John Cunningham, 'Popular protest and a "moral economy" in provincial Ireland in the early nineteenth century', in Francis Devine, Fintan Lane, and Niamh Puirséil (eds), *Essays in Irish Labour History: A Festschrift for Elizabeth and John W. Boyle* (Dublin, 2008), pp. 26–48.

8   Except where stated, the following account of Dublin craft unionism is based on D'Arcy, 'Skilled tradesmen in Dublin, 1800–50'.

9   Anthony D. Buckley, '"On the club": Friendly societies in Ireland', *Irish Economic and Social History* 14 (1987), pp. 39–58.

colleagues in other cities of Ireland or Britain; in 1836, Dublin shoemakers claimed to be in touch with France and Germany.[10] The practice of 'tramping' in search of work bound far flung societies together in a brotherhood of mutual hospitality, regulated by passes entitling the tramping artisan to a few days' sustenance while he enquired about a job. Locally, societies frequently assisted each other in industrial disputes. Occasionally, they lent money to support colleagues on strike in other cities. During the 1830s in particular, some attempts were made to federate societies on a United Kingdom (UK) basis. Though federations tended to locate centrally in Liverpool or Manchester, the logistical problems ultimately defeated them, and many broke up or withdrew from Ireland in the 1840s.

Dublin was the only part of the UK where a preponderance of trades was in continuous association in the early nineteenth century, and the city acquired a reputation for being the UK's strongest centre of trade unionism in the 1820s, with about 10,000 organised artisans. Twenty unions are known to have been active locally in 1820, 39 in 1840, and 45 in 1850; some trades contained more than one society. Union density varied. Figures for 1836 show that about ten unions had recruited more than half their trade; the hatters, cabinetmakers, and paper stainers claimed 100 per cent recruitment. The largest societies were the tailors, with 1,000 members out of 2,500 men in the trade, and the carpenters, who represented 900 out of a possible 1,500 men in 1838. Building unions were the best organised, and most active, with a reputation for violent militancy. Organisation was also extensive in textiles. The legendary 'Board of Green Cloth' may have functioned as a joint committee of the largest section in clothing, the woollen weavers. Woollen weavers sustained some kind of organisation between 1815 and 1824, though they never developed a recognised society. By 1850, nearly all trades were unionised to some degree.

Quite exceptionally, the gilds remained important in Dublin.[11] If their industrial function had virtually disappeared, they nonetheless demonstrated a model of organisation and regulation. In structure, style, and public expression, Dublin craft unions modelled themselves on the city's 25 gilds, often adopting gild rituals and symbols. It was common for gild and union alike to be called after the patron saint of the trade. This outward appearance has concealed, as it was intended to do, the comparisons between trade unionism and agrarian or Ribbon movements. In matters of conflict and solidarity, unions drew on Whiteboyism. Normally, the societies were run by a committee elected at an annual or quarterly general meeting. The committee usually met

---

10 John W. Boyle, *The Irish Labor Movement in the Nineteenth Century* (Washington DC, 1989), pp. 30–1.

11 J. J. Webb, *The Guilds of Dublin* (Dublin, 1929).

once a week in a public house to collect subscriptions and deal with routine business. Most societies also had executives and secretaries to handle emergency issues. By the 1840s, some maintained full-time secretaries. Unions involved with the tramping system were more likely to be federated. Eight Dublin societies, and others in Belfast and Cork, were linked to UK federations at some time or other between 1821 and 1835. One national federation formed in 1836 – the Irish Typographical Union – became the Western District Board of the British National Typographical Association in 1845. Uniquely, the UK Federation of Bookbinders was centred in Dublin from 1843 to 1848. Federation usually involved obligations to curb colts, assist tramps, and subscribe to strike funds. Otherwise, local branches made their own rules.

Membership of a society was open to all who had served the required apprenticeship; though strangers might be denied entry in times of poor trade. Some unions included small masters; others excluded them deliberately. Entry fees were lower for the sons of members, while strangers would be admitted at the highest rate; the required sums varied from 2s 6d to two guineas, one guinea being about average. Weekly dues ranged from 2d to 3s; the smaller the membership, the higher the subscription. There were fines for drunkenness, strike-breaking, or disorderly conduct. When necessary, members were levied for political, legal, charitable, or strike purposes. In addition to benefit and protection, unions offered their members the status of being a recognised artisan, an opportunity to defend the interests of the trade, and a social comradeship.

Such was the intensity of unrest in the city in the 1820s, and the degree of cooperation between unions, that employers believed them to be in conspiracy, coordinated by the 'Board of Green Cloth'. The practice, common in Dublin and Cork at least, of members of one society carrying out acts of violence on behalf of another society to reduce risk of recognition or conviction, lent credence to the myth. There is no certainty that the 'Board of Green Cloth' ever functioned outside the woollen trade, and it was not until August 1844 that unions in the city formed a trades council – the Associated Trades of Dublin – which was renamed the Regular Trades Association in October. By 1846, there were 37 societies affiliated to the association.

Ireland's first trades council had emerged in Cork about 1820, and was believed to represent all local crafts.[12] The Cork Union of Trades shared the same combative conception of industrial relations as its affiliates and aimed primarily to coordinate them in organisation and conflict. Cork trade societies

---

12 For details of trade unionism in Cork at this time see Seán Daly, *Cork, A City in Crisis: A History of Labour Conflict and Social Misery, 1870–1872, Vol. 1* (Cork 1978), pp. 253–314; for dates of the Union of Trades see pp. 21, 280.

paraded publicly, probably for the first time, in June 1832 to inaugurate the more respectable Cork Trades Association, but the Union of Trades survived into the 1840s. At least 19 craft unions existed in the city in 1845, some of them branches of British federations. In Galway, 200 men from all local trades took part in a Union of Trades procession in 1823. Limerick societies mustered occasionally as the Congregated Trades from the late 1820s onwards.[13] Whilst no similar councils operated elsewhere at this time, combination was carried on to a considerable extent, especially among bakers, coopers, printers, the building trades, and weavers. The National Association for the Protection of Labour formed in 1830 as a UK federation of trade unions by John Doherty[14] and linked to the cooperative movement of Robert Owen, attracted strong support in Belfast.[15] The Association had collapsed by 1832, but in 1834 about 1,500 artisans in over a dozen trades, chiefly in construction, were affiliated to the Belfast branch of a successor body – the Grand National Consolidated Trades Union. Craft societies in the provinces were broadly similar in style to their Dublin counterparts, though less extensive, more intermittent in activity, and shadowy in form.

There is some evidence of organisation among unskilled urban workers, like the 'Billy Welters' and 'Billy Smiths' who defended the interests of Dublin coalporters. Unlike the craft societies, these quasi-secret brotherhoods could sustain a protective function only. The British Parliamentary enquiry into trade unionism in 1837–8 was told that Dublin draymen and coalporters 'would not allow any man to be dismissed from his employment or at least if they were put out no one else went in their place, and if they did go they were beaten'. What enabled this limited bargaining power was the carter's effective control over his horse: 'one man was assigned to each horse, and while the proprietor kept that horse he was obliged to keep the man and could not dismiss the man without selling the horse'.[16] The horse was more valuable than the man. A similar system obtained on the canals and inland waterways,

13 Fergus A. D'Arcy and Ken Hannigan (eds), *Workers in Union: Documents and Commentaries on the History of Irish Labour* (Dublin, 1988), p. 3; Cunningham, '*A Town Tormented by the Sea*', p. 76.

14 John Doherty (*c.*1798–1854), born in Buncrana, Donegal and worked in a local mill; secretary of the Manchester Spinners' Union in 1828; founded the *Conciliator, or Cotton Spinners' Weekly Journal*, the *Voice of the People*, and the *Poor Man's Advocate*; retired from public life in 1838; remembered as a pioneer of the Labour press in Britain, and of attempts to build a national Labour movement; now commemorated in Buncrana. See R. G. Kirby and A. E. Musson, *The Voice of the People: John Doherty, 1798–1854, Trade Unionist, Radical, and Factory Reformer* (Manchester, 1975).

15 Vincent Geoghegan, 'Robert Owen, co-operation and Ulster in the 1830s', in Fintan Lane and Dónal Ó Drisceoil (eds), *Politics and the Irish Working Class, 1830–1945* (London, 2005), pp. 6–26.

16 Evidence of James Fagan, timber merchant, in BPP, *Report of the Select Committee on Combinations of Workmen* (1837–8) VIII, p. 388.

where the enquiry noted powerful combinations of boatmen, with violence applied against offending captains or owners.[17] In 1842 the Tory *Dublin Evening Mail* detailed a range of restrictive practices maintained by the Carrick-on-Suir boatmen who handled the flyboats and barges that plied between Waterford and Clonmel. According to the *Mail*, only a set number of vessels were allowed on the river, each new barge built having part of the old craft worked into it.[18] Labourers without such de facto property rights did combine occasionally to demand higher wages, but were in no position to sustain trade union practices.

Whiteboyism remained the most extensive form of labour defence up to the Great Famine. Agrarian secret societies were most active in the midlands, south-west Leinster, and Munster, in areas of desperate competition for access to plots of land where marginal men lived 'one degree removed above the lowest level of poverty', and normally emerged in times of stress occasioned by exceptional prosperity or hardship.[19] Composed mainly of cottiers, labourers, and subsistence tenants, they employed the traditional methods of threats and violence against landlords and farmers to prevent evictions, discourage grabbers, regulate rents and wages, prevent land being turned from tillage to grazing, and frustrate tithe proctors. Support levels varied. Agitation to restrain rent increases had a marked class composition, while the social base of unrest tended to broaden in times of falling prices. Societies operated within local economies; the Rockite agitation that spread across east and central Munster from 1819 to 1823 was one of the widest Whiteboy outbreaks before the Great Famine. These Rockites acquired a cohesion from the prophecies of Pastorini, which predicted the fall of Protestantism in 1825. However, their millenarianism was less a programme than a bonding ideology. A similar point may be made about the vague Defenderist nationalism of the Ribbonmen, the most political of Whiteboy factions, who might toast 'the rights of man' or 'no king', as easily as 'the end of heresy'. After 1815, Ribbonism spread from the border counties to north Leinster and north Connacht. Through the Ancient Order of Hibernians and the Molly Maguires, it would reach Glasgow, Manchester, Liverpool, and the United States. Quite exceptionally, Ribbonism became strong in the towns, especially Dublin, where it extended to both

17   BPP, *Report of the Select Committee on Combinations of Workmen* (1837–8) VIII, pp. 336, 506–11.

18   See an article reprinted in the *Waterford Mirror*, 2 Apr. 1842.

19   See George Cornewall Lewis, *Local Disturbances in Ireland* (London, 1836). For a general account of Whiteboy and Ribbon activity see Donal McCartney, *The Dawning of Democracy: Ireland, 1800–1870* (Dublin, 1987), pp. 63–109. For Rockism see James S. Donnelly Jr, 'Pastorini and Captain Rock: millenarianism and sectarianism in the Rockite movement of 1821–4', in Clark and Donnelly, *Irish Peasants*, pp. 102–39.

artisans and transport workers. Initially a Catholic anti-Orange movement, Ribbonism gradually blended into popular agitation movements, and became as generic a term as Whiteboyism. Leinster lodges particularly operated as labour leagues, with benefit and protective functions. Whiteboys achieved reasonable success in restricting the consolidation of farms and opposing evictions. But the acute inequality of the agrarian economy and social structure, in which both production and poverty were increasing, demanded that agitation be a recurrent battle against the tide of economic forces.

INDUSTRIAL CONFLICT

Once the Combination acts were repealed, trade unions immediately demanded higher wages to offset rising prices. Dublin police reports noted 53 incidents of violence relating to trade disputes between June 1824 and April 1825.[20] Thirty-two of them occurred in the building line, including the assassination of a jobber, bludgeoned for his refusal to dismiss non-body men. A meeting convened by the Lord Mayor in April 1825 to discuss the situation concluded by condemning the conspiracy 'for some time existing among the operative hands; not confined as hereto fore to any particular branch, but embracing all denominations of tradesmen, in a close confederacy. . .'.[21] It was agreed to establish a fund to reward informants of outrages. Some wished to go further and break trade unions. Master cabinetmakers, chairmakers, and upholsterers proposed to employ 'country operatives', who would be given adequate protection. For their part, 32 trade societies met in August to reiterate their belief in arbitration as the best means of ending strikes and avoiding violence.

Unrest persisted in Dublin, but by the end of the year it was employers who were on the offensive, seeking wage cuts in conditions of deep recession. The recession in British industry in 1825–6 was novel in the degree of its impact on Irish manufacture. Deflation caused by the assimilation of the Irish currency into sterling in 1826 sharpened the exceptionally industrial character of the crisis. As the Mayor of Waterford reported to his Relief Committee in March 1826, local distress stemmed from dismissals from employment, not from food shortages or food prices.[22] Perceptions of the resultant social problems had an industrial rather than pre-industrial aspect. Proposed solutions

---

20 The following accounts of craft unionism in Dublin are based on D'Arcy, 'Skilled tradesmen in Dublin, 1800–50.'

21 *Dublin Evening Mail*, 27 Apr. 1825. See also D'Arcy, 'Skilled tradesmen in Dublin, 1800–50', p. 23.

22 *Waterford Mirror*, 4 Mar. 1826.

emphasised job creation more than food distribution. The recession became most severe in the summer of 1826, when widespread unemployment coincided with high food prices due to an exceptionally dry season. Adding to the distress, many migrant workers returned from England. In July, Dublin artisans toured workshops calling out men to demand wage payment in English currency. Masters met the strike wave by forming an Association of Trades 'to arrest the programme of intimidation and violence . . . which has characterised the proceedings of journeymen . . .'.[23] Yet some trade unions won their demands immediately.

It was in textiles that the slump caused a long-term crisis. Bounties granted by the Linen Board for coarse weaving had been withdrawn in 1823, and the Board, established in 1711 to regulate and finance the industry, was abolished in 1828. With free trade and recession, imported British machine spun yarn undersold the native hand spun product. English woollens and cottons too were dumped on the Irish market. Following an unsuccessful strike of Belfast cotton workers in 1825, the recession dealt a terminal blow to trade unionism in Ulster's textile sector. Northern cotton weavers earned up to 24s per week in the early 1820s. In 1835, there were approximately 10,000 cotton weavers in the Belfast area living on 3s 6d to 8s per week. The 'cotton famine' during the American Civil War finally destroyed the industry in the north.[24] Almost 20,000 textile operatives were idle in the Liberties of Dublin in 1826, causing an outbreak of 'famine fever' and bread riots. Cork's textile operatives marched from Blackpool into Patrick Street behind a banner saying, 'We Want Employment – Ourselves and Our Families Are Starving'. Textiles engaged about 60,000 people in west Cork in 1822. Bandon supported over 1,500 cotton weavers up to 1829. Ten years later there were 150 weavers left in Bandon. In Cork city, employment in the textile trades fell from 6,600 to under 500 between 1800 and 1834.[25] Some mills survived precariously. In Drogheda, 1,900 linen weavers remained in part-time employment in 1840, earning about 4s per week. As Ulster adapted from cotton to linen, the south made a limited switch into cotton. Cotton mills continued to operate in Drogheda and Balbriggan, while Malcolmson's Portlaw Spinning Company,

23   Quoted in D'Arcy, 'Skilled tradesmen in Dublin, 1800–50', pp. 29–30.

24   Boyle, *The Irish Labor Movement in the Nineteenth Century*, pp. 26–7; Henry Patterson, 'Industrial labour and the labour movement, 1820–1914', in Liam Kennedy and Philip Ollerenshaw (eds), *An Economic History of Ulster, 1820–1939* (Manchester, 1985), pp. 158–83.

25   Maura Murphy, 'The working classes of nineteenth century Cork', *Journal of the Cork Historical and Archaeological Society* (1980), p. 28; Andy Bielenberg, 'Bandon weavers and the industrial revolution', *Labour History News* 3 (1987); and *Cork's Industrial Revolution, 1780–1880: Development or Decline* (Cork, 1991), p. 119.

established in 1825, employed over 1,800 operatives in what was claimed to be the biggest factory in the world.[26]

The conflict generated by the recession confirmed employers in their opposition to trade unionism per se. Even in Dublin, masters no longer appealed for a harmony of common interests. Once trade began to recover, industrial relations became increasingly bitter. In two sensational incidents in Dublin, a master builder was attacked with acid and a sawyer was bludgeoned to death by a gang of over 20 combinators. Four men were hanged for the latter crime.[27] In 1827, Dublin masters had initiated a national petition for the re-enactment of the Combination acts, inviting merchant bodies in Belfast, Cork, Limerick, and Waterford to lend support. Dublin trade unions replied with public meetings to refute employer allegations, arguing that violence was worse before 1824, and currently affected only five or six of the 70 trades in the city. Again, they called for arbitration. Strikers remained liable to prosecution under the Master and Servant Act, which made it a criminal offence for an employee to leave his work in breach of contract, and provincial employers still used the law to suppress strikes or attempts to maintain a scarcity of labour. In 1826, apprentices who struck at a calico printing works in Carrickfergus were promptly imprisoned. Two years later, a general turn out of mill labourers and storemen at Clonmel over wages and hours led to five men being sentenced to the tread mill in the local house of correction. One convict hulk which sailed regularly to the penal colonies, the *Essex*, transported seven men for combination offences between 1825 and 1834.[28]

Unrest intensified in the 1830s. The campaign for Emancipation had politicised the Catholic working classes, and the Emancipation Act in 1829 raised expectations. When Catholics in Graiguenamanagh withheld tithe payments in 1830, similar resistance spread throughout the country, escalating into a 'tithe war'.[29] Opposition to tithes united all social classes but, at a time of falling prices, Whiteboy groups called the Whitefeet, the Terry Alts, and the Poleens emerged in south Leinster, Clare/Limerick, and Waterford to turn the war into a wider social struggle. Disillusion with the fruits of Emancipation acted as a spur. 'Mr O'Connell and the rich Catholics go to

26 Gearóid Ó Tuathaigh, *Ireland before the Famine, 1798–1848* (Dublin, 1972), pp. 118–19; L. M. Cullen, *An Economic History of Ireland since 1660* (London, 1987), pp. 108–9.

27 F. A. D'Arcy, 'The murder of Thomas Hanlon: an episode in nineteenth century Dublin labour history', *Dublin Historical Record* 4 (1971), pp. 89–100.

28 Boyle, *The Irish Labor Movement in the Nineteenth Century*, pp. 37–8. For a report of the general turn out at Clonmel see the *Waterford Mirror*, 6 Oct. 1828.

29 For a concise account of the tithe question see Ó Tuathaigh, *Ireland before the Famine, 1798–1848*, pp. 173–82.

Parliament', a Whitefoot leader told Alexis de Tocqueville, 'We die of starvation just the same'.[30] Rural unrest, in England as well as Ireland, the 1830 revolutions in Europe, and Daniel O'Connell's new campaign for Repeal, prompted the government to take strong measures to curb popular agitation. Rural disorder was met with insurrection acts and increasingly frequent use of troops and police. After the introduction of a particularly tough coercion act in 1833, rural protest diminished. The long-standing friction over tithes was finally resolved in 1838 by a Commutation act, which converted tithes into a rent charge amounting to about 75 per cent of the old composition, effectively wrote off the arrears of 1834–7, and eliminated the hated tithe-proctors.

The law was also applied more pointedly against craft unionism after 1833. In addition to widespread convictions for attempts to restrict apprenticeships, intimidation, assault, conspiracy, and turning out in breach of contract, Cork magistrates sentenced eight men each to three months imprisonment for membership of a benefit society. In February 1834, 12 Dublin shoemakers were convicted of conspiring to reduce the livelihood of a colleague who had refused to join their society. The *Belfast News Letter* noted with satisfaction that 'every individual who is obliged to leave his situation in consequence of the decrees of Trades Unions [henceforth] has a valid action against the members of those Unions'.[31] George Kerr's *Exposition of Legislative Tyranny, and Defence of the Trades' Union* was a unique response to one such case of judicial browbeating. A leading figure in the Belfast Cabinetmakers' Club and an Owenite, Kerr was arrested while organising in Derry, charged with administering illegal oaths, maltreated in prison, and interrogated about trade unionism by the Mayor. Kerr's pamphlet recalling his experience and offering a high-minded, God-fearing defence of trade unionism contributed to his acquittal. The opening paragraph gives an idea of the impact of unrest in Belfast in 1834:

> Nothing has of late engrossed more of the public attention, nor occupied more space of the magazines and journals of the present day, than the subject of Trades' Unions. Hitherto, it was hard to find any journal or magazine deigning to take the least notice of the working class of society, unless for the purpose of stigmatising them with cognomens of *mob, lower order, swinish multitude,* or the *rabble.*

30 Quoted in K. Theodore Hoppen, *Ireland since 1800: Conflict and Conformity* (London, 1999), p. 22.
31 *Belfast News Letter*, 4 Feb. 1834. For conflict in 1834–5 see Boyle, *The Irish Labor Movement in the Nineteenth Century*, pp. 38–41. For Belfast see also Geoghegan, 'Robert Owen, co-operation and Ulster in the 1830s'. Kerr's pamphlet cited below is reprinted in Andrew Boyd, *The Rise of the Irish Trade Unions* (Tralee, 1985), pp. 122–40.

In April 1834, Kerr chaired a meeting of the Belfast branch of the 'General Trade Union' to petition on behalf of the Tolpuddle Martyrs. Fifteen hundred members attended and they were joined by 'several thousand' sympathisers. The assembly coincided with an upsurge of craft militancy in Belfast involving action by bakers, printers, flaxdressers, coopers, coachmakers, cabinetmakers, shoemakers, and stonecutters. Notable too was the absence of sectarian animosity in the proceedings; already the presence of Orange and Catholic trade unionists on the same platform had become an event worth congratulation in Belfast. However, before the year was out, employers had crushed the strike wave with law and lockouts, and then proceeded to establish an exchange for non-union labour in the city. No more was heard of the 'General Trade Union' in Belfast.

After years of relative tranquility from 1830 to 1833, union violence in Dublin reached a crescendo in 1836–7, when the price of bread rose to its highest level since the Famine year of 1817. In Dublin, most violence occurred subsequent to the outbreak of attacks on bakeries and bread carts in the summer of 1837. On this occasion, union aggression generated relatively little public odium, while the extent of hunger protests overstretched the police. Constables were severely beaten in October when they intervened in a trade union assault, and in November police stood by as an employer was attacked by 30 carpenters. There were 39 cases of assault in connection with combination in Dublin in 1836, and 97 in 1837; some incidents involved the unskilled societies, the 'Billy Welters' and 'Billy Smiths'. All assaults aimed to maintain wage levels, limit the employment of apprentices, or prevent the employment of colts.

IN SEARCH OF CONSENSUS

When food prices declined in 1838, violence fell sharply. By the 1840s, unions were turning to public pressure and moral force as a means of seeking redress. A severe slump from 1839 to 1842 depressed trade union activity. A dawning realisation that both masters and men were common victims of free trade encouraged class collaboration, and middle-class leaders began to join trade societies in appeals to promote native industry. In 1840, Fr Matthew Flanagan, a priest in the Dublin Liberties, set up the Operative Board of Trade to encourage self-help ventures in textile and footwear production. Renamed the Repeal Board of Trade following O'Connellite intervention, the Board ran 18 marts of local produce in Dublin in 1842, and had kindred bodies in Clonmel, Waterford, and Wexford. Lack of investment sent the Board into abrupt decline in 1843. There were other, less elaborate, efforts along these lines too, involving Tories as well as Repealers.[32] Also of significance in changing the social climate was the phenomenal success of Fr Mathew's temperance crusade, which emphasised material improvement through moral reform.

As unions recovered after the slump, they embarked on agitation that was more campaigning than combative. The 1840s were notable for three major trade struggles, unprecedented in extent or sophistication, involving bakers, tanners, and tailors.[33] In July 1842, Dublin bakers initiated a campaign to end night-work, offering to work from 6.00 am to 8.00 pm six days a week instead. Within weeks the demand was taken up by provincial colleagues. With a reputation for price fixing and adulteration, the master bakers were not popular men, and the operatives enjoyed broad public backing, including support from the *Freeman's Journal*. Temporary successes were recorded in securing the abolition of night-work in Derry, Belfast, Kilkenny, and Cork. After fruitless canvassing, Dublin bakers issued a formal strike notice in November. But the campaign petered out in 1843, and night-work was re-introduced in the provinces. Agitation by Dublin tanners in 1844 to raise wage rates led to a prolonged strike and lockout that summer. Whilst the conflict centred on Dublin, support came from all categories of leather operatives throughout the country, as well as from tanners in Leeds and Liverpool. Sympathetic action extended beyond financial assistance to joint employer and employee boycott of goods produced by the offending masters. In Wexford, agents recruiting for the masters were run out of town. From this dispute emerged the Dublin Regular Trades Association, formed as a 'moral and peaceful union' to articulate grievances, coordinate activities, and defend the 'character of our tradesmen from the many wanton and unfounded charges of combination. . .'.[34] The tanners' campaign did not survive long beyond 1844, but the association remained active until 1847.

Unlike the earlier unions of trades, the Regular Trades Association sought no role in managing internal union affairs, exalted the 'moral force principle' above combination, and operated largely as a public lobby. Over 1846 the association sent 47 deputations to employers in dispute, and deemed only 16 of them to have failed. During this year also, two labour papers were issued in Dublin, the *Argus* and the *Guardian and Tradesman's Advocate*. The *Guardian* especially reflected the trades' view that 'the interests of the employer and employed, when properly understood, are and ought to be identical. . .'.[35] To

---

32   See D'Arcy, 'Skilled tradesmen in Dublin, 1800–50', pp. 79–91.

33   For trade unionism in the 1840s see ibid., pp. 92–166; and Boyle, *Irish Labor in the Nineteenth Century*, pp. 47–53.

34   Quoted in D'Arcy, 'Skilled tradesmen in Dublin, 1800–50', pp. 122–3.

35   Quoted in ibid., p. 125.

contemporary eyes, the logical extension of this scenario was the revival of the gilds, moribund since the Municipal Corporations Act (1840) had abolished their political privileges. Calls for gild regulation of trade were not new. Faced with the chill winds of economic liberalism, artisans began to feel nostalgic for the old protections, and those who used the gilds for purely political purposes had abandoned them in 1840. From the outset, the Regular Trades Association was committed to the restoration of gild privileges.

On 12 June 1845 the courts upheld a claim of Benjamin Pemberton, sometime bricklayer and twice master of his gild, that the 1840 Act had not affected rights over trade granted to the Gild of St Bartholomew in a royal charter of 1670. Artisans and gildsmen united to revive the gilds. Coincidentally, in January 1845 journeymen tailors had begun the third major trade union agitation of the decade, against sweating. In October, the revived Gild of Tailors took up the cause, served writs on offending masters, and warned that from 1846 no master could operate without a licence from the gild. During the early months of 1846, Dublin Chamber of Commerce and the Regular Trades Association fought a political battle over the issue of gild authority. The former prevailed, and on 22 August a bill to abolish gild trading rights passed into law.[36] Interest in the Regular Trades slackened, and the Association fell into abeyance.

INTO POLITICS

The struggle for Catholic Emancipation first mobilised the working class in electoral politics. The Catholic Association was strong in the towns, where collectors for the Catholic Rent Committee could be drawn from any class to suit the occasion. Such social harmony would not be so easy to achieve in the Liberator's next campaign.

Dublin artisans greeted O'Connell's decision, in October 1830, to agitate for Repeal with relief.[37] The ill effects of the Union were felt keenly in the ex-capital. Though Repeal generally commanded even less support from

36 John Hogan and Gary Murphy, 'From guild to union: the evolution of the Dublin Bricklayers' Society, 1670–1888', *Saothar* 26 (2001), p. 21.

37 For Dublin craft societies and Repeal see F. A. D'Arcy, 'The artisans of Dublin and Daniel O'Connell, 1830–47', *Irish Historical Studies* 66 (1970), pp. 221–43; 'The National Trades' Political Union and Daniel O'Connell, 1830–1848', *Éire-Ireland*, XVII: 3 (1982), pp. 7–16; Boyle, *Irish Labor in the Nineteenth Century*, pp. 41–7; Rachel O'Higgins, 'Irish trade unions and politics, 1830–50', *Historical Journal* 4 (1961), pp. 208–17; Jacqueline Hill, 'The Protestant response to Repeal: the case of the Dublin working class', in F. S. L. Lyons and R. A. J. Hawkins (eds), *Ireland Under the Union: Varieties of Tension* (Oxford, 1980), pp. 35–68; and 'Artisans, sectarianism, and politics in Dublin, 1829–48', *Saothar* 7 (1981), pp. 12–27.

Protestants than Emancipation, inconclusive evidence suggests that Dublin's Protestant artisans, who comprised about 20 per cent of city tradesmen, endorsed the cause. So too did some of the minor gilds. However, the Catholic hierarchy and Catholic middle class, on whose social leadership O'Connell relied, preferred to await the benefits of Emancipation or press for moderate reforms of administration, tithes, and policing. With their former enthusiasm for Emancipation turning to cynicism about its consequences, artisans expected little from such palliatives. Repeal alone, they believed, would restore prosperity. The argument for Repeal assumed that an Irish government would make Dublin a centre of patronage, and protect and foster native industries, as the old College Green Parliament had done through tariffs, development boards, and grants. Repealers spoke constantly of the need to encourage indigenous industry, and by the 1840s tariff protection had become a standard nationalist demand.[38] Young Irelanders went furthest in rejecting the free trade ideas of the Manchester school; the philosophically liberal O'Connell actually remained a free trader, though he indicated that he would be flexible on tariffs if need be. The politics of industrial revival could be double edged for tradesmen. Both Old and Young Ireland were sometimes critical of trade unionism as a disincentive to enterprise. Nonetheless, the strategic interests of labour lay with self-government. However unsatisfactory that government might be, artisans saw no future for themselves, their societies, or their jobs under London rule. And they were convinced that only 'the great Dan' could deliver.

By 1831, the provinces too were active. In January, bodies of trades in Cork and Tullamore held Repeal rallies, determined to generate a tempo that would prevent O'Connell from dropping or compromising on the demand for self-government. On 19 August Dublin tradesmen reconstituted the Liberal Mechanics and Trades Association, founded in 1830, as the Dublin Trades Political Union to promote the cause. O'Connell then entered into discussions with the Union to bring it under his control and dilute its class orientation. In return for the admission of recommended artisans to O'Connell's association, the National Political Union, and the promise to build a hall for trades meetings, it was agreed to recast the Trades Political Union on a national basis and open membership to all. Primarily, the National Trades Political Union sought to win Repeal through political canvassing. It also agitated against tithes, petitioned for triennial parliaments and the secret ballot, and prepared reports on the decline of trade since 1800. Its own rules forbade it to interfere in industrial relations. Membership stood at about 1,000 initially, rising to about 5,000 by 1832, of whom 3,000 were electors. Though now largely middle

---

38   For the economic views of nationalists see Richard Davis, *The Young Ireland Movement* (Dublin, 1987), pp. 185–200.

class, the Union offered workers a platform for politics. In Cork, the 1832 elections saw the Trades Association became 'a significant force in local political life'. In Galway, a Trades Political Union was formed in 1831, and the trades were prominent in the Galway Reform Association, which denounced 'Tory Despotism, Tithes, and Corporation Monopoly'.[39] The growing political importance of organised labour was reflected in an ephemeral reform press. The radical *Comet* (1831–3), *Plain Dealer* (1832), and *Press* (1833), were joined by the more labour oriented *Repealer and Tradesman's Journal* (1832), and the *People* (1833). The O'Connellite *Express* (1832) also accommodated radical opinion.[40]

O'Connell's failure to subsume trade union politics into his movement ensured a thorny relationship with Labour. Friction hinged on tactical and class questions. O'Connell pursued a delicate political strategy in the 1830s. Though he believed, wrongly as it turned out, that Westminster would be more sympathetic to Ireland after the 1832 Reform Act, he knew that Repeal could not be won through parliamentary means alone. At the same time he supported the Whig administration, partly because he shared government concern about social unrest, partly to prevent his movement being suppressed, and partly in the hope of securing interim reforms. His supporters were less patient, and urged that Repeal be raised in the House of Commons. O'Connell eventually bowed to the pressure in April 1834, and proposed a House committee of enquiry into the effects of the Act of Union. Parliament dismissed the motion by 523–38 votes. The first phase of Repeal agitation was over. When the English radical, William Cobbett, visited Dublin in September, his enthusiastic reception from artisans was taken to imply a censure on O'Connell. O'Connell's relations with trade unions deteriorated further when he entered into the Lichfield House compact with the Whigs in 1835; it confirmed that Repeal had been dropped.

Class interests created deeper tension between Labour and the Repeal movement. As a liberal and a pacifist, O'Connell disliked unions for restraining trade and resorting to violence. In November 1837, after a crest of labour conflict in Dublin and a notoriously violent spinners' strike in Glasgow, he departed from his policy of public neutrality on industrial relations and condemned openly trade unionism as practiced in Ireland. Dublin trade union secretaries disputed O'Connell's charges, and in January 1838 the Liberator met his critics face to face in two extraordinary debates at the Old Chapel,

---

39   Fintan Lane, *In Search of Thomas Sheahan: Radical Politics in Cork, 1824–1836* (Dublin, 2001), p. 41; Cunningham, *'A Town Tormented by the Sea'*, pp. 118–20.

40   O'Higgins, 'Irish trade unions and politics, 1830–50', p. 213; Brian Inglis, *The Freedom of the Press in Ireland* (London, 1954), pp. 204–5.

Ringsend. O'Connell echoed a common supposition in contending that Irish trade unions were more militant than those in Britain, and were the cause of decline in Dublin's printing and shipbuilding industries. Spokesmen for the artisans made no attempt to justify violence, but defended restrictive practices as essential to the maintenance of employment and living standards. 'What advantage is it to the tradesmen of Ireland', they asked, carrying the attack into politics, 'that thirteen hundred situations have been thrown open by emancipation? . . . Has it given a loaf of bread to any of the thousand starving families of the poor operatives of this city?'[41] The artisans gave as good as they got in the first debate, where the atmosphere turned decidedly rancorous. In the second round, the seasoned counsellor got the upper hand. Evidently confirmed in his views, O'Connell then persuaded the House of Commons to appoint a committee of enquiry on trade unionism. The enquiry paid particular attention to Ireland, but neither of its reports made any recommendations.[42]

Although he had contrasted Ireland with the 'honest and praise worthy system of trade union' in Britain, the parliamentary enquiry alienated British Labour from O'Connell. Relations were already strained by his support for the Whigs. In 1838, O'Connell openly denounced the Chartists' People's Charter, completing his breach with British radicals. At home, O'Connell tried consistently to insulate Ireland from the British left. Ireland had featured on the agenda of British movements for democracy since 1815, and utopian socialist ideas crossed the Irish Sea in the 1820s. In response to near famine conditions in 1822–3, Captain Robert O'Brien invited Robert Owen to outline his plans for agriculture-oriented philanthropy in Dublin.[43] On foot of Owen's lectures at the Rotunda in 1823, Lord Cloncurry led O'Brien and other socially concerned squires to found the Hibernian Philanthropic Society as a solution to the twin evils of distress and Whiteboyism. The Society presented a memorial to parliament but achieved nothing else. A circle of philanthropic landlords remained, together with a brilliant Cork merchant, William Thompson.[44] Some practical experiments in Owenism were launched in 1830–1.

41   Quoted in D'Arcy, 'The artisans of Dublin and Daniel O'Connell, 1830–47', p. 221.
42   BPP, *First Report from the Select Committee on Combinations of Workmen: Minutes of Evidence* (1837–8); *Second Report on Combinations of Workmen: Minutes of Evidence* (1837–8).
43   On Owenism in Ireland see J. F. C. Harrison, *Robert Owen and the Owenites in Britain and America* (London, 1969), pp. 25, 29–30, 170–1.
44   William Thompson (1775–1833), born at Rosscarbery, Cork; his father was a leading reactionary and merchant in Cork City; Protestant turned atheist; socialist, feminist, and vegetarian; remembered for books on political economy and feminism, and practical ventures in cooperation; influenced by Bentham and Ricardo, and a radical critic of Owen's politics; attended the first three cooperative congresses in England, 1831–2, as a delegate of the Cork Cooperative Society, and clashed with Owen at the third congress; his memory has enjoyed a revival in recent years, especially in Cork. See Richard Pankhurst, *William Thompson (1775–1833): Pioneer Socialist* (London, 1991).

In January 1830, the Belfast Cooperative Trading Association was founded by artisans with ambitions to set up factories, farms, schools, libraries, hospitals, and boarding houses on Owenite principles. The Association initiated a library, two schools, and the monthly *Belfast Cooperative Advocate*, and by the end of the year six more cooperatives had been launched in Belfast, Armagh, Derry, Dungannon, Larne, and Monaghan. All had collapsed by 1834.[45] The Ralahine Agricultural and Manufacturing Cooperative Association, founded by John Scott Vandeleur in 1831 after an outbreak of disturbances on his estate, achieved international renown among Owenites. Vandeleur brought 52 people, tenants and their dependents, into the commune to improve their moral and material welfare and keep them out of the local Whiteboys – the 'Lady Clares'. All went well until Vandeleur's gambling addiction led him to wager away the estate. His creditors and the courts refused to accept that he was no longer the owner, and the Ralahine commune collapsed in 1833.[46]

While O'Connell amounted to a formidable obstacle for radicals, developing political consciousness in Ireland, emigration to Britain's burgeoning industrial cities, trade union contacts, and the influence in Britain of leaders like John Doherty, Feargus O'Connor,[47] and Bronterre O'Brien,[48] offered widening opportunities for radical cross-channel collaboration in the 1830s. O'Connor had begun his political career as a Repeal MP for Cork in 1832. Personality and policy differences with O'Connell, including O'Connor's suggestions for an alliance of Irish peasants and English industrial workers,

---

45   Rachel O'Higgins, 'Ireland and Chartism: a study of the influence of Irishmen and the Irish Question on the Chartist Movement' (PhD, TCD, 1959), pp. 92–3; Geoghegan, 'Robert Owen, cooperation and Ulster in the 1830s', pp. 9–21.

46   Owenites left three first-hand accounts of Ralahine: E. T. Craig, *The Irish Land and Labour Question, Illustrated in the History of Ralahine and Co-operative Farming* (London, 1882); William Pare, *Co-operative Agriculture: A Solution to the Land Question as Exemplified in the History of the Ralahine Co-operative Association, County Clare, Ireland* (London, 1870); and John Finch, 'Ralahine; or human improvement and human happiness', *New Moral World*, 31 Mar. to 29 Sept. 1838.

47   Feargus O'Connor (1794–1855), born in Connorville, Cork; Protestant; read law at TCD; elected an honorary member of the London Workingmen's Association in 1836; founded the *Northern Star* in 1837; undisputed leader of Chartism by 1841; MP for Nottingham from 1847 until committed to an asylum in 1852. Neither he nor Bronterrre O'Brien have been woven into the public memory of Irish labour. See Paul A. Pickering, *Feargus O'Connor: A Political Life* (Exeter, 2006).

48   James 'Bronterre' O'Brien (1804–64); born in Granard, Longford; Catholic; read law at TCD; wrote on Repeal and working-class issues for Carpenter's *Political Letters*, 1831; edited the *Poor Man's Guardian*, 1832; founded *Bronterre's National Reformer*, 1837; the ideologist of Chartism; his more intellectual style clashed with O'Connor's demagoguery and he condemned O'Connor's 'dictatorial' leadership of Chartism; advocated Babeufian schemes for land nationalisation; after 1848 he survived as an adult education teacher in London and died in poverty. See Alfred Plummer, *Bronterre O'Brien: A Political Biography* (London, 1971).

led to bitter enmity between the two. O'Connor lost his seat in 1835, and went on to lead Chartism in Britain, but never lost interest in Ireland. Chartism acquired support in Ireland in spite of O'Connell, and came under the leadership of another former O'Connellite, Patrick O'Higgins.[49] O'Higgins's paper, the *Tribune* (1834–6) established close links with Cobbett's *Political Register* and enjoyed a large circulation among the Irish in Britain. A Dublin Chartist group was formed in July 1839, only to have its first meetings smashed by the Trades Political Union, but Chartism recovered within the Irish Universal Suffrage Association, set up by O'Higgins in 1841. At its peak, the Suffrage Association claimed 1,000 members, the bulk of them in Dublin, Belfast, and Drogheda. Whilst small masters and tradesmen predominated at leadership level, Chartist activity in towns like Ballyragget, Cashel, and Loughrea reflected wider support from subsistence tenants and agricultural labourers. Irish Chartism took a more moderate line than its British counterpart. Its strategy was to maximise constitutional pressure on parliament. Physical force did not become an issue until 1848. The Universal Suffrage Association issued pamphlets, distributed newspapers, organised petitions on the charter, Repeal, and emigration, and popularised these issues in Britain, where it attracted stronger interest than in Ireland. In the face of O'Connellite opposition, clerical denunciation, and employer victimisation, it was rarely strong enough to mobilise publicly. By 1842, Chartist progress in the provinces had been checked.

When O'Connell revived the Repeal cause in April 1840, his relations with artisans improved immediately. In Dublin, the Repeal Association remained dominated by artisans and their grievances for the next two years. As had happened with the first wave of Repeal agitation, political reforms diluted support from the two groups whose backing O'Connell prized – the Catholic middle class and Protestants. The Municipal Corporations Act (1840) gave the former limited control over urban administration in the south. By the same token, the erosion of privilege alienated Protestants. Membership of the Orange Order had swelled to over 100,000 by 1835, and working-class Protestants became active in Tory politics. Even Dublin Protestant tradesmen, while still hostile to free trade, gave scant support to Repeal in the 1840s. Orange operative associations were formed in Dublin, Cork, Bandon, Youghal, and Belfast during the decade, though Belfast Chartists collected 2,000 signatures for the second Chartist petition of 1842, which included a

49   Patrick O'Higgins (1790–1854), born in Ballymagrahan, Down; apprenticed to the woollen trade in Dublin; expelled from National Trades Political Union for condemning the Whig Coercion Act; usually sided with O'Connorites in Chartism; wrote the tract *Landlord and Tenant* (1845); did not re-enter politics after the 1848 Rising; now largely forgotten. See Takashi Koseki, 'Patrick O'Higgins and Irish Chartism', Hosei University Ireland–Japan Papers, 2 (Hosei, *n.d.*).

demand for Repeal.[50] Repeal agitation gathered pace in late 1842, spurred on by bad harvests, widespread social unrest, and Young Ireland's phenomenally popular paper, the *Nation*. More than 40 monster meetings took place over the summer and autumn of 1843, proclaimed by the Liberator as 'the Repeal Year'. But there was no way that Westminster was going to grant Repeal without the kind of pressure O'Connell was unwilling to countenance. In October, the government banned the monster meeting planned for Clontarf. O'Connell backed down, and the cause foundered. It was a setback too for politics in the Dublin trades. They had lost faith in the Trades Political Union and, for the moment, Chartism held little attraction. The Universal Suffrage Association suspended activities as a gesture of solidarity following O'Connell's arrest on a trumped up conspiracy charge. Significantly, the rules of the new Regular Trades Association forbade discussion of politics.

1848

Young Irelanders offered fresh prospects for radicalism. Founded in 1842, Young Ireland represented advanced nationalism but gave conditional support to the Repeal Association. Debate on response to the Great Famine strained relations with O'Connell. Young Ireland demanded an embargo on food exports. O'Connell demanded that members of the Repeal Association sign a pledge renouncing violence. Young Ireland demurred. Starvation was already creating a sharp increase in agrarian crime, and popular disbelief in the logic of foodships sailing out from Ireland past relief ships sailing in was turning to violence.[51] Thomas Francis Meagher finally made the breach with his famous speech refusing to 'stigmatise the sword'. Young Ireland's expulsion from the Repeal Association in 1846 alienated many workers from O'Connell. Martin Crean, a shoemaker and former president of the Trades Political Union, led trade unionists to join dissident Repealers in drawing up a Remonstrance, which was signed by 15,000 people.[52] The failure of the potato crop that winter and the inadequacy of Whig measures to deal with the catastrophe discredited Old Ireland.

---

50 See Hill, 'The Protestant response to Repeal'; and 'Artisans, sectarianism, and politics in Dublin, 1829–48'; Hoppen, *Ireland Since 1800*, pp. 23–4; and Bernard Reaney, 'Irish Chartists in Britain and Ireland: rescuing the rank and file', *Saothar* 10 (1984), p. 98.

51 For rural crime figures see Charles Townshend, *Political Violence in Ireland: Government and Resistance since 1848* (Oxford, 1983), p. 24.

52 O'Higgins, 'Irish trade unions and politics, 1830–50', p. 216.

In response to pressure from artisans and shopkeepers, Young Irelanders founded the Irish Confederation in January 1847 to unite all nationalists at odds with O'Connell. A Trades and Citizens Committee was set up contemporaneously by artisans under the auspices of the Confederation. Support from urban workers and the imperative of separatism, propelled advanced nationalism steadily to the left.[53] Young Ireland had rejected appeals for an alliance with Chartism. Influenced by the Trades and Citizens Committee and radicals like Fintan Lalor,[54] who wanted to link nationalism with land agitation, some Confederate leaders took a more sympathetic view. On the British side, O'Connell's death in May facilitated a confluence of Repealers and Chartists. But the Confederation still baulked at the idea. Further confusion reigned over aims and methods. The Confederation demanded self-government but disavowed separatism or physical force. In February 1848, John Mitchel led a breakaway group to found the radical and separatist *United Irishman*, which gave extensive coverage to Chartism. With such internal dissent and no great support in the countryside, the Confederate movement appeared to be falling into disarray. Meagher struck out independently to challenge Old Ireland in a bye-election at Waterford. Though unsuccessful, he was elated with the popular response. The results were barely announced when news arrived that Louis Phillipe had been toppled and a republic declared in Paris. The fall of the last French king was hailed by workers and bourgeois liberals throughout Europe, and it revitalised the flagging Confederates.

Whiggish expectations that the revolution would be confined to a simple change of authority were to be disappointed. What began as a liberal challenge unleashed a rapid mobilisation of popular power. Moreover, Paris set off a chain of revolt in European capitals, triggering speculation as to when Ireland would follow suit. Now came the reckoning for advanced nationalism. Conservatives like William Smith O'Brien and Gavan Duffy argued initially for alliance with the Repeal Association to strengthen moderate opinion, but in March contacts with British Chartism developed quickly. Joint meetings of Confederates and Chartists were held in Manchester and Oldham. For the first time, the bulk of Irish emigrants in England's industrial north became

53   For relations between labour, Confederates, and Chartists see O'Higgins, 'Ireland and Chartism'; and 'Irish trade unions and politics, 1830–50'; Reaney, 'Irish Chartists in Britain and Ireland'; and John Saville, *1848: The British State and the Chartist Movement* (Cambridge, 1987).

54   James Fintan Lalor (1807–49), born at Tenakill, Queen's County, son of a Radical MP; crippled from birth; a powerful journalist in Young Ireland; formerly an icon of socialist republicanism, acclaimed for the slogan 'Ireland her own, and all therein, from the sod to the sky. The soil of Ireland for the people of Ireland'; neglected of late. See David N. Buckley, *James Fintan Lalor: Radical* (Cork, 1990).

involved with Chartism. Friedrich Engels wrote optimistically in the *Deutsche-Brusseler Zeitung* in January 1848: 'There can be no doubt that henceforth the mass of the Irish people will unite ever more closely with the English Chartists and will act with them according to a common plan'. On 22 March, the government tried to cripple this evolving union by arresting Mitchel, Smith O'Brien, and Meagher on a charge of seditious libel. After the great Chartist demonstration at London's Kennington Common on 10 April, in which Confederates were prominent, security legislation was rushed through parliament. In May, Mitchel was sentenced to 14 years' transportation. But the Crown failed to convict Meagher and Smith O'Brien, due to the dissent of the solitary Catholic on the jury. Meanwhile, Irish Chartism resurfaced to strengthen the alliance with Confederates. From late April, the revived Universal Suffrage Association organised public meetings to swing the Confederation behind universal suffrage, and a Chartist newspaper appeared – the *Irish National Guard* – the title echoing events in Paris. Thirteen trade unions paraded to greet Meagher in Cork in May, and observers described the city's 17 Confederate clubs as a 'union of trades'. Twenty thousand people welcomed Meagher to his native Waterford in July; bands from the industrial suburb of Ballybricken marched to Carrick to meet him.[55] The eventual military fiasco of 1848 and its middle-class leadership have concealed the extent and social composition of Confederate support.

As Confederate leaders prepared for insurrection, the government acted decisively on 22 July. Parliament suspended Habeas Corpus, the Confederate Clubs were suppressed, and arrests were intensified. Chartism too was crushed. O'Higgins spent seven months in jail on a charge of concealing arms. Whilst urban workers awaited 'the word', Confederate leaders still at large had fled to the country, where support was weaker. Aside from the fear of arrest in Dublin, they believed that the larger towns were too strongly garrisoned for a revolt to consolidate before facing the military. Remembering the slaughter of 1798, they reckoned the best place for badly armed insurgents to do battle was among small fields with plenty of hedges and walls. The plan was to spark the flame in Kilkenny city, mobilise west Kilkenny-east Tipperary, and then involve Waterford and Wexford. Kilkenny and Tipperary had the advantage of lying between the Confederate strongholds of Waterford, Cork, Limerick, and Dublin, and had been the location of major agrarian unrest in the Tithe war. Once an insurrection was under way, the Dublin clubs would join in. Poor preparation, informers, a want of guns, and Smith O'Brien's lack of audacity as a military commander combined to frustrate the plan, and the rising fizzled

---

55 Maura Cronin, *Country, Class or Craft? The Politicisation of the Skilled Artisan in Nineteenth Century Cork* (Cork, 1994), pp. 103–4; O'Connor, *A Labour History of Waterford*, p. 56.

out ingloriously in the widow McCormack's cabbage patch at Ballingarry. Some sporadic action continued, but essentially '1848' was over.

Against the odds, Confederates attempted a recovery. Bernard Fullam founded the *Irishman* in January 1849 as a successor to Mitchel's *United Irishman*. Lalor meanwhile regrouped the remnants of the Confederate clubs to prepare another rising. Trades sentiment in Dublin had not changed. The 'Famine Queen's' visit to the city that year drew a protest from an aggregate meeting of craft unions.[56] In nationalism's last appeal to insurrectionary spontaneity, Lalor made a vain effort to foment insurgency in the Waterford-Tipperary area. On 16 September, the day appointed for a general uprising, Cappoquin alone responded.[57] Lalor returned to Dublin in disappointment and died of ill health in December. A further blow to radicalism came when Gavan Duffy revived the *Nation* and siphoned support away from Fullam's *Irishman*. Fullam set about building the Irish Democratic Association, arguably the first Irish organisation with a socialist programme. With O'Connor's encouragement, branches were formed in Glasgow, Liverpool, Manchester, Wigan, and Barnsley as well as Dublin, Kilkenny, Limerick, Cork, and Carrick-on-Suir. Fullam claimed 2,000 members. In fact, there were only about 50 paid up supporters. By May 1850, the Association and the *Irishman* had folded.[58]

Working-class politics lost its revolutionary edge after 1848 as republicans and trade unions moved in opposite directions. The failure to effect a spontaneous revolt drove the former towards military conspiracy, while the latter continued to consolidate their legality. Not even James Connolly could reconcile the contradiction in 1916, when he was compelled to separate his union duties from his plans for the Citizen Army. '48 was a watershed too for British-Irish radicalism. As Irish Labour declined in importance after the Great Famine, its relationship with British Labour was degraded from fraternity to dependency. Increasingly, the Irish would adopt rather than adapt from their more successful neighbours.

56   *Freeman's Journal*, 22 July 1849.
57   Anthony M. Breen, *The Cappoquin Rebellion, 1849* (Thurston, 1998).
58   O'Higgins, 'Ireland and Chartism', p. 160; D'Arcy, 'Skilled tradesmen in Dublin, 1800–50', Appendix XII, pp. lix–lxi.

TWO

ATROPHY

THE UNMAKING OF THE IRISH WORKING CLASS 1849–88

Trade unionism is largely a thing of English growth and
development introduced into this country.
John Murphy, President, ITUC, 1908[1]

—

Post-Famine Ireland was a paradox of undevelopment and social progress. By exporting its surplus population and integrating into the UK economy, in a way that in turn accelerated depopulation, what had been one of Europe's poorest countries raised its income per capita to the point where it compared favourably with the continental average by the end of the century.[2] Rising incomes were paralleled by the emergence of modern state services. The national schools slashed the level of illiteracy from 53 per cent in 1841 to 18 per cent in 1891, and legislation for better housing finally took effect in the 1880s and 1890s, following the Labourers (Ireland) Acts and the Housing of the Working Classes Act. Though public health, housing, and welfare provision remained pitifully inadequate at the turn of the century, the material quality of working-class life had advanced more in the past 40 years than over the previous 400.[3]

Trade unionism similarly evinced a paradox of slow decline and incremental sophistication. The wealth generated by industrialisation began to trickle down to the British working class in the 1860s, and a quantum leap in the calibre of union organisation had an effect on Ireland, raising the question of forming a national Labour congress. It was a premature step in the short term;

1 University of Ulster, Magee College (UUMC), ITUC, *Report* (1908), p. 27.
2 The undevelopment thesis is argued a fortiori in Raymond Crotty, *Ireland in Crisis: A Study in Capitalist Colonial Undevelopment* (Dingle, 1986). For a discussion of income levels see Kieran A. Kennedy, Thomas Giblin, and Deirdre McHugh, *The Economic Development of Ireland in the Twentieth Century* (London, 1988), pp. 12–25.
3 See Mary E. Daly, *A Social and Economic History of Ireland since 1800* (Dublin, 1981); and *Dublin, The Deposed Capital: A Social and Economic History, 1860–1914* (Cork, 1984), for a closer look.

while in the long run, industrial trends threatened the very existence of an Irish Labour movement. After the Great Famine, the railways intensified the process begun by the steamships, facilitating unprocessed exports and cheap imports. When the mid-Victorian prosperity gave way to the first international slump in 1874, the vulnerability of Irish industry to free trade became ruthlessly exposed. The slump revealed a manufacturing base over-dependent on obsolescent minor crafts, and discouraged from modernising by depopulation and the fall in gross agricultural purchasing power. A flood of cheap British goods undercut native manufacture on the home market, while the recession threatened exports, sending the more advanced industrial sectors to join the obsolescent trades in terminal decay. The composition of the working class changed. Already decimated by the Famine, agricultural labourers continued to suffer a reduction in numbers. Their marginal role in the Land War reflected the eclipse of Whiteboyism by tenant right. In the towns, the demise of traditional handicrafts was compensated for partly by the growth in housing provisions trades. By the end of the century, building would rival manufacture as a source of craft jobs, and therefore the core of trade unionism. Conveyance employment shifted from carriage and sail to steam and rail. Together with the growing number of general labourers, transport would become of strategic importance to the resurgence of the Labour movement in the twentieth century.

Job opportunities for women contracted with the decline of employment in agriculture and a steady reduction in the number of fishmongers, egg dealers, fruiterers, dairy keepers, and hucksters. Their staple occupations however, domestic service and textiles, remained buoyant. Attitudes towards women in work changed. As the century wore on, heavy manual labour became less acceptable as suitable female employment and the view that, where possible, wives ought not to leave the home became prevalent.

Against the trend, the north east experienced a second industrial revolution as mechanised linen production primed an expansion of engineering in the 1850s, which complimented the development of iron shipbuilding in the 1860s, which in turn generated a marine engineering industry in the 1890s. Unlike textiles, shipbuilding and engineering employed a sizeable skilled artisanate, able to command an effective bargaining power through maintaining a scarcity of labour. Whereas Ulster's first industrial revolution generated no major differences in wage levels or the agenda of trade unionism north and south, the second produced a distinctive industrial relations environment in the Belfast metal trades. With the growth of shipbuilding and engineering, the prospect of Belfast being incorporated into an Irish Labour movement receded. Which way the rest of Ulster would lean was not to be decided until the First World War.

ATTEMPTS AT RECOVERY

Labour protest by urban workers during the 1850s kept within the bounds of 'moral force' trade unionism, and concerned itself mainly with reductions of hours. The length of the working day became an issue of general and persistent concern in the latter half of the nineteenth century. 'Nine hours' movements developed in Britain during the 1850s, and by the end of the next decade the 60-hour week was not uncommon.[4] Dublin drapers' assistants combined to win 6.oopm closing in 1855, but needed to address the question again within four years.[5] The greatest wave of agitation involved bakers. Dublin journeymen took up their old grievance against nightwork and Sunday work in 1859, and the cry was echoed in the provinces in 1860, leading to a national campaign the following year. The agitation achieved immediate successes but, as in the 1840s, bakers could not prevent masters re-introducing old hours in many areas. One permanent gain was Bakehouses (Regulation) Act (1863), which outlawed nightwork for journeymen under the age of 18 and empowered inspectors to visit bakeries. Movements to reduce work time, often involving grocers', drapers', or shop assistants, persisted through the 1860s. Usually they were concerned with seeking holidays on particular calendar days, such as church fêtes, and agitation took the form of annual appeals for public sympathy.[6] Unskilled workers too were caught up in the mood of militancy. Dublin paviours formed a union in 1860, as did Limerick dockers in 1863, and Dublin builders' labourers in 1864. Over 1,100 copper miners and face workers at Bunmahon, County Waterford, struck for wage increases in July 1860. After six weeks, the unorganised men were starved back to work. A similar fate awaited 200 Waterford dockers when they turned out in October 1862.[7]

Labour confidence extended to ambitions to restructure the movement. Dublin craft unions resolved in October 1862 to form a new trades council, the United Trades Association (UTA). By 1865 there were 25 societies affiliated, and the Association later claimed 10,000 members. The UTA lobbied employers on behalf of workers, defended affiliates in dispute by mobilising popular opinion and, in 1871, set up a committee to mediate in inter-union

4   Allen Hutt, *British Trade Unionism: A Short History* (London, 1975), pp. 27–8.
5   J. Dunsmore Clarkson, *Labour and Nationalism in Ireland* (New York, 1925), pp. 165–6.
6   The bakers' campaign was noted in some detail in Karl Marx, *Capital, Vol. 1* (Lawrence and Wishart edn, London, 1974), p. 241. See also Andrew Boyd, *The Rise of the Irish Trade Unions* (Tralee, 1985), pp. 55–8; John W. Boyle, *The Irish Labor Movement in the Nineteenth Century* (Washington DC, 1989), p. 55; Emmet O'Connor, *A Labour History of Waterford* (Waterford, 1989), p. 76.
7   Boyle, *The Irish Labor Movement in the Nineteenth Century*, pp. 104–5; O'Connor, *A Labour History of Waterford*, p. 76.

disputes. Not infrequently, it disbursed strike pay. A constant concern was the promotion of native products and the discouragement of imports. It was a measure of the straits to which the southern economy was being reduced that where foreign goods were concerned no item was too petty to be overlooked by the UTA, or indeed any other assembly of Irish craftsmen. Though strictly a body of artisans, the UTA assisted the formation of unions for general and semi-skilled operatives. Nor was their generosity confined to Dublin. Lurgan Damask Weavers, on strike against wage cuts, received a hearty reception from the UTA in 1874.[8] A number of trades councils were formed or re-formed in the early 1860s, and the laying of the foundation stone of the O'Connell monument in Dublin in August 1864 – an occasion to remember a man who clashed bitterly with trade unionists, and yet promised them the thing they wanted most – provided an opportunity for the trades to meet and take stock. A huge procession of the trades dominated the proceedings. To refresh the provincial delegates, the UTA provided a déjeuner at the Mechanics' Institute. On returning home, the delegates were quick to canvass trades unity. Cork trades formed their own, ephemeral, UTA shortly afterwards. Waterford Trades Guardians Association, founded in January 1862, wrote to Dublin suggesting an amalgamation of all trades to promote organisation, foster native manufacture, and develop a benevolent society. The UTA then urged that trades councils 'knowing neither politics nor religion, but trade and protection of tradesmen's rights alone' be formed locally, each federated to the UTA. In November, the UTA noted favourable responses from the Cork UTA, Limerick Congregated Trades, and the Waterford Guardians, to a call for a general union of trade unions. Galway, Ennis, Enniskillen, and Wexford were reportedly taking steps to form trades councils with a view to affiliating to the proposed confederation. However, the proposal never came to fruition.[9]

A glimpse of the dimensions to the real challenge confronting trade unionists, that of sustaining an effective general unionism, emerged in Cork in 1870.[10] Three societies catering for unskilled men appeared in the city in 1868–9; two of them – the Cork Working Men's Association and the Labourers' Society – were general unions in effect. In 1869, a Working Men's Society was formed at Mallow, and a Labour Club at Kanturk. A decade of fermenting unrest in Cork came to the boil in May 1870, when tailors struck for an upward revision of wage rates. Tailors also opposed the introduction of sewing machines. The dispute evolved quickly into a general strike and

8   Boyle, *The Irish Labor Movement in the Nineteenth Century*, pp. 54–61.
9   *Irish People*, 13–27 Aug., 19 Nov. 1864.
10 The Cork unrest is detailed in Seán Daly, *Cork, A City in Crisis: A History of Labour Conflict and Social Misery, 1870–1872, Vol. 1* (Cork 1978).

lockout of 240 tailors in the city. Cork's craft unions rallied behind the Tailors' Society and 22–27 June saw consecutive nights of rioting and streetfighting against the Royal Irish Constabulary (RIC) and military. During the second week of June, porters on the Cork and Bandon Railway turned out for a wage rise. On 22 June, a series of wage demands appeared from unskilled workers in the city. Over the next five days, wage demands flooded in from dockers, railway porters, flour millers, and timberyardmen; the rate requested soon settled on 15s per week. On Monday 27th, the gathering strike wave culminated in a general strike of unskilled operatives. Pickets toured factories and workshops calling out those still at work. Women and boys also joined the protest, textile girls striking on their own accord. Membership of the Cork Labourers' Society swelled to 1,400, whilst many others belonged to the Working Men's Society. This was a revolt of the unskilled. Shoemakers were the only trade to join the tailors in striking for higher wages and restriction of machinery. The unrest spread rapidly to the county, extending as far as agricultural labourers at Killarney and navvies on the Waterford and Lismore Railway. Queenstown boatmen came out on 27 June, and Glanmire bleach-workers and Mallow dairymen on the 28th; by 30 June, the agitation had reached farm labourers, railwaymen, and artisans in north and east Cork. Groups combined on a sectional basis, though in Charleville all classes united in a general local strike. Parity with city wage rates emerged as a common demand, while artisans also sought curbs on machinery or an end to the use of imported goods, and farm workers began campaigns of machine breaking.

After a hectic week of workers' parades and military policing in Cork city, the atmosphere relaxed on Thursday 30th. In most cases, workers' demands were granted, though sailors' and coalporters' disputes lasted into mid July and were less successful. Unrest in the county ended in the first week of July. Here too, employers had normally acceded to the men's pay demands. An end to agricultural machine breaking coincided with RIC intervention, but there is some evidence that the saboteurs were bought off with wage rises. A Labourers' Club was inaugurated at Glounthane on 31 July, and north Cork sustained a fragile 'club movement over the next decade'. The tailors' strike dragged on until 3 August, when a settlement was reached through the mediation of George Druitt, secretary of the London Operative Tailors' Association. A big increase in living costs sparked renewed unrest in Cork and Dublin in 1871, and the Cork Nine Hours League, initiated by the local branch of the Amalgamated Society of Engineers (ASE), achieved significant success in various industries the following year.

The recurrence of opposition to machinery in the Cork disputes illustrates the pressures facing obsolescent handicrafts at this time. After the slump in 1874, these pressures became overwhelming. The paradox of progress in decline intensified. Labour organisation enjoyed minor recoveries towards the end of the decade, and continued to mature during the 1880s. Following legal reverses in 1871, two acts of 1875 legalised peaceful picketing, and repealed the Master and Servant Act that had made employee breach of contract a criminal offence. The Trades Union Amendment Act (1876) finally confirmed some of the legal benefits recommended by the minority report of the Royal Commission on Trades Unions appointed in 1867. Unions now found it safer to register under the law, which gave protection to their funds.[11] Membership increased slowly. New trades councils were formed in Waterford in 1879, Cork in 1880, and Belfast in 1881. Some major disputes occurred, notably that of 1,100 milesmen on the Great Southern and Western Railway in September 1877 over wages and conditions.[12] However, small, selective, and unsuccessful strikes were more common. The deep pessimism that pervaded southern cities after 1874 reduced trade union preoccupations to a pathetic parochialism. Dublin United Trades Council – the direct forerunner of the present body – emerged from collaboration in support of an exhibition to promote craftwork in 1885, and the immediate prompt to its inaugural meeting was a deputation to the new Lord Lieutenant requesting His Excellency to provision the Viceregal household from native goods and services.[13]

'AN ELYSIUM FOR WORKING MEN'

As the south slipped into despond, the north's economy grew apace. The 1860s were a decade of tremendous growth in Belfast, when the city's population rose from 119,000 to 174,000. By 1911 Belfast had burgeoned to 387,000 souls, making it the biggest city in Ireland; with 8.8 per cent of the total population, it contained 21.0 per cent of all industrial workers. Like Dublin, the city enjoyed a sizeable trade in food, drink, and tobacco, but its near monopoly of other sectors gave it an exceptional importance. In 1907, the Belfast region accounted for £19.1 million of the total £20.9 million worth of manufactured exports, excluding food and drink. This performance was based mainly on textiles, engineering, shipbuilding, and marine engineering, the shipyards being the locomotive of progress. Belfast's 'big' and 'wee' yards were

---

11   Boyle, *The Irish Labor Movement in the Nineteenth Century*, pp. 67–71.

12   O'Connor, *A Labour History of Waterford*, p. 79; ibid., pp. 339–41; *Trade Union Information* 5: 28 (October, 1951), p. 9; *Waterford Mail*, 24 Sept. to 24 Oct. 1877.

13   Jim Cooke, *Technical Education and the Foundation of the Dublin United Trades' Council* (Dublin, 1987), p. 5; Séamus Cody, John O'Dowd, and Peter Rigney, *The Parliament of Labour: 100 Years of Dublin Council of Trade Unions* (Dublin, 1986), pp. 11–15.

employing a staff of 12,000 by 1900, and 20,000 by 1914. With lesser centres of manufacture scattered across the province, Ulster accounted for almost half of the industrial workforce in 1911. Working-class conditions were by no means easy, but compared favourably with those in the main British cities. Fifty thousand new houses were built in Belfast between 1880 and 1900: rows of red-brick 'Coronation Streets' becoming the city's urban signature. One per cent of Belfast families lived in one-room tenements in 1903, compared with 26 per cent in Glasgow, and 35 per cent in Dublin. This was the stuff of Lord Mayor Sir James Henderson's celebrated boast to the 1898 Irish Trades Union Congress that here was 'an elysium for working men'.[14]

Belfast's labour force can be divided into two major sectors – textiles and the metal trades. The linen industry survived the hiccups caused by the Crimean War, the American financial crisis of 1857–8, and the potentially disastrous loss of the American market in the 1860s, to profit from the substitution of linen for cotton after 1862. Boom times continued up to 1874. Thereafter, technical innovation and cheap wages allowed Ulster to maintain its position in a contracting market by consolidating its share of UK production. Employment in Irish linen rose from 62,000 to 65,000 between 1885 and 1904. Spin-off industries also developed, chiefly handkerchief-making in Lurgan-Portadown, and shirt production in Derry. By 1896 there were 20 shirt factories in Derry employing 10,000 people. Both linen and shirt making supported considerable outwork employment in dressmaking and 'making up'.[15]

Mechanisation of linen had accelerated in the 1840s and with the demise of domestic production it turned weaving and spinning, overwhelmingly, into women's work. Women and juveniles made up 60–70 per cent of the total labour force, and most women earned 7–8s per week, less fines for indiscipline or damage to goods. Men performed the skilled tasks, tended machinery, and did the more physical, semi-skilled work. Skilled men earned 30s per week or over; weekly rates for the semi-skilled flax roughers and dressers averaged about 21s. Conditions were difficult due to the climate required for each process. Weavers suffered bronchitis from the humidity caused by steam jets. Male hacklers and roughers worked in a constant cloud of fibre dust, which caused fits of coughing each morning. Spinners new to the job commonly

14   See L. A. Clarkson, 'Population change and urbanisation, 1821–1911', in Liam Kennedy and Philip Ollerenshaw (eds), *An Economic History of Ulster, 1820–1939* (Manchester, 1985), pp. 137–54; Michael Farrell, *Northern Ireland: The Orange State* (London, 1976), p. 18; L. M. Cullen, *An Economic History of Ireland since 1660* (London, 1987), pp. 16–62; James Henderson, *A Record Year in my Existence as Lord Mayor of Belfast, 1898* (Belfast, 1899). For housing figures see W. Coe, 'The economic history of the engineering industry in the north of Ireland (PhD, QUB, 1961), pp. 325–62.

15   Eithne McLaughlin, 'Women and work in Derry City: a survey', *Saothar* 14 (1989), pp. 35–45.

experienced 'mill fever' until accustomed to the noise and poor ventilation. Occupational health problems were accentuated by overcrowded housing, bad sanitation, and a staple diet for women of bread and sweet, stewed tea four times daily.[16] Why 90 per cent of women workers remained unorganised up to the First World War is a matter of contention. Certainly, the workforce was divided by pronounced distinctions of sex, grade, and religion. Weavers were 'the swanks'; the lower paid spinners were 'down'. And weavers were predominantly Protestant, while spinners were disproportionately Catholic. Underlying sectarian tensions erupted during the Home Rule crises. Yet the history of trade unionism in Ulster shows that religion and politics were dragon's teeth to class politics, not barriers to a narrow unity on wages and conditions. Plausibly, the key obstacles were that women were unskilled, easily replaced workers who saw their wages as supplementary to the household income; they faced anti-union managers and were wary of union officials, who tended to be men. Alternatively, it has been argued that women were not so docile, and rather than paying union dues, they preferred to exploit the solidarity engendered by their aggregation in the mills. Short, spontaneous strikes of non-union employees would be a distinctive feature of the industry up to 1914.[17] A government inspector described tactics in the prosperous 1860s:

> the workers consequently now are very independent of their employers. Small strikes for wages are often occurring, the girls sometimes appearing, in consequence, in the police courts, where they are lectured from the bench, and let off on contritely promising to return to work and fulfil their 'notice'. Occasionally they assemble in groups in the mill-yard, shouting and cheering, but determinedly refusing to enter the factory 'till prices go up'... The masters naturally refuse to be driven into concessions, but, in the long run, they have generally given way.[18]

Wage rates in linen rose by 15–20 per cent in the 1860s, and the cost of living fell. Many mill owners responded to the boom by stretching the working day from 12 to 14 hours. In Derry, shirt factories stayed open as late as 10.00pm.[19]

16   BPP, *Report upon Conditions of Work in Flax and Linen Mills* (1893–4), C.7287.XVII.

17   For an anthropology see Betty Messenger, *Picking Up the Linen Threads: Life in Ulster's Mills* (Belfast, 1988). The rationale and merit of strike tactics is discussed in Mats Greiff, '"Marching through the streets singing and shouting": industrial struggle and trade unions among female linen workers in Belfast and Lurgan, 1872–1910', *Saothar* 22 (1997), pp. 29–44; and 'Striking for the right to be late at work: workers' resistance to employers' time discipline in Lurgan power loom factories, 1899–1914', in Francis Devine, Fintan Lane, and Niamh Puirséil (eds), *Essays in Irish Labour History: A Festschrift for Elizabeth and John W. Boyle* (Dublin, 2008), pp. 118–34.

18   BPP, *Factory Inspectors' Reports for 1865–6* (1866), 3622.XXIV.

19   Ibid.

An increase in living costs in 1871–2 encouraged the men to unionise. A Flaxdressers' Union was formed in 1872, and demanded an extra 4s per week. The employers offered 2s. On 13 May Belfast flaxdressers came out, and within a week the strike had spread beyond the union to 2,500 workers, including flax roughers. Masters replied with a lockout on 31 May, closing the mills one by one. Support came from Belfast trade societies, and popular feeling ran high. At one point a crowd of about 250 workers attacked a mill owner's residence. But the strikers were ill prepared for a long struggle. On 17 June, they accepted the employers' original offer and went back. A second total lockout of linen workers in Belfast occurred in 1874. The Flaxdressers' Union survived, organising about 1,300 members in the 1880s. Two small societies – the Power-Loom Tenters and the Power-Loom Yarn-Dressers – were founded in 1877, and a tiny Hackle and Gill Makers' Union opened its books three years later.[20]

Though textiles remained the largest employment sector, the shipbuilding and engineering trades, with their higher quota of skilled men, became the strongest sector of trade unionism. By the 1850s, most engineering grades had assumed their modern form of patternmakers, moulders, turners, and fitters, though smiths carried on their traditional skills, and sheetmetalworkers continued the work formerly done by tinkers and braziers. Marine engineering later created a strong demand for boilermakers. The similarity of trades in Belfast and Britain, together with immigration of craftsmen from England and Scotland, encouraged the growth of British-based craft societies. The Ironmakers' had a branch in Belfast from 1826, the Boilermakers' from 1841, and the ASE from its inception in 1851. By the end of the century, the proportion of unionised men in the northern shipbuilding and engineering trades exceeded the UK average. Industrial relations in the trades were fairly harmonious. Unlike their British colleagues, Belfast engineering employers made no attempt to break trade unions in the 1860s and 1870s. As early as 1872, the Belfast Employers' Association negotiated directly with unions on conditions and hours. Between 1860 and 1900 skilled rates in Belfast rose faster than in Britain, though actual earnings tended to be lower due to the absence of piecework. Due to the scarcity of artisans and abundance of unskilled men, the differential between skilled and unskilled rates in the north exceeded the UK average, sometimes reaching a 3:1 ratio.[21] The ASE submission to the Royal Commission on Labour in 1893 claimed rates of 34–39s for a 53 or 54-hour week in engine shops, and a 56 1/2-hour week in the mills and factories.

---

20 Emily Boyle, 'The Linen Strike of 1872', *Saothar* 2 (1974), pp. 12–22; for union organisation and membership figures see Boyle, *The Irish Labor Movement in the Nineteenth Century*, pp. 98–9.

21 W. E. Coe, *The Engineering Industry of the North of Ireland* (Belfast, 1969), pp. 178–82.

Non-members usually worked for 2–6s less. The union complained of poor safety practices, lighting, and sanitation in the shipyards, but otherwise it was happy: 'Disputes in Belfast are very rare, as the employers generally meet their employees in a fair manner, and again the trade has never been the first to demand advance of wages, nor has the Society pushed demands to extremes'. Over the preceding 26 years the Belfast ASE had been involved in just one general dispute, when 500 members struck in 1880 against a 10 per cent pay cut. The Boilermakers' agent told the Commission: 'We are getting on very nicely . . . with our employers'.[22] In reality, disputes were not so rare, but a high proportion were sectional or about the demarcation of work between crafts.[23]

In contrast with the rest of Europe, urban and industrial growth in Ulster intensified sectarianism. In 1800, Belfast was over 90 per cent Protestant and known for its liberalism; by 1900, the erstwhile 'Athens of the north' was 24 per cent Catholic and notorious for sectarian violence. The influx of Catholics in search of work coincided with the rise of nationalism, Orangeism, and the politicisation of religion, leading to intermittent sectarian riots from the 1830s onwards. As early as 1835, one witness informed a Select committee on hand-loom weavers that there was 'so much political difference between the men, that they cannot permanently cooperate together'.[24] Catholics were ghettoised along the Falls Road, and being poorer, fewer, and less well connected they gravitated to unskilled occupations and the building trades. In 1901, they constituted half the number of linen spinners, one third of general labourers, 41 per cent of dockers, and 27 per cent of bricklayers. There is little corroboration of discrimination in employment, but in some contexts the circumstantial evidence is plain. Shipyardmen, who regarded themselves as the shock troops of Loyalism, were prominent in sectarian riots in 1857, and in attempts to expel Catholic workers in 1864, 1886, 1893, 1901, 1912, and 1920. It is hardly coincidental that the proportion of Catholics in the shipyards fell from 28 per cent in 1861 to eight per cent in 1911. Discrimination in public employment was virtually quantifiable. In 1901, Catholics held 28 per cent of central government jobs, and nine per cent of local government jobs in the city.[25]

22   BPP, *Royal Commission on Labour: Third Report* (1893–4), C.6894.XXXII.

23   Austen Morgan, 'Politics, the labour movement, and the working class in Belfast, 1905–23' (PhD, QUB, 1978), pp. 54–5.

24   Quoted in Patterson, 'Industrial labour and the labour movement, 1820–1914', p. 176.

25   Catherine Hirst, 'Politics, sectarianism, and the working class in nineteenth-century Belfast', in Fintan Lane and Donal Ó Drisceoil, *Politics and the Irish Working Class, 1830–1945* (London, 2005), pp. 62–86; A. C. Hepburn, 'Work, class, and religion in Belfast, 1871–1911', *Irish Economic and Social History* x (1983), p. 50; Boyd Black, 'Reassessing Irish industrial relations and labour history: the north-east of Ireland up to 1921', *Historical Studies in Industrial Relations* (autumn 2002), pp. 45–97.

Sectarianism was not the immediate problem confronting the mainly Protestant men who tried to build a Labour movement in Belfast. They struggled with two handicaps. The first problem was the exclusivism of the metal trades – the strongest sector of trades union. During the 1880s, the trades council's membership did not exceed 5,000, and it was composed largely of local craft unions in textiles, construction, and divers other trades.[26] While the council became more broadly based in the 1890s, it never enjoyed the committed backing of the metal trades. In 1899, out of 57 affiliates and a membership of 19,000, 25 affiliates were local, with a membership of 8,000, and of these nine linen unions accounted for 5,000 members.[27] For the pre-1914 period one can speak of a bipolarity in trade unionism between textiles and the metal trades. Textile unions were local, small, weak, and generally supportive of the trades council and its politics. Unions in the metal trades were British-based, well organised, Conservative in politics and suspicious of Labour.

A second problem was the contradiction between labour and Labour. The former was Conservative, the Liberals being seen as appeasers of Irish nationalists. Moreover, in so far as working-class representation in politics had been raised in Belfast, it had been promoted by radical Orangemen, who acted occasionally as a ginger group within Toryism. An early example was the formation of the Belfast Protestant Working Men's Association in 1868 at a rally in solidarity with 'the indomitable' William Johnston of Ballykilbeg, a landlord and senior Orangeman imprisoned for defying the Party Processions Act – under which Orange parades had been banned. Standing for the Association in the next Westminster elections, Johnston won a smashing victory over the Conservatives. But while he appealed to workers newly enfranchised in 1867, he stood primarily as a militant opponent of the Party Processions Act and subsequently mended his fences with the Conservatives and the Grand Orange Lodge.[28] Neither radical Orangeism or ties with the Conservatives offered avenues of advance acceptable to Belfast trades council: both ran counter to the values of British Labourism, which itself could be described at this time as social Liberalism. The Liberals were regarded as the party of labour, most British trade union leaders were Liberal-Labourites, or Lib-Labs, and Belfast trades council's usual contact at Westminster was the

26 Peter Gerard Collins, 'Belfast trades council, 1881–1921' (D.Phil, University of Ulster, 1988), pp. 10–16.

27 J. Dunsmore Clarkson, *Labour and Nationalism in Ireland* (New York, 1978), p. 348.

28 Hirst, 'Politics, sectarianism, and the working class in nineteenth century Belfast', in Lane and Ó Drisceoil, *Politics and the Irish Working Class, 1830–1945*, p. 77; see also Henry Patterson, *Class Conflict and Sectarianism: The Protestant Working Class and the Belfast Labour Movement, 1868–1920* (Belfast, 1980), pp. 1–18.

Lib-Lab MP, Henry Broadhurst.[29] To preclude contention, discussion of 'politics' – by which was meant party politics – was forbidden at council meetings. When its Liberal secretary, Alexander Bowman,[30] contested Belfast North in the general election of 1885, he stood on a Labour ticket, to avoid embarrassing the council. Bowman's manifesto combined Liberal radicalism with a demand for women's suffrage and improvements in workers' conditions. He was endorsed by Charles Stewart Parnell, but not Belfast trades council.[31]

William Gladstone's conversion to Home Rule shocked Belfast Liberals, and presented the trades council with its first major controversy. On 30 April 1886, large numbers of workers attended a rally in the Ulster Hall at which Liberals rejected Gladstone's Bill. To refute Gladstone's claim that only the upper classes of Ireland opposed Home Rule, local Liberals dispatched a group of trade unionists to Westminster to lobby MPs 'supposed to be identified with the interests of the artisans and working classes'. While the trades council dissociated itself from the deputation, a letter from Bowman to Broadhurst expressing his personal support for Home Rule was too much for council delegates. The ensuing furore compelled Bowman to resign as secretary. The council then recoiled from the Lib-Labs, declining to affiliate to the Labour Electoral Committee set up by the British Trades Union Congress in 1887, and hazarding no more than a tentative connection with the successor Labour Electoral Association.[32]

RURAL LABOUR

In the transformation of the rural social structure initiated by the Great Famine, the tenant farmer benefited at the expense of the landlord and the labourer. Between 1845 and 1851, the number of agricultural labourers declined from 700,000 to 500,000. Over the same period, the cottier class dwindled

---

29 Collins, 'Belfast trades council, 1881–1921', pp. 27, 42.

30 Alexander Bowman (1854–1924), born near Dromara, Down, raised in Belfast by his widowed mother; Presbyterian; began work in a spinning mill, aged ten; founding secretary of Belfast trades council; Ireland's first Labour candidate in a Westminster election; joined the Social Democratic Federation in London; moderated his views on returning to Belfast; president of the Irish Trades Union Congress in 1900; retired from politics to accept a municipal job in 1901; the best known Belfast socialist before William Walker, and enjoying some recognition of late. See Terence Bowman, *People's Champion: The Life of Alexander Bowman* (Belfast, 1997).

31 Ibid., pp. 38, 46.

32 Collins, 'Belfast trades council, 1881–1921', p. 42; Boyle, *The Irish Labor Movement in the Nineteenth Century*, p. 157.

from 300,000 to 88,000.[33] Unemployment and underemployment, low wages, and bad housing conditions, ensured continuing high rates of emigration for labourers. The 1881 census recorded 336,127 labourers, and by 1911 the figure had fallen to 199,901; still a significant fraction of the country's wage earners, but less impressive as a proportion of the agricultural community. In 1841, there were 2.71 labourers to each farmer. In 1911, the ratio stood at 1.31 to 1; and where the waged labour force was greatest, in the tillage counties of Munster and Leinster, only Waterford, Dublin, Meath, and Kildare contained more than two labourers to each farmer.[34]

Labourers' conditions improved little in the 1840s–1850s as low prices for wheat and barley caused a switch from tillage to pasture.[35] The replacement of the sickle by the scythe and the introduction of machinery in the 1850s brought further threats to the labourers, who relied on harvest bonuses for spare cash. Reports of Irish migrant harvesters to England and Scotland in 1862 remarked on their youth, in comparison with migrants of the 1840s. The bulk of migrants hailed from west Ulster and Connacht, and about two thirds were landless. Less is known of internal migration, which was more significant in Munster and Leinster. A rise in grain prices following the Crimean War drew additional spalpeens into the tillage counties. The harvest of 1858 saw protests against mechanisation in the south east. Threshing and hay-tedding machines were smashed and scythes broken in Waterford, Tipperary, and Kilkenny. Hundreds rioted at the hiring fair of Callan, County Kilkenny, in demand of 3s rather than 2s per day.[36] Agricultural wage levels rose considerably in the late 1860s. In 1870, average weekly rates for outdoor men varied from 10s to 12s around Dublin and Belfast to 6s in the poorer areas. Resident farm servants, normally engaged by small farmers, were paid from £8 to £14 per annum.[37]

These increases did nothing to diminish the almost universal discontent amongst farm workers, and they were the 'backbone of Fenianism' in rural areas.[38] A collusion of Fenians and English Lib-Labs undertook the first attempt to extend conventional trade unionism to the land. On 15 August 1873,

33   Joseph Lee, *The Modernisation of Irish Society, 1848–1918* (Dublin, 1973), pp. 2–3.

34   David Fitzpatrick, 'The disappearance of the Irish agricultural labourer, 1841–1912', *Irish Economic and Social History* 7 (1980), pp. 66–92.

35   The most comprehensive account of labourers' conditions, organisation, and politics, is John W. Boyle, 'A marginal figure: the Irish rural labourer', in Samuel Clark and James S. Donnelly Jr (eds), *Irish Peasants: Violence and Political Unrest, 1780–1914* (Dublin, 1983), pp. 311–38.

36   Ibid., pp. 316–17.

37   BPP, *Reports from Poor-Law Inspectors on the Wages of Agricultural Labourers in Ireland* (1870), C.35.XIV.1.

38   Fintan Lane, 'Rural labourers, social change, and politics in late nineteenth-century Ireland', in Lane and Ó Drisceoil, *Politics and the Irish Working Class, 1830–1945*, p. 119.

Joseph Arch and Henry Taylor, President and General Secretary of the English National Agricultural Labourers' Union, inaugurated the Irish Agricultural Labourers' Union at Kanturk, where a Labour club had been formed in 1869.[39] Prompted by the 1870 Land Act, the Kanturk Labour Club had aimed to secure legislative improvement of labourers' conditions; it played no part in encouraging the 1870 strike wave. Arch hoped that the new union would concentrate on pushing rates up to English levels, to staunch the flow of cheap or scab labour to Britain, and branches formed in Munster and south Leinster and achieved some success. The *Irish Independent: Trade and Labour Journal* came 'boldly before the public' on 13 September 1873 as the organ of the Agricultural Labourers' Union and in the interests of labour as a whole.[40] It survived until November 1874. If a union could complete the patient task of building membership and maintaining subscriptions among such scattered, isolated, subsistence-waged men, its bargaining position was made vulnerable by unemployment, the seasonal nature of the work, the low ratio of employees to employers, and the 'living in' system. The Agricultural Labourers' Union soon reverted to a strategy that would inform agricultural labour organisation up to 1918: alliance with the national movement and emphasis on legislative reform. Isaac Butt had been a patron from the outset. The union finally disintegrated in 1879 at a time of harvest failures and rising unemployment. A few cognate labour clubs which had emerged during the decade also collapsed.

The Land War brought fresh opportunities. Whilst labourers gave little active backing to the Land League, their refusal to work as 'emergencymen' for boycotted landlords was vital to the farmers' success. Landlords tried to sow dissent between labourers and farmers, suggesting that 'tenant right' would mean 'labourer wrong'. They were particularly scathing about the fact that while farmers shouted about injustice, their own record as employers was abysmal. Among a number of rural labour bodies to emerge in the 1880s was the County of Waterford and South of Ireland Labour League under the patronage of Villiers Stuart, MP. In 1884, Stuart funded a rally of over 400 League delegates from west Waterford, east Cork, and Limerick on his estate at Dromana, where he denounced the Parnellites to a respectful audience.[41] Parnell appreciated that the labourer had got nothing out of the Land War. Calling on masters and men to stand together, he promised to lead a labourers' movement if the farmers did give them fair treatment, and spoke vaguely

39   For rural labour unrest see ibid., pp. 113–39; Pamela L. R. Horn, 'The National Agricultural Labourers' Union in Ireland, 1873–9', *Irish Historical Studies* 17: 67 (1971), pp. 340–52; and Daly, *Cork, A City in Crisis*, pp. 109–37.

40   *Irish Independent: Trade and Labour Journal*, 6 Dec. 1873.

41   *Waterford News*, 17–24 Oct. 1884.

about settling men on reclaimed land. Labourers themselves were becoming restless. Workers around Kanturk struck for higher rates during the harvest of 1880. A Labour League was established at a convention in Limerick in 1881, where speakers advocated wage strikes after the manner of Arch's union in England. Over the coming months, north Cork experienced another spontaneous strike wave, with gangs of labourers touring farms calling out those still at work.[42] In October 1882 a list of labourers' demands was incorporated into the National League programme. With the scope for appeasing both labourers and farmers so restricted, Parnell focused on housing. The Dwellings for the Labouring Classes (Ireland) Act (1860) had encouraged landlords to obtain loans for the construction of labourers' cottages. However by the 1880s, most farm labourers still lived in one-roomed mud cabins with thatched roofs. The 'Parnell cottages' – in anti-Parnellite areas they would be called the 'Davitt cottages' – built under the Labourers (Ireland) Acts from 1883 onwards did nothing to tackle underemployment, low wages, or the persistence of the demeaning hiring fairs, but they offered rural labour a better return for its nationalism than urban workers received. And they provided in turn a platform for the Land and Labour Associations which emerged from 1894. Sixteen thousand cottages were built or authorised by 1900. By 1921, 54,000 cottages had been completed. Structurally, the dwellings set a standard for this class of housing, being generally superior to accommodation for unskilled urban workers, and occasionally better than neighbouring farm houses.[43] Housing was thus the one area where the rural worker acquired an advantage over his urban counterpart.

TOWARDS A NEW MODEL

Revolutionary politics revived after 1860 and skilled men were a key stratum of the Irish Republican Brotherhood (IRB). Some 60 per cent of those arrested for Fenianism in Dublin in the 1860s were artisans; ten per cent were labourers.[44] Yet, despite many and deep connections with Fenianism, and allowing for its secretive nature, trade unionists did not display the same revolutionary fervour in 1867 as in 1848. Workers were no longer as brutalised by social conditions. Their unions were becoming concerned with distinct organisational interests, separate from politics, and were being drawn into the

---

42 Boyle, 'A marginal figure', pp. 325, 332; Dan Bradley, *Farm Labourers: Irish Struggle, 1900–1976* (Belfast, 1988), p. 25.

43 Boyle, 'A marginal figure', pp. 332–3.

44 Shin-ichi Takagami, 'The Fenians in Dublin, 1858–79' (PhD, TCD, 1990), pp. 81–8.

values of social consensus and moderation. Furthermore, the closing decades of the nineteenth century saw a growing specialism in popular mobilisation. By the 1870s, the unprecedented wealth created by capitalism was finally percolating to the people through improvements in housing, services, and leisure. As organisations catering for social activities, sports, and party politics emerged, trade unions began to hive off these functions, restricting their ambit to industrial issues.

The Fenians had ever been favourable to labour organisation, and after the fiasco of 1867 some IRB elements redirected their energies into trade unionism. Cork's Working Men's Association, Labourers' Society, and Grocers' and Wine Merchants' Working Men's Society, all formed in 1868–9, were Fenian dens.[45] The post-Rising amnesty campaign, which allowed for the expression of Fenian sympathies without preaching sedition, drew open trade union backing. Cork trades passed a resolution for amnesty in 1868, followed by Dublin, and the campaign continued into 1869, with the trades of most towns heavily involved. On 10 October 1869, 45 Dublin unions paraded at an amnesty rally which reputedly attracted a crowd of 300,000 people. It was through a Fenian journalist, J. P. McDonnell,[46] that the International Working Men's Association made a brief foray into Ireland in 1872. The treatment of Fenian detainees had first aroused the International's interest in Ireland, though Karl Marx and Friedrich Engels had earlier apprized Ireland as the Achilles' heel of the British ruling class. In July 1871, Marx proposed McDonnell as the International's Irish secretary. McDonnell first organised Irish emigrants in London, and in late February 1872 the International set foot in Cork, then the most promising of Irish cities for the propagation of socialism. With pledges of financial aid, the Cork Internationalists recruited large numbers of Coachmakers on strike for a nine-hour day. Reports that ten other unions were considering association with the International sent panic signals through the Cork bourgeoisie. Within three months the International had sunk beneath a clerically induced red scare, the Catholic Church being in a violently anti-socialist mood in the wake of the Paris Commune. Branches in Dublin, Belfast, and Cootehill suffered a similar fate. The acronym of its Irish cover name – the

---

45   Seán Daly, *Ireland and the First International* (Cork, 1984), and Boyle, *The Irish Labor Movement in the Nineteenth Century*, pp. 75–91.

46   Joseph Patrick McDonnell (1864–1906), born in Dublin, son of a baker; educated at the Catholic University and considered entering the priesthood; elected to the General Council of the International Working Men's Association; a personal friend of Marx and Engels; emigrated to America in 1872; drifted from radicalism to supporting Samuel Gompers; chairman of the Federation of Trades and Labor Unions of New Jersey in the 1880s and 1890s, and died in Paterson. See Cormac Ó Gráda, 'Fenianism and socialism: the career of Joseph Patrick McDonnell', *Saothar* 1 (1975), pp. 31–41.

Hibernian Excelsior Labour League – would not have reassured the clergy. Engels remarked with disdain: 'Ireland still remains the *sacra insula* whose aspirations must on no account be mixed up with the profane class struggles of the rest of the sinful world'.[47]

Fenian echoes persisted in trade unionism. Many trades or trades councils commemorated the Manchester Martyrs until well into the new century. Parnell's efforts to incorporate Labour within the Home Rule alliance might have extended to urban workers the same tactical opportunities it afforded their rural colleagues. In 1881 Parnell restyled the Land League as the Irish National Land League and Labour and Industrial Movement; in 1882 he founded the Irish Labour and Industrial Union, and called for legislation to improve workers' conditions.[48] Workers remained convinced of the necessity of Home Rule to economic regeneration, but Labour's capacity for independent political mobilisation was nearing exhaustion, and trade unions could no more than limp along with the national movement. Like the economy, Labour had entered a tailspin of undevelopment after the Great Famine. And as with the economy, the most obvious symptom of decline lay in increasing dependence on Britain.

In 1851 the ASE introduced a 'new model' of organisation to British trade unionism. The Engineers set out to create a big, relatively centralised society, through a cautious policy of consolidation. Entrance fees and benefits were high. Strikes were discouraged, the tactical emphasis falling overwhelmingly on maintaining demand for labour through control of apprenticeships and enforcement of restrictive practices. Gradually other societies emerged, roughly similar in style to the ASE. New model unionism, as it came to be called, restricted itself to craftsmen. Politically, it sought to win public acceptance and legal toleration of trade unionism by advertising its responsibility and respectability. In social values it reflected the growing conservatism of the British craft elite, the 'labour aristocracy', during the era of mid-Victorian prosperity. The importance of British craft unionism was reflected in its spreading influence throughout the English-speaking world. Dublin and Belfast branches took part in the initiation of the ASE, and by 1891, the Engineers had 14 Irish branches with 2,228 members, 1,515 of them in Belfast. Other British engineering unions, notably the Ironfounders, the Boilermakers, and the United Patternmakers, also established a strong base in the north east. The Amalgamated Society of Tailors and Tailoresses included a Dublin branch on its formation in 1866, and spent considerable sums to surmount the difficulties of organising sweated employment in the main towns over the next 20 years. British printing unions

---

47 Friedrich Engels to Karl Marx, 9 Dec. 1869 in R. Dixon (ed), *Marx and Engels on Ireland* (Moscow, 1971), p. 283.

48 Boyle, 'A marginal figure', p. 332.

absorbed local societies in Dublin, Belfast, and Cork after 1877. By now, Ireland was firmly on the British takeover list, and local unions came to resent what they regarded as unfair competition from the amalgamateds, as British-based unions came to be called. The strongest resistance to assimilation came in the building trade. Bricklayers, plasterers, stonecutters, and slaters remained in local unions. The Dublin Regular Carpenters and the Ancient Corporation of Carpenters of Cork rebuffed the entreaties of the Amalgamated Society of Carpenters and Joiners until the 1890s.[49] The still important benefit function of trade unions gave the amalgamateds a major advantage over their smaller Irish rivals. As benefit societies, they were well run and reliable. Should a craftsman need to seek work in Britain, an amalgamated society offered him a recognised card. Outside the north east, new model unionism had a very limited application. To the mass of workers in unskilled or declining skilled trades it offered no effective means of establishing a bargaining power. Yet, limited though it could be, the spread of the amalgamateds was sufficient to establish them as the paradigm. With the backing of the mighty British Labour movement behind them, these unions tinted the values and outlook of urban Labour, preparing the way for an accelerated anglicisation of trade unionism during the 1890s. The moderation of rural labour protest and the anglicisation of urban society after the Great Famine reinforced this orientation towards the British model. The view that unions should address internal affairs alone, dovetailed neatly with the new model unionist conception of responsibility.

The anglicisation of Labour was all the more effective for being just one component of a broader process after the Great Famine, reflected most obviously in the language shift from Irish to English; the adoption of English social culture, such as songs, music hall, theatre, and sports like soccer, cricket, and rugby, and the increasing anglo-centrism of the Irish media. With their usual elitism, historians identify the period with a cultural renaissance because of the prominence of figures like W. B. Yeats and Lady Gregory in the 'Celtic twilight'; what prompted the 'twilight', the anglicisation of the masses, is ignored.[50] James Joyce caught the dynamic in *Ulysses*, his novel of Dublin on 16 June 1904, in which a fierce Gaelic zealot, 'the citizen', points to '*The Irish Independent*, if you please, founded by Parnell to be the workingman's friend', and rants against the English content of the births, marriages, and deaths

49   For the extension of British new model unions to Ireland see Boyle, *The Irish Labor Movement in the Nineteenth Century*, pp. 92–9, and Boyd, *The Rise of the Irish Trade Unions*, pp. 51–8.

50   A recent example of historiographical myopia is Betsey Taylor FitzSimon and James H. Murphy (eds), *The Irish Revival Reappraised* (Dublin, 2004).

columns.[51] When Waterford's first trades council was formed in 1862, the occasion was marked with an evening of romantic national airs, complete with the plaintive strains of a harpist dressed as a courtier of Brian Boru. In 1890, a successor body, the Federated Trades and Labour Union, was believed by the Special Branch to be a nest of Fenianism. Just over ten years later the local Gaelic League complained that 'it was found impossible . . . to introduce an Irish atmosphere into that institution . . . it was immersed completely in the "coon" swamp. . .'.[52]

51   James Joyce, *Ulysses* (Penguin edn: London, 1982), p. 296.
52   O'Connor, *A Labour History of Waterford*, pp. 77, 95, 109.

THREE

NEW UNIONISM AND OLD 1889–1906

Two bodies or communities cannot satisfactorily progress side by side except their starting point be identical and their rate of progress equal. When we contrast the industrial position of the richer island with that of the poorer ... we must recognise that ... the duty of trade unionists in the one set of circumstances is utterly unlike their duty in the other.

Alexander Bowman, secretary, Belfast Municipal Employees' Society and President, ITUC, 1901.[1]

we are not ashamed to admit that we took as our model the procedure and methods which resulted in bringing about material benefits to the workers of England during the past quarter of a century (hear, hear).

George Leahy, Plasterers' Society, Dublin, and President, ITUC, 1900.[2]

———

As the American and European economies pulled out of recession in 1887, an unprecedented burgeoning of trade unionism culminated in a great spasm of unrest that shook the industrial world between 1889 and 1891. This militancy challenged existing conceptions of labour organisation. In France it laid the seedbed of syndicalism. More moderately, British workers adopted a 'new unionism'. From the mid 1880s, unions catering for unskilled workers had been active in the English provinces, notably Tyneside and the Black Country. By 1889 the spirit had spread to the capital; the London dock strike that summer marked its arrival as a force. With an alacrity encouraged by the prominence of Irish émigrés amongst them, British new unions commenced operations in Ireland almost simultaneously.

New unions were distinguished by their focus on the unskilled; some recruited on a general basis. Unlike their craft counterparts, they offered low subscriptions rates and gave priority to winning improvements in wages and conditions rather than providing friendly benefits; and they aimed to defend their members' living standards through strike action, or the threat of it,

---

1   UUMC, *Report of the Eighth Irish Trades Union Congress, 1901*, pp. 8–9.
2   Ibid., *1900*, p. 6.

rather than the old craft union device of maintaining a scarcity of labour through control of apprenticeships. During the first flush of militancy they used tough strike tactics, including violence and blacking. New unionists believed also that labour interests should go beyond purely industrial matters to campaigns for legislative reform and political representation. The demand for an eight-hour day especially, which labour was raising throughout the world, became a symbol of Labour's social agenda and of its internationalism. Most workers, skilled or not, clocked up over 70 hours on the job each week. By 1890, there was a widespread determination to reduce this to under 60 hours.

New unionism therefore offered something for everyone, but it appealed to unskilled men mainly, and its recruitment strategy targeted employees in transport and essential services, sectors where strikes of unskilled workers were most likely to succeed. With little manufacture outside the north east, and a relatively high import-export trade, Ireland relied heavily on commerce. At the turn of the century, 'transport and general' defined the alliance vital to trade union success. Being located at the hinge of infrastructure, disputes in transport had an extensive impact, and from 1889 to 1913 transport constituted a 'leading sector' in the evolution of trade unionism. Moreover, the weakness of the craft echelon made plain the imperative of organising unskilled workers if labour as a whole was to win effective bargaining power, so that new unionism acquired an exceptionally inclusive nature in Ireland. In the smaller towns, artisans were often to the fore in replacing trades clubs with 'trades and labour' councils. Socialist ideas enjoyed an ephemeral vogue. And the option of forming a national labour centre reappeared.

The strength of new unionism depended absolutely on two external factors: the trade cycle and British support. The years from 1889 to 1906 were intersected by the recessions of 1891–4 and 1900–4. With the first of these, new unionism faded. Whilst British Labour retained something of its vigour and made slow progress throughout this period, once it lost its expansionist dynamic the Irish movement back-watered. Old unionism reclaimed its ascendancy until the advent of Larkinism.

NEW UNIONISM

New unionism represented the first serious attempt to modernise the Labour movement and it set the questions later taken up by Larkinite and syndicalist militancy: how to organise the unskilled, how to develop political consciousness, and whether the path of progress lay in building an indigenous movement or joining with the big battalions of Britain? Contemporary answers were ambivalent. Thirty Irish unions, many of them catering for unskilled and semi-skilled workers, were founded between 1889 and 1891. Dublin United Labourers' Society mushroomed to 2,300 members by 1890, when it restyled itself the United Labourers of Ireland. Some older bodies like the Bakers, the Brick and Stone Layers, and the United Corporation Workmen of Dublin were placed on a regular footing. Yet, membership of native general unions did not exceed 4,000 at maximum.[3] The amalgamateds played the key role, and new union- ism accelerated Irish assimilation into the British movement. The vintage phase of advance lasted from early 1889 to mid 1891; the most remarkable year of unrest being 1890, with 69 strikes compared with 30 in 1889 and 39 in 1891. The sudden growth of conflict reflected the diffusion of militancy beyond traditionally unionised sectors like engineering and construction to a range of employees as diverse as Jewish tailors in Sligo and gravediggers in Dublin. Newly recruited sectors continued to dominate unrest in 1891, but the high attrition rate, roughly two thirds of all strikes were lost that year, took its toll. Official records log just 18 disputes the following year, only five involving new sectors. Yet the new unionism never quite disappeared, and there were ripples of recovery in 1894–5, 1897, and 1900.[4]

Together with transport and essential services, general employment, the Belfast shipyards, textiles, and agriculture comprised the theatre of new union- ism.[5] As with Larkinism a generation later, waterside workers were in the van. In January and February 1889 the Tyneside-based National Amalgamated Sailors' and Firemen's Union struck with near complete success in Dublin,

---

3   John W. Boyle, *The Irish Labor Movement in the Nineteenth Century* (Washington DC, 1989), p. 105; for the official history of the United Corporation Workmen see Seán Redmond, *The Irish Municipal Employees' Trade Union, 1883–1983* (Dublin, 1983).

4   For official strike statistics for this period see the Board of Trade, *Reports on Strikes and Lock Outs* (BPP, 1889, C.6176; 1890, C.6476; 1891, C.6890; 1892, C.7403; 1893, C.7566; 1894, C.7901; 1895, C.8231; 1896, C.8643; 1897, C.9012; 1898, C.9437; 1899, Cd.316; 1900, Cd.689); National Archives of the UK (NAUK), Ministry of Labour reports on strikes and lockouts, 1901–6, LAB 34/1–6.

5   The following account of new unionism in transport is based on official records; Boyle, *The Irish Labor Movement in the Nineteenth Century*, pp. 99–103, 106–9; and C. Desmond Greaves, *The Irish Transport and General Workers' Union: The Formative Years, 1909–1923* (Dublin, 1982), pp. 4–7. The histories of the main societies concerned are A. Marsh and V. Ryan, *The Seamen: A History of the National Union of Seamen, 1887–1987* (Oxford, 1989); Eric Taplin, *The Dockers' Union: A History of the National Union of Dock Labourers, 1889–1922* (Leicester, 1986); Philip S. Bagwell, *The Railwaymen: The History of the National Union of Railwaymen* (London, 1963); Ken Coates and Tony Topham, *The History of the Transport and General Workers' Union, Vol. 1, Part 1 and Part 2, The Making of the Transport and General Workers' Union: The Emergence of the Labour Movement, 1870–1922* (London, 1991). For the collapse of the NUDL in Belfast in 1892–3 see also John Gray, *City in Revolt; James Larkin and the Belfast Dock Strike of 1907* (Belfast, 1985), pp. 24–5. The National Amalgamated Sailors' and Firemen's Union collapsed in 1894 and was replaced with the National Sailors' and Firemen's Union.

Belfast, Cork, and Derry, and extended its operations during 1890. As seamen's strikes frequently involved sympathetic action by dockers or carters, a close association developed between the Sailors' and Firemen's Union and the Liverpool-based National Union of Dock Labourers (NUDL). Commonly known in England as 'the Irish union', the NUDL followed the Sailors' and Firemen's Union to Ireland, spreading south from Belfast in late 1889. By mid 1891 it organised in 15 ports and claimed 2,000 members. The tide was on the turn, however. The railway and shipping companies, widely regarded as the most obdurate employers, had given a lead to their fellows by granting concessions initially. Now they set another example by weeding out activists and replacing them with 'nons', the polite term for non-unionists. Protest stoppages were then met with 'free labour'. Strikes were broken in Derry, Sligo, Dundalk, and Waterford, and a heavy defeat followed in Belfast in 1892 after four months of struggle. In this dispute the Unionist press had exploited the nationalist politics of the NUDL's Belfast organiser, Michael McKeown, to divide the men. These tactics killed the crippled Belfast branch during the second Home Rule crisis, when Protestant dockers withdrew. Decline continued over the next decade, and by 1905 the NUDL had dwindled to feeble outposts in Derry and Drogheda. Where and when possible, local societies or unorganised movements tried to carry on. In 1900, over 1,000 quaysidemen in Dublin, Limerick, and Newry struck for higher wages. But in this, as in many similar stoppages of unskilled grades, they were not successful.

A second growth area in transport was the railways. Like many long-standing unions the Amalgamated Society of Railway Servants (ASRS) espoused new unionism with enthusiasm. The ASRS had opened its first Irish branch in Belfast in 1885, and then commenced an all-grades recruitment drive. In December 1889, as Great Northern Railwaymen agitated for better conditions, a series of wage strikes broke out on the Great Southern and Western Railway and continued throughout the following year, spreading to the smaller systems. The biggest stoppage began in March when 1,500 Great Southern and Western Railwaymen struck in sympathy with two colleagues dismissed for blacking goods. Once the dispute became general, questions of wages and conditions were raised. On 5 May the strike ended with a promise to consider the men's grievances. Membership of the ASRS, which stood at 163 in 1889, had now soared to 3,659, giving the union about one third of its potential establishment. With the employers' counter-attack in late 1890, the ASRS lost ground in the south. When men on the Dublin, Wicklow, and Wexford Railway struck in protest at victimisation, they were replaced. Similar troubles befell Waterford and Limerick Railwaymen. A stronger presence on Great Northern lines largely accounts for the union's 2,893 members in 1893. Three years later, in step with a related drive in Britain, the

ASRS hazarded a comeback, boosting membership to 6,203 by 1897. Strike notices followed a 'national programme' demanding recognition, better conditions, and higher wages. But when the railway companies applied their standard threat of dismissal and replacement with scabs, the ASRS backed down. It was a crushing blow. The next year brought plummeting membership and defeat in a violent strike on the Cork, Bandon, and South Coast Railway, leaving the union with 1,100 members by 1900.[6]

Societies catering for unskilled men existed in most cities by 1890. Almost all such groups were local and sectional, representing builders', brewery, municipal, or quayside labourers. An exotic exception were the Knights of Labour assemblies. The Philadelphia-based Knights were a truly general union, operating 'mixed locals' in a masonic type brotherhood which preached temperance and thrift. In September 1888, they spread to Belfast from England's Black Country. Erin's First Assembly was instituted formally in Belfast the following March by organiser R. H. Feagan, a nationalist and later secretary of the local Fabians. Erin's First recruited about 300 shipyardmen and bootmakers. It was soon joined by a second Belfast assembly of ropemakers, and in August 1889, Alpha Assembly 1601 was inaugurated in Derry. Then disaster struck in Belfast. Loyalist opposition forced Feagan's resignation, and the ropemakers blundered into an ill-prepared strike. After 14 weeks, the strike was crushed, and the Knights with it. In contrast, Alpha Assembly flourished, reaching 800 members by 1891.[7] The greatest successes among general workers fell to the National Union of Gasworkers and General Labourers (NUGGL), launched in 1889 by a Birmingham Irishman, Will Thorne. With assistance from Eleanor Marx and others of the leading British Marxist group – the Social Democratic Federation (SDF) – Thorne recruited 20,000 members in England within four months, and prized the eight-hour day from a number of employers. Towards the end of the year the NUGGL was active in Belfast and Dublin, where its organisers, Michael Canty, Adolphus Shields, and William Graham, were all socialists. Belfast Corporation quickly conceded the principle of eight-hour shifts in its municipal gasworks. When Alliance Gas of Dublin followed suit in January, the union's reputation was made. It now turned its attention to general workers. A signal victory came in March, when 1,500 bricklayers' labourers in Dublin struck 25 firms to win a wage increase. Dublin coal merchants reacted by forming an employers' association and one of the biggest coal factors, McCormick's, dismissed two union

6   Joseph J. Leckey, 'The railway servants' strike in Co. Cork, 1898', *Saothar* 2 (1976), pp. 39–45.

7   Boyle, *The Irish Labor Movement in the Nineteenth Century*, pp. 105–7; see also Henry Pelling, 'The Knights of Labour in Britain, 1880–1901', *History Review* IX: 2 (1956); Shane McAteer, 'The "New Unionism" in Derry, 1889–1892; a demonstration of its inclusive nature', *Saothar* 16 (1991), pp. 11–22.

activists. On 1 July the NUGGL struck the entire trade for their reinstate-
ment. Two thousand members were affected. McCormick's brought in scabs
to keep business going. Pickets massed to halt coal transports, carts were
overturned, and scabs assaulted. Dockers in Dublin and Belfast blacked colliers
bound for McCormick's and there were strikes at firms which accepted
blacked coal. After two weeks of struggle the men agreed to resume work in
return for an employers' assurance that all future disputes would be referred to
arbitration. But before August had ended, strike notice in pursuit of a wage
demand was met with a lockout. On 10 September, the NUGGL recommended an unconditional return to work.[8]

Outside Belfast, general unionism was undermined fatally by the reverses
suffered in 1891. The year began with a series of wage strikes involving 1,400
railway navvies in the west and south west, all of which were quickly defeated.
In June, Dublin cornporters struck 39 firms to compel ship owners to employ
more tallymen. Lightermen, draymen, wharehousemen, brewers, millers, and
bakers came out in sympathy, bringing the total number on strike to 3,000. By
mid August the strike had been broken with scabs supplied through the
Shipping Federation. Of 18 disputes involving unskilled workers that year, just
two minor actions did not end in defeat; by contrast, roughly half of craftsmen's strikes succeeded, about the average rate for this era. Over one quarter
of disputes in 1891 resulted in some or all of the strikers being dismissed.[9] For
those without a recognised trade or union benefit to fall back on the price of
failure could be high. By August 1891, the Knights of Labour in Derry had
shrunk to 100 members. In 1892, the NUGGL's 12 Dublin branches disintegrated amidst persistent problems of keeping members in benefit and
recriminations over strike pay; Michael Canty fled from unpaid bills to work
for the new Irish National Labourers' Union. This Dublin body, bolstered with
stragglers from the Gasworkers, rose to a peak of 1,200 members in 1894, falling
back to 600 by 1897. The NUGGL enjoyed a slightly longer tenure in the less
militant north. In Belfast it had expanded to eight branches, representing 1,400
workers in municipal, building, and general employment. Four branches
operated in Derry, and others in Lurgan, Newry, Armagh and Portadown.
Decay set in 1893, and the Gasworkers had vanished from Ireland within two
years. Of general unions, only the Tyneside-based National Amalgamated
Union of Labour (NAUL) established a strong, enduring presence in Ireland.

8   Boyle, *The Irish Labor Movement in the Nineteenth Century*, pp. 109–14; Greaves, *The Irish
Transport and General Workers' Union*, pp. 4–7. For some detail of NUGGL activity in Dublin see
Dermot Keogh, *The Rise of the Irish Working Class: The Dublin Trade Union Movement and the Labour
Leadership, 1890–1914* (Belfast, 1982), pp. 93–104.
9   Based on Board of Trade, *Reports on Strikes and Lock Outs* (BPP, 1891), C.6890.

Founded in 1890, the NAUL's Belfast branch numbered 204 members by 1891. Its core support lay in the shipyards, where it organised semi-skilled men. Absorbing remnants of the NUGGL, the NAUL embraced builders' labourers, mineral water and other general workers in 1893. Membership peaked in 1897, with 2,856 members in 12 branches, including one in Dublin.[10]

New unionism had a little more success in the two largest employment sectors, textiles and agriculture. As male operatives seized the prevailing climate, the four existing craft and semi-skilled textile societies were supplemented by four more unions between 1889 and 1894. With little over 3,000 members on aggregate, they lacked muscle. When, in 1892, the Linen Lappers' Union demanded that weekly rates be raised from 15–20s per week to a minimum of 25s, the employers replied with a general lockout. Belfast trades council rallied 12,000 workers in a support march. To enhance the sense of solidarity, Catholic and Protestant bands were invited along and stewards sported orange and green rosettes. The linen lappers lost their fight, being replaced with machines and female labour.[11]

The first attempts were made to organise women. Backed by Belfast trades council, the London-based Women's Trade Union Provident League set up three unions in the mills in 1890, but all fell apart within a year. Eleanor Marx addressed a large meeting in Derry on 8 November 1891 on behalf of the NUGGL, which had opened a fifth branch in the city for female shirt operatives, prior to her visit. Marx complimented the trades council on its support, observing that English trades councils were not so helpful to unskilled or women workers.[12] The most enduring initiative was the Textile Operatives' Society of Ireland, launched with the help of Belfast trades council in 1893. This union enrolled about 1,000 members and was to be long identified with Miss Mary Galway,[13] a tenacious but none too radical lady who concentrated on signing up the better paid weavers. Female mill hands continued to employ their tactic of brief protest stoppages, usually lasting a day or two. Three thousand

10   Boyle, *The Irish Labor Movement in the Nineteenth Century*, pp. 105, 109–17. For NAUL activities in Belfast see also Henry Patterson, *Class Conflict and Sectarianism: The Protestant Working Class and the Belfast Labour Movement, 1868–1920* (Belfast, 1980), pp. 30–5.

11   Board of Trade, *Report on Trades Unions, 1896* (BPP, 1897), C.8644, XCIX.275; Patterson, *Class Conflict and Sectarianism*, pp. 37–8.

12   McAteer, 'The "New Unionism" in Derry, 1889–1892', p. 37. Marx's speech was reprinted in *Labour History News* 8 (1992), pp. 22–3.

13   Mary Galway (1864/5–1928), born in Moira, Co. Down; Catholic; moved to Belfast in the 1870s and worked as a machinist in the linen industry; general secretary of the Textile Operatives Society from 1897 to her death; a prominent moderate on Belfast trades council and in the ITUC; the best known female trade unionist of the pre-Larkinite era, but marginal subsequently. See Peter Collins, 'Mary Galway', *Labour History News* 7 (summer 1991), pp. 14–15.

girls in Lurgan struck against a wage cut in 1889. The Truck Act (1896), which compelled employers to list rules regarding fines and work penalties, provoked a series of stoppages by over 14,000 flax and linen operatives in 1897.[14]

Efforts at rural labour organisation took a more political direction. Kanturk again led the field with the formation of a local Trade and Labour Association in 1889. Similar bodies sprung up throughout central Munster. Michael Davitt[15] acted to coordinate this energy in January 1890, when he launched the Irish Democratic Trade and Labour Federation to reassert the claims of labour within the national movement. Davitt's programme demanded universal suffrage, free education, shorter working hours, and the provision of land and cottages. The Federation attracted agricultural and small town labourers mainly, extending to about 30 branches in and around County Cork.[16] The complications created by the Parnell split reduced it to total inefficacy. Davitt was the first to call for the Chief's resignation, whilst organised labour generally took the Parnellite side. But the split also politicised labour as rival factions competed for popular support. Backed by Davitt on the one hand, and powered by ubiquitous Fenian intervention on the other, divers groups attempted to continue the work. The Democratic Trade and Labour Federation recruited widely in Munster, while a more ephemeral Labour League mushroomed in the south east in 1891, forming 33 branches with 3,880 members, of whom 1,334 were in agriculture. In towns throughout the south, trade or workingmen's associations emerged, many of them under IRB control. Later, the Athy based Knights of the Plough became active in Leinster, under the patronage of Labour-Parnellite MP William Field.[17] To

14 Board of Trade, *Reports on Strikes and Lock Outs* (BPP, 1889, C.6176; 1890, C.6476; 1891, C.6890; 1892, C.7403; 1893, C.7566; 1894, C.7901; 1895, C.8231; 1896, C.8643; 1897, C.9012; 1898, C.9437); Board of Trade, *Report on Trades Unions, 1896* (BPP, 1897), C.8644, XCIX.275.

15 Michael Davitt (1846–1906), born in Mayo, raised in Lancashire, remembered especially for the 'New Departure' and leading the Land League; less well known for his increasing interest in labour and socialism; urged Labour to ally with the IPP, and the IPP to ally with British Labour; might have been the leader Labour badly needed in the 1890s, but preferred to champion various radical causes across the globe. See Laurence Marley, *Michael Davitt: Freelance Radical and Frondeur* (Dublin, 2007).

16 NAUK, RIC Intelligence notes, CO 903/2, 1887–92. For autobiographical comments on rural labour organisation at this time see Daniel D. Sheehan, *Ireland since Parnell* (London, 1921), pp. 168–86.

17 William Field (1843–1935), born in Dublin; elected 'Ireland's first Labour MP' (as he claimed) in 1892, defeating William Martin Murphy; held St Patrick's, Dublin, until defeated by Constance Markievicz in 1918; opposed to socialism, but 'an apostle' of nationalisation of public utilities, attended May day meetings and the ITUC, and acted for Dublin trades council; as a cattle-dealer, he took an interest in rural labour; caught Joyce's attention in *Ulysses* (Paris, 1922). J. F. Reid's eulogy, *The Irish Party's Work Epitomised: Biography of William Field, MP* (Dublin, 1918) illustrates the extent, limits, and style of the IPP's Labour-Nationalism.

the north, Richard McGhee, a founder of the NUDL and later a Nationalist MP, set up the Ulster Labourers' Union. The NUDL itself recruited a handful of farm workers in Wexford.[18] None of these groups could hope to meet the challenge of agricultural trade unionism. As ever, the labourer remained notoriously underpaid. In 1902 the Wilson Fox report estimated the cash value of weekly emoluments (including allowances in kind and extra payments) for male labourers in Ireland as 10s 11d compared with 17s 3d in Wales, 18s 3d in England, and 19s 3d in Scotland. A man dieted by a farmer might receive as little as 4s per week.[19] Nonetheless, new rural unionism showed that it was possible to agitate for cottages, for rent abatements, and for employment on road works. An increase in the statutory allotment with each cottage in 1892 from half to one acre added a further incentive to agitation. Labour pressure on the Boards of Guardians increased, sometimes spilling over into direct action. On 15 August 1894, the Irish Land and Labour Association was formed at Limerick Junction to pursue grievances such as these. Run by Nationalist politicians D. D. Sheehan and J. J. O'Shee as a labour lobby within the national movement, it would prove to be the most enduring of rural labour groups.[20]

With the ebb of new unionism, the more widely organised trades alone could strike with the prospect of victory. During 1892, general stoppages of building tradesmen in Belfast and of tailors and printers in Dublin were successful. In 1896, 4,500 building workers in Dublin stayed out for four months to win pay rises and a cut in the working week from 57 to 54 hours. In 1900, almost 1,000 woodworkers struck 70 firms in Belfast to reduce their standard week to 52 1/2 hours.[21] However, the skilled sector in the south was too small to exert a leading influence on working-class morale, whilst the numerically significant artisanate in Belfast was too sectional. Of the 40 recorded strikes involving shipbuilding and engineering workers between 1888 and 1913, 14 emerged from demarcation disputes.[22] New unionism raised possibilities of displacing craft with class-consciousness. In 1892, the NAUL

18 National Archives of Ireland (NAI), RIC District Inspectors' Crime Special reports on secret societies, DICS/3, 1891–4.

19 J. A. Venn, *The Foundations of Agricultural Economics* (Cambridge, 1933), p. 231; John W. Boyle, 'A marginal figure: the Irish rural labourer', in Samuel Clark and James S. Donnelly Jr (eds), *Irish Peasants: Violence and Political Unrest, 1780–1914* (Dublin, 1983), p. 334.

20 Dan Bradley, *Farm Labourers: Irish Struggle, 1900–1976* (Belfast, 1988), pp. 24–31; Pádraig G. Lane, 'The Land and Labour Association, 1894–1914', *Journal of the Cork Historical and Archaeological Society*, 98 (1993), pp. 90–108.

21 Board of Trade, *Reports on Strikes and Lock Outs*, 1892, 1896–7, 1900 (BPP, 1894, 1897–8, 1901), C.7403, LXXXI.1; C.8643, LXXXIV.239; C.9012, LXXXVIII.423; Cd.689, LXXIII.591.

22 Austen Morgan, 'Politics, the labour movement, and the working class in Belfast, 1905–23' (PhD, QUB, 1978), pp. 54–5.

won pay parity with Tyneside for its platers in Harland and Wolff and tried to end the system whereby plater's helpers were paid directly by the platers rather than by the company. But a recession the following year brought wage and staff cuts, for which the crafty trades council refused to condemn Mr Harland or Mr Wolff. As trade recovered in 1895, a fresh opportunity arose to promote labour unity. Hardened by new unionism, Belfast shipbuilders took the unusual step of joining with colleagues on Clydeside in a common front against wage demands. In a move deeply resented by craftsmen as a breach of the city's tradition of harmonious industrial relations, a strike in one area was to be met by layoffs in the other. In October, 1,100 ASE men struck to restore a cut of 2s per week; 190 ironfounders also came out for the same demand. Trade slumped, and by December 10,000 workers had been made idle, many of them labourers with no benefit to fall back on. In January the engineers accepted an extra 1s per week. The ironfounders held out a week longer and won the full florin. Despite the efforts of radicals to mobilise a class-based response, the sectionalist mentality of local trade unionism survived, and it was to be reinforced in 1897 by the British engineering trades agreement. This, the first such UK arrangement to include Belfast, still left wages to be decided on a district basis, and it soon embroiled Belfast in another upheaval, the general lockout of ASE men from July 1897 to February 1898. Yet it proved a stabilising influence in the long term and did not, as militants hoped, bring Belfast into the current of British labour politics.[23]

NEW POLITICS

Just as the new militancy effervesced from the unskilled to permeate main-stream trade unionism and become diluted within it in turn, so a new politics sprang from the socialists to fizzle and fade within labour. The impact of militancy on class-consciousness is evident in the introduction of May Day parades, the growth of trades councils, and the publication of papers like the new unionist *Irish Labour Advocate*, the more moderate *Irish Worker*, and Davitt's London-based *Labour World*. Responding to the Socialist International's designation of 1 May as a labour holiday, Dublin celebrated on the first Sunday of May from 1890 to 1896. Thousands marched each year, with 20,000 taking part in 1893. The initial parade, organised by the NUGGL, was largely confined to new unionists, but subsequent May days were convened by Dublin trades council and assembled a confluence of new and old unionists,

23 Patterson, *Class Conflict and Sectarianism*, pp. 23–4, 30–7; see also W. E. Coe, *The Engineering Industry of the North of Ireland* (Belfast, 1969), pp. 91, 178–86.

Parnellites, Fenians, and socialists. Parades were held also at Belfast, Cork, Dundalk, Drogheda, Newry, Derry, and Waterford during these years. Speakers usually appealed for the eight-hour day, legislative reform, and labour representation in politics. Trades councils provided a more mundane but enduring platform for radicals. Only Dublin, Belfast, and Cork boasted councils in 1886. Over the next ten years trades councils were formed in Drogheda, Derry, Kilkenny, and Newry, while those in Limerick, Sligo, and Waterford were revived or revamped.[24] Though still dominated by artisans, the councils now indicated a concern to unite 'trade and spade', and to speak for labour collectively. The very weakness of trade unionism gave the councils a role in promoting organisation for the unskilled.

Logically, the next step was to form a congress. After 1868, unions in Ireland were supposed to be represented by the British Trades Union Congress (BTUC), which assembled in Dublin in 1880 and in Belfast in 1893. These occasions aside, Belfast alone maintained a continual link with the BTUC, and even that was not substantial. Out of 380 delegates at the 1893 Congress, 34 were Irish based. Next year at Norwich, the Irish contingent numbered eight. The Belfast Congress noted the peculiar difficulties of the Irish by accepting a motion to guarantee them a seat on its executive.[25] It was not too little, too late. The problem went deeper and wider. The Irish were very conscious of the economic differences between the two countries, and felt they had got little out of the BTUC. Ireland had lower wage rates, worse working conditions, and fewer factory inspectors. Sending delegates to meetings in Britain was hardly worth the expense for societies too small to figure in the reckoning. And there was a niggling sense of neglect on the part of the Irish Labour elite, who was not finding much opportunity for self-advancement in the amalgamateds. Even William Walker, a staunch advocate of links with British Labour, remarked: 'unfortunately it seemed to be a canon of the amalgamated unions that "Irishmen need not apply"'.[26]

24 For details of trades council membership and foundation dates see Boyle, *The Irish Labor Movement in the Nineteenth Century*, p. 339.

25 Ibid., pp. 141–3.

26 UUMC, Belfast trades council minutes, 6 Apr. 1905. William Walker (1870–1918), son of a union official in Harland and Wolff, apprenticed as a joiner and later an officer of the Amalgamated Society of Carpenters and Joiners; the best known Labour leader before Jim Larkin; remembered for his attempt to reconcile Unionism and Labourism, and his polemic with James Connolly on the national question; in 1911 he left the Labour movement to become a government insurance inspector; his reputation remains controversial. See Henry Patterson, 'William Walker, labour, sectarianism and the Union, 1894–1912', in Fintan Lane and Dónal Ó Drisceoil (eds), *Politics and the Irish Working Class, 1830–1945* (London, 2005), pp. 154–71.

In attempts to build a national centre, Labour hovered between two contending conceptions of progress; its eventual choice would define the future framework of trade union political action. Labour nationalists – notably Davitt – wanted a congress which would be geared primarily towards legislative reform, inclusive in its definition of labour organisation, and open to tactical engagement with the national movement. The second option, one with no rationale other than the English example, was to replicate the BTUC, concentrate on building industrial strength in a congress confined to orthodox trade unions, and nurture a strictly trade union based politics detached from nationalism. At rank and file level and in the provinces the historic inclination towards labour nationalism remained vibrant. However, Dublin trades council took a more anglocentric view of things and, as the premier trade union forum, the ball kept coming back to its court. John Simmons, the council's secretary from its foundation to 1916, was a member of the Amalgamated Society of Carpenters and Joiners and a firm advocate of British practice. Simmons personified the way anglicisation was creating a sense of nationalism and Labour as dichotomous, and how workers would divide themselves between each. As secretary of the trades council, he insisted on neutrality towards all but a strictly Labour politics. When the BTUC established a Labour Electoral Association in 1888, the council kept in contact with the Association through Simmons, and Simmons was elated at the British Labour Party's breakthrough in 1906, proposing the council 'congratulate the Great Democracy of Great Britain on its Great triumph'.[27] In a parallel life, Simmons was sometime secretary of the Old Guard Benevolent Union, a harmless club of Fenian veterans living on their name.[28]

The first of four contemporary attempts at forming a congress was floated in 1888 by Dublin trades council. Trades council and other delegates from Dublin, Belfast, Clonmel, Cork, Derry, Dublin, Limerick, and Waterford assembled on 4 May 1889 to found the Irish Federated Trade and Labour Union. The Federated Union adopted a pragmatic programme, concerned chiefly with legislative improvement of working conditions, labour organisation, unions for women workers, native manufacture, technical education, and political representation. The real clue to its potential lay in its broad appeal to all labour bodies and the inspiration of the Parnellite constituency machine, the National League. High hopes were soon dashed by a row with Belfast trades council over

27 Séamus Cody, John O'Dowd, and Peter Rigney, *The Parliament of Labour: 100 Years of Dublin Council of Trade Unions* (Dublin, 1986), p. 34; Boyle, *The Irish Labor Movement in the Nineteenth Century*, pp. 155–7; UUMC, Dublin trades council, 5 Feb. 1906.

28 Owen McGee, "God save Ireland": Manchester-martyr demonstrations in Dublin, 1867–1916', *Éire-Ireland* (fall/winter 2001), pp. 39–66.

Sabbath breaking, and Dublin's commitment was not sufficient to get the project operational.[29]

Differences on the merits of the options facing labour were brought to the fore by the Parnell split. Like most advanced nationalists, from the United Irishmen to the Provisionals, Parnell turned to the men of no property when abandoned by the rich. Moderates saw only problems in the schism, and Dublin trades council declared its neutrality. Radicals grasped the opportunity for powerful allies. In February 1891, Michael Canty and Adolphus Shields announced a conference with Parnell on the labour question. On 14 March, a convention of urban and rural labourers met in Dublin to constitute the Irish Labour League. The adopted programme indicated a grey eminence of socialists behind the League; points included free education, nationalisation of land and transport, taxation of land values, and the removal of tax on food. Parnell addressed the afternoon session. It was all too advanced for most. Dublin trades council, the craft unions, and even the NUDL, stood aloof. The radical/nationalist Labour League died a death.[30]

Still the matter would not go away. In July 1891, Dublin convened a national conference of craft, labour, and trades council delegates to establish the nucleus of an annual trades congress. Three political resolutions were adopted: calling for labour representation in parliament, payment of MPs, and assimilation of the franchises. The conference accommodated an ambiguity on strategy. Its moving spirit, John Martin, president of Dublin trades council, believed that labour candidates should be independent of political parties. At the same time the conference included delegates from Davitt's Democratic Trade and Labour Federation and the Labour-Nationalist Michael Austin was elected vice-president. Martin's death in August caused the project to go the way of its predecessors. Meanwhile the 'Lab-Nat' idea was winning recognition, and the leading nationalist daily, the *Freeman's Journal*, suggested it was time for a genuine Irish Labour party at Westminster. Four 'Lab-Nat' MPs – distinguished by their involvement with trade unionism rather than mere sympathy towards it – were returned in the 1892 general election: Davitt, Field, and Austin and Eugene Crean, both former officers of Cork trades council.[31] But just as the Lab-Nat option was starting to gain traction, Simmons would lure his colleagues away from the political thickets to a neat and beaten path.

29 Boyle, *The Irish Labor Movement in the Nineteenth Century*, pp. 132–5; Fergus A. D'Arcy and Ken Hannigan (eds), *Workers in Union: Documents and Commentaries on the History of Irish Labour* (Dublin, 1988), pp. 106–10.

30 Boyle, *The Irish Labor Movement in the Nineteenth Century*, pp. 135–6.

31 Ibid., pp. 137–9.

BUILDING AN ILLUSION

In April 1894, following consultation with other trades councils, Dublin trades council convened the Irish Trades Union Congress (ITUC). Quoting the *Irish Worker*, the inaugural annual report affirmed the material need for an Irish congress.

> Like the Imperial Parliament, the Congressional machine has become overladen with the multifarious duties and interests committed to its care . . . they cannot be expected to understand the wants of a community largely agricultural, nor can we hope that they would, so to speak, cut their own throats, by assisting in reviving the languishing manufactures of Ireland.[32]

At the same time, oblivious to the contrasts in employment structure, trade unionism and politics between Ireland and Britain, the ITUC was a miniature version of the BTUC. Herein lay a damnable design fault. The BTUC's political influence rested on its industrial power. Trying to copy the British model meant that the ITUC would be primarily an industrial rather than a political body, pursuing its objectives on the basis of union organisation, where it was weak, rather than through the national movement, where it would have had some leverage. Congress rejected reality by abjuring the nationalism which most workers believed in for a strictly Labour politics which most of them did not. The result was not a seedling socialism, but depoliticisation. The only explanation for this bizarre self denial is mental colonisation. It was not a matter of adapting ideas from Britain, it was a wholesale rejection of native values as backward and an attempt to live in another people's reality. Congress became, in the words of the Dungannon Clubs, 'a mean tail to an English democracy'.[33]

The movement the ITUC purported to represent was weak at aggregate and sectoral levels. Immediately prior to its inaugural assembly, Congress claimed the backing of 21,000 trade unionists, or a little over two per cent of all waged workers. Membership figures were not supplied again until 1901, when it claimed an affiliation of 67,000, including trades councils and, therefore, a fair amount of double counting. Figures exclusive of trades councils are available

---

32   These points were repeated in the presidential address to the second annual congress. UUMC, ITUC, *Reports* (1894), pp. 3–5; (1895), p. 12.

33   The manifesto of the Dungannon Clubs, a short-lived political movement founded by republicans, proposed that trade unionism be 'reorganised and nationalised', much to the horror of the *Belfast Labour Chronicle*, 7–14 Oct. 1905.

from 1911, when 50,000 workers were in affiliation. So small a pool had many minnows: usually about 40 unions and five trades councils. The biggest society at the 1901 Congress, for example, was the Irish National Federal Union of Bakers, with 3,200 members. Before the foundation of the Irish Transport and General Workers' Union (ITGWU) in 1909, craft unions predominated, with printers, carpenters, and tailors featuring prominently on the parliamentary committee. Food and drink, transport and services, construction, and textiles were the main sectors represented.[34] The clerkly concern with conforming to British practice was encapsulated in the decision to debar Field, O'Shee, and Kendal O'Brien, from attending the annual congress as delegates of the Land and Labour Association on the ground that they were not employed in the occupation they represented. It didn't matter that Field and O'Shee were MPs – and O'Brien a future MP – that the Land and Labour Association was instrumental in securing decent housing for agricultural workers, or that a bridge to rural labour would be of major benefit to the ITUC. Their presence contravened standing order no 2, and that was that.[35]

Was Congress of any value? Lobbying government officials or MPs to give effect to Congress resolutions was supposed to be the chief function of the executive which, to that end, was called the parliamentary committee – though the name, like so much else, was borrowed from the BTUC. Issues like the eight-hour day, manhood suffrage, technical education, fair wages, and working conditions formed the staple of its debate. A few socialist voices achieved rare rhetorical success. Motions calling for the nationalisation of the means of production, distribution, and exchange were defeated by reformist amendments in 1895 and 1896, but passed comfortably in 1898. The parliamentary committee played a useful role in monitoring legislation, but it lacked any means of giving weight to its expression. In the first flush of enthusiasm, there were calls for action. Motions passed in 1895 and 1896 urged the parliamentary committee to establish a political fund and draw up schemes to unionise unskilled and rural labour. Nothing was done to implement them. Congress was hopelessly ill equipped for the task. It employed no secretariat. Finances were limited and uncertain; over one quarter of the annual budget came from voluntary subscriptions. In 1906, when a small level on affiliates was introduced, the annual income amounted to £190 10s 1d. As the years rolled by, delegates became a little more philosophical about all these resolutions that were never implemented. They sat back and enjoyed the occasion, the mock parliamentary pomp and circumstance, the patronising addresses of welcome from mayors,

---

34   Figures for the ITUC are based on ITUC annual reports, 1894–1914.
35   UUMC, ITUC, *Report* (1896), p. 27.

clerics, and other dignatories, and the hospitality of local employers. The irrelevance of Congress to its founding philosophy of self reliance is most evident in its failure to arrest the retreat of trade unionism into the British movement. Thirteen craft unions dissolved themselves into amalgamated societies in 1896, and six more between 1898 and 1900. New native unions kept popping up but, with the exception of the Draper's Assistants' Association, none achieved significance and few survived.[36] If Congress was better than nothing, it was too a treacherous illusion. In the vain assumption that BTUC strategy could be duplicated in Ireland, a delusion that blithely ignored the vast differences in economy, employment structure, and politics between both countries, it split the urban from the rural labour movement, widened the breach between artisans and labourers, and depoliticised a generation of trade unionists.

In defence of the ITUC, it is argued that the British model was necessary to avoid a breach with Ulster, and that the Lab-Nat alternative was precluded by the conservatism of the Irish Parliamentary Party (IPP). In truth, unity with the north was never an overriding concern of Congress, and despite itself, the ITUC was perceived as latently nationalist in any case. Not impressed that imitation might be the sincerest form of flattery, the BTUC deplored the existence of what it regarded as a treacherous breakaway, the more so when a Scottish TUC was established in 1897.[37] Up to the 1930s, and with some exceptions, the amalgamateds affiliated only where they recruited substantial numbers of nationalist workers. Aside from a few Derrymen, Belfast monopolised the Ulster contingent in the pre-1914 ITUC. Of all delegates to the Congresses Belfast residents accounted for 21 per cent between 1894 and 1906, and 26 per cent between 1907 and 1913; about half the representation the city might have claimed. Northern involvement was dictated more by industrial relations than politics. The craft unions in shipbuilding and engineering were hostile, but the NAUL, which included the most strident Loyalists, was a regular supporter, as was the political voice of Belfast Labour, the trades council. The council had usually sent one delegate annually to the BTUC, whereas it sent six, including a quota of two women, to the inaugural ITUC and an average of two or three thereafter.[38] Probably because it was a federation, it was naturally inclined to support federation. Forty-five unions in Belfast were represented at Congresses between 1894 and 1914, though a mere eight had a presence at more than half the Congresses; the weaker unions tended to be the

36 Board of Trade, *Reports on Trades Unions*, 1896, 1901 (BPP, 1897, 1902), C.8644, XCIX.275; Cd.1348, XCVII.377.

37 UUMC, ITUC, *Reports* (1895), p. 11; (1901), p. 21.

38 UUMC, Belfast trades council minutes, 28 July, 11 Aug. 1888, 10 Aug. 1889, 8 Aug. 1890, 4 Apr. 1894; ITUC, *Reports* (1894–1914).

most supportive. The parliamentary committee – which, to 1912, comprised the secretary and eight members elected by Congress – normally included two or three Belfast residents, while James McCarron, a Derry tailor, held a seat between 1895 and 1909. A more nationalist Congress would have been less attractive to unions in Ulster; on the other hand, a more effective Congress would have been more attractive.

There is an odd consensus between Connollyite and anti-republican historians on the much maligned IPP, which has been caricatured as 'petit-bourgeois', 'openly bourgeois', and even 'obesely bourgeois'.[39] In fact, several Nationalist MPs had labour associations, and John Redmond told the ITUC 'we will in future, as in the past, endeavour to fulfil for Ireland in the fullest sense the function of a Labour Party, believing that we are the Labour Party, as far as Ireland is concerned'.[40] Nor was this empty rhetoric. The IPP's voting record at Westminster won various tributes from British Labour leaders. Keir Hardie declared in 1901: 'The truest representatives of Democratic feeling in the House of Commons were the Irish Parliamentary Party, a fact which the workers of Britain would do well to recognise'.[41] This is not to suggest that the IPP was very left wing, but neither was the ITUC. The former wanted Labour, the latter wanted political influence. What was the problem? Pragmatism compelled the parliamentary committee to cultivate relations with some Nationalist MPs for lobby purposes; Austin acted as its liaison officer with the IPP to 1901, when he was replaced by J. P. Nannetti, a former president of Dublin trades council.[42] A balancing approach to Ulster Unionist MPs in 1902 and again in 1911 did not receive 'even an acknowledgement'.[43] Nonetheless, from 1901 to 1911, with the solitary exception of 1906, and that as a gesture of respect to an address from Nannetti, Congress approved Belfast resolutions calling for 'non-political' labour representation or for affiliates to set up branches of the British Labour Party.[44] Each year the motion was passed and each year nothing happened, because most trade unionists practiced in private what they abjured in public.

39   Emmet O'Connor, 'Problems of reform in the Irish Trades Union Congress, 1894–1914', *Historical Studies in Industrial Relations* 23–4 (2007), p. 39.

40   UUMC, ITUC, *Report* (1909), p. 10.

41   Quoted in Boyle, *The Irish Labor Movement in the Nineteenth Century*, p. 240.

42   UUMC, ITUC, *Report* (1901), p. 24.

43   Ibid., *Reports* (1902), pp. 24–5; (1903), p. 31; (1911), p. 18.

44   See Boyle, *The Irish Labor Movement in the Nineteenth Century*, pp. 224–32, 234–6, 239–43.

LABOUR AND SOCIALIST POLITICS

Closer to the grass roots, the social interests of trades councils drew Labour into the electoral arena. Even the self-consciously non-political Dublin trades council made frequent use of Field in lobbies on fair wages in government contracts, pensions, and protection of native industry.[45] As trades councils went, Belfast now boasted the biggest and best, with, in 1897, 56 affiliates and 17,500 members; by comparison, Dublin had 12,000 members, and Cork 2,000. Conservative control of the council declined after 1894 when the president and vice-president, Samuel Monro and Joseph Mitchell, resigned in a protest over the selection of delegates to the BTUC and alleged over-representation of labourers on the council. An extension of the municipal franchise in 1897 and public outrage at the state of the city's public health, encouraged the council to contest elections.[46] The council returned six members to the 60 strong Corporation, and subsequently published a short-lived paper – *Belfast Citizen*. The elections of John Murphy and Walker as president and assistant secretary in 1899 signalled an era of Labourite dominance; both had come to prominence in new unionist agitation.[47] It seemed as if the Local Government Act (1898) would generalise this shift to the left. The Act assimilated the local and parliamentary franchises and gave women who met the arcane franchise qualification the right to vote at local elections. Dublin's municipal electorate, for example, swelled from 8,000 to 38,000. Amidst much sunburstry about the new age of the people, trades councils and cognate bodies throughout Munster and Leinster launched electoral associations. The 1899 local elections whisked a candyfloss of popular power. 'Labour' candidates recorded spectacular success in the major towns. Limerick returned a labour majority; nine Labour men were elected in Cork; seven in Dublin; two in Waterford. But outside Belfast, where the trades council funded its candidates, the hustings soon brought disillusion in their train. In September 1899, Dublin trades council was demanding an enquiry into charges of bribery against its city councillors. Later attempts to reform Dublin labour representation met with repeated frustration. 'You can buy a Labour vote for a pint of beer' summed up a common view of Labour representation over the next decade.[48]

45 Cody, O'Dowd, and Rigney, *The Parliament of Labour*, pp. 32–3.

46 Patterson, *Class Conflict and Sectarianism*, p. 40.

47 Boyle, *The Irish Labor Movement in the Nineteenth Century*, pp. 278–80, 339.

48 For Dublin and Belfast see ibid., pp. 251–5, 278–8; Cody, O'Dowd, and Rigney, *The Parliament of Labour*, pp. 30–46; on Cork, Waterford, and Limerick see Maura Cronin, *Country, Class or Craft? The Politicisation of the Skilled Artisan in Nineteenth Century Cork* (Cork, 1994), pp. 84, 193–4; Emmet O'Connor, *A Labour History of Waterford* (Waterford, 1989), pp. 107–9; and C. Desmond Greaves, *The Life and Times of James Connolly* (London, 1961), p. 90.

Rural workers were quick to grasp the potential of local democracy for agitation for plots, cottages, and direct labour on council roadworks. Branches of the Land and Labour Association grew to 66 by 1899 and 98 by 1900, the bulk of them in Cork, Limerick, and Tipperary. In recognition of its enhanced importance, the Association was admitted to the National Convention that reunited the Home Rule factions in 1900. Due largely to the Local Government Act, the United Irish League made provision for greater rank and file representation at constituency level. Trades councils were entitled to send six delegates to selection conventions, as were Land and Labour associations, and constituency executives were free to invite representation from other Labour bodies.[49] Both Sheehan and O'Shee were elected subsequently as MPs, the former largely on a Land and Labour Association platform. After the Wyndham Land Act had met demands of tenant farmers, pressure mounted for comparable treatment for labourers. Labourers' Acts of 1906 and 1911 facilitated housing construction considerably. Though labour had now become entangled in the factionalism of the IPP – there were two Land and Labour associations after the 1906 general election, and three after that of 1910 – the work went on: 30,000 cottages were built between 1900 and 1916, compared with 15,000 over the previous 16 years.[50]

Meanwhile, for the first time since the International Working Men's Association had been hounded out of Ireland, socialist politics had reappeared. The Dublin Democratic Association, an echo of the SDF, and a Dublin branch of the Socialist League, a splinter from the SDF, surfaced in 1885. Neither lasted beyond 1887, but Dublin socialists remained active in a variety of contexts. Intervention in large demonstrations of unemployed workers in the spring of 1887 secured leftist control of the National Labour League, an agitational body with ambitions to organise all workers. By November, the League had lapsed, and socialists returned to their clubs, the most enduring of which was the Dublin Socialist Union, founded in 1890. Through new union-ism, and especially the NUGGL, the socialists came into positions of influence within mainstream Labour. The Gasworkers were instrumental in Dublin's early May Day festivities. On the heels of new unionism, Fabian Societies appeared in Belfast and Dublin, and branches of the British Independent Labour Party (ILP) emerged in Belfast, Dublin, and Waterford. The Belfast ILP was inaugurated in September 1892, one of a number established before the formal launch of the party. If Dublin had become a little more tolerant of socialists, the climate in Belfast could be aggressively hostile. The trades council dissociated itself from the branch and there were frequent disruptions

49   Boyle, *The Irish Labor Movement in the Nineteenth Century*, p. 222.
50   Bradley, *Farm Labourers*, pp. 26–31; Boyle, 'A marginal figure', p. 333.

of its public meetings by Arthur Trew and his Orange henchmen. When the engineering disputes of 1895–6 failed to generate the militant class response urged by the ILP, the branch sank into decline, to be replaced by an eclectic leftist forum, the Belfast Ethical Society. A Belfast Socialist Society was formed in 1898 and a Clarion Society in 1900. Both the Dublin and Waterford ILP branches began more promisingly, with support from local trades councils and prominent labour-nationalists. Within two years, each had contracted to middle-class debating societies. Dublin ILP'ers then re-formed as the Dublin Socialist Society and invited James Connolly[51] to become their full-time organiser.[52] Taking the comrades by storm, Connolly dissolved their society and formed a new party to prosecute his views; one whose energy, policies, and significance derived entirely from himself.

Connolly was born of Irish parents in Cowgate, the worst of Edinburgh's slums, in 1868. Leaving school aged ten or eleven, he went through a succession of menial jobs until 1882 when he joined the British Army. Army days had a radical effect on his thinking, and imprinted a passionate hatred of imperialism. After military desertion in 1889, he returned to Edinburgh and immersed himself in Marxist politics. Within a few years he had surmounted the drawbacks of limited schooling and a speech impediment to win a reputation as a promising thinker and agitator. Connolly took his Marxism from the SDF, in 1892 he became secretary of its Scotch wing, the Scottish Socialist Federation, but in one respect a Scots comrade, John Leslie, sowed the seeds of a distinctive perspective. Leslie's *The Present Position of the Irish Question*, published in 1894, argued that the Home Rulers had betrayed the Irish people and advocated an Irish party of workers and peasants. The pamphlet inspired Connolly to urge the British left to develop a rootedly Irish socialist party, an approach at variance with the left's prevailing 'internationalism'. Meanwhile, material prospects for Connolly and his bairns were bleak. He was considering emigration to Chile when, through an appeal from Leslie in the SDF paper *Justice*, Dublin offered him a precarious living.

The Irish Socialist Republican Party (ISRP) was a mighty mouse.[53] With, it was said, more syllables than members, it produced a paper, the *Workers'*

51   James Connolly (1868–1916) achieved a unique status as an Irish socialist theorist, the founding ideologist of socialist republicanism, and Labour's national martyr; much less influential than Jim Larkin in his day, but more mature, consistent, and principled; above all, his writings have made him more accessible and attractive and the subject of some 350 publications to date. His republicanism has always been controversial, but his reputation as a polemicist is consolidating. See Donal Nevin, *James Connolly: 'A Full Life'* (Dublin, 2006).

52   See Fintan Lane, *The Origins of Modern Irish Socialism, 1881–1896* (Cork, 1997).

53   See David Lynch, *Radical Politics in Modern Ireland: The Irish Socialist Republican Party, 1896–1904* (Dublin, 2005).

Republic, and eight pamphlets, sold other socialist literature, maintained an extensive international correspondence, held regular open-air meetings, contested local elections, led lively protests against 'the Famine Queen's' diamond jubilee and the Boer War – the Vietnam War of its day – and got its representatives recognised as a national delegation at the Paris congress of the Socialist International in 1900. Connolly would deservedly acquire international renown as a propagandist and theorist among socialists, but he was not so good at reaching out to the masses. Despite the enormous popularity of the Boers in Ireland, the ISRP made little headway. Programmatically, the ISRP drew on the SDF. At the same time, it was the first party to argue for an Irish road to socialism; earlier socialist groups were satellites of parent bodies in Britain. By 1896 Connolly had sketched his view of Irish history as a popular struggle against imperialism which the working class alone could complete. Whereas the British left generally gave a perfunctory approval to some form of Irish self determination but treated nationalism with disdain, the ISRP argued that the true socialist ought to be a republican, and vice versa.

After the pragmatic nationalism of trade unionists up to the 1890s, and the growing perception of Labour and nationalism as dichotomous in the 1880s and 1890s, Connolly's socialist republicanism offered a third position on the national question. Though plainly anti-colonial, it stemmed from thinking on the British left rather than Irish experience. There is a revealing parallel between Connolly's projection of Gaelic Ireland as a primitive communist society destroyed by Norman feudalism, and Chartist efforts to represent the English as a 'free-born' people before their enslavement under the 'Norman yolk'.[54] The central argument in his greatest work, *Labour in Irish History*, which he began to write in 1898, was a response to assumptions on the British left about socialism and nationalism. The story ends as trade unions emerge into legality, and 'the plan of the book . . . precluded any attempt to deal in detail with the growth, development, or decay of industry in Ireland', though this was the touchstone of Labour politics from 1830.[55] Historically, workers took nationalism for granted; Connolly treated it as problematic, starting from a presumed dichotomy between socialism and nationalism, albeit to reconcile them. Ironically it would have the effect of fixating socialists on the duality of the two. Socialists remember that Connolly turned the British SDF view of the Irish question inside out; they forget that it was a British view.

---

54 For a recent review of the myth see David Renton, 'Class language or populism: revisiting the nineteenth-century history of the Norman Yoke myth', *Socialist History* 35 (2009), pp. 1–19.

55 James Connolly, *Labour in Irish History* (Dublin, 1956), p. 121; for the history of the book see Aindrias Ó Cathasaigh, 'James Connolly and the writing of *Labour in Irish History* (1910)', *Saothar* 27 (2002), pp. 103–8.

In 1902, a new edition of Connolly's writings, *Erin's Hope*, indicated a transition from British Marxism to the American syndicalism of Daniel De Leon. Connolly helped to found a British section of the De Leonist Socialist Labor Party that year and undertook a lecture tour of America for De Leon. In his absence, the ISRP slid into financial chaos. Political funds had been used to subvent a licensed bar. The teetotal Connolly berated the comrades on his return. Bitterness welled up on both sides and Connolly broke with the party. In vain he cast about for similar employment. With his family reduced to desperate conditions, Connolly took the emigrant ship for America in September 1903. The Dublin comrades regrouped as the Socialist Party of Ireland the following year, keeping in touch with American developments, but remaining ineffectual at home.

As winter set in for the hard left in Dublin, it was springtime for social democrats in Belfast. British Labour took its first decisive step away from the Liberals in 1900 when it founded the Labour Representation Committee (LRC), later the Labour Party. The restriction of trade union rights in the Quinn *v.* Leathem case, in which Belfast and its trades council were directly involved, and the Taff Vale judgement, in which the Law Lords made trade unions liable for financial damages caused by strikes, nudged unions closer to the LRC. In Belfast, the sectarian tensions inflamed by the Boer War were dissipating. Even Orangeism developed a left wing. Orange dissident T. H. 'Tod' Sloan captured Belfast South from the Unionist Party in 1902 to become the city's first working-class MP.[56] Sloan subsequently launched the idiosyncratic Independent Orange Order, which posed a wider threat to official Unionism. Founded to combat Conservative appeasement of nationalists and 'Romanisation' in the Anglican Church, the Independents evolved into a vehicle of working-class resentment against the 'fur coat brigade'. In 1903 Belfast trades council was persuaded by Walker to abandon the local Labourism it had adopted in the wake of the first Home Rule crisis and initiate a branch of the LRC.

For Walker, whatever the problem, British Labourism was the answer. Voting British Labour, he argued, would provide more effective representation than the deferential municipal councillors sponsored by the trades council, show the democracy of England that not all pro-Union people were Tories and, ultimately, resolve the Irish question through good government in London. In the early 1900s, with Home Rule off the cabinet's agenda, linking up with the emergent LRC looked attractive. Sustaining local Labourism was expensive and had created problems of discipline. The trades council's municipal representation had fallen to three in 1902. And Walker, a fine speaker,

56   For Belfast politics at this time see Patterson, *Class Conflict and Sectarianism*, pp. 42–61.

seemed to be the coming man. There were high hopes that he would win Belfast North. Walker's pro-Union position has since been glorified as an ideology.[57] His comrades saw it as more of a makeshift stratagem, pending a resolution of the infernal Home Rule question. There was a glaring contradiction in claiming to be pro-Union by supporting a party that was largely pro Home Rule. But what else could they do if they wanted an effective Labour party in a Unionist city? What else could Walker do if he wanted to get to Westminster?

Well, he could be opportunist. Walker's ways of dealing with Unionist jibes that he was a Home Ruler ranged from the sublime to the slick and the shabby. Regarding himself as a patriotic Irishman, he appealed to all Irish workers to sink their differences in the British Labour movement. Hardie and Ramsay MacDonald, secretary of the LRC, made repeated visits to Belfast and emphasised that Walker could take his own line on the constitution. The *Belfast Labour Chronicle*, published jointly by the trades council and the LRC between 1904 and 1906, focused primarily on Belfast, Britain, and the Empire, and echoed Orange stereotypes in its assertions that Home Rule would mean 'Rome rule' and economic ruin. In its few references to the rest of Ireland, it scorned the demands of southern trade unionists for tariffs to revive Irish industry, and denounced 'the absurd and ridiculous craze' to restore the Irish language. Nationalism was dismissed as 'dead or dying', and imperialism commended as 'the transition stage to international union of the proletariat'.[58] Most dubiously, Walker cultivated Sloan, the Independent Orangemen, and their political cowcatcher, the stridently sectarian Belfast Protestant Association.

Walker fought Belfast North on three occasions. A bye-election arose in 1905, and when the Unionists nominated Sir Daniel Dixon – a man associated with the liquor trade and shady municipal land deals, rumoured to be headed for the divorce court, and, worse still, not an Orangeman – the scent of a Labour breakthrough created a huge interest throughout the UK. MacDonald acted as Walker's agent. Walker made it clear to him that he could leave his British politics at home: the fight against 'Dodger Dan' would be parochial and personal. Unfortunately for Walker, the campaign would be remembered for his endorsement of the Belfast Protestant Association's political programme. His friends pleaded that in an understandable anxiety to win the seat, he had caved in to pressure. But Walker was neither impulsive nor easily

---

57   Notably by Patterson in ibid.

58   *Belfast Labour Chronicle*, 12 July, 23 Sept., 7–14 Oct. 1905. The *Chronicle* was published monthly to July 1905, and then weekly from September.

intimidated, and he had been courting the Sloanites since 1904.[59] His calculated gamble lost him Catholic votes and probably cost him the seat. Walker edged closer to winning Belfast North in the 1906 general election, but yielded ground in a bye-election the following year. He never recovered from the third failure, and set his sights on a seat in Britain. Though Belfast received a fillip from hosting the British Labour Party's annual conference in 1907, and three ILP branches were formed locally that September, the city's Labourism had peaked. With the Liberals back in power, Home Rule was again in the realm of possibility and the scope for pro-Union Labourism already contracting.

59 Why Walker made the controversial decision to endorse the Belfast Protestant Association's questionnaire is discussed in Emmet O'Connor, 'William Walker, Irish Labour, and 'Chinese slavery' in South Africa, 1904–6', *Irish Historical Studies* XXXVII: 145 (May 2010), pp. 48–60.

FOUR

LARKINISM AND EASTER WEEK
1907–16

We don't deny that in most cases the cause of Labour is the same the world over; but that we should confess our inability to grapple with such problems by placing our headquarters in London or Glasgow, and sending Irish money to those centres, and seeking instructions from foreigners, is not the way to prove our ability to govern ourselves.
Irish Worker, 4 January 1913.

—

On Sunday 20 January 1907, Big Jim Larkin[1] disembarked from a cross-channel ferry at Belfast. He made his way with a slouching, gangly gait, without which Irish history might have been quite different. The cumbersomeness had denied him a place in the senior team at Liverpool Football Club, and he was not the man to stay in the reserves.[2] For the watching detectives, he was easy to read. A black broad-brimmed hat provided the bohemian touch affected by socialists of the fin de siècle, while his muscular frame, shovel-like hands, worn old great coat, and thick, droopy moustache, betrayed his 15 years as a Merseyside docker. Less obviously, Belfast was a kind of homecoming for Larkin. His parents had emigrated from Ulster to Liverpool and, though he is not known to have set foot in Ireland previously, he would insist, from 1909 at latest, that he too was an Ulsterman, born and bred in the maternal family homestead at Tamnaharry, south Down.[3] A dock strike in 1905 had brought his talents to the attention of the NUDL's general

1 James Larkin (1874–1947) revolutionised Labour between 1907 and the 1913 lockout, after which he left for a career as roving agitator in the United States; divisive on his return to Ireland in 1923; the lock-out earned him international renown as a brilliant agitator, but he was flawed as an organiser and leader; an ILP'er in Liverpool, then a syndicalist and republican; a communist from 1918; led Irish communism, 1924–9; rehabilitated from the 1960s as the personification of solidarity, his republicanism and post-1923 career conveniently forgotten. See Donal Nevin (ed.), *James Larkin: Lion of the Fold* (Dublin, 1998).
2 'The autobiography of Seán McKeown', p. 23. I am obliged to Neal Garnham for a copy of this unpublished memoir. Larkin appointed McKeown's father, Michael, as secretary of the NUDL in Belfast in 1907.
3 The family tradition is discussed in Jim Larkin, *In The Footsteps of Big Jim: A Family Biography* (Dublin, 1995), pp. 3–11.

secretary, James Sexton. Promotion and success followed rapidly, and in 1907 Sexton decided that the time was ripe to reorganise the Irish ports and Larkin was the man to do it.

What made Larkin so influential in Ireland? Employers coined the term 'Larkinism' as a shorthand for militancy, the cult of the agitator, and the sympathetic strike, and to distinguish these from what they called 'bona fide trade unionism'. In the extensive literature on the topic, little of which is both substantial and scholarly, Larkinism is usually equated with Big Jim.[4] There was certainly a personality cult, and Jim, a powerful orator with a flair for theatricality, would promote it shamelessly. There was too a method, involving tactics of sympathetic action, a strategy of industrial unionism, a politics of socialist republicanism, a morality of class solidarity, and an ambition to bring 'culture' to workers and class to 'culture'. What gave these a broad relevance was that they answered the two great questions facing trade unionists: how to build a bargaining power in an undeveloped economy where craft unions were too weak to be a leading sector and where employers were opposed to the unionisation of unskilled workers, and whether to stick with the big battalions of British Labour or build an Irish Labour movement? As ever, the international climate was also important. These years saw an acceleration of worker militancy throughout the industrial world, and Ireland reflected a wider pattern of violent strikes, generalised action, and use of police and troops against strikers.

The dimensions of Labour's industrial relations problem may be gauged from the census of 1911. Of some 900,000 employees, 348,670 were classed as agricultural or general labourers, 170,749 were in domestic or related service, and 201,717 worked in textiles and dressmaking. Thus, over seven out of every nine employees were to be found in largely unorganised, subsistence-waged employment. Trade unions were located mainly in the shipbuilding and engineering trades (30,234 workers); construction (which included 49,445 craftsmen); the tiny skilled grades in textiles and clothing; and the constellation of butchers, bakers, and candlestickmakers who held such a high profile in the pre-Larkinite ITUC. Labour's weakness was exacerbated by the concentration of manufacture in Belfast, and Ulster's increasingly fraught relationship with the south. By the same token, the unskilled were potentially powerful; any union that managed to recruit a fraction of general workers would be in a position to dominate the ITUC. Employees in transport and essential services remained crucial, being most favourably placed for industrial action. Transport was also a growth sector. The 1891 census noted 38,231 'persons engaged on

---

4 Nevin, *James Larkin*, while uneven in quality, is nevertheless a great compendium and includes a bibliography of some 500 books and articles referring to Larkin.

railways, roads, rivers, seas, storage, conveyancing messages etc', and by 1911 the number had risen to 62,947. Here was the Achilles heel of Irish employers. Between 1907 and 1912 transport accounted for an annual average of 12 per cent of strikers and under four per cent of strike days in the UK. In Ireland, it accounted for 22 per cent of strikes, 33 per cent of strikers, and 33 per cent of strike days over the same period.[5]

Larkinism began as a revival of new unionism. As it consolidated and addressed strategic questions, it evolved into an Irish variant on syndicalism. Originating in France (syndicat is the French for trade union) syndicalism surfaced in most advanced countries between 1890 and 1914. Syndicalists argued that politicians had failed to destroy capitalism because parties became hidebound by theory, corrupted by power, and dominated by declassé elites. In any case, political power merely reflected economic power. So the best means of struggle was directly – in workers' organisations and at the point of production – where the worker was most class conscious and most powerful. French syndicalists emphasised the promotion of strikes, culminating in a general strike, when workers would seize control of industry. In America, syndicalism was known as revolutionary industrial unionism, and identified especially with the Industrial Workers of the World, the 'Wobblies', founded in Chicago in 1905. The Wobblies argued that all grades of worker in each industry should be united in the same union. An injury to one should be the concern of all, and each industrial union should be federated, resulting ideally in One Big Union (OBU).

When Larkin broke from the NUDL to form the ITGWU, he had the basis of an Irish OBU. Making a virtue of necessity, the ITGWU set out explicitly to decolonise labour consciousness, arguing that Irish workers should rely on their own resources and build a movement geared to tackling native conditions. Coincidentally, where syndicalists pursued a 'dual union' strategy, creating specifically syndicalist unions rather than trying to 'bore within' existing bodies, they were forced to operate in sectors regarded by the established unions as too hard to organise. The Wobblies were most successful in the western states of America, among miners, migrant labourers, and timber workers; farm labourers made up half of the Unione Sindicale Italiana's pre-1914 membership; and in Canada a division emerged in the post-war struggle between craft unions, based in the industrial heartland of the eastern provinces, and the Canadian OBU, which had originated among

5   NAUK, Ministry of Labour reports on strikes and lockouts, 1907–12, LAB 34/7-12, 34/25–30; BPP, *Reports on Strikes and Lockouts*, 1907–12, Cd 4254, Cd 4680, Cd 5325, Cd 5850, Cd 6472, Cd 7089. Figures for 1913 have been excluded, as statistics for the lockout were not broken down by sector.

newly industrialised workers in British Columbia.[6] As a fringe area of trade unionism, nominally covered by British Labour, but in practice neglected by it, as an economically marginal region with a heavy reliance on primary production, and as an area where effective industrial tactics had to be militant, Ireland was a fairly typical centre of syndicalism.

TACTICS UNFOLD

By April 1907, Larkin had set up branches of the NUDL in Belfast and Derry.[7] The Belfast branch represented almost 3,000 dockers, and soon extended to carters and coalmen; these three groups were to make the first Larkinite revolt. Larkin's timing had two factors in its favour. Since 1906, the upturn in the trade cycle had been generating a resurgence of militancy, especially in Belfast. In May of that year, 17,000 spinners, weavers and others had struck for wage increases. Thirty-four strikes hit the city in 1907, beginning with a series of stoppages by textile operatives in February, and subsequently affecting engineering, the service trades, navvies and other labourers.[8] Secondly, the high tide of Edwardian Belfast's radicalism had only just begun to ebb. Hailing from Liverpool, Larkin needed no introduction to sectarianism, and tried to work around it. The NUDL's (Catholic) deep-sea section met at Bridge End, and the (Protestant) cross-channel men met in the Municipal Employees' Association's rooms at Victoria Street. The Association's general secretary, Alex Boyd, an Independent Orangeman, would be Larkin's deputy during the summer unrest. Larkin also took care to commend himself to the local Labour establishment, campaigning for William Walker in the Belfast North bye-election in April.

In some respects Belfast 1907 is a clearer guide to Larkinism than Dublin 1913, when the personalities of Big Jim and William Martin Murphy and the dramatic backdrop of the slums overshadowed the core issues in the lockout. In the public memory, the raw, class solidarity of 1913 came to be understood as a by-product of Dublin's appalling social conditions.[9] Yet Larkinism began

---

6   See Dick Geary (ed.), *Labour and Socialist Movements in Europe before 1914* (Oxford, 1989); P. F. Brissenden, *The IWW: A Study of American Syndicalism* (New York, 1920). The importance of marginal workers in the culture of the 'Wobblies' is captured vividly in Joyce L. Kornbluh (ed.), *Rebel Voices: An IWW Anthology* (Ann Arbor, 1964).

7   John Gray, *City in Revolt: James Larkin and the Belfast Dock Strike of 1907* (Belfast, 1985), is a very readable study of Larkinism in Belfast.

8   NAUK, Ministry of Labour reports on strikes and lockouts, 1907, LAB 34/6–7, 34/24–5.

9   For example, Curriculum Development Unit, *Dublin 1913: A Divided City* (Dublin, 1984), a text for secondary schools, said little about trade unionism and much about the city's social divisions.

in Belfast, where housing was comparatively good. The root of Larkinism lay in employer hostility to the unionisation of unskilled workers. Coalheavers at Samuel Kelly Ltd who joined the NUDL were dismissed, and, according to Gray: Kelly 'stated very clearly the prevailing view of Belfast's employers when he said, "the situation at issue had no reference to wages whatsoever; it was merely as to whether the dockers should associate themselves with a union which he considered should not embrace such a class of employment"'.[10] Belfast also illustrates Larkin's style. In line with NUDL policy, he set out to recruit dockers only and pursue improvements in conditions without strikes. Sexton believed that the NUDL's survival depended on minimising conflict with the notoriously militant Shipping Federation.[11] Within weeks, allied workers were pressing to join the union, and within months Larkin was being drawn into strikes by a combination of membership spontaneity and employers' militancy. When Kelly's men were sacked on 26 April, 400 colleagues stopped work in protest. On 6 May, 70 spellmen, or casuals, with the Belfast Steamship Company struck against the employment of two non-union members. Larkin opposed both strikes. Kelly had contracts with public authorities, and Larkin reckoned he might be more vulnerable to political or legal pressure. In the case of the Steamship Company, where Larkin had no such leverage, he went so far as to tender a personal apology to the company. Days later, Kelly agreed to settle, but Thomas Gallaher, chairman of the Steamship Company, tobacco factor and shareholder in the Belfast Ropeworks, was determined to quash the emerging organisation of unskilled labour. Gallaher had already arranged for the Shipping Federation to supply scabs and on 8 May 160 of the company's dockers found themselves locked out. It was typical of Larkin that he would oppose strike action at first, but once convinced that conflict was unavoidable, he would mobilise all possible forces behind it and extend action to over-stretch the employers and police. In June he escalated sectional disputes into a general strike in the port.

Two side effects of the strike would stand Larkin in good stead up to 1913. On 24 July the RIC buckled under the burden of their additional duties, assembled to demand better pay and conditions, and fraternised with the strikers. The government promptly rusticated 270 constables and rushed in 6,000 troops. A police mutiny in Unionist Ulster was bad enough. The prospect of similar action in Dublin made employers and the authorities think twice about confronting Larkin. Secondly, Larkin acquired a legendary reputation from his oratory and superhuman energy: an incalculable advantage in

10   Gray, *City in Revolt*, p. 59.

11   For a history of the NUDL, see Eric Taplin, *The Dockers' Union: A History of the National Union of Dock Labourers, 1889–1922* (Leicester, 1986).

evangelising or negotiating. It was said that he had led Catholics and Protestants in a 12 July parade, and incited the RIC mutiny. In fact, he spent the 12th in Liverpool with his ailing mother, and had no direct part in the police action. As with most myths, the facts embellished an essential truth, and Larkin did forge a brief, exultant unity across the religious divide, climaxing on 26 July when 100,000 people turned out for a trades council parade, which pointedly wound its way around the Falls and Shankill roads. The extraordinary atmosphere attracted a stream of visitors from the British left, and they were not disappointed. John Maclean, later to be Clydeside's most famous revolutionary, wrote home: 'Addressed strikers at night. Audience of thousands. Labourers mad to join trade unions'.[12]

What crippled Larkinism in Belfast? Larkin's willingness to generalise action alarmed Sexton, who took control of the strike in late July and negotiated the first of a set of sectional settlements. Repeatedly, Sexton would undermine the principles of solidarity and sympathetic action which Larkin was trying to establish. Then sectarianism threw Labour on the defensive. Since Tod Sloan's election in Belfast South in 1902 there had been hopes of a realignment in Unionism. The Belfast Protestant Association had helped Walker, and the Independent Orangemen supported Larkin. Events in August showed how fragile these developments were. The heavy security presence led to rioting in west Belfast. On 12 August, soldiers killed two rioters and wounded five others on the Falls Road. In the wake of the RIC mutiny, it was enough to convince some Protestant workers that the strike masked a Catholic revolt. Symptomatic of the paranoia was a trades council investigation into ludicrous accusations in the *Belfast Evening Telegraph* that the strike fund had discriminated against Protestants. Though the *Telegraph* was a standing joke in Labour circles for its bluff Toryism, the council decided it had better be seen to take the allegations seriously. Larkin concurred, and offered to submit the evidence to a jury of three Protestants.[13] Employers moved quickly to divide and conquer by sponsoring a company union for Protestants, the Belfast Coal Workers' and Carters' Benefit Society. Five hundred coalheavers struck on 14 November rather than work with members of the Society. Carters and cranemen – the skilled elite of the waterfront – came out in sympathy, and boats were blacked in Newry, Drogheda, Dundalk, and Derry. Again Sexton intervened. The strike collapsed on 26 November, and most strikers were victimised. A spirit of defiance persisted. Larkin received an illuminated address from the Belfast NUDL in July 1908, and Boyd affirmed that they would gladly stand with him again. But the stuff of Larkinism was too

12   B. J. Ripley and J. McHugh, *John Maclean* (Manchester, 1989), p. 30.
13   UUMC, Belfast trades council minutes, 5–12 Sept. 1907.

marginal to mount another assault on the hurdles of sectionalism and sectarianism. In Dublin and other cities of the de-industrialised south, Labour recognised that the alliance of 'transport and general' was the key to the revival of trade unionism; despite setbacks, they would return to it again and again. Industrialised Belfast had a well established craft unionism, and its most powerful sector, the metal trades unions, constituted a movement onto themselves, which had minimal contact with the trades council.

During the summer Larkin had visited Dublin to raise funds, and availed of the opportunity to expand the NUDL. A Dublin branch was formed on 4 August.[14] Within a year it had 2,700 members. As in Belfast, Larkin aimed to avoid confrontation initially, concentrating on recognition rather than the closed shop. But in July 1908 the Dublin Coal Masters' Association paid off 250 dockers for wearing their union badges. No one wanted another Belfast and Board of Trade intervention secured temporarily the status quo ante. Larkin was claiming victory when Sexton took the negotiations out of his hands. Sexton accepted employer demands that they not have to deal with Larkin and that members not sport the button at work, contrary to NUDL rules. Having embarrassed Larkin in Belfast and belittled him in Dublin, Sexton told him to organise Cork.

In April, painters in the building line had struck 18 firms in Cork to win improvements in pay and conditions. Prospects here seemed bright. Larkin despatched James Fearon, a former secretary of the NUDL's ill-fated Newry branch. Both Larkin and Fearon travelled to Waterford in October to address a meeting in the City Hall. Despite the disruptive tactics of henchmen engaged by a local stevedore, a branch based on cross-channel coalfillers was formed. November brought a series of strikes which boosted Larkin's standing. On 9 November, 179 dockers struck the City of Cork Steam Packet Company. A small dock strike a month previously had given forewarning, and the Shipping Federation was prepared. Scabs were imported, but the carters then refused to handle 'tainted goods'. Clashes with the RIC ensued. Larkin arrived in Cork on 11 November to arrange a truce which led to a favourable settlement. Shortly after this success 150 carters struck for recognition and better pay in Dublin, to be joined by dockers, labourers, canalmen, and malsters. By the end of the

---

14 C. Desmond Greaves, *The Irish Transport and General Workers' Union: The Formative Years, 1909–1923* (Dublin, 1982) provides a concise account of Larkin's career and ITGWU activities. A broader, but episodic, treatment of Dublin events at this time is found in Dermot Keogh, *The Rise of the Irish Working Class: The Dublin Trade Union Movement and the Labour Leadership, 1890–1914* (Belfast, 1982). See also Emmet Larkin, *James Larkin, 1876–1947: Irish Labour Leader* (London, 1965) and John Newsinger, *Rebel City: Larkin, Connolly and the Dublin Labour Movement* (London, 2004).

month 2,000 men were out. As in Cork, the conflict was marked by strike-breaking and violence. Sexton disowned the dispute, withheld funds, and suspended Larkin from his job on 7 December.

A STRATEGY DEVISED

For some years past, a circle of socialist republicans in Dublin had been advocating a break with British Labour. Larkin rejected the option as an unwarranted intrusion of nationalism into Labour affairs until his relations with Sexton snapped. He then became convinced, *mirabile dictu*, that only Irish unions could solve Irish problems. On 28 December, NUDL delegates from Belfast, Cork, Dublin, Dundalk, and Waterford agreed to secede as an Irish general union. Derry stayed with Sexton, whilst in Belfast, Sexton got Boyd to play the Orange card to win the Protestant cross-channel dockers back to the NUDL. The ITGWU was born in haste and confusion. Larkin was unsure if an Irish general union was viable, and anxious for legal, financial, and organisational reasons to represent the ITGWU as a 'continuity NUDL'. By May 1909 he was more ebullient. The rule book gave notice that the new union had a mission to revamp Irish Labour politically and industrially: 'Are we going to continue the policy of grafting ourselves on the English Trades Union movement, losing our identity as a nation in the great world of organised labour? We say emphatically, No. Ireland has politically reached her manhood'. The 'old system of sectional unions' was pronounced 'practically useless for modern conditions'. The ITGWU's ultimate aim was an 'industrial commonwealth', which would 'obliterate poverty, and help to realise the glorious time spoken of and sung by the Thinkers, Prophets and the Poets. . .'.[15] In 1910 Larkin attended the inaugural conference of the Industrial Syndicalist Education League at Manchester, where he told delegates that 'his union was formed on the industrial basis, and took in all workers in the transport industry. The transport industry held the key, for they could stop the whole of the rest of the trades'.[16]

Larkin's early years as a union leader were an anticlimax, characterised by caution on wage movements. With a meagre war chest and a trade recession in 1908–9, he had reason to be cautious, yet those factors had not deterred him before. In Dublin, some 50 per cent of NUDL members had not transferred to the ITGWU. Over 1,500 workers joined up in 1910, bringing ITGWU membership to 3,000, scarcely more than the NUDL had mustered in Dublin

15 Keogh, *The Rise of the Irish Working Class*, pp. 63, 139–40.
16 *Industrial Syndicalist*, Dec. 1910, p. 30. I am obliged to Conor McCabe for this reference.

two years earlier. Where possible, recruitment was achieved at the expense of other unions, and Dublin trades council found itself involved in regular poaching wrangles involving the ITGWU. Larkin also neglected the provinces. Dublin being the limelight, he never led another strike outside the capital. One after another, the branches disintegrated. With passive assistance from the NUDL, Belfast employers introduced a system of victimisation that gutted the local branch. Dundalk and Waterford branches dwindled to a paper existence. Disaster overtook the Cork branch in 1909. On 14 June, the Cork coalporters' section refused to work with members of the British-based Workers' Union, which they claimed was a 'yellow' union. Other quaysidemen came out in sympathy and railway porters blacked 'tainted goods'. A rebel spirit had survived in Cork. Tramwaymen had struck for a pay rise in April, and in May builders' labourers, supported by craftsmen, won an extra shilling a week in a general stoppage. The city's first Labour Day demonstration for years took place on 16 May. Not content to rely on the inevitable Shipping Federation scabs, a Cork Employers' Federation was formed to blacklist anyone taking sympathetic action. In the first example of Larkinism without Larkin, the dock dispute spread to 2,000 employees, including mineral water operatives, railwaymen, flour millers, building workers, and bacon factory hands. Larkin visited the city, but when he failed to persuade employers to compromise, he left the Cork branch to disintegrate. Cork trades council split on 12 August when tradesmen withdrew, tired of strikes and Larkinism. Another twist of the knife came the following week when Larkin, Fearon, and two others of the Cork branch were arrested and charged with 'conspiracy to defraud'. Larkin had spent NUDL dues collected in Cork on struggles elsewhere. On 17 June 1910, the court gave him 12 months hard labour. So harsh a sentence, widely regarded as a piece of class vindictiveness, won Larkin some badly needed sympathy. Public opinion compelled his release on 1 October. Larkin also made progress in the ITUC. Prior to the 1909 Congress, Sexton had instigated his expulsion from the parliamentary committee on the ground that he had been elected to it as an NUDL member. Larkin went to the Congress in any case, interjecting from the gallery as his supporters on the floor argued for the ITGWU's affiliation. They lost the vote, 49–39. Technically, the ballot hinged on the rights and wrongs of the NUDL–ITGWU split, but Larkin had made it a division about whether Congress should tolerate Larkinism. When the 1910 Congress resumed its discussion of NUDL objections to the ITGWU, the majority of 'old unionists' took the view that it was time to accept the new realities. By 42–10 votes, the ITGWU won affiliation to Congress.

Change was in the air. The Liberal government was trying to contain the growth of the Labour Party with a rolling agenda of social reform. The Trades

Disputes Act (1906) was virtually written by the BTUC and would remain the basic statutory instrument in Irish industrial relations up to 1990. The 'people's budget' of 1909 included a land tax and a supertax, and provision for workers' compensation, old age pensions, trade boards, and labour exchanges. Congress lobbying helped to ensure Ireland's inclusion in the Trade Boards Act (1909), which provided for the appointment of committees to enforce wages in 'sweated' occupations. Five trade boards were in operation by May 1916, catering for workers in clothing, textiles, and food preparation.[17] Grist to the mill was the Osborne judgement in which the Law Lords found that unions could not lawfully use their funds for political purposes. Like the Taff Vale judgement before it, so blatantly partisan a decision proved counterproductive. It was repealed partially by the Trade Union Act (1913), which allowed unions to maintain a political fund if approved by members and provided members were allowed to 'contract out' of the political levy if they so desired. The National Insurance Act (1911) was particularly significant. To avoid displacing the benefit provision of unions and friendly societies, the Act allowed these bodies to become 'approved societies' under the state system. This proved to be an incentive to join unions and was the major factor behind the 60 per cent surge in BTUC affiliation over the next two years.[18]

Big changes were afoot in British industrial relations. Trade had begun to improve in 1909, reversing two years of high unemployment, falling wages, and falling union membership. But employer militancy kept wages lagging behind rising prices, most notoriously so through the Shipping Federation's scabbing. In November 1910 the British Transport Workers' Federation was formed to create a network of direct action sufficiently extensive to make scabbing ineffective. The ITGWU applied for affiliation, but the NUDL had it blackballed.[19] First to move in this new round of class warfare were seafarers who refused to sail the SS *Olympic*, the largest liner afloat, as she lay at Southampton. On 14 June 1911, with rockets and naval flags signalling 'war', the National Sailors' and Firemen's Union took up the general clamour for wage movements with a strike at all ports for a uniform pay scale.[20] Unrest

17 Brendan Mark Browne, 'Trade boards in Northern Ireland, 1909–45' (PhD, QUB, 1989), pp. 45–56, 340.

18 Henry Pelling, *A History of British Trade Unionism* (London, 1974), pp. 128–33; details of unrest are in Board of Trade, *Report on Strikes and Lockouts in the United Kingdom* (BPP, 1912), Cd 6472, XLVII.43. For the impact on Ireland see Greaves, *The Irish Transport and General Workers' Union*, pp. 59–75; and Larkin, *James Larkin*, pp. 89–94.

19 Ken Coates and Tony Topham, *The History of the Transport and General Workers' Union, Vol. 1, Part 1* (London, 1991), p. 329. For unrest in Britain see also Pelling, *A History of British Trade Unionism*, pp. 123–48.

20 *Irish Independent*, 15 June 1911.

spread to dockers and carters. Sectional stoppages on the railways led to a UK strike on 18–19 August. Although the spasm had passed in Britain by the end of August, the greatest outbreak of social disaffection since 1889 surged on to the brink of the First World War and contained revolutionary stirrings within it. Syndicalism inspired an interest in industrial unionism, culminating in the foundation in 1915 of the 'Triple Alliance' by the Transport Workers' Federation, the Miners' Federation, and the National Union of Railwaymen (NUR), as the ASRS was to become.

Ireland was ripe for militancy. In Dublin, the cost of food on which workers lived – tea, sugar, milk, white bread, butter, potatoes, bacon, and eggs – had risen by 15 per cent since 1900, with sharp increases in 1906–7, and 1911–12, without any general improvement in wages.[21] Clearly, English unrest provided the spark, but when workers moved, Larkin responded, and the ITGWU did make a difference to the diffusion of militancy to new sectors. The 18 strikes in the traditional industries of the north east in 1911 were distributed evenly throughout the year. By contrast, 32 of the 36 disputes in other sectors took place after mid June. The large number of 'miscellaneous' militants included paperboys and golf-caddies, sandwichmen and bill-posters. Agitation spread to the smaller towns and in Wexford, scene of a six month, cast-iron fight of foundrymen, brushed farm labourers with its wingtip.[22] Larkin also availed of the unrest to form a union for women, on the incredible pretext that 'member' in the ITGWU rules meant a man. If Larkin was no misogynist, he had a weakness for nepotism: the Irish Women Workers' Union was launched on 5 September, with Jim's sister, Delia, as general secretary.[23] The most powerful and contentious demonstration of class solidarity took place on the railways. During the UK rail strike ITGWU members refused to handle 'tainted goods'. Dublin timber merchants retaliated with a lockout. When the rail strike ended the timbermen would not go back without a pay rise. On 15 September the timber merchants tendered a 'black' consignment at Kingsbridge. Two Great Southern and Western Railway porters refused to touch it and were dismissed. As the dispute extended through unofficial sympathetic action, the ASRS attempted to assert its authority by calling a national strike on 21 September. The largest company, the Great Southern and Western, locked out a further 1,600 workers by closing the railway workshops and imported

21   Séamus Cody, John O'Dowd, and Peter Rigney, *The Parliament of Labour: 100 Years of Dublin Council of Trade Unions* (Dublin, 1986), pp. 49–50.

22   NAUK, Ministry of Labour reports on strikes and lockouts, 1911, LAB 34/11, 34/29; Michael Enright, *Men of Iron: Wexford Foundry Disputes 1890 & 1911* (Wexford, 1987).

23   Greaves, *The Irish Transport and General Workers' Union*, p. 64; Mary Jones, *These Obstreperous Lassies: A History of the Irish Women Workers' Union* (Dublin, 1988), pp. 1–5.

labour from England. When the strike collapsed on 4 October, the Great Southern dismissed ten per cent of the strikers, and re-engaged others at reduced rates. So pleased were the directors with crushing Larkinism on the railway, that they marked the occasion with the gift of a clock to each of 121 station masters.[24]

The unrest of 1911 alarmed employers. In June, Dublin bosses formed an Employers' Federation modelled on the Cork namesake that had smashed the 1909 dock strike. The rail strike raised a storm of criticism in the media against 'foreign' ideas in Irish industrial relations. Dublin Chamber of Commerce met in emergency session and urged employers to mobilise against what one termed 'not a strike in the ordinary sense . . . but the beginning of a social war'.[25] Within weeks, local employers' federations were being formed throughout the country. In reality, 1911 was far from a triumph of militancy. The high proportion of strikes over trade unionism per se confirmed that Labour was still struggling for recognition, and 55 per cent of those who took industrial action encountered complete defeat.[26] Congress affiliation doubled from 50,000 in 1911 to 100,000 in 1913, but the growth owed something to the National Insurance Act; in contradiction of their alarmism, employers reckoned it owed a very great deal.[27] Larkin made steady rather than spectacular progress with the ITGWU, boosting membership from 5,000 to 8,000. He might have done better had he taken an interest in the provinces or had his jealousy allowed him to create a chain of command.[28]

So why the alarm about Larkin? How can we reconcile his underwhelming performance with the ITGWU, occasional aversion to militancy, and support

---

24 Irish Railway Record Society Archive, Dublin, Great Southern and Western Railway, files 1019, 1069. I am obliged to Conor McCabe for these references.

25 Thomas J. Morrissey, *William Martin Murphy* (Dundalk, 1997), pp. 44–6.

26 Based on NAUK, Ministry of Labour reports on strikes and lockouts, 1911, LAB 34/11, 34/29.

27 Arnold Wright, *Disturbed Dublin: The Story of the Great Strike of 1913–14, with a Description of the Industries of the Irish Capital* (London, 1914), pp. 94–5.

28 Estimates of ITGWU membership during these years vary enormously. There is broad agreement that the union had under 5,000 members in mid 1911. Based on returns to the Registry of Friendly Societies, and a presumptuous multiplication of known recruitment to the no 1 branch, Greaves puts membership at 18,000 by the end of 1911, rising to close on 30,000 by mid 1913. Greaves, *The Irish Transport and General Workers' Union*, pp. 70, 82–3, 91. Emmet Larkin rejects the Registry of Friendly Society returns in favour of the ITUC affiliation figure for 1912: 8,000, and the number of contributors under the National Insurance Act in 1913: 9,580. Larkin, *James Larkin*, pp. 108–9. Insured membership figures are probably the most reliable indicator, as they were less likely to be exaggerated. O'Brien claimed that insured membership was close to total membership. In November 1913 there were 12,829 ITGWU men in receipt of support from the BTUC lockout fund. Pádraig Yeates, *Lockout: Dublin 1913* (Dublin, 2000), p. 459.

for compulsory arbitration with his reputation and his syndicalism? The explanation is that he wanted to agitate, not organise. His preferred weapons were a newspaper, the *Irish Worker*, and the development of social and cultural centres for workers like Liberty Hall and Croydon Park. The *Irish Worker* appeared on 27 May, and sold about 5,000 copies. The second issue sold 8,000 copies, and the third 15,000. Thereafter, sales were something above 20,000 a week. For a political weekly, this was phenomenal; the more so as wholesalers and many newsagents refused to handle it. It was Larkin's triumph. He was the editorial board, and the paper would foster his brash personality cult. Over 41 months, he edited 189 issues, and wrote the editorials and more than 400 articles.[29] Larkin's ambivalence on militancy in no way softened his belief in sympathetic action as the hinge of solidarity, or diminished his conviction in industrial unionism. In 1912, the year he became chairman of a largely Larkinite parliamentary committee of the ITUC, he called for an OBU. 'Tomorrow', he declared on the eve of the annual Congress, 'We are going to advocate one society for Ireland for skilled and unskilled workers, so that when a skilled man is struck at, out comes the unskilled man, and when an unskilled worker is struck at, he will be supported by the skilled tradesman'.[30] Twenty-three votes were cast in favour of an Irish Federation of Trades, indicating wide support from Irish unions as the ITGWU contingent at the Congress numbered eight. Unfortunately for the Irish, the British unions had 45 delegates, and as an OBU would entail the end of the amalgamateds in Ireland, they voted against it.[31] Similar problems would arise in 1919 and 1939.

THE EMERGENCE OF SOCIALIST REPUBLICANISM

In June 1909, realignments on the Dublin left led to the formation of the Socialist Party of Ireland (SPI). Over the following year William O'Brien[32]

29   For studies of the paper see Donal Nevin, 'The *Irish Worker*, 1911–1914', in Nevin, *James Larkin*, pp. 152–8; and John Newsinger, 'A lamp to guide your feet: Jim Larkin, the *Irish Worker*, and the Dublin working class', *European History Quarterly* 20 (1990), pp. 63–99.

30   *Irish Worker*, 8 June 1912.

31   UUMC, ITUC, *Report* (1912), p. 61.

32   William O'Brien (1881–1968), born in Cork and worked as a tailor in Dublin until 1917, when he joined the ITGWU; a veteran of the ISRP, but ultimately pragmatic; an effective *éminence grise* in various Labour initiatives, and one of the most powerful union leaders from 1917 to his retirement in 1946; his cold, dictatorial, managerial style and bitterness towards Larkin from 1923 made him the most vilified Labour leader of the twentieth century. The one substantial biography is Thomas J. Morrissey, *William O'Brien, 1881–1968: Socialist, Republican, Dáil Deputy, Editor and Trade Union Leader* (Dublin, 2007).

and other comrades tried to facilitate James Connolly's return from the United States.[33] Tired of America's sectarian far left, Connolly himself yearned for a politics more homely and more mainstream. In January 1910, he transferred his ethno-socialist paper the *Harp* to Dublin with Larkin as editor. He also penned *Labour, Nationality, and Religion* as the SPI's reply to the Jesuit preacher Fr Kane, whose Lenten lectures had denounced socialism. 1910 saw too the publication of *Labour in Irish History*, the first critical analysis of the subject. This classic of scholarly empathy and originality was to have a seminal impact on agitational writing in labour history. Connolly debarked at Moville on 26 July 1910. That autumn the SPI issued a manifesto which confirmed Connolly's drift to the centre. Although Connolly remained heavily influenced by American syndicalism, it was broadly social democratic in philosophy and remarkably open-ended on method and aims. Connolly wished to concentrate on politics. The SPI agreed to engage him as an organiser, but found it difficult to pay his weekly stipend of £2. O'Brien advised him to seek work with the ITGWU. Connolly demurred. He combined acknowledgement of Larkin's influence with doubts about his judgement, describing him privately as 'an overgrown schoolboy'.[34] For his part, Larkin had no desire to share his union with another big name. But in June 1911 the Sailors' and Firemen's Union pressed him to appoint an experienced agent in Belfast. Reluctantly, Connolly accepted the job.[35]

Though associated with Connolly, it was Larkin who made socialist republicanism a force. Everything followed from his decision to form an Irish union. A British Labourite in Belfast, he became an ardent separatist as head of the ITGWU. By 1910 a loose alliance of socialists and advanced nationalists controlled Dublin trades council, and the *Irish Worker* would be thoroughly enthusiastic for an Irish Ireland. From within the Irish revival movement, W. P. Ryan[36] promoted a broad front of rank and file Sinn Féiners, Gaelic Leaguers, and Larkinites.[37] The events of 1911–13 differentiated nationalists on

33 Ibid., pp. 39–45.

34 Keogh, *The Rise of the Irish Working Class*, p. 159.

35 Austen Morgan, *James Connolly: A Political Biography* (Manchester, 1988), p. 89.

36 William Patrick Ryan (1867–1942), also Liam P. Ó Riain and 'Kevin Kennedy' (pseudonym); born near Templemore, Tipperary; raised in London where he became a successful journalist; returned to Ireland in 1905 to edit the *Irish Peasant*, which folded after Cardinal Logue denounced it as anti-clerical; then edited the *Irish Nation and Peasant*; active in the SPI; moved back to London in 1910, becoming assistant editor of the *Daily Herald*; a prolific author of novels, plays, poetry, and prose; died in London. See Martin J. Waters, 'W. P. Ryan and the Irish Ireland movement' (PhD, University of Connecticut, 1970).

37 Peter Murray, 'Irish cultural nationalism in the United Kingdom state: politics and the Gaelic League, 1900–18', *Irish Political Studies* 8 (1993), pp. 66–7.

the social question. With the prospect of an Irish parliament and exchequer in sight, the IPP cast a more parsimonious eye on public spending. Trade unions were particularly annoyed that the party did not have the National Insurance Act's provision for medical benefits extended to Ireland; they said nothing about the Catholic Church's opposition to the Act per se.[38] The rail strike especially made Larkinism a topic of nationwide debate, and challenged the labour proclivities of Redmondites. Conversely, advanced nationalists gave scattered support to the strike wave; in Wexford, the Gaelic Athletic Association organised benefit matches for the striking foundry workers.[39] Sinn Féin had withdrawn from electoral politics in 1910 to concentrate on propaganda work, and the resultant vacuum both helped Labour and strengthened the overlap between radicals and advanced nationalists. Dublin trades council formed a Labour Representation Committee in January 1911, and six of the 13 Dublin Labour councillors elected between 1912 and 1915 were former Sinn Féin candidates. The Dublin Labour Party, like the cognate initiatives that emerged in Cork, Castlebar, Sligo, Tullamore, Waterford, and Wexford, met with limited success.[40] The politicisation of senior and middle level trade unionism had yet to impress the masses.

Developments which led to sluggish progress in the south had the opposite effect in Belfast, where all of the Protestant-based anti-Unionist forces were in decline. The Independent Orange Order faded, and Sloan lost his Westminster seat in 1910. The once mighty Belfast trades council suffered a steady fall in affiliations, from 63 in 1907, to 40 in 1911, and 32 in 1913.[41] This was all the more remarkable as the Liberal government's social reforms gave trades councils a role in campaigning for, providing explanatory public lectures on, and, in some cases, helping to administer legislation through appointments to local committees. The reforms provoked fierce Tory opposition and, in Unionist eyes, created an anti-constitution alliance of Labourites, Liberals, and Home Rulers. Ramsay MacDonald had concluded an electoral pact with the Liberals in 1906, and the 1910 elections left the Liberals reliant on Labour and the IPP to stay in office.[42] In 1911, the restriction of the veto of the House of Lords, which had rejected the 'people's budget', also removed a bulwark

38　UUMC, ITUC, *Report* (1914), pp. 84–5; Sophia Carey, *Social Security in Ireland, 1939–1952: The Limits to Solidarity* (Dublin, 2007), pp. 82–3.

39　Enright, *Men of Iron*, p. 31.

40　Peter Murray, 'Electoral politics and the Dublin working class before the First World War', *Saothar* 6 (1980), pp. 8–22. For the wider picture see Arthur Mitchell, *Labour in Irish Politics, 1890–1930: The Irish Labour Movement in an Age of Revolution* (Dublin, 1974), pp. 27–30, 52–3, 63–4.

41　UUMC, Belfast trades council balance sheets, 1899–1928, D/1050/6/F1.

42　Henry Pelling, *A Short History of the Labour Party* (London, 1976), pp. 18–20.

against Home Rule. The famous 'Connolly–Walker controversy' across the pages of the Glasgow socialist paper *Forward* on the merits of forming an Irish Labour party or continuing to support the British Labour Party is a deceptive guide to the dilemma of Belfast Labourites in 1911.[43] Walker's 'internationalism' was now a beaten docket. The problem was how to cope with the consequences of the Home Rule bill. The leakage of pro-Union delegates left Belfast trades council finely poised. On the right was a residue of conservatives, willing to break with the ITUC on the national question and retreat into the localism embraced by the council in the wake of the first Home Rule crisis. On the left, a socialist republican circle acquired a profile following Connolly's arrival in Belfast. It appealed to old Walkerites like Tom Johnson[44] and D. R. Campbell[45] who wanted Belfast to advance with Congress. Holding the balance was a fraying band of more cautious Walkerites, most of whom intended to wait till the midnight hour, and then go with Irish Labour.

The immediate consequence of the Home Rule bill was a shift in the ITUC's position on an Irish Labour party. The 1910 Congress rejected Larkin's call for an 'Irish ILP' by 39–18 votes. The 1911 Congress defeated a similar motion, and accepted Walker's amendment commending affiliation to the British Labour Party by 32–29 votes. A combination of Larkinism and the perceived advantage of having a party ready for the first elections to an Irish parliament tipped the scales in 1912. Connolly's resolution 'that the independent representation of Labour upon all public boards be and is hereby included among the objectives of this Congress' was passed by 49–19 votes, with 19 delegates not recorded.[46] The Irish Labour Party was founded, notionally at least. Efforts to make it a reality made fitful progress. Not being a team player, Larkin insisted on being awkward. Connolly, O'Brien, Johnson, and Campbell pressed ahead. A constitution was framed in 1913 and adopted at the 1914 Congress. It bore the imprint of Connolly's syndicalism. Connolly's first aim

43 See *The Connolly-Walker Controversy: On Socialist Unity in Ireland*, Cork Workers' Club, Historical Reprints no 9 (Cork, *na*).

44 Thomas Ryder Johnson (1872–1963), born in Liverpool of English parents; worked in Ireland as a commercial traveller from 1892; his dedication and talents as a secretary and facilitator brought him to prominence in the ITUC; as the only personality not encumbered with a union job, he emerged as the ideologist of post-1916 Labour, and first leader of the parliamentary Labour Party; a nice man, but a terrible tactician, unsuited for the leadership thrust upon him from 1917 to 1927. See J. Anthony Gaughan, *Thomas Johnson* (Dublin, 1980).

45 David Robb Campbell (1875–1934), an insurance agent, like his father; on the ITUC executive, 1909–18; ITUC president in 1911, and treasurer, 1912–18; declined an offer to become secretary of the Irish Labour Party in 1920, not wishing to leave Belfast; led the Labour group on Belfast Corporation and remained prominent on Belfast trades council until the late 1920s; a barrister at law from 1926.

46 UUMC, ITUC, *Reports* (1910), pp. 48–9; (1911), pp. 39–42; (1912), pp. 12–19.

was to politicise the movement without encouraging electoralism. Thus, the party and Congress were to be the same. Congress rejected a Belfast proposal that socialist groups and cooperatives be allowed to affiliate. Replying for the executive, Johnson stated that the true function of the party 'was propagandist merely – to educate, not to form a political party'. So the ITUC and Labour Party (ITUCLP), as it was called, would contest elections without forgetting Connolly's dictum that politics was no more than the 'echo' of industrial warfare. By confining membership to trade unionists Connolly intended to exclude 'the professional politician who was doing as much harm as good' in the British Labour Party. The BTUC's failure to authorise sympathy strikes during the 1913 lockout had reinforced Connolly's abiding aversion to 'fakirism' – the derogatory American term for union officials who put the organisation before the cause. He rejected the introduction of 'card-voting' (whereby a union had a vote for each member) into Congress on the ground that the smaller unions were often the more militant. Connolly's second objective illustrates a concern of his 'mature' years: to link revolutionaries with mainstream Labour without compromise. Thus, he opposed renaming Congress 'the Labour Party' for fear of provoking a breakaway, envisaging instead a dual arena of left agitation, in the catch all ITUCLP and in socialist parties. To that end, shortly before the 1912 Congress, he had formed the Independent Labour Party (of Ireland). The Irish ILP united the SPI with the Belfast branch of the British Socialist Party and four of Belfast's five ILP branches – Walker's old comrades stayed out, though Walker himself had since retired from the Labour movement.[47]

THE HIGHEST POINT OF MORAL GRANDEUR

The upheaval of 1911 did not resolve the problem of keeping wages in line with escalating living costs. 1912 brought a mild recession and unemployed protests onto the streets. Exceptionally favourable economic conditions the following year enabled an unprecedented level of wage militancy, but early results were mixed. During the first six months of the year, employers in the north's staple industries recorded considerable success against these movements. In Belfast, the Flax Roughers' Union lost a two-month stoppage against dilution. In Derry, 1,200 shirt factory workers were locked out for three weeks to enforce a pay cut.[48] Other sectors fared better. A succession of disputes in construction over the summer secured pay increases for craftsmen and labourers. Transport workers too won modest advances. By the summer of 1913 the ITGWU stood at the summit of its pre-war strength, numbering about 15,000 men, unskilled

---

47 Greaves, *The Life and Times of James Connolly* (London, 1961), pp. 224–8.
48 NAUK, Ministry of Labour reports on strikes and lockouts, 1913, LAB 34/31.

Dubliners in the main. Provincial outposts were making slow progress. Shipping companies had crushed Waterford's embryonic Larkinism with ease in 1912. Limerick dockers and carters lost a dispute over 'nons' in the new year. But in May the ITGWU won a favourable settlement to a violent generalised strike in Sligo. A recruitment drive amongst Dublin farm labourers commenced the following month.[49] The tramwaymen were next.

Employers were dismayed that the defeat of the railwaymen in 1911 had not stopped the strike wave or sympathetic action. They blamed Larkin, but they also blamed the Liberal government for the Trades Disputes Act 1906 and the National Insurance Act 1911, and its minions in Dublin Castle who were nervous about confronting Larkin after the RIC mutiny in Belfast.[50] In mid-1913 it seemed as if the balance of power might produce a stable equilibrium. In May a leading shipping company recognised the ITGWU in return for one month's notice of industrial action. In July, trade unions and employer organisations agreed to nominate delegates to a conciliation board sponsored by the Lord Mayor. But nationalist Ireland's puissant capitalist – William Martin Murphy – owner of the *Irish Independent*, the Imperial Hotel, Clery's department store, and was chairman of the Dublin United Tramway Company, was determined never to recognise Larkin's union. Murphy made no secret of the fact that his quarrel with Liberty Hall was not about wages and conditions. Business, he told his colleagues, could not survive the 'system known as "syndicalism" or "sympathetic strikes"'.[51] He hated Larkin. If the *Irish Worker* had vilified Murphy repeatedly as the epitome of sweating capitalism, that was Larkin's way: it served his compulsion to put a face on the enemy. He had no ulterior motive in challenging Murphy. He had always believed that the financial future of the ITGWU depended on pushing into steady employment areas such as the railway and the trams, where workers with a regular wage could pay regular union dues. On the other hand, when Murphy called Larkin a 'mean thief' and expressed surprise that artisans should associate with 'scum like Larkin and his followers', he was not playing to the gallery.[52]

Throughout July the ITGWU consolidated within Murphy's empire.[53] In Independent Newspapers, Murphy countered with cajolery and threats, telling

---

49 Ibid.; Greaves, *The Irish Transport and General Workers' Union*, pp. 86–93; Emmet O'Connor, *A Labour History of Waterford* (Waterford, 1989), pp. 124–5.

50 Wright, *Disturbed Dublin*, p. 94.

51 Morrissey, *William Martin Murphy*, pp. 56–7.

52 R. M. Fox, *Jim Larkin: The Rise of the Underman* (London, 1957), p. 81; ibid., p. 57.

53 The definitive account of the lockout is Yeates, *Lockout*. For the report of the government enquiry see BPP, Dublin Disturbances Commission, *Official Report on Riots, 30 August to 1 September 1913 and Minutes of Evidence of Enquiry* (1914, Cd 7269, XVIII.513–990); see also Board of Trade, *Report on Strikes and Lockouts in the United Kingdom in 1913* (1914, Cd 7658, XXXVI.489).

employees that they were able enough to form their own union; but, should they side with Larkin, then starvation awaited. Still the men continued to join up. On 15 August, the dismissals commenced. Independent newspapers were blacked immediately, and approaching 10.00 am on 26 August, the start of Horse Show week, ITGWU men left the trams where they stood. Murphy had prepared his ground well. One week before the tram strike, he visited Dublin Castle and emerged with firm assurances of adequate protective measures in the event of trouble. Special constables and RIC were quickly deployed to supplement the Dublin Metropolitan Police. 'I think I have broken the malign influence of Mr Larkin and set him on the run', Murphy informed the *Irish Independent* of 27 August. The tougher security policy was soon in evidence. On 28 and 29 August, Larkin, Connolly, and Dublin trades council officers were arrested for sedition. Sunday 31 August – 'Bloody Sunday' – is framed in Labour memory as an identikit of class brutality. Police had banned a demonstration due to be held in Sackville Street. Larkin promised to be there 'dead or alive'. All morning crowds hung about the street not knowing what would happen. At midday, a bearded figure appeared on the balcony of the Imperial, Murphy's hotel, and began to address the people. It was Larkin, disguised to avoid arrest. Within minutes he was taken into custody. Down below, the police waded into the crowd, swinging their batons at will. Many who fled were chased into the tenements, where homes were invaded and ransacked. The rioting continued the following day. Two workers were killed. About 200 police and at least twice as many civilians were injured. Hundreds more were arrested. In September the conflict expanded to its full proportions. On 3 September, 404 employers weighed in behind Murphy with a pledge to lockout any employee who refused to sign 'the document' denying   or renouncing ITGWU membership. In the county, where the union had recently won a harvest strike, the Farmers' Association followed suit. So too did the Master Builders, although building workers were not connected with the ITGWU. In other instances men were locked out for refusing to handle 'tainted goods'. By 22 September almost 25,000 workers were affected, in a city of little over 300,000 people.

While '1913' was fundamentally about the right to organise, and has gone down in Labour legend as such, the protagonists had no doubt that syndicalism lurked at the heart of the matter. The Board of Trade conciliator, George Askwith, recalled that whereas British strikes of the period were 'chiefly based upon economic issues, the serious riots in Dublin, although founded on poverty, low wages and bad conditions, included the determination to establish the transport workers' union as "the one big union" in Ireland and put into practice the doctrines of syndicalism'.[54] It is easy to find both Labour and employer voices in

54   Quoted in Newsinger, *Rebel City*, p. 16.

agreement with him.[55] Middle-class opinion divided. Though most blamed Larkin, the blatant assault on trade unionism, the aggressive policing, and the seeming indifference of employers to the misery of tenement life rallied the literati round Labour. Politically, the conflict intensified the differentiation of nationalists. The IPP was hostile. Sinn Féin was silent – Arthur Griffith consistently opposed Larkinism. And many advanced nationalists supported the workers.[56]

As the masters put their trust in starvation, Labour cast about for allies before time ran out. Being little more than a talking shop, the ITUC played no part in events. Apart from County Dublin, the Belfast docks, and Sligo, provincial workers confined their solidarity to finance; and in some instances the clerical criticism of Larkin made public backing extremely tentative. Liberty Hall turned to England, where 'Bloody Sunday' had generated enormous concern, and the *Daily Herald*, champion of the 'rebels' on the British left, gave regular coverage to events. Larkin appealed for sympathetic action. In early September three Liverpool railwaymen blacked Dublin-bound goods. Dismissals led to a snowball of unofficial action involving over 2,000 railwaymen in Liverpool and central England. Since 1910, the growth of syndicalism in Britain had stimulated direct actionist rank and file movements hostile to what they regarded as the class collaboration of union officialdom, and BTUC leaders desperately wanted to avoid the lockout becoming a bandwaggon for the rebels. The NUR general secretary, J. H. Thomas, a resolute opponent of the 'tainted goods' doctrine, quickly effected a return to work. Instead, the BTUC and some trade unions opened 'fighting funds', while the Co-operative Wholesale Society helped to provision a series of relief ships to burst the boom of starvation.

On 29 September a Board of Trade enquiry embarked on the patient task of seeking the compromise, which British Labour and Liberal opinion earnestly desired. The ITGWU offered to limit the sympathetic strike in return for union recognition, and to consider a conciliation scheme. Within days the employers replied that the locked out workers would not be reinstated. Public attitudes shifted. AE[57] expressed the indignation of intellectuals in his famous

---

55   W. P. Ryan, 'The struggle of 1913', in Donal Nevin (ed.), *1913: Jim Larkin and the Dublin Lock-out* (Dublin, 1964), p. 7; William O'Brien, 'Nineteen-thirteen: its significance', in ITGWU, *Fifty Years of Liberty Hall: The Golden Jubilee of the Irish Transport and General Workers' Union, 1909–59* (Dublin, 1959), pp. 34–9; Wright, *Disturbed Dublin*, pp. 29, 94.

56   See James McConnel, 'The Irish Parliamentary Party, industrial relations, and the 1913 lockout', *Saothar* 28 (2003), pp. 25–36.

57   George William Russell (1867–1935) – also known by his pseudonym AE – born in Lurgan, educated in Dublin and London; remembered for his interest in mysticism, theosophy, literature, and editing of the *Irish Homestead*, the journal of the Irish Agricultural Organisation Society; less well known for his interest in guild socialism and Larkinism; moved to England in 1932 and died in Bournemouth. See Henry Summerfield, *That Myriad-Minded Man: A Biography of G. W. Russell, 'AE'* (Gerrards Cross, Bucks, 1975).

open letter 'To the masters of Dublin' in the *Irish Times* of 7 October. As the pressure on Liberty Hall's soup kitchens tightened, Mrs Dora Montefiore proposed a 'Save the Kiddies' scheme to board the children of distressed parents with families in England for the duration. It was a veteran syndicalist tactic. On 20 October, Archbishop Walsh condemned this 'most mischievous development' which would put Catholic children in the care of, presumably, Protestant homes. Hysterical scenes ensued when priests and zealots physically frustrated their evacuation. It was all very embarrassing and Connolly, deputising for the absent Larkin, was happy to scuttle the scheme. He then suspended free dinners at Liberty Hall for a week to bring the magnitude of the problem home to the Archbishop.

With the rejection of Board of Trade proposals the struggle entered its critical, middle phase. Amidst expectations that the 'Save the Kiddies' blunder would crack the ITGWU, employers began importing scabs from England on 29 October. Connolly retaliated with mass pickets. When this failed he closed the port, invoking a higher moral duty to justify this breach of the 26 May agreement with the shipping companies. Connolly also assented to Captain Jack White's proposal for a workers' defence force. From the outset, Larkin had suggested that workers should take their cue from Edward Carson's Ulster Volunteer Force to arm themselves against the police. White formulated a plan in October, and on 23 November two companies of the Irish Citizen Army paraded at Croydon Park. Meanwhile, Larkin spent as much time as possible in England whipping up support for sympathetic action. On 27 October he was sentenced to seven months imprisonment for sedition, but released on 13 November. Immediately, he returned to England to raise the 'Fiery Cross', a campaign of torch lit meetings. The reception was enthusiastic; popular pressure for action mounted, especially following the importation of scab labour to Dublin. But making Dublin part of the battle between rebels and officialdom was a dangerous gamble. On 9 December, the BTUC summoned a conference to consider its response. Larkin had already alienated the BTUC parliamentary committee with personal attacks on trade union leaders. He now infuriated the conference with an intemperate speech. The delegates rejected overwhelmingly a rebel motion calling for the blacking of all Dublin goods until the locked out workers were reinstated. Instead, they condemned Larkin's attacks, and expressed confidence in the parliamentary committee's ability to secure a settlement. The conference signalled the beginning of the end. Labour had played its last card. It remained simply to get as many back to work as possible. On 14 December the ITGWU executive decided that members should return without signing 'the document'. Larkin could never abide admitting defeat. He finally agreed to make the decision known publicly on 18 January. The British relief fund closed on 10 February.

A week later there were still 5,000 workers locked out. The defeat was a severe set back for trade unionism in Dublin and for general unionism throughout Ireland. Labour candidates performed poorly in the municipal elections of January 1914. Nevertheless, the attempt to break general unionism had not succeeded. There had been no split in the ITGWU, no rejection of Larkinism, and there would be no acceptance of 'yellow unions'. Unlike the 1890s, unlike Belfast in 1907, the clock had not been put back.

Ideologically too, the outcome was a pyrrhic victory for employers, as it reinforced the interplay of republicanism and syndicalism. Patrick H. Pearse had denounced the employers in the IRB's *Irish Freedom*. Joseph Plunkett and Thomas MacDonagh opened their literary monthly, the *Irish Review*, to Connolly. Larkin later named a union hall after Thomas Ashe in gratitude for his help in 1913. At AE's prompting, Ryan wrote the pamphlet *The Labour Revolt and Larkinism: The Later Irish Pioneers and the Cooperative Commonwealth*, which envisaged Larkinism, the cooperative movement of Horace Plunkett and AE, and politico-cultural forces like Sinn Féin and the Gaelic League remaking the Gaelic communism of Connolly's *Labour in Irish History*. Larkin's interest deepened in the syndicalist idea of underpinning industrial struggle with a working-class counter-culture based on collectivist values like sharing and solidarity, in opposition to the bourgeois ethic of possessive individualism. Croydon Park House and three acres of ground had been leased in August 1913 as a social, sports, and educational centre for ITGWU families. As Larkin put it, 'We make our family life focus around the union. . .'.[58] At the height of the lockout he spoke of extending this counter-culture into commerce through producers' cooperatives, and later toured England raising funds for a programme of practical cooperation. His sister Delia subsequently launched a small shirt manufacturing cooperative to employ girls victimised after the dispute.[59] Connolly too was prompted to reassert the fundamentals of syndicalism. *Old Wine in New Bottles*, provoked by the limits of cross-channel solidarity with Dublin, argued that industrial unionism without syndicalism merely strengthened bureaucratic control over the rank and file. 'Fighting spirit,' he warned, 'is of more importance than the creation of a theoretically perfect organisation.'[60]

58 Quoted in Bob Holton, *British Syndicalism, 1900–1914* (London, 1976), p. 188.
59 Larkin, *James Larkin*, pp. 167–9; *Daily Herald*, 3–4 Feb. 1914.
60 James Connolly, *The Axe to the Root and Old Wine in New Bottles* (Dublin, 1934), p. 35.

The ITGWU emerged from the lockout more aggressively nationalist. Up to the eve of Easter Week, 1916, it would criticise republicans not only for not being socialist but for not being republican. Larkin initiated the shift in emphasis: he lost his appetite for union work after the lockout and took a keener interest in politics at home and freelance agitation in Britain for various groups on the far left. In March 1914 he revamped the Citizen Army as a uniformed force with a republican constitution, and in April the army marched behind the Starry Plough for the first time. Larkin's support for Seán O'Casey's aversion to cooperation with the Irish Volunteers extended only to a suspicion of Redmondite influence. In June, after a section of the IRB dissented from John Redmond's demand that the Volunteers come under his control, he led the Citizen Army to join the IRB at the annual Wolfe Tone commemoration.[61]

Meanwhile, Labour rallied against partition, arguing that it would weaken the working class or was a device to that end: Connolly's observation that it would mean 'a carnival of reaction both North and South' was exceptional only in its eloquence. Larkin, who liked to call himself an Ulsterman, was beside himself with anger at the prospect. MacDonald delivered a parliamentary philippic on the 'Curragh mutiny', and told the government: 'pass Home Rule as quickly as possible and take the consequences'.[62] Congress sponsored an anti-partition meeting on 5 April 1914. Its annual conference in June, with 20 delegates from Ulster and four from Britain in attendance, condemned partition by 84–2 votes with eight delegates unrecorded.[63] The Ulstermen may not have spoken for the majority of their members, but they reflected the views of northern Labour activists, most of whom were not nationalists, but were fearful of being locked into an Orange state. Belfast had seen another round of workplace expulsions in 1912, when Loyalists forced 3,000 workers from their jobs. About 600 of the expelled men were Protestant, and targeted for being Labourites, Liberals, or Independent Orangemen. Campbell helped to organise an Expelled Workers' Committee, which raised relief funds and lobbied the authorities to protect those willing to go back to work. The ITUC made similar representations to Redmond and the British Labour Party.[64] Belfast trades council tried hard to avoid antagonising Unionist workers,

61   Donal Nevin, 'The Irish Citizen Army, 1913–16', in Nevin, *James Larkin*; pp. 257–65.

62   *Northern Whig*, 26 Mar. 1914.

63   UUMC, ITUC, *Report* (1914), pp. 70–3.

64   Ibid., (1913), pp. 11, 13; Austen Morgan, *Labour and Partition: The Belfast Working Class, 1905–23* (London, 1991), pp. 127–39 provides the most detailed account of the expulsions.

distancing itself from the expellees, and – though Unionist leaders had condemned the violence – refusing to even mention the disturbances in its annual report for 1912.[65] The council never voted on Home Rule or partition, though the minutes suggest that a narrow majority of delegates opposed the former and almost all opposed the latter.

The outbreak of world war in August acted as another catalyst in driving the militant left into Fenianism. No sooner had the Liberal government caved in to army insubordination and Carson's threats, than the Socialist International's much vaunted promise to prevent war disintegrated as socialists in France, Belgium, Germany, and Britain swung in behind their governments. Again, Larkin set the pace. Even before the crisis in the Balkans engulfed Europe, the *Irish Worker* called on 'every man who believed in Ireland as a nation to act now. England's need: our opportunity. The men are ready. The guns must be got, and at once'. A few were 'got', smuggled from Liverpool by Larkin's boyhood friend, Fred Bower.[66] Larkin was appalled at Redmond's support for the war and gave short shrift to O'Casey's ultra-leftism. In his persona of the hard-bitten lad from the slums, the cantankerous O'Casey could not resist attacking the middle-class people on whom a Labour-separatist alliance depended. O'Casey overreached himself in trying to have Countess Markievicz[67] expelled from the Citizen Army because of her republican connections. With no support from Larkin, he resigned as Citizen Army secretary. Never one to let life subvert art, he would later denounce Connolly's politics in his purple prosed *Story of the Irish Citizen Army*, and lionise Big Jim as Connolly's antithesis.

It would be 20 years and more before Larkin's mental health recovered from the lockout. He had become near impossible to work with and had no stomach for rebuilding his crippled union. Increasingly, the no 1 branch committee – the union's de facto executive – took up the slack, and by August 1914 its relations with the Larkins were beginning to sour. In September, Delia was requested to remove the Women Workers' Union from Liberty Hall. Before matters came to a head, Jim announced his departure for the

---

65 UUMC, Belfast trades council minutes, 3 Apr. 1913.

66 Nevin, 'The Irish Citizen Army, 1913–16', p. 260; Fred Bower, *Rolling Stonemason: An Autobiography* (London, 1936), p. 182.

67 Constance Markievicz (1868–1927), born in London of Anglo-Irish ascendancy stock; educated privately at Lissadell, Sligo; influenced by the national revival; Sinn Féiner and suffragist; made an honorary member of the ITGWU in 1913, and a Citizen Army officer in 1916; Minister of Labour in the Dáil cabinet, 1919; devoted to Connolly, and wrote *James Connolly's Policy and Catholic Doctrine* (1924); caricatured unfairly as a 'lady bountiful' and not taken seriously as a socialist, but not effective as a left republican and died a member of Fianna Fáil. See Diana Norman, *Terrible Beauty: A Life of Constance Markievicz* (London, 1987).

United States. Publicly, he pretended he was leaving on a fund-raising mission. Most thought he was taking a break to recuperate and would be back within a year. Privately, he had been thinking of a new career as a globe-trotting freelance agitator since December 1913. He had no plans to return, though he remained titular general secretary of the ITGWU and kept himself informed of Irish affairs. He worked secretly for the German embassy in the United States from 1915, and spoke of going to Germany to help Roger Casement raise an 'Irish brigade' from prisoners of war.[68] Larkin had wanted P. T. Daly[69] to take his place in Dublin. O'Brien and Tom Foran[70] prevailed on him to choose Connolly instead.[71]

During the first half of the war, social conditions for urban workers worsened steadily. The lockout had shown how dependent Labour was on Britain, and the industrial truce between British Labour leaders and the government promised to preclude militancy for the duration of hostilities. But there were glimmers of hope. Inflation and food shortages were generating resentment against the farmers, employers, and shopkeepers who seemed to be doing well out of the war. Trade union membership underwent a slow recovery. If strike action remained largely within the craft sector, movements of transport workers gathered pace from late 1914 onwards.[72] In August 1915 Connolly felt sanguine enough to propose a unity conference of unskilled unions. After September, the ITGWU won a series of pay increases for Dublin dockers. During a strike in the Burns Laird line, Citizen Army weapons were

---

68 Larkin, *James Larkin*, pp. 210–11.

69 Patrick T. Daly (1870–1943), born in Dublin, son of a printer; an IRB man and an isolated advocate of Irish Labourism in the pre-Larkinite ITUC; his ambitions in the ITGWU and ITUC were repeatedly frustrated by O'Brien, who regarded him as untrustworthy and too close to Larkin; after 1918 they became open enemies in a feud that was very damaging to Labour unity in Dublin; worked for various small unions, served on Dublin Corporation, and had his revenge on O'Brien at the ITUC special congress in 1939. See Séamus Cody, 'The remarkable Patrick Daly', *Obair* 2 (1985), pp. 10–11.

70 Thomas Foran (1883–1951), born in Dublin and worked as a docker; nominated as first president of the ITGWU by Larkin, retiring in 1938; interned after the Easter Rising, though not a participant and critical of Connolly's involvement, favouring concentration on industrial issues; wrote *The Lines of Progress* (1918); approved of Labour's withdrawal from the 1918 general election; friendly with Larkin, but sided with O'Brien in 1923; a senator, 1923–36 and 1938–48. See D. R. O'Connor Lysaght, 'Labour lives, no 7', *Saothar* 30 (2005), pp. 99–100.

71 Greaves, *The Irish Transport and General Workers' Union*, pp. 128–38.

72 David Fitzpatrick, 'Strikes in Ireland, 1914–21', *Saothar* 6 (1980), p. 36; Board of Trade, *Fourteenth Abstract of Labour Statistics of the United Kingdom, 1908–9* (BPP, 1911), Cd 5458, CX 307; Board of Trade, *Report on Strikes and Lock Outs for 1912* (BPP, 1913), Cd 7089, XLVIII.363; Greaves, *The Life and Times of James Connolly*, p. 299.

lent to pickets. Indeed, Connolly's difficulty lay in keeping dockland militancy within the resources of his financially crippled union. Spontaneous organisation of ITGWU members in the provinces commenced in early 1916.[73] Winds of political change were evident in May 1915 when the College Green division fell vacant on the death of J. P. Nannetti. Dublin trades council convened a conference of 150 delegates to reconstitute itself as the Dublin United Trades Council and Labour League and fight the bye-election. Standing on an anti-war, anti-partition manifesto drafted by Connolly, the council's president, Thomas Farren, polled 1,846 votes to 2,445 votes for the IPP's John D. Nugent.[74] The result was promising enough to catch Larkin's attention. When a vacancy arose in the Harbour constituency in August, he cabled from San Francisco: 'Boys here think I should fight Harbour Division – money forwarded'.[75] No money arrived, and Connolly advised against entering the lists, pleading lamely that it would be a waste of resources.[76] In all likelihood, he didn't want to cross Larkin by fielding another candidate, and neither did he want his volatile boss back in Dublin as he pressed republicans for insurrection.

Why did Connolly not await the ripening of time? V. I. Lenin would say, in October 1916, that the Irish 'rose prematurely, when the European revolt of the proletariat had not yet matured'.[77] One can explain Connolly's strategy and urgency. The collapse of socialist opposition to the war magnified the Fenian option, and there was cause for revolutionary pessimism. The Irish, for the first time in their history, were backing Britain in a war. Labour complained of 'economic conscription'. Unskilled labourers, who made up 28 per cent of men between the ages of 20 and 45, comprised 70 to 80 per cent of recruits into the army's other ranks in wartime Ireland; some 30 per cent of recruits were illiterate.[78] But whatever the spur to enlistment, the war was sealing bonds of blood and welfare between working-class families and the

---

73   Greaves, *The Irish Transport and General Workers' Union*, pp. 150–6. For attitudes to the loan of arms to pickets and Connolly's difficulties see Frank Robbins, *Under the Starry Plough: Recollections of the Irish Citizen Army* (Dublin, 1977), pp. 31–3.

74   Mitchell, *Labour in Irish Politics*, pp. 63–7; Cody, O'Dowd, and Rigney, *The Parliament of Labour*, pp. 110–14.

75   ITGWU, *The Attempt to Smash the Irish Transport and General Workers' Union* (Dublin, 1924), pp. 70–1, 133.

76   William O'Brien, *Forth the Banners Go: Reminiscences of William O'Brien as told to Edward MacLysaght* (Dublin, 1969), p. 71.

77   V. I. Lenin, *British Labour and British Imperialism* (London, 1969), p. 166.

78   Thomas P. Dooley, *Irishmen or English Soldiers? The Times and World of a Southern Catholic Irish man (1876–1916) enlisting in the British Army during the First World War* (Liverpool, 1995), p. 8; see also Niamh Puirséil, 'War, work, and labour', in John Horne (ed.), *Our War: Ireland and the Great War* (Dublin, 2008), pp. 183–94.

British state, eviscerating the gut anti-imperialism of the Irish people. Connolly was by no means alone in believing that wartime labour regulations presaged the displacement of the liberal capitalism by a new servility that would enslave the proletariat in the shackles of statism; sections of the British Labour movement would denounce the introduction of conscription as 'Prussianism'.[79] But this is to rationalise. The oddity is that the great theorist had a simple prescription for revolution in Ireland: just do it, and do it now. If it works, then the time was right. If it doesn't work . . . better luck next time. He had urged Griffith, of all people, to lead a revolt during the last big war, against the Boers, and was determined not to let this opportunity pass.[80]

Still the Irish Volunteers refused to ally with the Citizen Army, leaving Connolly to conclude that under Eoin MacNeill's command they would never seize the moment. It was only to forestall unilateral action by Connolly that, in January 1916, he was informed of IRB plans and the union of Easter Week was sealed. The insurrection was not intended as a blood sacrifice, but after MacNeill's countermanding order Connolly reckoned there was no chance of success. When the Citizen Army marched out of Liberty Hall on Easter Monday it left Labour behind it. Even the ITGWU had come close to repudiating Connolly ten days previously for hoisting a green flag over Liberty Hall, and he, quite responsibly, did not implicate the union in the Rising.[81] The 210 Citizen Army men and women who turned out were positioned mainly in St Stephen's Green, the Royal College of Surgeons, and the General Post Office, where Connolly commanded the garrison. All were impressed by his cool efficiency. Twelve of the Citizen Army were killed in action, and two later died of wounds. Michael Mallin, its chief of staff and secretary of the Silk Weavers' Union, was shot by firing squad on 8 May, and Connolly himself was executed on 12th. Markievicz was reprieved 'only on account of her sex'. Contrary to rumour, she displayed courage and composure at her trial.[82] As Connolly anticipated, international socialist opinion was baffled by his involvement in a 'Sinn Féin' revolt, with the notable exceptions of Lenin and Leon Trotsky.[83] He himself had no regrets, satisfied that nothing would have been worse than the failure to fight. And it cannot be denied that the Rising became an astonishing political success.

79   Pelling, *A Short History of the Labour Party*, pp. 38–9.
80   Donal P. McCracken, *Forgotten Protest: Ireland and the Anglo-Boer War* (Belfast, 2003), pp. 65–6.
81   Greaves, *The Life and Times of James Connolly*, pp. 323–34; Greaves, *The Irish Transport and General Workers' Union*, pp. 163–4.
82   Brian Barton, *From Behind a Closed Door: Secret Court Martial Records of the 1916 Easter Rising* (Belfast, 2002), pp. 77–82, 267–98, 316–8.
83   For a discussion of the left and the Rising see Newsinger, *Rebel City*, pp. 135–55.

Easter Week threw Labour on the defensive. The British had shelled Liberty Hall and seized trade union leaders, including Daly, Congress secretary, and his papers. Into the vacuum stepped the Belfast based Johnson and Campbell. As none had been held in 1915 because of the War, the August 1916 Congress was the first in wartime. Johnson's presidential address masterfully blended a generous acknowledgement of Labour's irreparable losses in Easter Week with tribute to those 'who have laid down their lives in another field . . . for Love of their Country'. Worried about employer demands that Labour should be held responsible for the damage to property during the Rising, the Congress report refuted allegations of trade union involvement in the Rising and tried to dissociate the ITGWU from the Citizen Army. Foran declared that his union 'was proud of the actions taken by the Irish Citizen Army', but did not seek to change the report.[84]

84 UUMC, ITUCLP, *Report* (1916), pp. 3, 12, 21–33, 36–7.

FIVE

SYNDICALISM 1917–23

The young working class of Ireland, formed as it was in an atmosphere saturated with heroic memories of national rebellion, and coming into conflict with the egotistically narrow and imperially arrogant trade unionism of Britain, has wavered accordingly between nationalism and syndicalism, and is always ready to link these conceptions together in its revolutionary consciousness.

Leon Trotsky, *Nashe Slovo*, 4 July 1916.

—

Within three years of the Rising, Labour was on the march to the Workers' Republic, more syndicalist than ever before. The primary cause of this change of fortune was the World War. Secondary factors were the climate of revolution, at home and abroad. If the first half of the war stored up social grievances, production demands and the growing manpower shortage after 1916 provided the means of redress. The pre-conditions of wage improvement materialised in two ways; through government intervention to increase pay in war-related industries, and, later, through the all-round economic improvement. After the war, the release of 'pent-up' consumer demand generated a brief economic boom. Wages generally rose faster than prices from 1916, overtaking pre-war levels by 1919–20, until the economy hit a disastrous slump in 1920–1. Given the nature of capitalism, the money was only for those who could get it. Trade unionism exploded in all directions; from under 100,000 in 1916, membership affiliated to Congress reached 225,000 in 1920.[1] As workers spontaneously revived pre-war Larkinite tactics, their leaders adopted industrial unionism as an organisational strategy. To this was added the promise that through industrial unionism Labour would ultimately realise the Workers' Republic. The ascent of Sinn Féin politicised wage militancy. In breaking the hegemony of conservative nationalism, separatists subverted the social consensus, creating the scope for native echoes of international radicalism to flourish. All over Europe, workers moved left in 1917. After the armistice, workers demanded recompense for their wartime sacrifices. A spirit of change was in

---

[1]   UUMC, ITUCLP and ILPTUC, *Reports* (1916–20).

the air. The war, it was felt, had discredited the old ways. The future would be democratic, surely, and socialist, probably. Congress was finally transformed from a talking shop for a loose collection of trade unions with few ideas beyond assumptions borrowed from Britain, into a voice of Labour, with a mission to create an integrated movement, geared to tackling native reality. The confluence of tactics, strategy, and promise made the syndicalist moment.

THE WAGES MOVEMENT

State intervention remained a key determinant of wage movements for the first three years of the war. Though the initial effect of statutory control was to freeze wages, from 1915 onwards, state intervention became a means of securing war bonuses or minimum rates. Importance to the war effort and good organisation were therefore essential for successful militancy. Ireland's piecemeal integration into the war economy created a time lag in wage movements between employment sectors.[2] 'Old sectors' – ie: those in trade unions – were the first to recoup lost ground. Seamen and dockers won pay advances in 1915. The government took control of the shipyards and railways in 1916, making provision for the payment of war bonuses. Aerodrome and other military construction, together with the repair of Dublin's shell torn city centre, revived the building line in 1917–18. Building became particularly strike-prone after mid 1918, with three general stoppages hitting Dublin and Belfast. Almost 19 per cent of all strikers between 1914 and 1921 were building workers.[3] The introduction of statutory minimum rates in agriculture in 1917 finally enabled 'new sectors' to join the wages movement over the next two years. To minimise industrial unrest, government intervention and regulation persisted into the post-war era. The recommendations of the Whitley Committee, appointed to investigate wartime industrial relations in Britain, led to the Trade Boards Act (1918). An Irish Department of the British Ministry of Labour was set up in July 1919, and 15 new trade boards were established in little over a year. By August 1920, there were 19 trade boards covering 148,000 employees, the bulk of them in Ulster's textile and clothing industries.[4]

2   The following account of the wages movement is based on Emmet O'Connor, *Syndicalism in Ireland, 1917–23* (Cork, 1988), pp. 20–53.
3   For strike statistics during these years see NAUK, Ministry of Labour annual reports on strikes and lockouts 1914–21, LAB 34/14–20, 34/32–39. See also David Fitzpatrick, 'Strikes in Ireland, 1914–21', *Saothar* 6, pp. 26–39, for its fine statistical analysis.
4   Brendan Mark Browne, 'Trade boards in Northern Ireland, 1909–45' (PhD, QUB, 1989), pp. 146–57, 340.

The war mobilised industry without restructuring the workforce. Ulster was the main beneficiary. Textiles, clothing, engineering, and shipbuilding were soon harnessed to military needs, but no sizeable munitions sector developed in Ulster, while Unionist and British employer determination to freeze nationalist Ireland out of lucrative war contracts kept the south deindustrialised. The few munitions factories distributed to mollify nationalist outrage did not commence production until 1917, and employed a mere 2,169 persons by the armistice.[5] As a result of the bias in government policy, southern wage movements were compelled to be the cause as much as the consequence of state intervention. This, together with the more primitive condition of industrial relations in which they operated, gave them a more militant character, and strikes lit the path of trade unionism to new sectors and new regions. Strike activity increased steadily from 1915 to the armistice. The level of conflict declined in 1919 as rising unemployment yielded quickly to an economic boom, but militancy reached new heights in 1920, before receding sharply with the onset of the slump and the gradual fall in the cost of living towards the end of that year.

Railwaymen led the first big push for government intervention in the south. Inspired by British NUR men, who had emulated munitions workers in developing a shop stewards' movement, Dublin and South Eastern Railwaymen spearheaded a threat of unofficial action in September 1916 for a 10s per week wage rise. Most railwaymen still earned under 14s weekly, a rate that ignored soaring prices since 1914. After inconclusive discussions, the NUR sanctioned a strike for 18 December. As private interests could not, or would not, meet the pay demand, the government stepped in to keep the war effort running smoothly and took control of Ireland's 32 railway companies shortly before Christmas. On 29 December, the men were awarded a 7s per week war bonus. Over the next nine months the NUR's Irish affiliation surged from 5,000 to 17,000 members.[6] It was a victory not alone over the railway companies. In 1917 NUR men launched the monthly journal *New Way*, and developed the most sophisticated rank and file movement in Ireland during these years. Up to the rise of the ITGWU in 1918, they were the van of progress.

The major state intervention came in agriculture. Social conditions worsened alarmingly over the winter of 1916–17 as food and fuel supplies dwindled. To provide more basic foodstuffs the government introduced tillage

5 A further 8,000 or so Irish worked in munitions in Britain. See Imperial War Museum, London, French MSS, Memorandum from Sir Thomas Stafford and Sir Frank Brooke to the Viceroy's Advisory Council, 20 Nov. 1918, 75/46/12; Fitzpatrick, 'Strikes in Ireland, 1914–21', pp. 29–34.

6 Philip S. Bagwell, *The Railwaymen: The History of the National Union of Railwaymen* (London, 1963), pp. 356–7.

orders under the Corn Production Act, obliging farmers to bring at least ten per cent of their arable land under the plough in 1917, and a further five per cent in 1918. As tillage was labour intensive, the Act gave farm workers a scarcity value. Moreover, the Department of Agriculture accepted that if there was not an absolute manpower shortage on the land, the quality of labour suffered from the attraction of higher wages in Britain. Initially, the Department appealed to farmers' better nature. It was soon compelled to be serious. An Agricultural Wages Board was established in September 1917 to determine compulsory minimum pay and conditions. Tillage orders stirred the old rural labour unions and encouraged the formation of new local societies. Broadly, these bodies had three main objectives: wage improvement, land redistribution, and government aid for plot holders. Land hunger remained strong, but agricultural trade unionism gradually turned aside to the more urgent goal of wage improvement. After January 1917, labourers aimed at parity with their urban counterparts, requesting pay rises of up to 100 per cent. Though the introduction of the Agricultural Wages Board reduced the likelihood of conflict, where organisation was strong, labourers sought to ensure that 'legal minimums' did not become 'legal maximums'. It was the ITGWU that grasped the potential of this development.[7] From the beginning of 1917 its organisers were in the countryside, mopping up the rural labour unions as farm workers threw in their lot with the urban working class. By 1920 the union mustered 60,000 members in agriculture, the bulk of these in the 12 south easterly 'tillage counties'.

Surmounting the enormous difficulties of organising farm workers copperfastened trade unionism in the provinces, and was of immense psychological importance in taking Labour from the more anglicised urban fringe to the very heart of the Irish condition. It also facilitated an equally remarkable rise of general unionism in the towns. As unrest spread, the coincidence of pay claims from so many disparate occupations turned wage movements into 'the wages movement'. Trends towards general action first cohered in Dublin in October 1917 when strike notices affecting 2,000–3,000 employees were pending. The *Irish Independent* feared another 1913. Dublin trades council offered to coordinate demands and promote the convening of unions in industrial groups. If the promise of inter-union coordination at the grand level was never realised, generalised action re-emerged to enable the ubiquitous 'miscellaneous' workers to become militant. The ITGWU mushroomed from 5,000 members in 1916 to 120,000 four years later. Craft and clerical unions expanded too, with the latter displaying a strong and unusual affinity with Labour. Trades

---

7 For ITGWU activities see especially C. Desmond Greaves, *The Irish Transport and General Workers' Union: The Formative Years, 1909–1923* (Dublin, 1982).

councils multiplied, to 15 by 1918 and 46 by 1921, and now styled themselves 'workers' rather than 'trades and labour' councils. Reflecting the myriad of minor struggles making up provincial wage movements, the proportion of strikes in Dublin and Belfast fell from 50 per cent between 1914 and 1918 to 20 per cent from 1919 to 1921; the corresponding proportion of strikers fell from 67 to 57 per cent.

In what ways was Labour syndicalist? There were no card carrying syndicalists in Ireland, and the term was rarely used, though 'industrial unionism', 'OBU', 'cooperative commonwealth', and 'Workers' Republic' were coming into common currency. One could also argue that union leaders were fair weather syndicalists. Equally, it was a measure of the impact of syndicalism that they were swept along in its path.

Sympathetic action again became central to strike tactics. In some cases the principle was extended to generalised action. Between 1917 and 1920 there were 18 local general strikes, mainly in small towns where almost all workers had joined the ITGWU and put forward common wage demands. During these strikes the town was usually taken over by the strike committee, which controlled business and transport through a system of permits. The permits were a means of getting everyone – including employers – to accept the authority of the union as well as enforcing solidarity. Strikes, especially in rural areas, were also more likely to be accompanied by sabotage or violence during these years. Workplace seizures – or soviets as they were called – almost all involving the ITGWU, emerged from November 1918 onwards, substantially as strike tactics but indicating too a political ambition. The most extensive seizure, that of 13 Limerick creameries owned by the Cleeve company, was a well planned affair, directed by three revolutionary ITGWU officials. On 16 May 1920 a red flag was hoisted over the central creamery at Knocklong and a banner proclaimed: 'We make butter, not profits. Knocklong Creamery Soviet'. The plants were returned to Cleeve's on 22 May after demands on wages and conditions had been met.[8] The 'Knocklong soviet', as the occupations came to be called, was the first to attract widespread interest. In September, the ITGWU paper, the *Watchword of Labour*, began to publish on related developments in Italy, and featured items on the earlier seizures of Mazzoni's and FIAT which, the paper conceded, were 'an advance on Knocklong'. The lessons drawn by the *Watchword* were: form revolutionary councils, organise a red guard, make friends with soldiers, and get railwaymen to maintain supplies.

---

8   See D. R. O'Connor Lysaght, 'The Munster soviet creameries', *Saotharlann Staire Éireann* 1, pp. 36–9.

For strategy, Labour turned to industrial unionism. The ITGWU was facing a novel problem for an Irish union: how to make best advantage of the tens of thousands joining up. On 1 July 1918 it issued *The Lines of Progress*, a pamphlet inspired by James Connolly's *Socialism Made Easy*, and intended to 'advance Connolly's OBU idea' as 'a scientific solution to the Labour question'. 'With this machine [the OBU] in their possession,' it promised, 'the workers of Ireland can break all their chains with ease and from the mere rallying cry of political parties turn Freedom into a glorious reality.'[9] In 1921 the ITGWU published the first Irish edition of *Socialism Made Easy* together with other Connolly writings on industrial unionism in the pamphlet *The Axe to the Root*. Industrial unionism was also promoted in the NUR's *New Way*.[10] Under the impact of nationalism and industrial unionism, growth reshaped the movement. Nineteen of the 37 affiliates to the 1916 congress were British. Five years later, the number of Congress unions had risen to 42, but the amalgamateds had dropped to 13, and now represented under 25 per cent of total membership. Between 1917 and 1923, 11 new unions were founded by breakaways from the amalgamateds, and four of these adopted an industrial union structure. The NUR's rank and file movement combined nationalism with industrial unionist arguments to win a semi-autonomous Irish executive. Partially successful ventures in industrial unionism resulted in the formation of the Local Government Officials (Ireland) Trade Union and the Irish Union of Distributive Workers and Clerks.

Syndicalism was evident too in efforts to develop a working-class counter-culture, through cooperatives, May Day parades, aeríochtaí [festivals], and labour newspapers. The ITGWU's annual report for 1919 directed members to conceive of the union 'as a social centre, round which they can build every activity of their existence, and which, wisely used, can be made to remedy all their grievances'. In 1919 trade unions funded the James Connolly Labour College, which enrolled over 200 students in classes in history, economics, and public administration. An appeal for lecturers in the *Watchword of Labour* advised that 'the working class outlook' was an essential requirement 'for unless ye become as proletarians ye cannot enter the Workers' Republic'. The College flourished up to November 1920, when it was raided and ransacked by the British military.[11] One measure of the greater importance of Labour at

---

9   O'Connor, *Syndicalism in Ireland*, pp. 62–3.

10   See Conor McCabe, 'The Amalgamated Society of Railway Servants and the National Union of Railwaymen in Ireland, 1911–1923 (PhD, University of Ulster, 2006).

11   Emmet O'Connor, '"True Bolsheviks?": The rise and fall of the Socialist Party of Ireland, 1917–21', in D. George Boyce and Alan O'Day (eds), *Ireland in Transition, 1867–1921* (London, 2004), p. 213.

this time was the Catholic Church's heightened interest in the social question. The *Irish Messenger* published 28 pamphlets on the church and labour in 1918, compared with five in 1913. There was even, mirabile dictu, an academic study of labour, George O'Brien's *Labour Organization*, published in 1921.

The post-war years confirmed the divergent evolution of northern and southern trade unionism. Ulster wage movements never gelled into the wages movement. In the key engineering and shipbuilding sectors, war production brought few changes in working practices. Skill displacement or dilution, which pushed west Canada craftsmen into the Canadian OBU and created 'Red Clydeside', were resisted successfully by the craft unions. Government control of shipbuilding did lead to a narrowing of wage differentials between skilled and unskilled, and a big increase in membership of the NAUL and the Workers' Union. However, the craft unions went some way to restoring the differentials in 1917, and the issue provoked the only major strike of the war years in Belfast. In the uncertain aftermath of the armistice, it looked briefly as if sectionalism might be rattled. On 25 January 1919, 30,000 Belfast engineering and shipbuilding workers struck unofficially for a 44-hour week. Soon the trouble spread to municipal employees. Control of power supplies gave the strike committee some administrative authority and the establishment of a permit system, enforced by pickets, led journalists to refer to the 'Belfast Soviet'. Alarmed at the contagion of 'Bolshevism' and the prospect of Sinn Féin winning Protestant support through it, Dublin Castle sent in troops on 14 February to take over the gasworks and electricity station. The strike collapsed within a few days, and marked a deceleration of northern wage movements. In truth there was little cause for alarm. Sensitive to its fragile base, the strike committee had strained to moderate radical impulses. Offers of help from Congress and the ITGWU were ignored.[12] Though 1919–20 were paramount years for Belfast Labourism, the massive dispute carried a tentative import.

There were possibilities of bringing unskilled and textile operatives into communion with Dublin. Their bargaining problems approximated to those of southern workers. Like the mass of southern workers, they had historically proved too difficult for the British unions to organise, and the small craft societies in textiles had, of all unions in Ulster, been most supportive of Congress. Whilst Protestants held Dublin unions in suspicion, there was no enthusiasm for Loyalist alternatives. The Ulster Workers' Trade Union, launched in December 1918 by James Turkington, encountered stiff opposition from other unions. Faced with the option of Irish or Loyalist

12   Henry Patterson, *Class Conflict and Sectarianism: The Protestant Working Class and the Belfast Labour Movement, 1868–1920* (Belfast, 1980), pp. 92–114.

unions, Protestant workers might have chosen the former. However, the earlier mobilisation of the northern and British economies for the war effort allowed the amalgamateds to preclude this dilemma and then camouflage sectarianism with a veneer of British secular ideology. When Liberty Hall was ready to push north in late 1918, the NAUL and the Workers' Union had already established a firm presence among general workers outside Belfast. With textile operatives, the story was similar. The ITGWU recorded some successes in recruiting Protestant and Catholic workers in Monaghan and Caledon, County Tyrone, but otherwise its resolute Ulster campaign found itself sided into the nationalist ghetto. Smaller Dublin unions, such as the Brick and Stonelayers, the Irish National Teachers' Organisation, and the Drapers' Assistants, lost northern branches after the general strike against conscription.

CONSENSUS AND CONSTITUTION

Congress policy during these years has always been something of a puzzle; on the social question, an ambiguity of revolutionism and restraint; on the national question, a more enigmatic juxtaposition of republicanism and detachment. The explanation is that Congress leaders were syndicalists while militancy paid dividends. Syndicalism looked like a good investment in 1917. William O'Brien revived Connolly's SPI in January. It soon included key players like Tom Johnson and Cathal O'Shannon,[13] and became the best connected, best resourced Marxist party in Irish history.[14] Similarly, Labour was republican where a consensus for republicanism existed. Where there was no consensus, it retreated into neutrality and constitutionalism. Indeed Labour policy on nationalism from 1916 onwards, amounted to either tailing the consensus or wrapping itself in the constitution. The difficulty of engaging with the national revolution at home, made Congress all the more anxious to assert its radical credentials abroad, and the SPI sought to position Irish Labour on the left of the international socialist movement.

The sea change in the character of Labour began to affect Congress in late 1916. With widespread talk of famine, the ITUCLP called a special conference

13 Cathal O'Shannon (1893–1969), born near Randalstown, Co. Antrim, the third of four children of a locomotive engine driver; a lifelong republican, Gaeilgeoir, and socialist; worked with Connolly in Belfast, and tried to join the Easter Rising; as an editor of ITGWU papers from 1918, he encouraged militancy and Bolshevism; ultimately loyal to the union, he moved to the centre after 1923 as ITGWU political secretary (1924–6), and head of [wage] movements (1926–41); secretary of the ITUC (1941–5), and the CIU (1945–6), and a workers' representative on the Labour Court (1946–69).

14 O'Connor, 'True Bolsheviks?', pp. 209–22.

in December 1916 to demand price control and a ban on selected exports. It was the first such conference, and the first time that Congress had acted for workers as a class rather than the interests of its affiliates. The food supply crisis also widened the ambit of industrial struggle. Workers – especially NUR men – responded to profiteering by setting up consumer cooperatives which, though limited in scale, and mostly of brief duration, were of demonstrative importance for the inchoate anti-capitalist sentiment welling up in popular consciousness.

The conscription crisis had a similar ice-breaking effect on Labour politics. In 1917 all of the main parties were becoming nervous about the anticipated post-war radicalism. Sir Edward Carson would establish the Ulster Unionist Labour Association (UULA).[15] Joe Devlin, the IPP's labour spokesman, proposed a 'New Democratic Movement', committed to co-partnership in industry and profit sharing. Devlin also maintained that Sinn Féin's policy of abstention from Westminster was tantamount to saying 'Labour must wait' for the dim and distant republic before any progress could be made on legislation for social reform. The phrase got legs, and the fiction that Éamon de Valera had actually declared 'Labour must wait' survived as one of the great myths of Irish history. In truth, no politician with a modicum of intelligence would have dared to suggest anything of the sort at this time. Sinn Féin wanted Labour to join the revolution, and hoped for a deal with Congress.[16] Labour still had its doubts about any association with nationalism until the conscription crisis acted as a gateway to the national question. The conscription issue had a Labour pedigree, having met strong opposition in the British and Australian Labour movements, and Congress had no qualms about joining the resistance committee Comhdháil Chosanta Gaedheal with Nationalists and Sinn Féin.[17] On 20 April 1918, 1,500 trade union delegates assembled in Dublin's Mansion House to call a protest for 23 April. For the *Irish Times*, the success of Ireland's first general strike made 23 April 'the day on which Irish Labour realised its strength'.[18] The tremendous upsurge of union membership over the next three months seemed proof positive of the synergy of the industrial and political struggles.

15   Henry Patterson, 'The decline of the collaborators: the Ulster Unionist Labour Association and post-war Unionist politics', in Francis Devine, Fintan Lane and Niamh Puirséil (eds), *Essays in Labour History: A Festschrift for Elizabeth and John Boyle* (Dublin, 2008), pp. 238–9.

16   Arthur Mitchell, *Labour in Irish Politics, 1890–1930: The Irish Labour Movement in an Age of Revolution* (Dublin, 1974), pp. 82–3; D. R. O'Connor Lysaght, '"Labour must wait": the making of a myth', *Saothar* 26 (2001), pp. 61–5.

17   The most detailed account of Labour involvement in the anti-conscription campaign is in J. Anthony Gaughan, *Thomas Johnson* (Dublin, 1980), pp. 86–122.

18   *Irish Times*, 24 Apr. 1918.

Self confidence was unmistakable at the 1918 Congress in August. Two hundred and forty delegates attended, compared with 99 the previous year. O'Brien's presidential address strained to strike a historic note, invoking Connolly and his influence on 'the great Russian Revolution'. Equally conscious of history, the delegates passed unanimously a motion entwining support for the Bolsheviks, peace in Europe, and self-determination for all peoples. A more comprehensive Labour policy now began to take shape, with Johnson and O'Brien exerting a guiding influence on political and industrial strategy respectively. The Congress took as its objective the promotion of working-class organisation socially, industrially, and politically in cooperatives, trade unions, and a party. Liberty Hall subsequently formulated a scheme to develop the cooperative angle to this trinity in syndicalist style. Taking its cue from the workers' cooperatives formed to combat profiteering, it recommended branches to start by forming distributive outlets, connecting ultimately into a 'Workers' Food Committee laying down food policy for the country'. The annual Congress also addressed political action. It seemed that the war would drag on for another year, but with the threat of a German victory gone forever, there was speculation about a general election, none having been held since 1910. It would be a watershed election. All men over the age of 21 and all women over the age of 30 would be entitled to vote for the first time, expanding the Irish electorate from 700,000 to just under two million. It was agreed to enlarge 'the scope and authority' of Congress, instruct the executive to formulate proposals by 15 September, and hold a special conference on a revised constitution not later than 15 November.[19] Predominantly native in organisation and Fenian in mindset for the first time since the 1890s, with the old dependency on the rhythm of British militancy finally broken, Labour looked set to make its mark. However, in three crucial areas the Congress leadership was to prove unable to surmount the legacy of colonialism.

POLITICS

The most immediate failure occurred in relation to the 1918 general election. On 6–7 September the Congress executive agreed unanimously to Johnson's proposal that Labour contest the election on an independent and abstentionist basis. Johnson defended abstentionism because of 'the proved futility' of attending Westminster during the war, the importance of 'undermining' Britain's moral authority to govern Ireland, and the need to secure separate

19   UUMC, ILPTUC, *Report* (1918), p. 58.

Irish representation in the Socialist International.[20] Sinn Féin, which had
been chasing Labour for 'a deal' since 1917, stepped up the pressure.[21] Secret
talks between the parties were held on 22 September. The Labour representatives spoke of fielding 15 candidates, but said the number might be closer to
six, and wanted Sinn Féin to stand aside in four Dublin constituencies. Sinn
Féin offered a clear run in the Dublin seats if Labour would not fight
elsewhere and its candidates pledged support for the Republic and abstention
from Westminster. Two days later, Dublin trades council nominated five
possibilities – O'Brien, Louie Bennett,[22] Thomas Farren, Jim Larkin, and
Thomas MacPartlin[23] – for four seats: Harbour, College Green, St Patrick's,
and St Michan's. Complications set in October. The provinces showed no
great enthusiasm for entering the lists. In Dublin, P. T. Daly made mischief
for O'Brien by canvassing a withdrawal in favour of Sinn Féin. Crucially, the
Central Powers began to crumble. A peacetime election meant the collapse of
the consensus created by conscription, and made abstention controversial.
The Congress executive divided. Given what had happened in 1916, was it
worth tying their unions to the wheel of Sinn Féin for the sake of four seats?
When the special conference convened on 1–2 November, the executive
recommended withdrawal. Opening the debate, Johnson explained that in
September they had been expecting a wartime election, whereas a post-war
election would become a referendum on Ireland's constitutional status in the
post-war world. The suggestion that it was not Labour's business to take a
unilateral stance on the constitution appealed to most delegates. Opposition
came from the more radical elements, like O'Shannon, who saw no reason for

20   National Library of Ireland (NLI), Thomas Johnson papers, Ms 17249. 'National Executive
circular (handwritten).'

21   Brian Farrell, *The Founding of Dáil Éireann: Parliament and Nation-Building* (Dublin, 1971),
pp. 34–46 offers the most detailed account of Labour's decision to withdraw. See also Gaughan,
Thomas Johnson, pp. 118–20.

22   Louie Bennett (1870–1956), born into a Protestant family of prosperous Dublin merchants;
educated in Dublin, London, and Bonn; became involved with suffragism in 1911 and trade unionism
in 1913; invited by Tom Foran to reorganise the Irish Women Workers' Union in 1916, and general
secretary of the union, 1916–55, drawing no salary; first woman president of the ITUC, 1931; a pacifist
and internationalist, insistent on the need for a women's union, but moderate as a feminist and
socialist. See Rosemary Cullen Owens, *Louie Bennett* (Cork, 2001).

23   Thomas MacPartlin (1879–1923) was born in Sligo and raised in Dublin; left school aged ten to
become a carpenter; active in the Gaelic League, Dublin trades council, and the ITUC; elected to
Seanad Éireann in December 1922; he and Tom Johnson were the workers' representatives in the first
Irish delegation to the International Labour Organisation in Geneva, where he died of a heart attack.
See Charles Callan and Barry Desmond, *Irish Labour Lives: A Biographical Dictionary of Irish Labour
Party Deputies, Senators, MPs, and MEPs* (Dublin, 2010), pp. 168–9.

not giving a lead on the constitutional question, and worried about the implications of not having parliamentary representation for membership of the Socialist International. The famous fudge was approved by 96–23 votes.

In other respects, the radicals had more cause for satisfaction, as the special conference went on to rename the ITUCLP as the Irish Labour Party and Trade Union Congress (ILPTUC), and adopted a socialist programme, demanding collective ownership of wealth and democratic management of production. Rifling syndicalism to rationalise political inaction and affirming long-term revolutionary aims in place of immediate demands would become typical of Congress policy during these years of wasted opportunity.

After the electoral landslide for Sinn Féin, Labour tucked in behind the new consensus. In January 1919, O'Brien and Séamus Hughes, ITGWU, asked Richard Mulcahy, Teachta Dála (TD), for something to offset Labour's lack of parliamentary representation as it strode onto the world stage at the first post-war socialist conference at Berne. In return they offered to canvass support for Ireland's national aspirations. The upshot was the 'Democratic Programme', drafted by Johnson and adopted at the inaugural assembly of Dáil Éireann on 21 January. The 'Democratic Programme' was neither democratic nor a programme, but the staggering sight of a party with 73 parliamentary seats adopting the manifesto of a party with none testified to Sinn Féin malleability on social issues.

On the main issue at Berne the Irish delegates, Johnson and O'Shannon, sided with the left minority, voting for a resolution demanding a 'dictatorship of the proletariat' rather than one supporting parliamentary democracy, on the ground that the latter 'tended to condemn the Soviet system of government'. The republican weekly *New Ireland* was so delighted with Labour's assertion of the Irish cause at Berne, that it published a variety of features on Russia, Bolshevism, and soviets over the coming weeks.[24] Acknowledging that 'When we wanted the help of Labour in Berne, Labour gave it to us', de Valera urged the Sinn Féin Árd Fheis in April to support the May Day general strike called by Congress 'for international proletarian solidarity and self-determination for all peoples' in line with a recommendation at Berne. Persuading kindred bodies, especially the British Labour Party and its commission on Ireland in 1920, to endorse self-determination, became the Labour leadership's special role, and regular meetings were held with Sinn Féin agents regarding the promotion of the Irish cause on the left internationally.[25]

The Congress executive would have been happy to leave it at that, but pressure from the rank and file and the consolidation of the national consensus

24 *New Ireland*, Feb.–Apr. 1919.
25 Mitchell, *Labour in Irish Politics*, p. 112; Gaughan, *Thomas Johnson*, pp. 162–9.

drew Labour deeper into the struggle for independence. There were three major rank and file led actions. In April 1919 Limerick trades council coordinated a nine-day general strike 'against British militarism', which came to be known as 'the Limerick soviet'. In November, the Irish Automobile Drivers' and Mechanics' Union struck in protest at the introduction of compulsory permits for vehicle drivers; a move by the authorities designed to assist the monitoring of transport. And in May 1920, dockers, and then railwaymen, commenced a seven-month selective stoppage, refusing to handle or convey British munitions.[26] The January 1920 local elections saw widespread collusion with republicans, despite a Congress manifesto which devoted half a line to the independence struggle. Labour did well, winning 18 per cent of first preferences and 324 seats, compared with 422 for Sinn Féin, 213 for the Nationalists, and 297 for the Unionists.[27] Far from diluting class-consciousness, the revolution was politicising workers. In building its skeletal republic, Sinn Féin provided a tutorial in state power, while the Irish Republican Army (IRA) paralysed state agencies, encouraging direct action in wage movements. Workers' action against British militarism was not just about political freedom, it was also about workers' control, however inchoate that was. The dialectic of political and social aspirations climaxed in the spring of 1920. In March, dockers responded to the government's decontrol of food prices by threatening to halt food exports.[28] As the Congress executive tried to defuse the crisis, 100 political prisoners in Mountjoy Jail began a hunger strike on 5 April, generating a huge emotional response. On 12 April, Congress called an immediate, indefinite general strike for their release. Coordinated by workers' councils, many of which assumed a 'soviet' style command of local government for the occasion, the stoppage was a breathtaking display of Labour discipline. According to the *Manchester Guardian*: 'The direction of affairs passed during the strike to these [workers'] councils, which were formed not on a local but on a class basis. . . . It is no exaggeration to trace a flavour of proletarian dictatorship about some aspects of the strike'.[29] Fearing the infection of the Sinn Féin struggle with 'Bolshevism', the authorities released the prisoners after two days. On 15 April, Congress secured a modification of the food embargo pending talks, and meanwhile advised trades councils to form food

26   Liam Cahill, *Forgotten Revolution: Limerick Soviet, 1919, A Threat to British Power in Ireland* (Dublin, 1990); Charles Townshend, 'The Irish railway strike of 1920: industrial action and civil resistance in the struggle for independence', *Irish Historical Studies* XXI: 83 (1979), pp. 212–82.

27   UUMC, ILPTUC, *Report* (1920), pp. 5–9; Mitchell, *Labour in Irish Politics*, pp. 122–9; Gaughan, *Thomas Johnson*, pp. 188–9.

28   For the food control crisis see Gaughan, *Thomas Johnson*, pp. 179–84; for the political prisoners strike see Mitchell, *Labour in Irish Politics*, pp. 119–20.

29   *Manchester Guardian*, 20 Apr. 1920.

control committees and be prepared to enforce price fixing. After conferences with farmers and bacon curers, an arrangement was reached whereby 30 per cent of certain produce would be retained for the home market. It was the first time that Congress had sanctioned direct action on a purely social issue. It was also an example of how the Congress executive used the national question as a safe outlet for the social revolutionary dynamic bubbling up at the base of the movement. It is no coincidence that the three general strikes of 1918–20 occurred on or before May Day, and provided an excuse for avoiding a general strike on the socialist holiday or, as in 1919, invoking a nationalist pretext to celebrate it.

The escalation of British counter-insurgency in 1920 – with over 4,000 military raids in February alone – inevitably affected the increasingly republican Labour movement. The *Voice of Labour* had been suppressed in September 1919. Weekly seizures of its successor, the *Watchword of Labour*, culminated in suppression in December 1920. In November, the military had closed the James Connolly Labour College. More than a dozen ITGWU officials were arrested; branch meetings were disrupted by soldiers, and union offices and Liberty Hall searched repeatedly. In Cork, the ITGWU hall was burned and Tadhg Barry, an outstanding organiser of rural workers, was imprisoned and later shot. By October 1921, the ITGWU reckoned that 115 of its 583 branches had collapsed because of the military terror. The Irish Union of Distributive Workers and Clerks, the third largest Irish union, claimed that 500 of its 7,560 members were imprisoned, interned or otherwise prevented from working because of military activities.[30] This was just what union leaders had feared in 1918, and it partly explains Congress's formal detachment from the revolution. Labour never recognised Dáil Éireann, lest it prejudice its industrial relations with British state agencies, and endorsed 'Ireland's right to self-determination' as if it were a principle of foreign policy. By the same token, Labour was not a Sinn Féin satellite. As noted above, Congress used the national question to manage militancy. It also insisted on the benevolent neutrality of Dáil Éireann and the IRA towards the wages movement; a concession which contrasted with the Republic's suppression of the much less disruptive anti-rancher agitation by small farmers in the west in 1919–20.

Could Labour have demanded more from the Republic? The revolution was not without a radical dimension. Aside from the 'Democratic Programme', Dáil Éireann backed Seán Etchingham, a former union leader in Wexford and Dáil Director of Fisheries, in trying to reorganise the fishing industry along cooperative lines in the face of proprietary opposition.[31] The Republic

---

30 *Watchword of Labour*, 31 Jan. to 21 Feb., 13 Mar. 1920; O'Connor, *Syndicalism in Ireland*, p. 90.
31 NAI, Dáil Éireann MSS, DE 2/27, 2/52, 2/111, 2/333–34.

created a Department of Labour, with Constance Markievicz as minister. Labour arbitration courts and a Central Conciliation Board were established in 1919.[32] And the better known Dáil courts of justice promised a more democratic judicial system. In the temper of the times, this was not much, and the rationale of the Republic's administration was to displace the agencies of colonial regime rather than lay the foundations of the future. But it was up to Congress, not Sinn Féin, to fight Labour's corner, and the evidence suggests that the revolution stayed narrowly political by default. Sinn Féin's satisfaction with Labour's detachment should not be confused with a reluctance to treat. The most remarkable indication of how far republicans were prepared to go was de Valera's decision to seek aid from Soviet Russia in 1921, despite a British propaganda campaign to depict Sinn Féin as 'Bolshevist', and accurate advice from Congress that the mission would be fruitless.[33]

INDUSTRIAL RELATIONS

A second great challenge came on the industrial front. As wage movements intensified, pressure mounted for coordinated action. In February 1919, the Congress executive responded with a special conference on minimum pay and conditions. The conference set as its objectives a 44-hour week, a 50 s weekly minimum wage, and a general 150 per cent increase on pre-war wage levels.[34] To match the mood, the executive reminded employers that wage increases could be an interim palliative only, pending workers' control of production. May Day was set as the deadline for employers' compliance, but no practical steps for action were taken and, not surprisingly, nothing happened. The Congress executive then served employers with a May Day manifesto, explaining its case and warning of dire consequences should the manifesto be ignored. Affiliates were circulated with a document on a 'Proposed United National Wages and Hours Movement'. These papers merely represented an appeal to others to act and served to underline the executive's inefficacy. Embarrassed into further initiative, the executive appointed a subcommittee to examine ways of strengthening the movement. Their report came before the annual Congress in August. It recommended its 70 affiliates to reorganise in ten industrial sectors with the intention of making Congress 'a single, all-inclusive Irish Workers' Union' which, through its political and industrial

32 *Dáil Éireann Proceedings*, 19 Aug. 1919; 27 Oct. 1920.
33 Emmet O'Connor, *Reds and the Green: Ireland, Russia, and the Communist Internationals, 1919–43* (Dublin, 2004), pp. 26–9.
34 See O'Connor, *Syndicalism in Ireland*, pp. 60–9.

activities, would eventually realise 'the taking over control of industry by the organised working class'.[35] Opposition came from the amalgamateds. As in 1912, their British ties could not be reconciled with an OBU. Though the report was approved by 131–50 votes, progress on implementation was sluggish, and further retarded by the death of M. J. O'Lehane.[36] Representing distributive workers with a weak bargaining power, O'Lehane was a keen proponent of trade union rationalisation. For others, there seemed no urgency. While the appeal of industrial unionism was strong, the necessity, in these propitious times, was not. The ITGWU was virtually an OBU onto itself. The NUR was caught in the contradiction of being a British union. The Congress executive passed the buck to its affiliates, suggesting they initiate the scheme at local level. The failure to grasp the opportunity for reform in 1919 would return to haunt trade unions in subsequent decades.

THE NORTH

Ulster was the third area of policy failure. While historians usually cite the north as the reason for Labour's reluctance to bargain with Sinn Féin, Congress scarcely attempted to accommodate Belfast Labourites, the bulk of whom were averse to Sinn Féin but ready to accept Home Rule rather than partition. Differences with Belfast trades council became evident in 1917 when the British government launched its latest effort at resolving the Irish question – the Irish Convention. Seven of the 95 seats in the Convention were offered to the trades councils of Dublin, Belfast, and Cork. Congress was not consulted. Johnson's suggestion that the executive seek representation was defeated on the casting vote of O'Brien. The southern trades councils declined the invitation, but Belfast agreed unanimously to accept, and three Belfast Labour delegates were joined by two Labour–Nationalists. All five signed the Convention's majority report, favouring Dominion Home Rule.[37] The report was already doomed by Sinn Féin's boycott of the Convention and Unionist

35 UUMC, ILPTUC, *Report* (1919), pp. 49–55, 61–5, 99–112.

36 Michael O'Lehane (1873–1920), was born near Macroom, and apprenticed to the drapery trade in Cork. An early advocate of an Irish-based trade unionism, he formed the Irish Draper's Assistants' Association in 1901, and later represented Sinn Féin on Dublin Corporation. A member of the Congress executive from 1909, treasurer 1910–11, and chairman in 1912, his ambitions for industrial unionism were partly realised in the trade with the formation of the Irish Union of Distributive Workers and Clerks. See Dermot Keogh, 'Michael O'Lehane and the organisation of linen drapers assistants', *Saothar* 3 (1977), pp. 33–43.

37 Austen Morgan, *Labour and Partition: The Belfast Working Class, 1905–23* (London, 1991), pp. 193–4.

refusal to compromise on partition. Belfast was included in Labour's anti-conscription campaign, the trades council having voted against the introduction of conscription in Britain in 1916.[38] On 14 April 1918 Johnson and D. R. Campbell addressed Congress's first anti-conscription meeting at the Custom House steps. Three days later, a meeting at the City Hall was broken up by a 'group of young Queen's Islandmen . . . spearheaded by a lorry, used as a tank'. Johnson was struck by a missile and the crowd dispersed in panic. Rioting followed, late into the night.[39] Thereafter, Congress left the north to itself.

Labour politics in Belfast, moribund since the third Home Rule crisis, was revived in April 1918 when the trades council summoned a conference of trade union delegates and the city's two ILP branches to form the Belfast Labour Party.[40] Far from being a gesture to all-Ireland unity, Congress's withdrawal from the 1918 election was taken as a snub: Campbell protested that it would 'give a walkover to the Conservative crowd in the North'.[41] Belfast Labour proceeded unilaterally and ran four candidates in the city. They polled a respectable average of 22 per cent of the vote, but the only 'Labour' victors of the 1918 election were three UULA MPs.[42] The Belfast Labour Party was Walkerite at heart. In 1919 it applied to join the British Labour Party, only to be told to redirect its enquiries to the Irish Labour Party.[43] But it was also predominantly anti-partition. Three of its four candidates in the 1918 general election were Home Rulers, as were the majority of its 22 candidates in the municipal elections of 1920, Labour's highwatermark. The outgoing Corporation of 52 Unionists and eight Nationalists yielded to a council of 37 Unionists (including six UULA men), 12 Labour councillors, one Independent Labour Unionist, five Nationalists, and five Sinn Féiners. Labour formed the official opposition, under Campbell.[44]

During the negotiations for the Anglo-Irish Treaty, Labour made three demands of any settlement: withdrawal of British forces, self-determination for Ireland as a whole, and the maintenance of Irish unity.[45] Yet Congress had done little to foster the political unity of Labour.

38   Peter Gerard Collins, 'Belfast trades council, 1881–1921' (D.Phil, University of Ulster, 1988), p. 271.

39   Ibid., pp. 272–4; Gaughan, *Thomas Johnson*, p. 88.

40   Morgan, *Labour and Partition*, pp. 252–3.

41   UUMC, ILPTUC, *Report of the Annual Congress and of the Special Congress* (1918), p. 107.

42   Morgan, *Labour and Partition*, pp. 254–7.

43   Boyd Black, 'Reassessing Irish industrial relations and labour history: the north-east of Ireland up to 1921', *Historical Studies in Industrial Relations* (autumn 2002), p. 82.

44   Collins, 'Belfast trades council', p. 296.

45   Mitchell, *Labour in Irish Politics*, pp. 144–53.

THE SLUMP

Massive expansion of the world's productive capacity during the First World War, followed by a further increase in output to meet the first demands of a peacetime market, led to a crisis of overproduction in the autumn of 1920.[46] Food prices were the first to tumble, causing a severe depression in agriculture. During 1921, Irish manufacturing trade was almost halved. By December, over 26 per cent of workers were idle. Rising unemployment depressed consumer demand, sending the economy tail spinning into long-term recession. Employers clamoured for the restoration of pre-war wage levels. In Britain, wages were getting 'back to normal' following the collapse of the Triple Alliance of railwaymen's, miners', and transport unions on 'Black Friday' and the subsequent isolation and defeat of the miners' strike against pay cuts. A similar pattern was anticipated in Ireland, with the railwaymen providing the initial sacrifice following government decontrol of the railways on 14 August 1921. Largely fulfilled in Northern Ireland, employer expectations were frustrated in the south by the effect with which militancy could be deployed in the near anarchic conditions obtaining during the Anglo-Irish truce and the Civil War. In contrast with rank and file heroics, the Labour leadership emerged from the crisis with its credibility in tatters.

Congress's initial response to the looming economic crisis looked resolute. *The Country in Danger!*, its most detailed and practical programme to date, disturbed the Dáil cabinet with warnings against any reduction in tillage acreage. A series of meetings took place in April 1921 involving representatives of the cabinet, the Irish Farmers' Union, and Congress. If *The Country in Danger!* suggested that Labour was awakening belatedly to the need to confront the national revolution with social demands, the Congress executive was unwilling to push the point. It agreed unanimously not to contest elections for the second Dáil in May. On this occasion the reason given for abstention was blunt: 'to defeat the obvious design of the British Prime Minister to divide the democratic forces'.[47] There was, of course, no possibility of withdrawing from the industrial war. The annual Congress in August pledged to 'hold the harvest' of wage gains, and prioritise unity in the impending struggle. Speaker after speaker affirmed conviction in industrial unionism as a strategic riposte to the employers' counter-attack, pledging that there would be no 'Black Fridays' in Ireland. Tom Foran's presidential address captured the confident spirit of defiance:

46 Except where stated the following account is based on O'Connor, *Syndicalism in Ireland*, pp. 96–164.
47 UUMC, ILPTUC, *Report* (1921), p. 18.

> The employers in this country are combining and studying what is taking place in England . . . poor deluded employers! The course of events that will certainly follow any general attack upon the standard of living in this country will be very very different. There is in this country different machinery – different human material . . . different methods entirely. . . . The Irish Labour Party has advised that in all industries where notice of reduction in wages or attacks on working conditions are made, all the unions in this trade or that industry should come together . . . and pledge themselves to stand firmly together to the bitter end (applause).[48]

But when it came to the crunch, inter-union solidarity crumbled. The Congress executive did propose direct intervention to assist the railwaymen, the first major sector into the breach, only to learn that the railway unions had agreed to arbitration under the Carrigan tribunal and had no need of Congress. Thus ended the first and last effort to forge a united response to the slump. From this on, employers held the initiative; they would dictate the pace and pattern of events as best they could.

J. H. Thomas, the NUR leader and a steadfast opponent of sympathetic action, had persuaded a reluctant membership to accept the Carrigan tribunal as an alternative to a national strike, and the 'railway crisis' produced six months of tense uncertainty as union leaders battled to restrain sporadic unofficial disputes. It was precisely to avoid such divisive and ultimately unsuccessful conflict that NUR men appealed for national action. Their fears were confirmed when the Carrigan tribunal found in favour of reductions and an extension of hours. Under strong rank and file pressure, the NUR's Irish council opted to fight for the eight-hour day, calling an unofficial national stoppage from 15 January 1922. In Cork, industrial unionists formed the Industrial Cooperative Workers' Committee to coordinate a take over of local lines. Intervention by the Belfast and Dublin governments secured a postponement of action pending further negotiation. On 10 February a settlement was announced which suspended the Carrigan award for six months and guaranteed the eight-hour day in principle. Lunging at the heels of a vanishing era, the Industrial Cooperative Workers' Committee seized all four railway systems in Cork on the following day, and ran its own timetable for 24 red hours: a belated gesture of what might have been. Strikes continued and in August the threat of serious unrest prompted further state intervention to delay proposed wage cuts, but the 'railway crisis' was over.

The 'railway crisis' had not tumbled the domino effect anticipated by employers, and a second false dawn of decisive conflict following the ratification of the Anglo-Irish Treaty on 7 January 1922 confirmed the

48 Ibid., pp. 76–7.

dependency of the wage cutting offensive on state help. For most of 1922, direct action kept employer ambitions in check. Following the abolition of the Agricultural Wages Board in October 1921, violence and sabotage became more important in farm strikes, and played a crucial role in enabling the ITGWU to settle four major disputes in Dublin, Meath, Cork, and Waterford. In late January, the first of about 80 soviets that year took place at Mallow, where the Quartertown Mills were seized. With such minimal scope for compromise on wage grievances, soviets now acquired a serious revolutionary intent. All were disowned by the ITGWU and created friction within the union. Unable to guarantee property protection, the Provisional Government tried to restrain employers, hoping to minimise disorder by staggering wage deflation. Dáil Éireann's Labour Department intervened widely in disputes during the first quarter of 1922. The cabinet approved the formation of conciliation boards to deal with unrest in printing and dairying, and sponsored commissions of enquiry into the railways, canals, tailoring, and the postal service. Most remarkably, the Provisional Government overruled objections from Cleeve's to appoint two ministers to a subcommittee to formulate a scheme that would enable employees to buy out the proprietary creameries. By mid May, neither ownership nor Cleeve's demand for wage cuts had been resolved. When Cleeve's locked out its 3,000 employees on 12 May, a workers' Council of Action directed the seizure of the company's extensive network of creameries and milk factories. As the red flags fluttered in Munster, it seemed initially that the soviets might realise their motto 'the sovereign people'. Even Liberty Hall offered tacit assistance with the storage and export of butter. However, the economic and infrastructural disorder which facilitated occupation, frustrated the financial success of the soviets. Moreover, farmers had now become violently hostile to 'Russian methods'; most withheld milk supplies, some resorted to arson or sabotage. The end came in August as the Free State Army rolled up the 'Munster Republic' along the Waterford–Limerick line. By September, the Provisional Government had established its authority over virtually all of the 26 counties. Its newfound confidence revealed itself in a willingness to face strike action in the civil service. Since February, the cabinet had played for time in negotiations with postal workers. In September, it rejected the findings of its own commission of enquiry into the cost of living for postal employees and fought a tough 18-day strike to enforce pay cuts. In the spring of 1923, state defences were reviewed to enable more effective intervention against popular unrest. The Criminal Investigation Department's intelligence system was redirected against 'agrarian irregularism', and, to avoid compromising the new Civic Guard, a Special Infantry Corps was raised from the army to act as 'armed police'. Six hundred Specials were subsequently deployed in the Waterford farm strike in 1923.

O'Brien's survival strategy for the ITGWU involved ditching syndicalism while retaining the OBU ideal and a cautious wage militancy. Having clawed his way to the top in the union by removing his rivals, and graduated from a dutiful backroom servant to an arrogant superior, he was not the most sensitive man to manage the awkward transition from advance to retreat. Frugal and abstemious in his personal life, he could also be priggish and petty. In a signpost to history, he split Dublin trades council rather than deal with people he deemed to be venal, and had the ITGWU lead the formation of a rival Workers' Council in 1921.[49] Using the slump to consolidate his grip, he reduced the ITGWU's organising staff from 21 in 1920 to nine by July 1922, and promoted a 'big branch' scheme to increase the number of full-time branch secretaries; replacing the colonels of contemporary radicalism with subalterns of central control. Dissatisfaction mounted with the growing authoritarianism, and the union suffered the indignity of a strike at head office in 1922. The OBU ideal was corrupted as the ITGWU tried to offset losses by poaching. In particular, it exploited the amalgamateds' disposition to accept wage cuts in line with the more rapidly falling cross-channel rates. 'This poaching business,' explained one senior ITGWU man, 'was not such a terrible thing as represented. It was merely the natural development [of industrial unionism] . . . ultimately the craft unions will come into one great body'.[50] By 1922–3 a needling anglophobia vitiated the rivalry, aggravated by the inaction of British Labour in the face of northern sectarianism and its stubborn intention to remain in post-colonial Ireland. Other unions came to regard the ITGWU's industrial unionism as thin camouflage for empire-building; the OBU they jibed, meant 'O'Brien's Union'. The ITGWU still had much to be proud of in 1922, with 100,000 members, most on peak wage rates. There were omens in the spring of 1923 that hopes of weathering the storm without general conflict might be realised. Agricultural workers in Wicklow and Cork were settled with little difficulty. Nine thousand labourers struck in Dublin, Meath, and Louth to hold weekly rates of 30s or more. Then the union was ambushed by Larkin.

After roving agitation, bankrolled by the Germans, Larkin had settled in New York in 1918, joined the Socialist Party of America, and immersed himself in a project to turn the party into a Communist party.[51] Imprisoned on a charge of 'criminal anarchy' in 1920, he was released in 1923, and subsequently deported. When he landed in Dublin on 30 April to resume his job as ITGWU

49 Séamus Cody, John O'Dowd, and Peter Rigney, *The Parliament of Labour: 100 Years of Dublin Council of Trade Unions* (Dublin, 1986), pp. 126–33.
50 UUMC, ILPTUC, *Report* (1921), p. 100.
51 For the Larkin's career in America and the split see Emmet O'Connor, *James Larkin* (Cork, 2002), pp. 54–79.

general secretary, everyone expected trouble. Incredibly, nothing happened. O'Brien knew he was not strong enough to challenge Big Jim. Instead, he had the union rules revised to lock the general secretary into a five-man collective leadership. Larkin raised no objections. He didn't want union work. His goal was to get the Soviets to fund him as a freelance agitator and continue the lifestyle he had enjoyed in America. With his characteristic secrecy and dislike of explaining himself, none of this was made clear, and on a tour of the branches in May Larkin found he couldn't stomach the idea of others running 'his' union. On 3 June, the fragile truce was shattered when Larkin denounced O'Brien in an incoherent and vituperative rant. The best case he could make to the ITGWU executive on 5 June was that as a salaried TD O'Brien was not entitled to hold a union office. He then put the executive in the dock by claiming that recent changes to union rules were invalid. Plainly, if Larkin got his way, no union official was safe. After he tried to dismiss union officers and seize Liberty Hall, the executive suspended him as general secretary. In another bewildering turn of events, Larkin made no attempt to offer an alternative politics or rally support at large, confining activities to a few close followers in Dublin. The *Irish Worker*, revived on 15 June, denounced O'Brien, Johnson, and the 'God save the King Labour Party' without making the cause any clearer. As Moscow would discover, Larkin was not a well man in the 1920s.

A convergence of strikes brought the industrial war to a head in the autumn. The wages crux in the portal trades had hung fire for two years as stubborn resistance prevented a conclusive adjustment of rates. On Friday 13 July, employers announced a reduction of 2 s in the dockers' average daily rate of 16s. About 3,000 dockers and others struck on Monday. The strike dealt a body blow to the economy. Cattle exports fell by 60 per cent. The meat industry virtually shut down, reducing staff and lowering wages in the process. With trade depressed, employers had little to lose in industrial action. By late September, Dublin was experiencing a series of selective strikes. A violent farm strike in south Kildare approached its first anniversary. Since May, Waterford had been convulsed in a major farm strike that had extended to urban employees, and on 21 August 6,000 workers in building, manufacture, distribution, and transport turned out against demands of the Cork Employers' Federation for staff cuts. About 20,000 trade unionists were affected by the autumn unrest. Here was the bosses' 'big push' dreaded by Congress since 'Black Friday', and rampant sectionalism left it ill equipped to respond.

Where was the Labour Party? The Anglo-Irish Treaty in December 1921 reconfigured politics. Labour was annoyed that it had never been consulted during the negotiations. The *Voice of Labour* reckoned Labour had more in common with the social and political outlook of the 'anti-ratificationists'. An early draft of an executive recommendation to a special conference in

February 1922 proposed a deft combination of support for peace and for the republicans should Labour deputies hold the balance of power in Dáil Éireann. O'Shannon's thumbprints on the passage are evident in a reference to the Bolsheviks' willingness to accept the punitive diktat of Brest-Litovsk.[52] The final draft, however, offered no opposition to the Treaty, and probably reflected Johnson's influence. Johnson welcomed the Treaty and canvassed for it privately. For all his English nonconformist conscience, he had a duplicitous streak, which infuriated his critics. A rhetorical revolutionary when called upon, he now believed that the revolution was over. In his British Labour mindset, a constitutional settlement promised an end to the national question and an open road to 'normal' class politics. Hours after the Provisional Government had replaced its revolutionary predecessor, Johnson led the first ever Labour deputation to Dáil Éireann, to protest about social conditions. At the special conference, Johnson presented the case for contesting the next elections arguing that it would enable Labour 'to frustrate reactionary measures' and influence the new state's constitution.[53] All Labourites were beholden to the assumption that it was not their business to give a lead on the national question, and the abstentionists had little to offer but more waiting. The absentionist opposition also illustrates the disarray among critics of executive policy. First, there were those who dismissed electoral activity as a vain diversion from the industrial front. Secondly, there was the argument, tendered by straightforward separatists, Larkinite antagonists to the Johnson–O'Brien leadership, and Communists, that entering Dáil Éireann and taking the controversial oath of allegiance would legitimise the regime. An abstentionist resolution was defeated by 115–82 votes.

Only the Communists believed that nationalist difficulty was socialist opportunity. Communist policy on Ireland was made in Moscow, if not always applied as Moscow intended. When V. I. Lenin founded the Communist International, or Comintern, in 1919, he insisted that it should not be a talking shop, like the Socialist International, but the controlling body of all Communist parties and the 'general staff' of the world revolution. The Comintern's second world congress in 1920 marked the beginning of its Irish policy, and a consistent theme would be the cultivation of the IRA. After various attempts by competing factions to develop an Irish section, Roddy Connolly[54] took over

52   *Voice of Labour*, 17 Dec. 1921; 7–14 Jan. 1922; Charles McCarthy, 'Labour and the 1922 general election', *Saothar* 7 (1981), pp. 115–21.

53   UUMC, ILPTUC, *Special Conference on Election Policy* (1922), p. 63.

54   Roddy Connolly (1901–80), was born in Dublin and served as aide-de-camp to his father in Easter Week; after 1916 he conspired to win Comintern approval for his leadership of the CPI; too headstrong for Moscow, his standing never recovered from being displaced as CPI leader in 1923;

the SPI in September 1921, expelled the 'reformists', and got it affiliated to the Comintern as the Communist Party of Ireland (CPI). The CPI claimed a membership of 300 initially, but the number of activists had dwindled to 50 or so by 1923. Whilst Communists organised unemployed protests and had contacts with some of the Munster soviets, Connolly, headstrong and impatient, rejected the slow grind of building up grass-roots support for the quick fix of vaulting to power through capturing the IRA. Though Roddy was always his father's young pretender in politics, he had a far more sceptical view of the bourgeois-dominated republican movement. Nonetheless he was convinced that the negotiations for the Anglo-Irish Treaty would eventually split the republicans and the 'die-hards' would turn to the Communists for help. He was right. After spurning CPI overtures in the first half of 1922, IRA leaders signed a secret pact with Comintern agents in August. In return for a shipment of arms from Germany, the IRA was to set up a new political party which would adopt the CPI programme. Liam Mellows's famous 'Notes from Mountjoy', urging the IRA to apply a social programme, was the tip of the iceberg. Ultimately, the deal unravelled as the Comintern feared the consequences for Anglo-Soviet relations.

Congress meanwhile had sought to consolidate its neutrality on the republican split. A general strike, the last of that vintage, 'against militarism' took place on 24 April 1922, the sixth anniversary of the Easter Rising. Coevally the ITGWU moved to incorporate the Citizen Army within a 'Workers' Army', ostensibly to defend Labour interests, but probably to prevent Labour entanglement in a civil war. The initiative failed and 143 members of the Citizen Army fought with the IRA in the Civil War.[55] The elections in June reassured the Congress leadership. Contesting its first general election, in which the Treaty was the big issue, Labour returned 17 of its 18 candidates, the 18th missing a seat by 13 votes. Undoubtedly the circumstances of an election in which pro and anti-Treaty Sinn Féin colluded to ensure that many constituencies went uncontested were exceptionally favourable to third parties. Labour, with a handful of Farmers' Party and independent candidates, offered the only alternative to continued Sinn Féin dictatorship. On the other hand, it is not likely that Labour attracted the moderate voter in these 'red flag times', and it would surely have won more seats with more candidates. The results showed that despite the slump, the bulk of trade unionists were in fighting form, and revealed the extent to which their leaders had underestimated

worked with various revolutionary groups in the 1920s and 1930s, and drifted steadily to the right from the 1940s, becoming a firm and controversial supporter of the Labour Party leadership in the 1970s. See Charlie McGuire, *Roddy Connolly and the Struggle for Socialism in Ireland* (Cork, 2008).

55 R. M. Fox, *The History of the Citizen Army* (Dublin, 1944), pp. 216–23.

their strength. That strength was magnified by the abstention of the 36 anti-Treatyite TDs. When the third Dáil met in September – the Provisional government having repeatedly deferred a meeting until it got the upper hand in the Civil War – Labour became the official opposition. But beware the thing that you wish for. Reconciling the grim and gritty dynamic of industrial struggle with the shadowboxing of parliamentary opposition was a tricky business at the best of times. An inexperienced team of TDs was taking it on at the worst of times. And their pointman was Johnson.

Johnson had come into his element as a parliamentarian. Arguing that democracy depended on Labour playing the role of opposition, he insisted on draining the poisoned chalice, whatever the cost. Unfortunately for Labour, he was not seen to be getting anything in return, and what Johnson regarded as principle and self-sacrifice, others saw as humbug and hollowness. Cumann na nGaedheal derided his humanitarian criticism of security practices, and dismissed his efforts to influence the Saorstát constitution. Bitter about its desertion of the cause, Sinn Féin targeted Labour, Johnson especially, as the underbelly of the Free State. The more he denounced the terror against them, the more abusive republicans became of him and his English background. Labour started to look pathetic. A rally in Waterford City Hall turned farcical when Johnson tried to silence republican hecklers by singing the national anthem. Mercifully, the chairman brought the evening to a close.[56] Being in the eye of the storm at least dealt Labour an ace; it could turn the tables on its detractors and trump the cabinet's dismissal of republicanism as a cloak for anarchy by raising the spectre of industrial agitation merging with 'irregularism' unless the government agreed to restrain employers. Financial opinion in Britain, which the government was anxious to reassure, believed that republicans might commence a campaign of economic sabotage, aided and abetted by Larkin and his Communist friends. The cabinet took seriously a threat by Larkin to prevent the general election, scheduled for August 1923, failing a settlement of strikes. Concluding that 'an atmosphere of industrial unrest, necessitating, perhaps, the presence of bodies of military to prevent breaches of the peace during the elections should be avoided at all costs', the cabinet agreed on 1 August to request that employers postpone wage cuts for three months, during which conferences would be convened under government auspices. Johnson had no taste for that sort of power politics. He had already refused appeals to withdraw his deputies from Dáil Éireann in protest at the partisan deployment of the army in strikes.

56 *Munster Express*, 2 June 1923.

The Labour Party sailed into the hustings with pamphlets entitled *How to Get Houses* and *If You Want Your Child to Get a Fair Start in Life*.[57] 'It is certain,' predicted the *Voice of Labour*, 'that the Labour Party in the new Dáil will be considerably stronger' – a measure of its detachment from mounting disillusionment among the rank and file.[58] Labour paid the price of irrelevance to the industrial war, and was clipped to 14 deputies and saw its share of the poll reduced from 21 to 11 per cent. Only 60 per cent of electors bothered to vote. The game was almost up. Though vilified for the Civil War, Sinn Féin had polled surprisingly well, and the government's position worsened over the next two months. Despite vigorous pruning of public spending, war expenditure had created a deficit of £2.5m. With the first Saorstát loan to be floated, public confidence needed to be bolstered urgently to meet this fiscal test of statehood. Congress pleaded for an across-the-board settlement of strikes, based on mutual economic cooperation, but again refused to imperil democracy by pulling its deputies out of Dáil Éireann. Both Larkin and the Congress leadership stooped to bidding against each other for government favour. With no compulsion to do otherwise, President W. T. Cosgrave rejected general discussions, arguing that a resolution of the dock dispute would pave the way for industrial peace. An ignominious end to the dock strike in early November did just that. Within two weeks the spirit of post-war trade unionism had been crushed.

Labour had known defeat and disillusion in the past, and it would be unfair to blame unions for not 'holding the harvest'. Economic reality was against them. But never before had Labour leaders promised so much and delivered so little. The scale of the 1923 catastrophe was unique.

57 Mitchell, *Labour in Irish Politics*, p. 186.
58 *Voice of Labour*, 25 Aug. 1923.

SIX

UNFINISHED BUSINESS 1924-39

The English unions in Ireland . . . are 'outposts of British imperialism'
Report to the Comintern, 27 December 1924.[1]

—

The modern Labour movement was formed between 1917 and 1923. The principle of trade unionism for all, for the labourer and the clerk as well as the craftsman, was established, and Labour, in the Free State at least, was now substantially Irish based, with a more effective Congress, an operational political wing, and a larger number of trades councils. The two steps forward were followed by one step back. The 1923 defeats led to the collapse of general unionism in small towns and on the land, and contraction elsewhere. Craft and clerical unions suffered too, if less severely, and Congress membership dropped from 175,000 in 1924 to a low of 92,000 in 1929.[2] The great challenge first posed by new unionism, how to build a bargaining power for the mass of workers, remained uncompleted.

For trade unions, the prospects were not good. Though the worst of the slump was over by 1924, trade remained sluggish. Saorstát Éireann inherited a small, undeveloped, open economy, tied to Britain. Agriculture employed over 50 per cent of the labour force, industry a mere eight per cent. Food and drink accounted for 85 per cent of merchandise exports, and 98 per cent of exports went to the UK in 1924. Faced with this crushing dependency, and beholden to the ranchers and the handful of major capitalists, the cautious Cumann na nGaedheal government chose to leave well alone, jettisoning the industrialisation through self-sufficiency aim indelibly associated with Sinn

1   The phrase 'nachposten der britischen Imperialismus' was quoted by John Pepper, pseudonym of József Pogány, and Comintern emissary to the Irish Worker League. He was probably quoting Big Jim or Peter Larkin. See Rossiiskii Gosudartsvennyi Arkhiv Sotsial'no-Politischeskoi Istorii (Russian State Archive for Social and Political History, RGASPI), Moscow, John Pepper, 'Der Konflikt der Irish Workers [*sic*] League mit der Communist Party Gross-Britanniens', 27 Dec. 1924, 495/89/26–22; and memorandum by Big Jim or Peter Larkin, undated, 495/89/26–25/37.
2   For Congress affiliation figures see Charles McCarthy, *Trade Unions in Ireland, 1894–1960* (Dublin, 1977), p. 635.

Féin. Reliance on beef exports as the engine of economic progress produced an impressive rise in farm incomes for the Saorstát's 25,000 or so graziers, but little growth in employment.[3] Cumann na nGaedheal opposed public enterprise, and the two exceptional cases of state enterprise – the Shannon hydro-electric scheme and the Carlow sugar factory – reflected the weakness of the private sector. Public policy had no use for trade unions, and the Labour departments established by Dáil Éireann and the British Ministry of Labour in Ireland in 1919 were discontinued. Labour added unstintingly to its own misfortune with a suicidal sectionalism. Divided between two trades councils, and Jim Larkin and William O'Brien, Dublin Labour indulged in its own civil war.

Politically, the years to 1927 gifted the left a unique window of opportunity. Revolutionism was not yet dead, nor was its staid successor yet established. Symptomatically, the Catholic Church was fairly quiet, still coming to terms with the dislocation of the conservative consensus after Easter Week. No Irish governments would be as easy to oppose as those of W. T. Cosgrave. Finding their rationale in reaction, clinging to a treaty imposed by British guns and likely to survive only as long as its subversion did not require Irish guns, Cumann na nGaedheal's 'ministers for hardship' courted unpopularity. 'People may have to die in this country,' warned Patrick McGilligan, Minister for Industry and Commerce, 'and die through starvation'.[4] And starve they did, as famine hit the west in 1925. The best alternative Sinn Féin could offer was another round of civil war. Into the vacuum stepped the experts in revolution, the Bolsheviks. Working with Larkin and with the IRA, the Comintern contributed to the development of a socialist republicanism that would reach its apogee in the Republican Congress. Unfortunately for the Communists, their intervention in Ireland would not mature until after the recovery of clericalism in the 1930s. Prospects for the more moderate Labour Party were better. But Labour, stolidly, gave a blank cheque to Cumann na nGaedheal on the constitutional question, and continued to see itself as essentially a parliamentary group. Not until 1932 would the party rid itself of those encumbrances and put its political interests first. Meanwhile, it fell to Fianna Fáil to exploit the opportunities.

With the election to power of Fianna Fáil, a new consensus took shape. The flourish of radical politics in the immediate aftermath of Éamon de Valera's victory proved to be short-lived. Fianna Fáil created a novel set of difficulties for Labour in politics and industrial relations. De Valera's indus-

3 See James Meenan, *The Irish Economy since 1922* (Liverpool, 1971); Kieran A. Kennedy, Thomas Giblin, and Deirdre McHugh, *The Economic Development of Ireland in the Twentieth Century* (London, 1988), pp. 34–40. The figure for graziers is cited in Raymond Crotty, *Farming Collapse: National Opportunity* (Dublin, 1990), p. 5.

4 Quoted in R. F. Foster, *Modern Ireland, 1600–1972* (London, 1988), pp. 519–20.

trialisation programme gave trade unions a new importance. Membership expanded, as did strike activity and inter-union competition. Fianna Fáil identified multiplicity, wherein two or more unions competed for the same members, as the root cause of militancy, and called for the rationalisation of trade unions. This in turn would divide unions between traditionalists favouring the inherited mode of sectionalist trade union organisation and an antagonistic Labour–state relationship, and reformists favouring industrial unionism and a more collaborative relationship with the state. Now, the unfinished business was back on the Congress agenda.

RED DUBLIN

Strike activity fell steadily after 1923, and Labour opted to fight with itself.[5] In February 1924 the Master of the Rolls dismissed several legal actions taken by Jim Larkin to show that ITGWU rules were invalid.[6] On 14 March the ITGWU executive voted unanimously to expel Larkin. Larkin still hoped to win back his old union, and an opportunity arose in May when members at Dublin Gas struck over a personnel issue. Refused backing from the executive, they invited Larkin to represent them. Within a week he had won the strike and his supporters occupied Liberty Hall until ejected by the army. Leaving for Moscow on 2 June, to address the Comintern and its trade union counterpart, the Profintern, he told his brother, Peter,[7] to stick with the ITGWU. Instead, Peter and Young Jim[8] moved quickly to form the Workers' Union of Ireland

5   Statistics for industrial conflict are found in the *Irish Free State Statistical Abstract*.

6   The dispute with Larkin and the WUI's early history is discussed in Emmet O'Connor, *James Larkin* (Cork, 2002), pp. 70–9; and Emmet O'Connor, *Reds and the Green: Ireland, Russia, and the Communist Internationals, 1919–43* (Dublin, 2004), pp. 94–104.

7   Peter Larkin (1880–1931), born in Liverpool; represented Liverpool dockers at the foundation of the British Industrial Syndicalist Education League in 1910; like Big Jim, he embraced Communism as the latest form of revolutionism, and remained more of a syndicalist; imprisoned as a Wobbly in Australia in 1916; settled in Dublin in 1923; national organiser of the WUI from 1924; seen as a 'primitive', but in the 1920s he was more stable than his brother, who gave him a secular, 'red funeral' on his death in Dublin.

8   James Larkin, Junior (1904–69), eldest son of Big Jim; born in Liverpool; attended the International Lenin School, Moscow, but withdrew from the CPI during the Spanish Civil War, probably to avoid embarrassing his father; general secretary of the WUI from 1947; a Labour TD, 1943–57; retired from Dáil Éireann to concentrate on union work; the antithesis of his father, a judicious advocate of unity and progress, and widely regarded as the best leader Labour never had. See Manus O'Riordan, *The Voice of a Thinking Intelligent Movement: James Larkin Junior and the Modernisation of Irish Trade Unionism* (Dublin, 1995).

(WUI) on 15 June. Sixteen thousand members, two thirds of the ITGWU muster in Dublin, defected to the WUI, along with 23 of 300 provincial branches. The bulk of branch officials, Dublin and country, stayed with Liberty Hall. Whereas Big Jim's quarrel with the ITGWU executive was personal, the 1924 split had an ideological basis, and echoed the schism in European Labour movements between Communists and social democrats.

The WUI was founded as a Communist trade union. Young Jim applied immediately to the Communist Party of Great Britain (CPGB) for financial aid, with the promise that a 'workers' party' would soon compliment the Workers' Union. The CPGB declined to help, citing the Comintern's policy of opposing the creation of parallel unions, and underestimating the lengths that Moscow was prepared to go to accommodate Big Jim. The WUI became the biggest anglophone affiliate of the Profintern. The future of Irish Communism looked fairly promising at this point. In addition to the WUI, about 5,000 workers were affiliated to the 'all red' Dublin trades council, which had called for Congress to join the Comintern in 1920, and sent delegates to conferences of the Minority Movement – the British section of the Profintern, which included Communist fractions in all unions – in 1925, 1926, and 1928.[9] The basis of a party existed in the Irish Worker League (IWL), which Big Jim had launched in 1923 as an auxiliary to the *Irish Worker*, with some 500 supporters. There were also 13,000 volunteers in the IRA, bewildered by the Free State's facile victory over Liam Lynch and his 24 generals, and, in Moscow's eyes, ripe for the plucking. Mixing admiration for their implacable spirit with a Marxist-Leninist hauteur towards their politics, the Comintern assumed that working-class IRA men could be detached from their 'putchist ideas' and 'petit bourgeois' leaders to bolster the fragile insurrectionary tradition in Irish socialism.

Whatever potential the Communist Labour movement had was destroyed by Peter's reckless militancy and Big Jim's hidden agenda. From June 1924, the WUI began a series of strikes in building, the fishmarkets, the docks, the cinemas, and the railway, to prevent the recognition of ITGWU cards. Jim was furious on his return to Dublin in August. Peter had saddled him with the post of WUI general secretary, and the direction of strikes he believed could not be won. Reluctant to lead the strikes, or compromise his reputation by calling them off, he allowed the situation to drift. The Larkins hoped the WUI would be augmented by the withdrawal of British-based unions from Ireland, and the Comintern and Profintern agreed that Communists should launch a campaign to this effect. In a further setback for the WUI, the CPGB refused, pleading that it would 'stir up more difficulties' for the Minority

9   UUMC, ILPTUC, *Report* (1920), pp. 96–109.

Movement.[10] Jim attacked Dublin trades council for its continued association with the Minority Movement, and frustrated the council in its efforts to launch an Irish Minority Movement.

Though confident the Larkins would bankrupt their union, O'Brien was prepared to help the police and employers to accelerate the process. On 29 November a police detective reported that he was having informers enrolled in 'Larkin's mob' 'through the medium of the ITGWU'.[11] That same day the *Voice of Labour* announced that in future ITGWU members would take the place of WUI strikers. There was a propaganda war too, as both sides lambasted each other in the *Voice* and the *Irish Worker*, and in abusive handbills. The turning point came in July 1925 when the Dublin Coal Merchants' Association locked out ITGWU and WUI workers 'until a satisfactory guarantee is obtained that the men . . . will work amicably together'. Many employers had long been urging similar action, and the Dublin Employers' Federation pledged its support to the coal merchants. On 12 August, the ITGWU men resumed work 'to end the tyranny of the Larkin family organisation in the coal trade'.[12] The animosity reached new depths in September when WUI men assaulted ITGWU dockers at the North Wall. In mid September, the WUI ordered its members back to work. The union was broke. Apart from a gallant gesture of solidarity with the British miners in 1926, its role as a revolutionary force was over. Membership had dwindled to a low of some 5,000 by 1929, when it withdrew from the Profintern. Squeezing out all dissidents through a simple policy of 'my way or no way', Jim thereafter ran the WUI as his fief. The last vestige of Communist trade union organisation in Dublin disappeared in 1929 when the 'all red' trades council merged with Dublin Workers' Council.

If there was honesty in Peter's aggression, Big Jim's designs were shabby. His real reason for going to Moscow in 1924 was to persuade the Soviets to establish a commercial venture in the Free State, in which he would obtain a sinecure that would allow him to finance a life as a freelance agitator. The Comintern reckoned that Ireland had some potential as a flashpoint, as a country with an extensive diaspora, and as a cause with a potential to embarrass Britain, the linchpin in the circle of enemies around the Soviet Russia. And an internationally renowned figure like Larkin seemed to be the obvious man to lead Irish Communism. Aware of his volatility, they flattered him with election to the Executive Committee of the Communist International (ECCI), and made vague promises of trade and pledges of aid, conditional on the establishment of a Communist party in Ireland. Jim had already insisted that the CPI be dissolved in favour of the IWL, and agreed that the IWL would be

---

10   O'Connor, *Reds and the Green*, pp. 102, 113.
11   NA, Department of Justice, Larkin file, JUS 8/676.
12   O'Connor, *Reds and the Green*, p. 107.

transformed into a Communist party in 1925. Jim was a genuine Communist, at least to the extent that he was a revolutionary and admired the Bolsheviks; he had no time for theory. But he knew that the Comintern would use a party to control him, and he had a horror of being accountable and was insanely jealous. Despite the secondment of full-time agents, and offers of generous funding, from Moscow, he found one excuse after another to delay the formation of a party. Nor would he allow others to take up the slack. Suspecting an intrigue against him, he opposed Comintern collusion with republicans. When Roddy Connolly despaired of the IWL, launched the Workers' Party of Ireland and sought recognition from the Comintern, Jim persuaded the ECCI to demand its dissolution.[13] The crisis that followed the assassination of Kevin O'Higgins, Minister for Justice, on 10 July 1927, prompted the ECCI to issue Jim with an ultimatum for activating the IWL. He responded by fielding three candidates in the ensuant general election. The outcome was a fleeting triumph. Collaborating with Fianna Fáil and fixing its venom on Labour, the IWL won 12,500 votes, compared with 9,000 votes for the Labour Party in Dublin.[14] Big Jim became the only Communist ever elected to Dáil Éireann. However, as an undischarged bankrupt he was not allowed to take his seat. The Comintern offered to clear the debts, but as they arose out of litigation against the ITGWU and Tom Johnson, Jim refused.

Jim cut the painter with Moscow in 1929. Russian Oil Products, a division of the Soviet oil trust Neftetrest, had opened a depot in Dublin the summer of 1928. Here at last was the commercial activity which Jim had been pushing for, and he was livid at being excluded from it. In January 1929 he made his fifth and final trip to Moscow to appeal to the highest authorities. The case was heard by Josef Stalin at a meeting of the politburo on 7 February. It was agreed to review the Russian Oil Products apparat in Dublin, and instruct it to give preference to WUI members in recruitment, but no deals were to be done with Larkin on the sale of oil. The WUI disaffiliated from the Profintern. The ECCI gave no credence to the claim that the IWL would continue as a Comintern section under the leadership of Jim's fidus achates, Jack Carney.[15] Moscow had other plans for Ireland.

13   Charlie McGuire, *Roddy Connolly and the Struggle for Socialism in Ireland* (Cork, 2008), pp. 94–124.

14   For election results see Cornelius O'Leary, *Irish Elections, 1918–1977: Parties, Voters, and Proportional Representation* (Dublin, 1979).

15   Jack Carney (1886 or 1887–1956), born in Dublin or Liverpool; met Larkin in Liverpool in 1905, and worked with him in Ireland and the United States; represented the IWL in Moscow in 1925; pushed out of the WUI in 1936 (probably for financial reasons), and worked in London as a journalist; more anarcho-syndicalist than Communist, he gave some support to anti-Communism during the Cold War; died in London. See Richard Hudelson, 'Jack Carney and the *Truth* in Duluth', *Saothar* 19 (1994), pp. 129–39.

COMMUNISTS AND SOCIALIST REPUBLICANISM

In November 1925 an IRA army convention voted to break with Sinn Féin. The more military-minded volunteers were disturbed by rumours of Sinn Féin preparing to take its seats in Dáil Éireann. Others, notably Peadar O'Donnell,[16] wanted the IRA to become a force for social revolution. The Soviets may have been instrumental in the split. The Comintern had been renewing direct contacts with the IRA since 1924, aware that it would be foolish to make its Irish operation dependent exclusively on Jim Larkin. An even more secretive link emerged between the IRA and Razvedupr – Red Army intelligence. By 1927, the IRA had become heavily reliant on Soviet funding, in return for which it supplied information on British weaponry.[17] It was Soviet policy to keep Razvedupr activities separate and hidden from all but the highest people in the Comintern. The IRA too concealed its ties with Razvedupr. Nonetheless, there is evidence that some top functionaries in the ECCI encouraged links with republicans in 1927–8 because of the IRA's espionage value, and it would be odd if Soviet money did not cause the militarists on the IRA army council to take a more indulgent view of socialist republicanism. At the same time, the politics had a rationale of its own. The army council refused to work for Razvedupr after 1928 on account of the latter's insistence on treating its Irish informants as individual agents rather than as representatives of the IRA, a caution dictated by its chronic fear of the implications for Anglo-Soviet relations should the British get wind of the collusion.

Pending the creation of a party, the Comintern sought to consolidate its association with republicans through its various front organisations. In 1925, sections of Workers' International Relief and International Class War Prisoners' Aid were established in Ireland. From 1927, a plethora of organisations emerged to connect republicans, CPI veterans, trade unionists, the unemployed, and small farmers within the rubric of Communism, notably the League Against Imperialism, Irish Friends of Soviet Russia, the James Connolly Workers' Club, the Trade Union Unity League, the Irish Labour Defence League, and

16   Peadar O'Donnell (1893–1986), born of peasant stock in Donegal and trained as a teacher; introduced to Marxism as an ITGWU organiser in 1918; joined the IRA in 1920; a prominent champion of socialist republicanism from 1922; started the campaign against land annuities; offered to join the Communists in 1930 if he were made leader, but the ECCI regarded him as too independent-minded, a view widely shared in Ireland; stayed close to the Communists, and was outraged by their treatment of his friend, Seán Murray (see note 19 below), in the 1940s; best known as a freelance agitator and writer; the subject of four biographies.

17   For Irish-Soviet espionage connections see Tom Mahon and James J. Gillogly, *Decoding the IRA* (Cork, 2008), pp. 245–80; for the politics see O'Connor, *Reds and the Green*, pp. 116–60.

the Irish Working Farmers' Committee. The Comintern's next step was to build a party that would be 'Bolshevised', ie loyal to Moscow. In the wake of the IWL's electoral performance in 1927, the ECCI decided that Larkin had to be bypassed, and invited Irish students to its 'cadre-forge', the International Lenin School in Moscow. The first Irish candidates were 'delegated' to the school in November 1927, and 19 Irishmen, and one Irishwoman, would eventually be enrolled. With well-founded suspicions, Big Jim was hostile, but Young Jim was keen to go, and he was reluctant to stand in the way of his favourite son. Following Big Jim's break with Moscow, the Comintern sent a three-man commission to Ireland to found a party. The commission set up the Revolutionary Workers' Groups (RWG) in 1930. Surviving attempts by Cosgrave and the Catholic bishops to generate a red scare in 1931, the RWG would have a heroic record of struggle, with outdoor relief workers in Belfast, miners in Castlecomer, building workers in Dublin, and small farmers in Leitrim, and be remembered as the most vigorous Communist organisation in Irish history.[18]

Two factors crippled the Communists. The first was the contradiction in their relations with republicans. On the one hand, the Comintern wanted to push them to the left; on the other, it feared a socialist republicanism that would displace Irish Communism. Comintern policy was currently governed by the theory of the 'third period' and the slogan 'class against class'. In 1926, Nikolai Bukharin – then leader of the Comintern – had argued that the Bolshevik revolution had led to a period of advance for socialism. Then, from 1921, in a period of stabilisation, the right had checked the advance of the left. During this second period, it made sense for Communists to work with others on the left. Now, the capitalist world was entering a third period, of a profits squeeze, intensified class conflict, and greater threat of war. Capitalists would turn increasingly to fascism to crush the left, and as non-Communists were basically pro-capitalist, they should be unmasked as 'social fascists'. For the moment, the line was modified for Ireland, to preclude criticism of Larkin or the IRA. In the event, Larkin simply ignored the Communists, offering neither the help they had hoped for, nor the disruption they had dreaded. He also kept them out of the WUI, and their inability to permeate the trade unions made them more dependent on republicans, who became their only friends in Ireland. Manipulating the IRA proved to be more tedious than the ECCI had envisaged. A premature initiative to detach working-class elements from the IRA in June 1930 backfired badly. When the IRA moved left in 1931 and launched a socialist political movement, Saor Éire, Moscow regarded it was a rival and was happy to see it suppressed by the government. After Fianna

---

18 See Mary M. Banta, 'The red scare in the Irish Free State, 1929–37' (MA, UCD, 1982).

Fáil's triumph in 1932, Seán Murray[19] persuaded the ECCI to allow the RWG
to place a greater emphasis on anti-imperialism. The revision led to a promising
collaboration with republicans until the RWG hit a second obstacle, from
which there was no escape. The Catholic Church's relaxed attitude towards
the left had changed profoundly after Stalin imposed severe limits on the
toleration of religion in Russia in late 1929. Pope Pius XI retaliated in 1930 by
virtually excommunicating Communists, and the Irish Catholic press and the
hierarchy – then awakening to its power in the new Irish state – seized on
anti-Communism as a means of flaunting its authority. Initially republicans
had challenged the clergy, but by 1933 the intensity of anti-Communism was
causing the IRA leadership to distance itself from the RWG. In Belfast, the
RWG faced equally trenchant hostility from Protestant clerics, the Unionist
Party, and the Orange Order. Despite the increasingly unfavourable circumstances – membership had fallen from a peak of 339 to about 250 – Murray
bowed to ECCI pressure to transform the RWG into the second CPI in June
1933. In reaction to allegations that it was behind the party, the IRA formally
abjured Communism for the first time. The army council did not see this as a
shift to the right, and sought to strengthen links with mainstream Labour. It
simply decided that the Communists were more trouble than they were worth.

This was too much for the CPI's greatest fellow traveller. O'Donnell had
tabled a motion at the 1933 IRA army convention for an alliance with other
radical groups. When the proposal was defeated again in 1934, he and his
supporters proceeded unilaterally to call for a Republican Congress. Within
months a sprouting network of social agitation was blossoming into a 'united
front' of some 8,000 republicans and trade unionists. To the CPGB, which
handled Irish communications with Moscow through a secret radio transmitter,
it was a 'most dangerous situation'.[20] Like the Comintern, it feared that
Murray was too close to O'Donnell, and that the Communists would end up
joining the republicans, rather than vice versa. The CPI meanwhile struggled
to reconcile its third period strategy of supporting 'united fronts from below'
with the united front strategy of the Republican Congress. To begin with, the
CPI offered joint action with the Congress only on specifics, such as anti-
fascism. As luck would have it, the ECCI was allowing national sections to
drift from third period thinking in response to the left's failure to prevent a

19   Seán Murray (1898–1961), a farmer's son from the glens of Antrim; joined Sinn Féin in 1917, the
IRA in 1919, and the IWL in London in 1924; a student in the Lenin School, 1927–30; de facto leader
of the RWG and CPI general secretary, 1933–41; led the Communist Party, Northern Ireland from
1950; a Connolly republican and a confidante of Peadar O'Donnell, but always loyal to Moscow. See
entry *Dictionary of Labour Biography*, XI (London, 2003).
20   O'Connor, *Reds and the Green*, p. 201.

Nazi dictatorship in Germany. On 1 September the CPI was able to endorse a united front with the Congress on the central issue of anti-imperialism.

On 28–9 September 1934, Rathmines Town Hall hosted a star-studded inaugural conference of the Republican Congress. Delegates attended from 14 trade unions and trades councils, together with comrades from almost every shade of radical opinion, under the chairmanship of William McMullen,[21] a senior ITGWU official and vice-president of the ITUC. A disastrous division emerged on strategy. Michael Price, with the backing of a majority of the Congress's organising bureau, proposed that the conference endorse a new party, and a workers' republic. O'Donnell drafted a minority resolution calling for the continuation of a united front, committed to 'a republic'. Both sides cried foul. O'Donnell described what he saw as last minute proposals from Price as an ambush and a 'weird stunt', although the Congress paper, *Republican Congress*, had appeared to back a new party as early as 16 June, and the Communists had long been worried about this possibility. The Price faction blamed Moscow for turning O'Donnell. The allegation was plausible. The CPGB sent Willie Gallacher to Dublin on 19 or 20 September with instructions to vote for a united front. According to Nora Connolly, Gallacher persuaded O'Donnell to row in with the Communist line after an all-night argument.[22] There was also a second disaster in store. On 21 or 22 September, the politsecretariat, the executive organ of the praesidium, and the highest policy making body within the ECCI, radioed London with detailed directions for the CPI. The party was to 'fight for the leadership of the Congress'. While supporting a united front against 'hunger, fascism, and war', it was to 'bring forward the main slogan "Workers' and Farmers' Republic"' against O'Donnell's slogan – the slogan was very important for the Communists. Harry Pollitt, the CPGB general secretary, confirmed receipt of the message, and never bothered to forward it to Dublin.[23] When the conference convened, O'Donnell called for 'a republic', and Price for a 'workers' republic'. The sizeable Communist contingent should have called for a 'workers' and farmers' republic'. But they didn't. They sided with O'Donnell, and the united front motion was passed by 99–84 votes. Price's people with-

21 William McMullen (1892–1982), born in north Belfast; Protestant; ILP'er turned Connollyite and a strong critic of Labour anglocentrism; expelled from Harland and Wolff in 1912; ITGWU official in Belfast; NILP MP in 1925; moved to Dublin in 1932; a vice-chairman of the Republican Congress at Rathmines in 1934; member of the ITUC executive from 1925, and the CIU central council from 1945; general president of the ITGWU, 1946–51; a senator, 1951–4; close to Fianna Fáil during the CIU years.

22 Nora Connolly O'Brien, *We Shall Rise Again* (London, 1981), p. 72.

23 RGASPI, to the secretariat CPI, 19 Sept. 1934, 495/14/334–24/27; Memo to the CPI, 16 Sept. 1934, 495/89/96–46/47; NAUK, London, Government Code and Cypher School decrypts of Comintern messages, 1930–45, HW 17/17. I am obliged to Eunan O'Halpin and Barry McLoughlin for drawing my attention to these decrypts.

drew in disgust.

The Republican Congress never recovered from the schism. Neither did Murray. Moscow blamed him for dividing the Congress and bracketing the CPI with the 'right' rather than the 'left' at Rathmines. The ECCI re-established the CPGB's 'fostering role' over the CPI and considered replacing Murray. In the short term, the Communist–republican nexus deepened as the O'Donnellite rump of the Congress and the CPI had few other friends. In the long term, prospects were not good. The powerhouse of socialist republicanism, the ECCI, switched tack in 1935. The Comintern's seventh World Congress endorsed a new strategy: the popular front. Communists were now to seek alliances with all anti-fascists, and the Comintern was to relax its management of affiliates and reduce the level of logistical support. The Spanish Civil War brought an unexpected Indian summer. There was no avoiding the Spanish question in Ireland in the 12 months after July 1936. It is possible that per capita the Irish accounted for more volunteers in Spain than any other nation. While most 'fought' for Franco, and half of the 250 or so in the Connolly Column – the blanket term for all Irishmen on the Republican side in Spain – were emigrés, the Irish contribution to the International Brigades was remarkable for a country with a Communist party of about 150 members, confined organisationally to Dublin and Belfast.[24] The Republican Congress and the CPI formed the twin pillars of opposition to Franco in the Free State, and a popular front atmosphere emerged on the far left as writers and middle-class liberals supported projects like the Left Book Club and the New Theatre Guild. It was the swansong of socialist republicanism, the end of an era that began with Larkin's decision to found an Irish trade union in 1908.

THE LABOUR PARTY

The Labour Party, during the Cumann na nGaedheal era, had two major handicaps, its structure and its leadership. The ILPTUC format meant that the party did not have a conventional constituency organisation, and as trade unions, trades councils, and the annual Congress were unable to act in place of dedicated branches, the party was, in effect, the TDs and senators and their henchmen.[25] A structure designed to politicise the unions and democratise the party elite had the opposite effect. Moreover, the notional dynamo of it all,

24 The best source on Ireland and the Spanish Civil War is Ciarán Crossey's website, http://www.irelandscw.com

25 The most comprehensive history of the Labour Party is Niamh Puirséil, *The Irish Labour Party, 1922–73* (Dublin, 2007).

the unions, were in decline. Some British unions found that their rules did not allow them to subvent candidates for Dáil Éireann. The bulk of the Dublin ITGWU had gone Communist in 1924, and as the fountainhead of sectionalism, Dublin remained embarrassingly barren territory. Up to the 1960s, Labour TDs tended to come from the agricultural labour-intensive tillage and dairying counties of south Leinster and Munster, where the party polled double its vote in Dublin.[26] Ironically, Johnson attributed this to the politicising effect of Labour nationalism, in the form of the Land and Labour Associations.[27] The oddest thing about the Labour Party was that it demanded mediocrity of its politicians. Most TDs of the early intake were trade unionists, who had come to prominence in the heyday of direct action. When trade unionism disintegrated about them, those who wished to survive rebuilt their electoral bases on clientelist lines. Over the next 40 years the party was dependent on personal constituency machines, led by politicians who relied on some level of support from Fianna Fáil or Fine Gael voters, and for whom being on the left meant little more than looking after the forgotten people of Ireland's property-obsessed society – urban and rural labourers, public housing tenants, and social welfare recipients; anything more assertive was a threat to their election prospects. Paradoxically, an efficient, centrally directed, policy driven party was not in their interests.

After stepping down from the 1918 general election, and refusing to play the republican card during the Civil War, Labour squandered its last big opportunity of this vintage between 1923 and 1927. Republicans were stubbornly leaving an ace in the pack: Labour was in Dáil Éireann, Sinn Féin was not, and abstentionism was becoming increasingly unpopular as the public grew into the new dispensation. The sensible thing would have been to keep republicans withering on the vine, and steal their thunder. Indeed, this scenario was a factor in prompting de Valera to decamp from Sinn Féin and found Fianna Fáil.[28] Good results for Labour in the 1925 local elections and subsequent bye-elections were followed by the peak achievement of returning 22 deputies in the general election of June 1927. Perversely, Johnson both recoiled from the faintest republicanism – 'We have had one revolution and one revolution in a generation is enough' was his response to a suggestion that he might oppose the oath of allegiance – and worked hard to lure the cuckoo into the nest, convinced that having Fianna Fáil in Dáil Éireann would bring

26 Michael Gallagher, *Political Parties in the Republic of Ireland* (Manchester, 1985), p. 158.

27 Arthur Mitchell, *Labour in Irish Politics, 1890–1930: The Irish Labour Movement in an Age of Revolution* (Dublin, 1974), p. 241.

28 Henry Patterson, *The Politics of Illusion: Republicanism and Socialism in Modern Ireland* (London, 1989), p. 36.

stability and lead eventually to 'normal' politics.[29] He was, of course, reflecting a mentality embedded in trade unionism by its anglicisation in the late nineteenth century. Johnson was not so much a bad leader as an anti-leader, adept at rationalising inertia. Labour, ran his favourite rhetorical theme, could do the easy thing and make itself popular, and might be forced to do so if the government did not heed the people, but, for the moment, it would, in the public interest, sit on the moral high ground. Typical was his position on the land annuities, which also came under the rubric of his severe constitutionalism:

> if the Labour Party were to adopt the strategy of the Communists and aim at disturbing and disintegrating the existing social order . . . [it] then might become popular at least with the disinherited masses. A few imprisonments would add to its popularity and we should receive the plaudits of the 'Left Wing Republicans'! . . . But if we are to act as a party with a sense of responsibility . . . we should not follow this course . . .'[30]

Johnson busied himself with parliamentary duties, never missing a division until overwork forced him to take a respite in 1927. His interest in policy formulation and personal example helped to raise Labour above the other minnows in Dáil Éireann. But not even he believed that this was of value to the working class. He was particularly troubled by unemployment. Almost one in four insured workers were idle, and thousands were exhausting their insurance benefit and having to rely on the demeaning home assistance provided by local authorities. Notwithstanding Larkin's obstructionism, Roddy Connolly's faction staged some impressive 'work or maintenance' protests.[31] At least the Communists were trying. The Labour Party was doing nothing. In July 1925 Johnson startled his colleagues by resigning as party leader and secretary of Congress. In an extraordinary cri de coeur, raw with the pain of personal attacks against him, dripping with guilt at his inability to make any impression on Cumann na nGaedheal's stone-hearted conservatism, and plaintively reproachful of class politics, he pleaded: 'I am a 'community-ist', a 'nation-ist', before I am a 'trade-union-ist'.[32] Plainly, he was stressed, and telling the party that if it wanted a chief it should find someone else. It was a measure of the lack of alternative talent that he was prevailed upon to withraw his resignation. It could not have helped Johnson's self-confidence that Cosgrave was not completely impervious to Labour influence. Cosgrave took

29   Mitchell, *Labour in Irish Politics*, p. 245.
30   *Irishman*, 4 Aug. 1928.
31   O'Connor, *Reds and the Green*, pp. 119–20.
32   Quoted in J. Anthony Gaughan, *Thomas Johnson* (Dublin, 1980), p. 287.

a positive view of the International Labour Organization (ILO) in Geneva. Established under the Treaty of Versailles as a gesture to the left at the height of post-war radicalism, the ILO's primary function was to improve working conditions internationally. Happily for Ireland, the third most important man in the ILO was Ned Phelan.[33] Phelan persuaded Cosgrave to ratify ILO conventions, and it was in the ILO that the Free State first asserted its independence of Britain on the world stage. When Labour Senator Thomas MacPartlin died suddenly in Geneva while a member of the first Irish delegation to the ILO, Cosgrave provided what was virtually a state funeral. Congress had an ILO enthusiast in its assistant secretary, R. J. P. Mortished,[34] who later became chief of the ILO's maritime service.

Fianna Fáil continued to baulk at taking the oath of allegiance until the assassination of O'Higgins rocked the party system. Johnson offered to join a government of national stability. Cosgrave dismissed this soother and introduced bills to toughen public safety legislation and require Dáil candidates to abjure abstention. When de Valera moved to elude his impending pickle, both Larkin and Johnson scrambled to help him. De Valera and Larkin proposed a conference of opposition groups to discuss an alternative government. Labour would have nothing to do with Larkin, but Johnson cobbled together support for a Labour-led coalition government that would be sustained from the backbenches by Fianna Fáil. It was an unlikely scenario that would have harnessed such adversaries as Fianna Fáil and the Redmondites. Yet had it not been for the inexplicable absence of the Redmondite deputy for Sligo, the famous Mr Jinks, the opposition would have defeated the government in a confidence vote. Cosgrave dissolved the 'short Dáil', went to the country, and won his majority. The September general election squeezed the smaller parties. Labour lost nine seats, including Johnson's. When Fianna Fáil entered Leinster House in August 1927, Labour's fate was sealed. Fianna Fáil blended economic and political nationalism with an amorphous social radicalism. Politics now assumed a classic post-colonial format, with Cumann na nGaedheal

33 Edward J. Phelan (1888–1967), born in Tramore, son of a master mariner; the family moved to Liverpool in 1895 and he later joined the British civil service; appointed chief of the ILO's Diplomatic Division in 1920, rising to director-general in 1946; an ardent Irish nationalist, and a social liberal rather than a socialist, he regularly advised Cosgrave on the ILO and the League of Nations, but was not so popular with Fianna Fáil or in touch with Irish Labour. See ILO, *Edward Phelan and the ILO: The Life and Views of an International Social Actor* (Geneva, 2009).

34 Ronald J. P. Mortished (1891–1957), born in London of Irish Protestant parents, educated at the London School of Economics, and joined the civil service in Dublin in 1909; a member of the ILP and SPI, and an Esperantist; critical of Irish imitation of British trade unionism, he founded the Irish Civil Service Union as an OBU for civil servants; assistant secretary of the ILPTUC, 1922–9, when he joined the ILO staff in Geneva; chairman of the Labour Court, 1946–52, then rejoined the ILO in Rome. See Charles Callan, 'Labour lives, no 9', *Saothar* 32 (2007), pp. 45–8.

representing the compradors – those with a material interest in existing economic relations with Britain – and Fianna Fáil appealing to those who wished to reduce ties with the metropole. In Labour's mindset, this was just an irrational continuation of the Civil War divide.

In 1930 the party separated from Congress. Plainly, the ILPTUC had become dysfunctional. Syndicalism was dead, and its format survived as a sarcophagous. Instead of politicising the unions, it was depoliticising the party. Congress carried on, largely as before, and the party established its own branches and an administrative council. The restructuring made little difference to Labour's second leader, Thomas J. O'Connell,[35] who outdid his predecessor in shunning 'politics'. O'Connell's primary concern was that the party would not embarrass the unions. Weeks before succeeding Johnson, he had asked that teachers' opinions be respected through 'strict neutrality' on 'purely political' questions. Once Fianna Fáil accepted the role of official opposition, neutrality became impossible and discipline crumbled. Five TDs bucked the whip to vote with Fianna Fáil on a land annuities motion; two more suffered expulsion for supporting Cumann na nGaedheal's public safety legislation during the red scare of 1931.[36] Identity faded as circumstances pushed both Labour and Fianna Fáil into the same division lobbies. Labour's neutrality attained farcical dimensions in the watershed election of 1932. O'Connell requested 'five or ten years truce' on questions relating to the Ango-Irish Treaty. On tariffs, Labour speakers approved a 'low wall', going half way with Fianna Fáil. On land annuities, the party programme pleaded: 'political parties [are] not qualified to pronounce judgement'. Extreme moderation in a moderately extremist climate paid no dividends. The Labour vote fell to 7.7 per cent. Seven Labour deputies were returned, and the party's immediate requirement in the 7th Dáil was a replacement for its unseated leader.

The succession fell to William Norton.[37] Professional and pragmatic, Norton was the party's first real leader. Johnson had put the constitution first;

---

35   Thomas J. O'Connell (1882–1969) born in Bekan, Mayo, and qualified as a teacher in St Patrick's College, Drumcondra; a primary teacher from 1902, general secretary of the Irish National Teachers' Organisation from 1916; TD for Galway, 1922–7 and South Mayo, 1927–32; co-founded the Educational Building Society in 1935; was nominated to the Seanad in 1938; his *History of the Irish National Teachers' Organisation, 1868–1968* (Dublin, 1969) was only the second trade union history to be published.

36   An account by Johnson of the party's 'first internal crisis' is quoted in Gaughan, *Thomas Johnson*, pp. 471–4. Johnson was not impressed with O'Connell's leadership.

37   William Norton (1900–63), born in Dublin; a postal messenger in 1916; general secretary of the Post Office Workers' Union, 1924–57; won a bye-election for Labour in 1926, and was TD for Kildare, 1932–63; instrumental in the separation of the party from Congress in 1930; a good speaker and parliamentarian, and an effective Minister for Social Welfare, 1948–51, but his jaded leadership after 1951 tarnished his reputation.

O'Connell put the unions first; Norton put the party first. That Labour survived the nadir of 1932–3 at all owed much to Norton. Synonymous with the aching conservativism of his TDs in the 1950s, he showed himself to be a shrewd tactician in the preceding decades. He soon ditched Labour's ambiguity on nationalism for a straightforward acceptance of consensus republicanism, dismissing the oath of allegiance as a 'relic of feudalism'. Labour and Fianna Fáil met to discuss cooperation on 8 March 1932. Next day, Norton pledged backbench support for a minority Fianna Fáil government. In return, Labour expected work or maintenance for the unemployed, the construction of 40,000 houses, pensions for widows and orphans, the re-organisation of transport on a national basis, protection for the flour milling industry, control of food prices, and economic development. Labour gave conditional support to Fianna Fáil from the backbenches up to 1938, extracting a few social reforms in return.

Fianna Fáil more than met Labour expectations. A comprehensive tariff policy created opportunities for enterprise that expanded industrial employment from 110,000 in 1931 to 166,000 in 1938, proportionately a performance comparable with Stalin's massive industrialisation programme – the second five-year plan. New semi-state industries and public spending programmes were launched, agricultural policy laid greater emphasis on labour-intensive tillage, and working conditions were improved through the introduction of Joint Industrial Councils, new trade boards, and the Conditions of Employment Act (1936). A notable prize for rural Labour TDs was the reappointment of an Agricultural Wages Board in 1936 to set minimum rates for 150,000 farm workers.[38] While gross national income virtually stagnated as the Economic War depressed farm prices, incomes of those in industry and services increased. The slump in livestock exports during the Economic War improved diet for the urban poor. Between 1926 and 1936, consumption of cattle rose by 79 per cent, of lamb by 37 per cent, and of eggs by 14 per cent.[39] Greater efforts were made to tackle housing. Twenty-seven per cent of the population lived in bad

38 As K. Theodore Hoppen, *Ireland since 1800: Conflict and Conformity* (London, 1989), p. 211 has noted, 'Irish historians (for reasons of social background, ideology, and academic fashion)' have been unsympathetic to Fianna Fáil's policies in the 1930s. More recent economic studies have emphasised the underlying achievements. See Brian Girvin, *Between Two Worlds: Politics and Economy in Independent Ireland* (Dublin, 1989), pp. 88–130; and Kennedy, Giblin, and McHugh, *The Economic Development of Ireland in the Twentieth Century*, pp. 40–9. M. E. Daly, 'The employment gains from industrial protection in the Irish Free State during the 1930s: a note', *Irish Economic and Social History* 15 (1988), pp. 71–5 examines the debate on employment creation and upholds the Soviet comparison. For improvements in labour law see R. J. P. Mortished, 'The Industrial Relations Act, 1946', *Journal of the Statistical and Social Inquiry Society of Ireland* 17 (1946–7), pp. 670–90; *Trade Union Information* 1:3 (July, 1949), p. 7; and Dan Bradley, *Farm Labourers: Irish Struggle, 1900–1976* (Belfast, 1988), pp. 93–111.
39 David Johnson, *The Inter-War Economy in Ireland* (Dublin, 1985), pp. 40–1.

housing – ie: a density of more than two persons per room – in 1926. State credit schemes allowed 17,680 local authority houses to be built between 1932 and 1936, over twice the number completed during the previous seven years. By 1936, the proportion of people badly housed had fallen to under 23 per cent.[40] The Unemployment Assistance Act (1933) provided for all unemployed men, insured or not, introducing the 'dole' in April 1934. A Land Allotments Act subsidised local authority in letting plots to the unemployed for food cultivation. It became easier to qualify for blind and old age pensions, and widows' and orphans' pensions were introduced in 1935.[41] There were limits to Fianna Fáil achievement, and basic differences with Labour would surface before the decade closed. The growth in total employment, from 1,220,284 in 1926 to 1,235,424 in 1936, was unimpressive. The extra jobs created were insufficient to absorb rural depopulation, whilst the worldwide depression discouraged emigration, severely so in the case of America. Rising unemployment figures reached 145,000 in January 1936.[42] And once the great industrial leap forward was over, new growth areas were not obvious. Efforts to diversify the export market met with meagre results. High input costs for industries in a small home market meant high consumer prices. Nonetheless, from a Labour viewpoint, short-term trends at least were encouraging. If unemployment remained high, the workforce was being restructured in a way favourable to union organisation, while the Control of Manufactures Acts, designed to promote native ownership of industry, enhanced trade union bargaining power. Congress membership rose from 95,000 in 1933 to 161,000 in 1938.[43]

Unlike Cumann na nGaedheal, Fianna Fáil was both opponent and rival, and presented Labour with unprecedented challenges. In addition to offering more intense competition at the hustings, de Valera was never happy to be reliant on Labour support in Dáil Éireann. Each time Labour held the balance of power, as in 1932 and 1937, de Valera called snap elections the following year. Fought on the pretext that minority governments were unstable, these elections saw the Labour vote squeezed and de Valera win his majority.

How was Labour to oppose Fianna Fáil ideologically? Initially, Norton took the obvious course of adopting a more republican and left-wing position. He gave unwavering support in the Economic War, and made himself useful by lobbying British Labour leaders during negotiations over the land annuities issue, and arranging a meeting between de Valera and the British Prime Minister, Ramsay MacDonald. The fascist menace also pushed Labour to the

40   *Irish Free State Statistical Abstract*, 1931–6.
41   John Curry, *The Irish Social Services* (Dublin, 1980), pp. 24–5, 31.
42   Census, 1926, 1936; *Irish Free State Statistical Abstract*, 1936.
43   McCarthy, *Trade Unions in Ireland*, p. 621a.

left. Though General Eoin O'Duffy's National Guard was proscribed in August 1933, fascism acquired a deadlier import in September when Cumann na nGaedheal, the National Centre Party, and the Blueshirts merged as Fine Gael under O'Duffy's leadership. Labour then agreed to support the government in return for concessions on pensions, unemployment benefit, housing, and working conditions. A joint Labour–ITUC manifesto on the 'Fascist Danger' appeared in October, and Congress, after some prodding from Dublin trades council, sponsored a series of anti-fascist rallies in May.[44] O'Duffy finally overreached himself in the local elections of June 1934. When his promised big advances failed to materialise, Fine Gael pressured him into resigning. Fascism had never tempted Labour to collaborate with red republicans. Weeks after the schism in the Republican Congress, Labour's annual conference slapped down a motion of Roddy Connolly's to unite republicans, Communists, and Labour in a common anti-fascist, anti-imperialist alliance, resolving instead to resist the introduction of 'anti-Christian communist doctrines into the movement'.[45] Subsequent popular front overtures from the CPI met a similar response. Arguably, they made little sense for Labour, and Norton was brave enough to seek to attract the remnants of the Republican Congress. In 1936, Labour adopted a constitution committing it to a 'workers' republic', and in 1937 it opposed the adoption of Bunreacht na hÉireann for the status it gave to private property and for not declaring the state a republic. However, the Spanish Civil War indicated that Labour would never be so radical as to step outside a prevailing consensus. With the Catholic Church rallying support for Franco, the ITUC declined to take a stand on the war. In some cases, workers in British-based unions which funded humanitarian aid to Republican Spain made formal protests or disaffiliated.[46] Even Larkin banned WUI officials from speaking out on Spain. After doing its best to avoid the issue, Labour published an evasive pamphlet, *Cemeteries of Liberty: Communist and Fascist Dictatorships*, written by Norton and introduced by O'Brien. Skirting both Spanish and Irish politics, Norton treated fascism as Nazism, and equated Nazism with Stalinism. Labour, as Norton would have it, was anti-fascist and anti-communist equally, but not pro- or anti-Franco. As the last embers of post-1916 radicalism faded, Norton endorsed a request from the Irish National Teachers' Organisation to have Labour's new constitution vetted by the Catholic hierarchy. Two sections found 'contrary to Catholic social teaching' by

44 Gaughan, *Thomas Johnson*, pp. 357–61. For Dublin trades council and fascism see also Séamus Cody, John O'Dowd, and Peter Rigney, *The Parliament of Labour: 100 Years of Dublin Council of Trade Unions* (Dublin, 1986), pp. 167–70.

45 Puirséil, *The Irish Labour Party*, p. 54.

46 Fearghal McGarry, *Irish Politics and the Spanish Civil War* (Cork, 1999), pp. 182–90.

the hierarchy were amended and the workers' republic objective was deleted. Norton could claim to have buried the pre-1932 inanity about his party's political nature, and assured that it would survive the Fianna Fáil challenge, but he had also affirmed that it would be opportunist and conformist.

Another problem was posed indirectly by Fianna Fáil. When Labour separated from the ITUC, provision was made for union affiliation, and the party liked to project itself as the political wing of the trade union movement. The power of this comforting image was rooted in British experience, and it served to cloud Irish realities. It is likely that most trade unionists voted Fianna Fáil, and most Labour voters were not trade unionists. Unions still provided the party with finance, organisation, and activists. By contrast, a party with little hope of forming a government was of limited value to the unions, and just 13 of some 40 Congress unions bothered to affiliate in 1930. Unions would present the party with four challenges between 1936 and 1945, three of them a consequence of their new relationship with the state. Norton's handling of the first would be one of Labour's biggest mistakes.

INDUSTRIAL UNIONISM THIS TIME?

Trade unions had a grim decade under Cumann na nGaedheal. The ITGWU claimed 40,000 members in 1926, when Larkin had done his worst. Three years later, enrolment had fallen to 15,500.[47] The number of trades councils, an indicator of the geographical spread of trade unionism, fell from 46 in 1921 to ten by 1930. A few 'Back to the Unions' campaigns were mooted at local level in the mid decade, particularly after the British general strike of 1926, which quickened the pulse of Irish workers. In a feeble attempt at recovery, a special ITUC conference on organisation in 1927 addressed two problems: the multiplicity of unions and the amalgamateds. Both were related as in some cases British unions had duplicated Irish societies in the nineteenth century, and Irish unions then emerged subsequently as alternatives to British unions. Aside from multiplicity, having some 25 per cent of members in unions with their senior officials, head offices, and resources in another jurisdiction was in itself a source of weakness. Ineffectually, the conference commended mergers of cognate unions and urged the amalgamateds to appoint an 'Irish organiser or secretary' and 'in addition some form of representative body for the consideration of matters of peculiar or special concern to the Irish membership'.[48] As yet, the ITUC did not wish to raise the divisive demand that British unions withdraw from Ireland.

47   C. Desmond Greaves, *The Irish Transport and General Workers' Union: The Formative Years, 1909–1923* (Dublin, 1982), p. 321.
48   Gaughan, *Thomas Johnson*, pp. 363–4.

Industrialisation after 1932 triggered a significant escalation of trade union militancy. Yet despite Communist, and even IRA, involvement in some disputes, industrial struggle carried little radical import. In contrast with the syndicalist era, Labour was fatally divided; primarily, expansion meant new opportunities for inter-union rivalry. Sometimes unions fought over their respective merits, sometimes over the advantages of craft or industrial unionism, sometimes over the principles behind Irish or British-based unionism; always they fought over members. The most strike prone sectors – transport and construction – were also the most faction-ridden areas of trade unionism. Sixteen unions operated in transport, 12 of them British based, making it a cockpit of the general friction in the movement between the ITGWU, the WUI, and the amalgamateds. A protracted tram strike in 1929 prompted Congress to adopt a system of adjudication for inter-union disputes, and show greater concern to discourage the affiliation of small or splinter unions.[49] Such tentative action became hopelessly inadequate in 1934 when moves by the Amalgamated Transport and General Workers' Union (ATGWU) to block the defection of Dublin tramwaymen to the ITGWU provoked a renewal of opposition to British-based unionism per se. Preoccupied with Larkin, O'Brien had been fairly conciliatory towards the amalgamateds over the preceding decade. *Three Men and Three Days: A Fight For Irish Trade Unionism*, the ITGWU's version of the tramway dispute, indicated that the gloves were off, again. Moreover, the ITUC executive sided with the ITGWU, and the annual Congress that August uncovered a broad opinion among Irish unions that the accelerating economic and legislative divergence between both countries should cause the British unions to review their position in Ireland.

Trade unions were no less sympathetic to Fianna Fáil than the Labour Party. The international depression had strengthened their belief in protectionism, and a convergence of Labour and Fianna Fáil views was evident at the 1931 Congress. To rally the movement against unemployment, the Congress adopted an 'Industrial Charter' demanding: a living wage; a 40-hour week; work or maintenance for the unemployed; national programmes of house and road building, and afforestation; public ownership of banking, power supplies, and transport; and import controls and the establishment of an exports boards. Congress instructed the executive to pursue implementation of the Charter through parliamentary channels.[50] By 1934 Congress could list nine items of legislation on housing, welfare, or industry featuring some Labour input.[51]

---

49 McCarthy, *Trade Unions in Ireland*, p. 121. Except where stated, the following is based on McCarthy's detailed account, pp. 118–68, though the interpretation differs.

50 *Waterford News*, 7 Aug. 1931.

51 Brian Girvin, 'Protectionism, economic development, and independent Ireland, 1922–60' (PhD, UCC, 1986), pp. 148–56.

In 1936, Seán Lemass, as Minister for Industry and Commerce, advised Congress that the government would intervene unless something was done about the continuing internecine friction.[52] Congress responded in April with the appointment of a high-powered commission of inquiry to examine five main areas, of which the most important was the merger or grouping of unions, a delicacy that kept repeating; previous committees had toyed with it in 1927 and 1930. Forty-nine societies represented the 134,000 workers in Congress; two had more than 10,000 members; 17 had under 500. None were strong enough to play a leading role; the ITGWU's share of Congress membership had fallen from over 40 per cent in 1919 to under 25 per cent. Taking his colleagues by storm, O'Brien dusted off a relic of old glory and recommended that Congress membership be regrouped in ten industrial unions catering for building and furnishing; engineering, shipbuilding, and vehicle building; the marine; transport; printing and paper works; bakeries; distributive, clerical, and supervisory staffs; teaching; the civil service; and general employment. To accommodate the North what were to be all-Ireland structures, Northern Ireland would receive 'the fullest measure of autonomy'. O'Brien's goal was less ambitious than the syndicalist resolution for a 'single Irish Workers' Union' adopted in 1919, but more specific. It envisaged that Congress should take the initiative in implementation, and whereas the 1919 resolution stemmed largely from the 'pull' of ideology, 'push' factors were now much stronger.

In addition to the demarcation disputes which caused internal annoyance and external calls for statutory reform of trade unionism, a broader question materialised with increasing menace in the late 1930s. With the import substitution phase of industrialisation evidently nearing its limit, would further advance be at the expense of living standards? Employers said yes, arguing that wage costs should compare with rates in agriculture rather than in British manufacture. Initially, the more important partner in economic direction seemed to say no; the Conditions of Employment Act (1936) allowed for the registration of wage rates throughout a given industry. Then, to trade union dismay, the government resisted application of the Act in this respect, raising apprehensions that Fianna Fáil's policy of 'ruralising' industry would serve as a cover for the pursuit of industrialisation on a cheap wages basis. It was a serious grievance for the more geographically dispersed bodies – the ITGWU and the Distributive Workers' Union in particular – and threatened to generate a fundamental tension between unionisation and job creation. O'Brien believed that industrial unionism would enable Labour to outflank the government 'through a large accretion of strength from the general reorganisation of all

52   Finbarr Joseph O'Shea, 'Government and trade unions in Ireland, 1939–46: the formulation of labour legislation' (MA, UCC, 1988), p. 39.

workers', that reorganisation to include a bluff, vintage 1919 demand that 'all within the industry must be either in their respective union or out of the job' by a certain date. Others were less sanguine, but the emergence of the first major difference in perceptions between unions and the Fianna Fáil government at a critical time in national economic history – when Labour–state relations were still in their infancy and fascist or corporatist ideas were advancing in Europe – made O'Brien's plan look all the more attractive. The commission encoded it as Memorandum 1.

There is no evidence for the canard that O'Brien's secret goal was to eliminate the British presence and make himself king of the movement. O'Brien pointedly declined to press for a giant 83,000 member marine, transport, and general union to allay fears of empire-building, opting instead for three industrial unions to cater for these workers. Under his proposals, the ITGWU would hive off members to some industrial groupings, and merge the remainder with the remnant of nine other unions. O'Brien would swap control of a 35,000 member union for, presumably, a less dictatorial seat within a 38,000-member industrial union. Far from making himself king, O'Brien stood to lose more from the shake-out than probably any other senior officer. If there were accusations of anglophobia and empire-building, there were also testimonies to O'Brien's bona fides from amalgamated officials, and Memorandum 1 secured remarkably wide support. No alternatives appeared until 11th-hour back pedalling from the amalgamateds. In what became Memorandum 2, Sam Kyle – the senior ATGWU man in Ireland since 1932 – rejected O'Brien's scheme as impractical, suggesting instead that Congress formulate plans to merge small unions, and that unions agree to recognise each others' cards. The blunt closed shop ultimatum, he feared, would merely provoke a hostile reaction! Kyle's intervention split the 12-person commission between five Irish union delegates for Memorandum 1, five amalgamated delegates for Memorandum 2, one undecided, and Norton. As head of a sectionalist union, Norton agreed with Kyle but, in a pretence at fence-sitting, tendered cognate recommendations as Memorandum 3.[53] That Memorandum 2 did not appear until September 1938, almost two years after Memorandum 1, generated suspicion that the amalgamateds were acting under orders from London.

The British were watching the growing consensus for reform. Since 1934 the amalgamateds had been boosting their affiliation from Northern Ireland, and UK unions now accounted for 77,000 members, compared with 83,000 for unions based in the state.[54] It had also become more common for British

53 For Norton's views see Dáil Debates, Vol. 84, 3 July 1941.
54 NLI, ITUC, *Report of the Trade Union Conference, 1939, with Terms of Reference and Memoranda of the Commission of Enquiry* (Dublin, 1940).

officials to attend annual congresses. They made up nine per cent of delegates in 1937, for example, and usually being senior officers, exerted a disproportionate influence.[55] Just a few defections from the more sectionally conscious Irish societies would scupper O'Brien's plan. It was a dilemma for Congress. To debate the commission's reports might deepen internal dissention: to shelve them would fortify employer calls for statutory reform. A special conference finally convened on 9 February 1939. The British sent a weighty team, including the general secretary of the NUR, John Marchbank, the assistant general secretary of the ATGWU, and the general secretaries of the Associated Society of Locomotive Engineers and Firemen and the National Union of Boot and Shoe Operatives. The Irish were outmanoeuvred by Marchbank and O'Brien's vindictive old antagonist, P. T. Daly, who chaired the session. Rejecting pleas by several prominent Irish trade unionists for a vote on Memorandum 1, Daly let Marchbank present Kyle's memorandum as the key motion. In a card vote, 21 unions representing 85,211 members voted for Memorandum 2; 18 unions representing 70,836 members voted against. That was it, Daly decided: no more voting. After a debate which took the motion at face value to begin with, but touched increasingly on the glaring breach between Irish and British unions, Daly's ruling was dangerously insensitive. O'Brien walked out, furious that the amalgamateds should batten on Irish sectionalism to hamstring the movement for their own vested interests; furious that he should be belittled by Daly. Daly was rattled enough to suggest the conference be closed, and the old Fenian suffered the indignity of being rescued by a patronising intervention from Marchbank. On 23 May, a Council of Irish Unions (CoIU) was formed as a lobby within the ITUC. Fissures criss-crossed trade unionism at various angles, but the fault line was now the divide between Irish and British conceptions of strategy.

There were strategic consequences too for the Labour Party. Norton had sided with the British against the bulk of Irish unions, and Labour TDs would take the same line on the Trade Union Act (1941). The ITGWU would turn to Fianna Fáil in its quest for reform of industrial relations.

55   McCarthy, *Trade Unions in Ireland*, p. 149.

SEVEN

THE CHRONIC MADE ACUTE
1939–45

War makes the chronic acute
James Douglas, Seanad Éireann, 14 March 1940.

—

The Emergency is often recalled in a cosy, nostalgic light; a time when a brave little country cheerfully shouldered its crosses to chart its own path through danger, oblivious to the great turmoil swirling about it. The quaint character of wartime social hardship is conveyed in tales of the ubiquitous glimmerman; while the plain people of Ireland's good humoured response is summed up in the jingle 'Bless de Valera and Seán MacEntee, for giving us brown bread and a half-ounce of tea'. Reality was not so funny. Over these years, the cost of living rose by two thirds, whereas wages increased by one third. Neither was Éire so isolated. People followed the war closely, and if they blessed Éamon de Valera for anything, it was for keeping them out of it. Equally, popular values were affected by the war. The percentage of births outside marriage births increased each year from 3.18 in 1939 to 4.03 in 1944, a peak figure not exceeded until 1977.[1] Unemployment, poverty, and, above all, the social inequality of the Emergency regime, swung public opinion to the left. So too did Europe's hopes for a fairer society after the peace, and Britain's plans for a welfare state. Coincidentally, all-party backing for neutrality collapsed the differences between Fianna Fáil and Fine Gael, leaving the latter drifting towards implosion. It was Labour's last chance to break out of third party status.

For trade unions, the Emergency was a period of experiment in labour-state relations, which harvested the conflict of philosophies between Irish and British trade unionism, and seeded the post-war industrial relations system. The depth of the economic difficulties, coupled with the unprecedented authority assumed by the government under its Emergency powers, led to statutory wage control and the Trade Union Act (1941) – the first attempt at legislative reform of industrial relations since the foundation of the state. Initially, Labour appeared to unite against what appeared to be an attack on

1 *Statistical Abstract of Ireland*, 1939–44.

workers' rights. However, the bigger private sector Irish unions shared the Fianna Fáil view that the key to better industrial relations lay in the rational-isation of trade unions. And while the introduction of the Act was mismanaged by the trenchantly right-wing MacEntee, who replaced Seán Lemass as Minister for Industry and Commerce between 1939 and 1941, Lemass, on returning to his old portfolio, drew unions into a more positive attitude towards state intervention. Lemass's long-term aim was to use the windfall of wartime controls on capital and labour to shift the basis of industrial relations from the voluntary to a statutory mode, and introduce a tripartism in public policy. Ultimately, this was going too far for the unions, but they divided on the merits of collaboration with the state. With a high proportion of low-paid workers, for whom wage militancy was not an option, private sector Irish unions began to take a more favourable view. The amalgamateds were opposed to rationalisation, and wanted to preserve the voluntary mode, partly because that was the British way, and partly because, having filleted the workforce in the nineteenth century, they were more likely to represent wage militants who felt they had little to gain from greater state regulation. Public sector unions, which inherited a deep and anglocentric sectionalism, and for whom the state was their employer, shared their apprehensions.[2]

The Trade Union Act (1941) was the first of three crises which the trade unions created for the Labour Party during the Emergency. As William Norton had done at the ITUC conference in 1939, the party sided with the tradition-alists against the reformists. It seemed the opportune thing to do, though it drove some unions closer to Fianna Fáil. A second crisis arose in 1943–4 after Norton flouted party rules to endorse Jim Larkin's candidature for Dáil Éireann. William O'Brien split the party rather than accept Larkin as a Labour TD. O'Brien created a third crisis in 1945 when he pushed the divisions in Congress to their logical conclusion.

EMERGENCY

Once Hitler overran Czechoslovakia on 15 March 1939, few doubted that a general conflagration could be avoided. International affairs peppered the 1939 Congress agenda. The executive's report condemned Japanese militarism in China and urged affiliates to enforce Congress's boycott of Japanese goods! A donation of £10 was made to the Irish Committee for the Relief of Austrian Refugees. Larkin tried to raise Frank Ryan's imprisonment under the Franco

---

2   On the appeal of the British model for civil servants, see Martin Maguire, 'Civil service trade unionism in Ireland (part 1), 1801–1922', *Saothar* 33 (2008), pp. 18–19.

regime.[3] War clouds over Europe recalled memories of shortages and profiteering during the Great War, and there was little to reassure delegates that Congress was any better prepared for the Second World War than it had been for the First. Charged with devising a programme, Luke Duffy and Eamonn Lynch, secretaries of the Labour Party and the ITUC, drafted *Planning for the Crisis*, an 18-page pamphlet proposing the creation of a consultative economic council of representatives of government, industry, labour, and agriculture. With opposition from the left, *Planning for the Crisis* was adopted by a joint ITUC– Labour Party conference in January 1940.[4] The left might have saved its breath. Duffy was much influenced by the corporatist thinking of Alfred O'Rahilly,[5] but, as the Emergency would show, neither Labour nor Fianna Fáil were ready for corporatism. *Planning for the Crisis* was perfunctory window dressing, another manifesto which exposed the want of original thinking in the Labour movement.

If war itself never came, its social and economic consequences were inescapable.[6] Prices increased immediately, and people were soon complaining bitterly about inadequate price control, profiteering, and the black market. Selective rationing, of imports like petrol, was introduced incrementally from

3   NLI, ITUC, *Annual Report* (1939), pp. 150–5, 160, 184–7. Frank Ryan (1902–44) was born in Elton, County Limerick, where his parents were national school teachers; educated at UCD; joined the IRA in 1922, and worked as a journalist; prominent in socialist republicanism and the Republican Congress; acknowledged leader of the Connolly Column; captured by the Italians, 1938, imprisoned in Burgos, and released to the Abwehr, 1940; died in Dresden; despite some controversy about his time in Germany, his reputation has enjoyed a revival with the upsurge of interest in the Connolly Column. See Adrian Hoar, *In Green and Red: The Lives of Frank Ryan* (Dingle, 2004).

4   Niamh Puirséil, *The Irish Labour Party, 1922–73* (Dublin, 2007), pp. 84–6; Charles McCarthy, *Trade Unions in Ireland, 1894–1960* (Dublin, 1977), p. 194.

5   Alfred O'Rahilly (1884–1969), born in Listowel; professor of mathematics and maths-physics in University College Cork; prolific polymath and Catholic actionist; keenly interested in labour affairs; a delegate to the ILO in 1924–5 and 1932; an eminence grise in the Labour movement in the 1940s, playing a role in the split in the Labour Party and National Labour's decision to join the inter-party government in 1948; fiercely anti-communist and active in promoting Catholic workers' education after 1945. See J. Anthony Gaughan, *Alfred O'Rahilly* (Dublin, 1986).

6   For impressions of Emergency life see Bernard Share, *The Emergency: Neutral Ireland, 1939–45* (Dublin, 1978); strike statistics are in the *Statistical Abstract of Ireland, 1939–45*; for aggregate trade union membership see W. K. Roche and Joe Larragy, 'The trend of unionisation in the Irish Republic', in UCD, *Industrial Relations in Ireland: Contemporary Issues and Developments* (Dublin, 1987); on the economic impact see James Meenan, *The Irish Economy since 1922* (Liverpool, 1971), pp. 33–6; L. M. Cullen, *An Economic History of Ireland since 1660* (London, 1987), p. 181; on wages see NLI, ITGWU, *Annual Report* (1942); Dan Bradley, *Farm Labourers: Irish Struggle, 1900–1976* (Belfast, 1988), pp. 109–10; on health, see J. J. Lee, *Ireland, 1912–1985: Politics and Society* (Cambridge, 1989), p. 314.

1939, and general ration books came into operation in June 1942. As Ireland produced most of the foodstuffs it consumed, the basic problem was not scarcity but price. Inflation produced a high level of strike activity over the first eight months of the Emergency, but increasing use of the Emergency Powers Act to restrain wage demands, slackening trade, and industrial dislocation had depressed wage movements and union membership by late 1940. The proportion of strikes in which workers were wholly or partly successful dropped sharply.

Nonetheless, the government moved steadily towards statutory control of wages. Civil service salaries were frozen in May 1940, and from August MacEntee argued in cabinet for a general pay freeze. With the proviso that protected industries and essential services only should be affected, he got his way. On 7 May 1941, Emergency Powers Order no 83 – more usually known as the Wages Standstill Order – introduced an absolute wage freeze for employees in these sectors, and removed legal immunity from trade unions in respect of action in breach of the order.[7] Conditions really began to bite from this point on. Adding to the distress, an outbreak of foot and mouth disease suspended cattle exports from January to October that year, and Britain retaliated for its failure to obtain trans-shipment facilities at Irish ports by restricting vital imports. By 1943, petrol supplies had dwindled to 20 per cent of pre-war levels, gas to 16 per cent, and textiles to 22 per cent. Domestic coal was unobtainable. Unemployment and emigration rose steeply. Already, the building industry had virtually shut down. Railwaymen were laid off as train services were curtailed. Deep-sea docks lay idle, and cross-channel shipping fell. Factories closed for want of fuel or raw materials. Output slumped by 27 per cent between 1938 and 1943, reducing industrial employment from 166,000 to 143,000. The gap between wages and prices continued to widen. In February 1942, prices were 37 per cent above the pre-war level; wages had increased by about ten per cent. By 1945, the average weekly industrial wage stood at 70s 8d, an increase of just under 30 per cent on the 1937 figure. The cost of living rose by 74 per cent over the same period. The hard reality of these figures did not stop at frugal sustenance: they meant disturbing levels of malnutrition, infant mortality, and tuberculosis.

The one group of workers to benefit from the adversity was rural labourers. Price controls in Britain denied a repeat of the Great War profits boom, but farmers at least held their own; prices for agricultural products rose by 90 per cent from 1937 to 1945. Furthermore, to meet the food shortage, orders were introduced from 1940 to 1948 requiring 3/8ths of arable land in each holding to be under tillage. Tillage acreage rose from 1.5 million acres in 1938 to 2.6

7   Finbarr Joseph O'Shea, 'Government and trade unions in Ireland, 1939–46: the formulation of labour legislation' (MA, UCC, 1988), pp. 28–35.

million in 1945. The coal shortage also created an urgent demand for turf
cutters. The need to keep labour on the land compelled the government to
make a relative improvement in agricultural wages. The Agricultural Wages
Board weekly rate rose from 27s in 1939 to 30s in 1940, and 40s 3d by 1945 – an
82 per cent advance on the 1937 level. However, the improvement was from an
abysmally low base rate, and did not keep pace, in absolute terms, with
industrial earnings.[8] So serious was the want of skilled agricultural and turf
workers, that the government prohibited men ordinarily resident outside
towns of over 5,000 in population from emigrating.[9] The shortage of rural
labour, together with the evident scope for improvement in wage levels, raised
the question of reviving trade unionism on the land. A motion that 'all road-
workers and bog workers should be members of the Union' was put to the
ITGWU annual conference in 1942. Recalling the painful experiences of 1923,
the executive quashed the idea.[10] Larkin took up the gauntlet in 1943 and in
1946 the WUI reconstituted its agricultural section as the Federation of Rural
Workers, with Seán Dunne as organising secretary.[11]

FIGHTING WITH SHADOWS

From early 1940, the focus of the government's labour policy expanded from
wages to industrial relations, and there were sympathetic nods at employer
calls for statutory intervention. Pay restraint remained the primary concern: in
the short term to check inflationary pressures, and in the long term to improve
the competitiveness of exports to Britain. When Dublin Corporation workers
struck for an extra 8s per week in March, threatening municipal services and
cattle exports, the government broke the strike, and MacEntee seized the
opportunity to prepare legislation to deal with similar disputes.[12] A draft bill,
based on Britain's Emergency Powers Act (1920) and Trades Disputes and
Trades Union Act (1927), proposed that if strikes disrupted public utilities or
essential services, the government be empowered to introduce a state of

8 Bradley, *Farm Labourers*, pp. 110–11.
9 Share, *The Emergency*, p. 91.
10 NLI, ITGWU, *Annual Report* (1942).
11 Bradley, *Farm Labourers*, pp. 74–92.
12 A trade union view of the strike is found in Seán Redmond, *The Irish Municipal Employees' Trade Union, 1883–1983* (Dublin, 1983), pp. 104–7. The most thorough account of the framing of the Trade Union Act (1941) is O'Shea, 'Government and trade unions in Ireland, 1939–46', pp. 36–80; see also McCarthy, *Trade Unions in Ireland*, pp. 181–206; and Fergus A. D'Arcy and Ken Hannigan (eds), *Workers in Union: Documents and Commentaries on the History of Irish Labour* (Dublin, 1988), pp. 200–2.

emergency. Employees might then be instructed to perform normal work by ministerial order; failure to comply could lead to fines, dismissal, imprisonment, or loss of welfare benefits, including pension rights. This emphasis on economic penalties reflected MacEntee's conclusion that physical force would be counterproductive. One breathtaking stroke of vindictiveness recommended that traders might be debarred from supplying goods to recalcitrants. Any strike could be declared illegal, and deprived of the protection of the Trades Disputes Act (1906), if its objects were other than a trade dispute or if it inflicted hardship on society, and one month's notice was to be given of all strikes or lockouts. MacEntee's draft alarmed his colleagues, who considered some of its provisions to be provocative or unworkable. Surprisingly, a second draft, confined to 'lighting strikes' in essential services as the cabinet had directed, was also rejected by the government, this time without any alternative guidelines. Possibly the reason was that trade unions were now aware that something was afoot and the ITGWU annual conference in June had threatened to fight restrictions on the right to strike. On the other hand, the cabinet endorsed the principle behind the second draft, quibbling mainly with its provisions for the loss of pension and social security rights.

Either way, MacEntee was in a quandary. He still hankered after tough measures, and in August suggested that the legislation be extended to imposing demarcation lines on unions. This was a departure in theme, and it prompted civil service advice for a consultation with William O'Brien. O'Brien had initiated secret contacts with a principal officer of the Department of Industry and Commerce in May, sending him a copy of the Memorandum 1 submitted to the special ITUC conference in 1939. If this wasn't hint enough, O'Brien later forwarded – again 'in strict confidence' – extracts from a speech he delivered to the ITGWU conference in June, in which he warned that the ITUC's inability to reform itself 'was a direct invitation to the government to interfere in their movement'. MacEntee authorised meetings with O'Brien and Tom Kennedy,[13] the ITGWU president, in August. When the Department finally discussed its proposals with the ITUC executive in October, O'Brien had already shifted the content of the Bill from industrial disputes to trade union regulation. Though MacEntee drafted a separate anti-strike Bill, it was never presented to the Oireachtas. O'Brien also supplied his civil service confederates with a rationale for their action, locating the origins of the Bill

---

13   Thomas Kennedy (1886–1947), born in Dublin; became an apprentice portmanteau-maker on leaving primary school; moved to Scotland after serving his time, and joined the socialist movement; returned to Ireland in 1913, joined the ITGWU, and worked closely with William O'Brien from 1917; a justice of the Dáil courts during the War of Independence; elected to the ITGWU executive in 1918 and general secretary from 1946; elected to Dublin Corporation in 1920; a senator, 1934–6, and from 1943.

not in the Dublin Corporation strike, but in the failure of the ITUC commission of inquiry. It was a neat mutual accommodation; O'Brien nudged the state away from coercion of industrial relations, while allowing the government to say it was implementing a trade union agenda. However, he could not claim credit for derailing the initial anti-strike thrust of MacEntee's proposals. Though later to be the source of speculation, his contacts with the Department remained secret; for O'Brien had committed the unpardonable sin of inviting the state to meddle in union affairs.

The published Bill had three aims: to clarify the legal position of trade unions, to whittle away the smaller unions, and to eliminate multiplicity. Part II of the Bill stipulated that to enjoy legal immunity and the right to negotiate for wages and conditions, unions must obtain a licence. This in turn required them to register under the Trade Union Acts of 1871–1935, or be a union under the laws of another jurisdiction, to maintain a registered office in Ireland, to submit details on rules, officers, and members to the Minister for Industry and Commerce, and to lodge a deposit of between £2,000 and £10,000 with the High Court. Part III proposed to establish a tribunal with powers to grant one or more unions sole rights to negotiate for a category of workers where that union, or unions, represented a majority of those workers. Radical as these measures were, the government believed them to be broadly palatable to the ITUC. The tribunal was O'Brien's idea, though he demurred at the requirements for lodging a deposit. Both the CoIU and the ITUC executive were briefed by the Department of Industry and Commerce on the basic points of the draft Bill in late October 1940. Far from tendering reservations, both bodies indicated an acceptance of the legislation in principle. Congress warned its affiliates to expect a curtailment of organisational rights in 1941, but gave no details.

Observers detected no unease in Labour circles when the terms of the Bill were published on 30 April 1941. The feared encroachment on union rights had not materialised. Congress deferred comment to a special conference, scheduled for 16 May. Then, on 6 May, Dublin trades council condemned the Bill outright and started a snowball of rank and file dissent that led the special conference to express its 'emphatic opposition' to an 'unwarrantable invasion of the constitutional and historic rights of the Trade Unions'.[14] Whatever obligation O'Brien felt to defend the Bill evaporated with the untimely promulgation on 7 May of the Wages Standstill Order; given the government's record on price control and its slack attitude to profiteering, this was downright

14   For the reaction to the Bill see O'Shea, 'Government and trade unions in Ireland', pp. 81–123; McCarthy, *Trade Unions in Ireland*, pp. 207–43; and Séamus Cody, John O'Dowd and Peter Rigney, *The Parliament of Labour: 100 Years of Dublin Council of Trade Unions* (Dublin, 1986), pp. 171–7.

inflammatory. The left promptly spancelled the two as a coordinated assault. Yet, if the ITGWU baulked at an endorsement of state intervention, O'Brien's covert sympathy for the Bill was sufficient to dissuade the Congress executive from taking a strong line. The special conference, which widened the agenda from the Bill to the Wages Order, implied that the onus of opposition should fall to the Labour Party. Labour obliged quite happily but, to the Congress executive's embarrassment, the dynamo of resistance sprang from a Council of Action formed by Dublin trades council. The trades council was uniquely placed for united effort as the ITGWU had disaffiliated following its decision to admit the WUI. With no internal diplomacy to worry about, the Larkins led the council's fight against what many suspected, in a reference to O'Brien, to be 'Bill's Bill'.

Critics of the Bill were therefore divided into many camps and two layers of thinking. At one level, there were the pragmatic, focused objections of the CoIU. Contrary to common recollection, the original Bill was not anti-British and the effective riposte came from Irish unions; London's outposts were usually slower on the uptake. On 17 June, the CoIU requested MacEntee to withdraw the Bill, pleading that its requirement for a financial deposit discriminated against the small unions and treated Irish societies unfairly, as the British could borrow funds from England. Liquidating the small fry, of course, was the whole point of the exercise. Moreover, MacEntee's mandarins had hoped that the absence of a pro-Irish bias would be seen positively as a signal that the Bill was not designed to 'nationalise' the movement. In a fateful revision of policy, MacEntee not alone agreed that the deposit might be reduced by up to 75 per cent for Irish unions in straitened circumstances, thereby blunting the impact of the legislation considerably, but explicitly, and gratuitously, redirected the venom of the Bill from the small unions to the amalgamateds. Speaking in Dáil Éireann on 4 June he had recited the familiar case for rationalisation in order to end internecine conflict without apportioning blame to any quarter, in line with government advice to attract the widest possible trade union assent. However, in late June and July he vilified the amalgamateds as the root of industrial disruption, the obstacle to efforts of patriotic Irishmen to secure voluntary reform in 1939, and the source of the campaign against the Bill. When William Norton pointed out that amalgamateds might obtain sole negotiation licences under Part III of the Bill, MacEntee introduced a second crucial amendment reserving such licences to Irish unions. This change of tack was patently intended to split the unexpected resistance to the Bill.

On 22 June – the day the Wehrmacht crashed into Soviet Russia – members of 53 trade unions marched from Dublin's Parnell Square to College Green, where Larkin dramatically burned a copy of the Bill before an estimated 20,000 people. Impressed by the biggest demonstration of working-class resolve since 1923, Norton pledged that Labour would escalate its selective criticism of the Bill into blanket opposition. It was the climax of the campaign. But it seemed at the time as if Congress would be trundled into action against the government. Given the notorious tensions between Irish and British unions – Kennedy's presidential address to the ITGWU conference in June complained that the Bill would not 'confine the organisation of Irish workers to Irish unions' – and the more constructive attitude of the CoIU, the gritty, confrontational MacEntee could not forego a tempting opportunity to divide and conquer. The government would learn eventually that a bifurcated movement was not in its interest.

The 22 June rally bolstered the ideologues. Dublin Council of Action projected the Bill, with the Wages Standstill Order, as the first step towards 'corporative organisations made up of both workers and employers under the control of the Government'.[15] Superficially, this seemed plausible. Corporatism, and its Catholic variation, vocationalism, were voguish in the 1930s. De Valera had appointed a Commission on Vocational Organisation in 1939 to examine 'the practicability of developing functional or vocational organisation in the circumstances of this country'. Comprising 25 leading persons from the fields of industry, trade unionism, agriculture, social studies, and the churches, the Commission collected extensive evidence from voluntary bodies and presented a weighty report in 1943, recommending the creation of six vocational chambers representing agriculture, industry, commerce, transport, finance, and the professions. These in turn would elect a National Vocational Assembly to operate in parallel with existing political structures.[16] The Federation of Irish Manufacturers offered a gothic view of labour, productivity, and economic development in its submission to the Commission. The problem, it contended, lay in the character of the Irish worker, the answer in his subordination to the needs of a fragile, developing economy; a mental readjustment which the British unions militated against.[17]

---

15 Dublin Council of Action circular, quoted in McCarthy, *Trade Unions in Ireland*, p. 209.

16 Commission on Vocational Organisation, *Report* (Dublin, 1944). The CIU later endorsed the report, but with its industrial aspects in mind; some CIU leaders suspected its general thrust as proto-fascist. Whilst vocationalism continued to be championed by Catholic action groups into the 1950s, the public saw it as a relic of the 1930s, out of tune with post-war ideas. See Joseph Lee, 'Aspects of corporatist thought in Ireland; the Commission on Vocational Organisation, 1939–43', in Art Cosgrove and Donal McCartney (eds), *Studies in Irish History* (Dublin, 1979), pp. 324–46; J. H. Whyte, *Church and State in Modern Ireland, 1923–79* (Dublin, 1980), pp. 96–119; McCarthy, *Trade Unions in Ireland*, pp. 116–17, 379–82.

17 See McCarthy, *Trade Unions in Ireland*, pp. 186–9.

One feature of the Emergency labour regime had already introduced an uncomfortable element of moral re-education. Plans drawn up by the Department of Industry and Commerce for labour camps for the unemployed were partially implemented in 1940, in response to the shortage of turf workers. Out of this initiative emerged the Construction Corps. The corps recruited boys, mainly from deprived urban backgrounds, and set them, in army fashion, to work 'of national importance'. It was an experiment in social rehabilitation, as well as an attempt to mobilise labour for necessary but unattractive employment. At its peak in 1943, the corps was 2,000 strong. The concept was badly managed by the authorities and met with dogged uncooperation from unemployed men themselves, despite loss of welfare benefits.[18] Leftists were not reassured by the qualified approval given the corps by the Congress executive, granted after a meeting between de Valera and O'Brien, or by the ITGWU's loan of £50,000 to the state to help it through the Emergency.[19] It all implied a corporatist collusion between O'Brien and Fianna Fáil that made the Trade Union Bill's bias against the smaller unions and the amalgamateds appear sinister.

In truth, there was no connection between the wage freeze and the Bill, no fascist corporatism in government policy, no Machiavellian ploy to 'nationalise' Labour, even after MacEntee's amendments to the Bill; and, whatever the justification for shopfloor suspicions, the Congress executive should have known this or made it its business to find out. Neither was the Commission on Vocational Organisation more than a diversion to fob off the vocationalism lobby. Larkin, who sat on the Commission with three other Labour representatives, never took it seriously.[20] The government received its report coldly; ministers and civil servants opposing its demands for greater consultation with social organisations and a diffusion of decision-making powers. The corporatist red herring caused Labour to confuse a genuine threat of legislative intervention in industrial relations and a policy of wage depression with the question of rationalising the movement. Instead of exploiting its consent to the Bill as a bargaining chip in a power play against the wage freeze, union leaders confronted the rationalisation issue with such ineptitude as to make the government's case for it. O'Brien regarded allegations of corporatism as hypocrisy. The ITGWU remained scathingly critical of Fianna Fáil's 'criminal' record on wages and prices. It had led the charge against statutory control of

18   See J. P. Duggan, *A History of the Irish Army* (Dublin, 1991), pp. 229–30, 289–90, and Bryce Evans, 'The Construction Corps, 1940–48', *Saothar* 32 (2007), pp. 19–31.

19   Other unions loaned lesser sums. An Comhaltas Cána for example offered £500. See John Campbell, '*A Loosely Shackled Fellowship': the History of Comhaltas Cána* (Dublin, 1989), p. 55.

20   Emmet O'Connor, *James Larkin* (Cork, 2002), p. 103.

industrial relations in Éire at the 1940 Congress, whereas the amalgamateds were working hand in glove with Stormont to maintain war production, though wartime regulations in Northern Ireland effectively debarred strikes. Yet this never came before Congress.[21] As for campaigns against the Bill, that was just Larkin stirring things up, again. Outside Dublin there was little street protest. Speaking to the 1941 Congress in July, O'Brien condemned the Wages Standstill Order, but implied that if one could not commend the Trade Union Bill, it should be accepted as an inevitable consequence of the movement's incapacity to reform itself. O'Brien's indifferent, 'take it or leave it' attitude as chairman of the Congress suggested that the old dog was tired of playing games. He had tried to persuade from within. It remained only to let the law, or 'the surgeon's knife' as he put it, take its course. From here on, Congress became of lesser consequence to O'Brien, and the process of alienation was exacerbated by a hardening of opinion against the ITGWU. In a break with convention the 1941 Congress saw a contested election for vice president, with Michael Keyes, NUR, defeating Kennedy by 101–84 votes.[22]

When the Trade Union Bill was enacted, a joint meeting of the Congress executive and the Labour Party administrative council asked the executive to recommend unions not to take out negotiation licences. The party was understandably bullish; the trickle of recruits since the beginning of the Emergency had swelled in response to the Bill and the Wages Standstill Order. Kicking to touch, the executive summoned a special conference in October. The move merely pushed the CoIU closer to the government. To steal some of the conference thunder, the CoIU made a prior approach to the government to amend the Act. At the conference, where London's foreboding was evident in the presence of 23 British delegates, nothing conclusive emerged on the thorny question of taking out negotiation licences. Resigned to his failure to carry Congress opinion into some accommodation with the government, and fatigued with the endless fudge, O'Brien said nothing in the debate, and the ITGWU did not obstruct a motion from Norton for a joint campaign with the Labour Party against the Act. Implicitly, it sidestepped the licence issue. As O'Brien anticipated, the campaign drummed up little enthusiasm in the provinces.[23] Unions were eventually compelled to treat with the Act. Lemass, who resumed responsibility for the Department of Industry and Commerce in August 1941, relaxed the pay freeze on 9 April 1942. Emergency Powers Order no 166 allowed wages tribunals to award cost of living bonuses in certain circumstances. Turning pay restraint from a source of hostility to a lever for

21 ITGWU, *Annual Report* (1942); McCarthy, *Trade Unions in Ireland*, pp. 197, 260–1.

22 McCarthy, *Trade Unions in Ireland*, pp. 207–20.

23 Ibid., pp. 230–42.

compromise, Order 166 recognised licensed unions only in applications for bonus awards. Outmanoeuvred, the 1942 annual Congress agreed nem con to tail the CoIU in parleying with the government. Lemass responded quickly with the Trade Union Act (1942), which made minor amendments to the parent Act and of symbolic importance in restoring a consensual style to Labour-state relations.[24]

Lemass had no intention of allowing Congress to undo the substance of MacEntee's work. Appointed to a cabinet sub-committee on post-war planning with de Valera and Seán T. O'Kelly in November 1942, he envisaged the long-term retention of Emergency controls on labour to advance the 1930s industrialisation drive, and had proposals drafted for a Ministry of Labour to coordinate all aspects of policy, including wages, industrial relations, unemployment, emigration, and welfare services. In addition to the anticipated problems of demobilisation and the return of 'conditionally landed' workers from Britain's war economy, Fianna Fáil were anxious about the impact on expectations of Sir William Beveridge's 1942 report – *Social Insurance and Allied Services* – which became the blueprint for Britain's welfare state; a concern borne out by the enthusiasm for Bishop John Dignan's paper on radical reform of social security. In the teeth of resistance from the Department of Finance, Lemass and de Valera pushed through a scheme for children's allowance payments in 1944. Though MacEntee gave short shrift to Dignan, Departments of Health and Social Welfare were hewn out of the Department of Local Government and Public Health in 1947.[25] Lemass believed that if Ireland could not match British living standards and levels of welfare benefit, it could achieve full employment through a policy of economic self-sufficiency embracing extensive state direction of capital and labour. In placing priority on wages, the unions, he held, militated against full employment. It was no longer tolerable that they should pocket a dividend from Ireland's relatively high degree of state economic regulation without conceding changes in the voluntary basis of labour relations. By 1943 Lemass was thinking of a totally new conception of trade union–employer–state interaction, geared to creating, not redistributing, wealth. Now was the time to entice unions into that

24   O'Shea, 'Government and trade unions in Ireland, 1939–46', p. 138; McCarthy, *Trade Unions in Ireland*, pp. 237–8.

25   See Sophia Carey, *Social Security in Ireland, 1939–1952: The Limits to Solidarity* (Dublin, 2007); Lemass's evolving labour policy is discussed in Brian Girvin, *Between Two Worlds: Politics and Economy in Independent Ireland* (Dublin, 1989), pp. 137–57; O'Shea, 'Government and trade unions in Ireland, 1939–46', pp. 124–92; Most Revd J. Dignan, *Social Security: Outlines of a Scheme for National Health Insurance* (Sligo, 1945). Dignan was Bishop of Clonfert and chairman of the National Health Insurance Society.

framework. Whilst Lemass proposed draconian controls on labour, such as legal restrictions on wages, industrial relations, trade unions, labour mobility, and access to unemployment benefit, his was not the corporatism of the Commission on Vocational Organisation. If Dublin Council of Action's talk of assault on trade union liberties stumbled blindly over a truth, the knee-jerk reflex to defend voluntarism obscured rather than clarified the issues. There was a conflict of interests in a post-colonial, unevenly developed economy between wage militants with a stake in the status quo and those without; the lower paid, the unemployed, and emigrants. Lemass intended to offer something to the have-nots, and to proceed through consensus. The wages tribunals set up under Order 166 were granted approval to link pay to the cost of living index; an important gain in principle for the lower paid. For the very first time, the bulk of workers did not need to establish a bargaining power through militancy. And as licensed bodies alone could apply for bonus orders, the tribunals acted as an incentive to join trade unions, contributing to an expansion of membership to new sectors after 1942.

Circumstances remained difficult. Unions criticised the procedures under Order 166 as deliberately cumbersome. Above all, there was seething resentment at the absence of effective price control. 'No government in Europe,' declared the ITGWU annual report for 1942, 'has done more to depress the standard of living of the members of the working class than the Government of Éire . . . Grave dissatisfaction pervades all ranks of the workers at the unbridged gap between wages and prices'. Labour's most successful campaign of the Emergency mobilised a series of protests in the autumn, and trade union nominees on the tribunals helped to secure over 800 pay awards in 1942/3. Lemass responded on 2 March 1943 with Emergency Powers Order no 260, which made a significant concession to Congress in providing for a further relaxation of pay restraint, and encouraged a convergence of views between Lemass and trade union leaders on mechanisms of wage adjustment in peace time.[26]

Hopes that none would dare invoke the controversial Part III of the Trade Union Act, scheduled to take effect in April, were raised by a short rapprochement between the two big general unions following the appointment of a Congress committee on inter-union friction. In a gesture sympathetic with the ITGWU's well known position on Larkin, the executive departed from custom to list its reasons for rejecting the WUI's regular application for affiliation at the 1942 Congress, citing the WUI's 'record as a cause of disruptive action . . . and a promoter of libels against officers'; Larkin had recently been back in court for libelling Denis Cullen, a Bakers' Union official and member of the executive. Emphasising his solidarity with O'Brien on the point, Sam

26 McCarthy, *Trade Unions in Ireland*, pp. 245–9.

Kyle, ATGWU, proposed that Congress exclude members of unaffiliated unions; a move intended solely to remove Larkin, who normally slipped in the back door with a nomination from Dublin trades council. Again, Congress grappled with the old chestnuts of eliminating multiplicity and encouraging mergers: with the same old results. By 1944, time was running out. Applications had been made under Part III. All were refused. More would follow.[27]

DIVISION

Reaction to the inequity of wartime social hardship, and what looked like a bout of union bashing from Fianna Fáil, reaped rewards for Labour. The party made a breakthrough in the 1942 local elections, becoming the largest group on Dublin Corporation. In the 1943 general election the Labour vote jumped from 10 per cent – in 1938 – to 15.7 per cent nationally, and from 6.7 per cent to 16.2 per cent in Dublin; its best showing since 1922.[28] In one respect, success was to be its undoing. Larkin's role in the campaign against the Trade Union Act had done much to reconcile him with the Dublin left. In December 1941, he was readmitted to the Labour Party and later selected as a Dáil candidate. The party's administrative council refused to ratify the nomination, but only because the absence of two persons gave ITGWU members a majority. With the ITGWU isolated, a breakthrough on the cards, and activists enthusiastic for Larkin, Norton pressed on. Contrary to the rules, Larkin was nominated by the party's Dublin executive and openly supported by Norton. That was the year the ITGWU published the pamphlet *Nineteen Thirteen: Its Significance* without once mentioning Larkin's name, and admitting the unperson to the Dáil party was more than O'Brien could stomach. Immediately, the ITGWU demanded his expulsion. With Norton making every effort to defuse the crisis, the controversy dragged on until 3 December, when the administrative council defeated the expulsion motion 8–9.[29] On 7 January 1944, the ITGWU disaffiliated from the party, and on 15th O'Brien circularised branches with a defence, citing Larkin's ancient enmity to the union, and arguing that his acceptance into the Labour Party was facilitated by Communists. Norton countered with accusations that the roots of the split lay in the ITGWU's

27   Ibid., pp. 238–43, 250–1.

28   For electoral details see Michael Gallagher, *Political Parties in the Republic of Ireland* (Manchester, 1985), pp. 75–6, 109–10.

29   On the split see Puirséil, *The Irish Labour Party*, pp. 101–7; J. Anthony Gaughan, *Thomas Johnson* (Dublin, 1980), pp. 377–8; for O'Brien's view see Thomas J. Morrissey, *William O'Brien, 1881–1968: Socialist, Republican, Dáil Deputy, Editor, and Trade Union Leader* (Dublin, 2007), pp. 334–55.

secret backing for the Trade Union Act, and that the union was acting from 'a thirst for revenge' against Larkin, and 'without any reference to their own members'.[30] These charges were widely believed, and the trouble was perceived as an illustration of how far O'Brien was willing to take his private war against Larkin; even within the ITGWU, officials shook their head in disbelief at Labour being nobbled for an old man's spite.[31] Three of the eight ITGWU TDs refused to resign from the party. O'Brien hastily reshuffled his arraignment. Revising and emphasising what had been presented originally as a secondary reason for disaffiliation, he now purported that his real concern lay with a Communist conspiracy to control Dublin Labour.[32] The claim was echoed by the five ITGWU deputies who sealed the split by forming the National Labour Party, challenging Norton to accept an investigation by 'the bishops or any impartial body'. O'Brien added a second coat of camouflage to his vindictiveness by conniving with O'Rahilly and the *Standard* – correspondent of this Catholic weekly was one of O'Rahilly's many hats – in prosecuting an anti-Communist witch-hunt over the next five months. Norton thought it prudent to appoint an internal enquiry.

There was a pretext for the scaremongering. When the Nazis invaded Russia, the CPGB – the CPI's 'foster party' – was doubtful about how the Comintern's demand for total support for the war could be applied in neutral Ireland, pro-war and pro-British being near synonymous up to that point.[33] In July 1941 the CPI was pressured to dissolve its organisation in Éire – in effect, its Dublin branch – and comrades were told to join the Labour Party and work for an alliance with Fianna Fáil to bring Éire into the war. The liquidation was probably as unnecessary as it was unwise. The party's *Irish Workers' Weekly*, which continued until November, urged the government to barter neutrality for concessions from Britain on trade and cross-border unity. The CPI might have become the home of a small but virtually voiceless minority which disapproved of neutrality on left-wing grounds. Instead, Communists and fellow travellers came to direct Labour's Dublin central branch and its Dublin executive. It was symptomatic of the more tolerant climate generated by the Allied–Soviet alliance that only fanatics like MacEntee were bothered about the entryism. The Communists were few – their Dublin branch had 20 members on its dissolution – and not very radical. O'Brien concocted a confection of old news and half-truths to link them with Larkin. The idea of Larkin as a

30   University College, Dublin, Archives (UCDA), Seán MacEntee Papers, Mss P/67/535(7), P67/535(12).
31   NLI, William O'Brien and Thomas Kennedy Papers, Ms 33718/I(272).
32   UCDA, Seán MacEntee Papers, Ms P67/535(12).
33   CPI, *Communist Party of Ireland: Outline History* (Dublin, 1975), p. 31.

conspirator was risible to those who knew Big Jim's volatile temperament – and who didn't? – and it was common knowledge that he had been at daggers drawn with the Communists since the 1920s. Even National Labour would show little evidence of its supposed fears of Communism, and relations between both parliamentary parties remained amicable. On foot of Norton's enquiry, 17 members were summoned for investigation and six were expelled for attending a CPI conference in Belfast in October 1943. The central branch and the Dublin executive were dissolved. Both Larkins were investigated, but not expelled. Norton refused to regard previous membership of any organisation as a ground for expulsion.[34] The disruption took its toll. The Labour vote sank to 8.8 per cent in the 1944 general election and the Dáil party dwindled to eight. National Labour held four seats, with 2.7 per cent of the vote. As Labour usually suffered in snap, second elections, the real damage was to the party's prospects of capturing the immediate post-war mood for change, and positioning itself to displace Fine Gael as the main opposition in the first post-war general election. It was a disastrously untimely reverse.

The split confirmed the ITGWU's imperious isolationism and prepared the drift of allied unions from the prevailing, anglicised thinking towards a pointedly indigenous labourism, distinguished by emphases on corporatism, nationalism, Catholicism, and anti-communism. This retreat into authenticism was driven too by Northern Ireland's embarrassingly good war. The stark contrast with Éire's proud but painful neutrality was hammered home to Irish unions in the more rapid expansion of the amalgamateds. The former affiliated 80,000 members to Congress in 1944; the latter 108,000, an increase of 40,000 on the 1937 figure.[35] Congress elected Bob Getgood as president in 1943, the first Belfast-based delegate to hold that office since Tom Johnson in 1917, and for the first time since 1918 British unions secured a majority on the executive in 1944.[36] As the bulk of amalgamated membership lay north of the border, there was no real threat to Irish domination in Éire. Nor did the amlagamateds indicate any desire to control Congress. Indeed the true outcome of these trends was the creation of a special Northern Ireland Committee in 1945 to activate the ITUC presence in the six counties. But in terms of prestige, of competition for members, and of the fading prospects for collaboration between Congress and the government to restructure trade union organisation, developments were deeply frustrating for the CoIU. Adding

34   Emmet O'Connor, *Reds and the Green: Ireland, Russia, and the Communist Internationals, 1919–43* (Dublin, 2004), pp. 231–3; Mike Milotte, *Communism in Modern Ireland: The Pursuit of the Workers' Republic since 1916* (Dublin, 1984), p. 199.
35   McCarthy, *Trade Unions in Ireland*, pp. 260–1, 274–5.
36   Ibid., pp. 260, 273.

insult to injury, the reactionary, sectarian Tory statelet of inter-war imagery metamorphosed as Hibernia anti-fascista to tilt with neutral Éire for the moral high-ground. This was too much for the jealousies endemic in cross-border exchange. With little ado, Congress condemned fascism in 1939, but similar resolutions in 1942 and 1943 tread unwittingly on sensitivities about neutrality. Speakers from Irish unions made plain their dislike of taking sides publicly on the war.[37]

Here was the nerve-end of a visceral clash of world views; between the inchoate Weltanschauung of Irish unions – an unprepossessing offspring of their clumsy quest for a Labour strategy geared to native conditions, and all the more techy for its immaturity – and the hegemonic anglo centrism of the amalgamateds. In January 1944, the Congress executive declined an invitation to attend a world trade union conference on the war economy and reconstruction, to be hosted in London by the BTUC. Although the BTUC proposed to restrict congresses from neutral countries to the debates on reconstruction, and the ITUC was invited as a neutral, Irish unions objected to representation at an assembly identified with the Allied powers. When Kyle tabled a motion regretting the decision, O'Brien warned that were it passed, it would be 'the first step in the break-up of this Congress'. Passed it was, by 96–51 votes, and the incoming, amalgamated controlled, executive reversed the decision and appointed two delegates to the London conference, which met in February 1945. Fifteen unions, ten of them affiliated to the ITUC, then resolved that a British-dominated congress could not represent 'the opinions and aspirations' of Irish workers. On 25 April they withdrew formally from the ITUC. The CoIU, together with its new accretions, became Comhar Ceárd Éireann – the Congress of Irish Unions (CIU).[38] The schism hardly ruffled Northern Ireland, where the CIU presence rested entirely in the ITGWU's 2,500 or so members; a trifle compared with the ITUC muster of over 70,000. But the southern cleavage went deep, with the CIU claiming 75,000 members to the ITUC's 72,000.[39]

The split is usually remembered in the way the ITUC would have it, as one between right-wing nationalists, and left-wing internationalists. But the make-up of the rival Congresses reveals a more concrete basis. With one minor exception, the 15 unions that formed the CIU operated mainly in the private sector.[40] They were elements with something to gain from a new relationship with the state; like the ITGWU with a membership potential closely dependent

37   NLI, ITUC, *Report* (1939); ibid., pp. 261–7.

38   McCarthy, *Trade Unions in Ireland*, pp. 272–7.

39   Ibid., p. 277.

40   For a list of affiliations to both Congresses see ibid., pp. 615–21.

on national industrial policy, or like the Irish Union of Distributive Workers and Clerks, with a high proportion of members for whom wage militancy was not an attractive option. The need for machinery 'that will be completely effective in all relations with both of these Governments [North and south] and their Parliaments and Departments' was one of two points emphasised in the CIU's founding manifesto, the other being the right of Irish workers to control their movement, and in CIU eyes the two were linked.[41] British Labour was based on a strong trade union movement in a strong economy, capable of pursuing workers' interests through a voluntary system of industrial relations, and a political agenda through a powerful Labour Party in a party system divided along class lines. None of these conditions applied in Ireland, yet ITUC values took no cognisance of this. The ITUC represented those with vested interests in the status quo; the amalgamateds, who had creamed off the better paid workers in the late nineteenth century and were well situated for wage militancy in free collective bargaining, and who feared that a shift from the voluntary principle of industrial relations would carry an attack on their British roots; and the public sector unions, who had maximised their membership and did not want trade union rationalisation or need a closer relationship with their employer. It was telling that the public sector unions stayed with the ITUC, as many had a marked Gaelic ethos, which, like the civil service itself, they juxtaposed with an ingrained anglocentrism. The ITUC also retained support from unions at odds with the ITGWU or CIU values for their own particular reasons. The Bakers, for example, included Northern Ireland members; the Women Workers' Union nursed an old fear of being assimilated into the ITGWU; and the WUI naturally opted for the ITUC, and secured admittance shortly after the departure of O'Brien. Leaders of each of these unions – John Swift, Louie Bennett, and Larkin, respectively – had favoured an Irish-based industrial unionism until alienated by its association with O'Brien.

Ideologically, the split was a tangle of contradictions. The reformist CIU combined anti-colonialism with an ostentatious association with Fianna Fáil, the Catholic Church, and anti-communism, whereas the conservative ITUC was a little more secular, liberal, and internationalist. How seriously should the ideologies be taken when the upheaval evoked such little shopfloor enthusiasm? In all cases, union executives chose between the Congresses.[42] Most

41 D'Arcy and Hannigan, *Workers in Union*, pp. 209–12.
42 Examples of membership indifference and lack of consultation with members are given in Ken Hannigan, 'British based unions in Ireland; building workers and the split in Congress', *Saothar* 7 (1981), pp. 40–9; Terence Gerard Cradden, 'Trade unionism and socialism in Northern Ireland, 1939–53' (PhD, QUB, 1988), p. 353.

trades councils remained united until CIU affiliates received instructions to form separate Councils of Irish Unions. Inured to the contradictions of a British paradigm and native reality, of a leftish elite directing Fianna Fáil voting masses, of a secular movement in a Catholic society, and of an all-Ireland Congress embracing the Loyalist North, workers accepted that there were things in trade unionism one didn't question. Whilst a treacherous signpost to ideology, and derivative ideologies are usually deceptive in post-colonial societies, the split says much about the inability of Labour to cultivate an organic politics, the want of vision in the Labour Party, and the lack of internal union democracy.

EIGHT

LABOUR IN TWAIN 1946–59

so long as two separate Governments exercise jurisdiction in two different areas in Ireland, as they have done since 1919–20, the Trade Union movement must operate machinery that will be completely effective in all relations with both of these Governments and their Parliaments and Departments. To persist in any other course would be fatal self-deception and folly.
CIU, founding manifesto, 1945[1]

—

Nineteen forty-six is a watershed in labour history. Before the Emergency wages orders, trade unionism was characterised by struggle for survival; not always and everywhere, but basically, success depended on militancy. About a quarter of employees were unionised, roughly the same as when the state was founded. By 1955, union density stood at 46 per cent.[2] The Industrial Relations Act (1946) made unions a part of the social furniture. The Act set up the Labour Court to offer services of conciliation and adjudication in the rush of wage claims that would follow the revocation of Emergency Powers Order no 260. The Court consisted of employers' and workers' representatives under a neutral chairman appointed by the government. In providing for wages orders, the Labour Court made it possible for low paid employees to pursue pay claims without first establishing a combative bargaining power. As the Court recognised licensed trade unions only, it not alone accorded a more secure status to unions, it was a direct incentive to join them. Voluntary reform of industrial relations was taken a step further when statutory wage control yielded to joint agreements on wage levels under the national pay rounds. Like the Labour Court, the pay rounds encouraged a broader accept-ance of unions and the standardisation of rates for comparable employment. Along with the Labour Court and the pay rounds, the economy was the third factor behind the rapid expansion of membership after 1945 was, of course,

1   Reproduced in Fergus A. D'Arcy and Ken Hannigan (eds), *Workers in Union: Documents and Commentaries on the History of Irish Labour* (Dublin, 1988), pp. 209–12.
2   W. K. Roche and Joe Larragy, 'The trend of unionisation in the Irish Republic', in UCD, *Industrial Relations in Ireland: Contemporary Issues and Developments* (Dublin, 1987), p. 22.

economic. The economy recovered at an impressive rate. Industrial output was double the 1943 level before the end of the decade, and by 1953 there were 228,403 people engaged in industry.[3] However, ambitions to keep pace with European economic reconstruction came unstuck in the 1950s. Agricultural output and exports did not match the growth in consumption. Record levels of imports led to successive balance of payments crises. Large budget deficits in 1951 and 1955 were followed by deflationary policies and a credit squeeze, causing economic stagnation and a fall in gross national product between 1955 and 1958. By 1958, industrial output barely exceeded the 1953 level; industrial employment had fallen to 210,324. Unemployment again became a major problem. Emigration reached figures not seen since the 1890s. With the rest of Europe enjoying the novelty of sustained full employment, and moving towards free trade, Ireland's underdevelopment created a crisis of national self-confidence.

POST-WAR TRADE UNIONISM: EXPANSION AND STAGNATION

The Industrial Relations Act originated in a proposal from Seán Lemass in 1944 for a commission of inquiry on wage policy and its relation to economic development, comprising representatives of Congress and the Federated Union of Employers (FUE).[4] Congress responded positively in 1945, indicating an enthusiasm for wage negotiation machinery, but a desire to deal separately with matters of economic development. Following the split in Congress, Lemass confined his initiative to the more urgent problem of securing agreement, especially trade union agreement, on negotiation machinery. He now believed that wage control could not be imposed forcibly, rejected FUE and civil service suggestions for a strong compulsory element in the Industrial Relations Bill, and accepted requests from both Congresses not to grant transitional wage control functions to the Labour Court. Reflecting the greater leverage of organised Labour over the weak private manufacturing sector on state policy on industrial relations, Lemass developed a closer liaison with the Congresses than with the FUE. His ties with the CIU were strongest, and while both Congresses

3   For economic developments during these years see Kieran A. Kennedy, Thomas Giblin, and Deirdre McHugh, *The Economic Development of Ireland in the Twentieth Century* (London, 1988), pp. 55–65.

4   For the background to the Industrial Relations Act see Finbarr Joseph O'Shea, 'Government and trade unions in Ireland, 1939–46: the formulation of labour legislation' (MA, UCC, 1988), pp. 147–92. The Act itself is dissected in R. J. P. Mortished, 'The Industrial Relations Act, 1946', *Journal of the Statistical and Social Inquiry Society of Ireland* 17 (1946–7), pp. 670–90.

endorsed the Bill, the ITUC's suspicion of government intervention was evident in negative speeches from the floor at its 1946 annual conference.

Simultaneous with the Industrial Relations Act coming into effect, Emergency Powers Order no 260 lapsed on 23 September. The 'general adjustment of wages' over 1946–7 came to be known as the first national pay round. On average, wage increases of about 25 per cent were secured as unions sought to make up the ground lost since 1941.[5] Discussions on a second round commenced on 1 December 1947. Representatives of both Congresses met the FUE under the auspices of the Labour Court. On 11 March 1948, the parties issued a 'Joint Statement on Principles to be Observed in Negotiations for the Adjustment of Wages'. Wage claims for men were not to exceed 11 s per week; claims for women were to be 'in accordance with existing practices'. The second national pay round lasted from 1948 to 1950. On average, weekly rates for men rose by 8–10 s, and for women by about half these amounts. Up to the re-establishment of the Employer–Labour Conference in 1970 subsequent pay rounds followed the practice of one or other of the first two. Demands for pay increases mounted in 1950, and talks on a general agreement were opened. As economic trends worsened, the FUE refused to negotiate a new arrangement. Both Congresses then ended their commitment to the 1948 'Joint Statement on Principles', and the third national pay round took the form of a general wage movement. The fourth was partially negotiated, being preceded in May 1952 by an agreement between the CIU and the FUE. Again reverting to a general adjustment, the controversial fifth round brought an upsurge of strike activity and widely diverging wage advances. The sixth round involved a 'Joint Agreement on Guiding Principles relating to Wage Claims', while the seventh emerged from another general movement.

The national pay rounds were a long way from the centralised bargaining of the 1970s, but they marked a decline in the autonomy of local industrial relations. Plant level bargaining continued, but within a national matrix strung together with a new jargon of parity, differentials, inequities, and anomalies. Guidelines of the fourth pay round for example, though endorsed by one congress only, were generally implemented. This process of standardisation in wage claims and wage bargaining, together with the work of the Labour Court and the easier acceptance of trade unions by employers after 1945, initiated a change in the character of unions and branch officials. Their

---

5   The pay rounds are discussed in Charles McCarthy, *Trade Unions in Ireland, 1894–1960* (Dublin, 1977), pp. 539–40, 633–4; Donal Nevin (ed.), *Trade Unions and Change in Irish Society* (Cork, 1980), pp. 160–7; and Brian J. Hillery, 'An overview of the Irish industrial relations system', in UCD, *Industrial Relations in Ireland* (Dublin, 1987), pp. 1–12.

The banner of the Drogheda Labourers' Society dates from the 1870s, but reflects the style of the first banners of Irish unskilled unions in featuring nationalist heroes to emphasise their opposition to the Act of Union, the cause, they believed, of Ireland's economic decline. (Reproduced courtesy of the Millmount Museum)

Bookends of the industrialisation of textiles and clothing in Ulster. Spinning near Bushmills (above) and shirt-factory workers in Derry, 1960 (below). Most workers hated the regimentation brought by the factories. (Magee Community Collection, reproduced courtesy of the University of Ulster Archives)

Old unionism and new: the Parliamentary Committee of the ITUC, aldermanic in waistcoats and watchchains, in the People's Park, Waterford during the 1897 Congress. The President, P. J. Leo, a porkbutcher, sports a cane and cigar.

Unlike the craft unions, the general unions needed a small army of full-time officials to hold them together, creating opportunities for advancement. Here, Peter Larkin tries some poses for a professional photographer, Poole of Waterford, in 1913, preparatory, perhaps, to an intended career as an organiser. (Reproduced courtesy of the National Library of Ireland)

Contrasting views of Belfast Labour. Larkin (above) in 1907, composed and commanding amidst apprehension. Directly behind him in the straw hat is leading Loyalist Alex Boyd. (Reproduced courtesy of Dr Frank Boyd). Unfurling a banner of the Amalgamated Society of Woodworkers in the Independent Labour Hall, York Street, Belfast, 1 May 1935 (below). William Walker is wearing his trademark high, white collar. (Reproduced courtesy of the Trustees of the National Museums, Northern Ireland)

Revolution and reaction. The Bruree Soviet, August/September 1921 (above, reproduced courtesy of the Limerick City Museum) and farmers saving the hay with Special Infantry guards during the Waterford farm strike, 1923 (below). Soviets and the Special Infantry Corps symbolised the rise and fall of 'the red flag' times in rural Ireland.

What to do about unemployment? The Construction Corps, mobilised in Meath, 1942 (above). Labour saw uncomfortable parallels between the Corps and fascism. (Reproduced courtesy of the Irish Military Archives) Dublin Unemployed Protest Committee march, 1957 (below). High unemployment during the Emergency returned again in the 1950s. (Courtesy of Lensmen & Associates, Dublin 3)

Labour history in a frame. International Brigaders pay their respects to Jim Larkin in Dublin, 1991, with the GPO in the background. Larkin, 1913, Connolly, 1916, and the Connolly Column are the few elements of Labour history that have become part of public history. (Reproduced courtesy of the ILHS)

Propaganda for a new left. 'Cher' Guevara, Free Derry Wall, International Women's Day, 2004. (Reproduced courtesy of Jim Collins, photographer, and the women who painted the wall)

operations became more businesslike, more bureaucratic, more taxing intellectually, and less demanding of physical stamina and courage. In acknowledgement of the times, the ITUC appointed a Research Officer in February 1949, the post going to Donal Nevin, and issued the first bulletin of *Trade Union Information* in May.[6]

Although the national pay rounds reduced the likelihood of conflict over wage levels, difficulties persisted, compounded by inflationary trends in 1947 and again in 1950–1 when a wave of price hikes caused by the outbreak of the Korean War led to an upsurge of wage militancy, including a six-week bank strike.[7] Workers also began to use the strike weapon more readily in protest against conditions, dismissals, or personnel grievances. Before the Emergency, about half of all strikes involved wage questions. After 1945, this proportion fell, significantly so in the 1950s. Unofficial strikes also became more common. The frequency of disputes, especially of lightning or unofficial action, and the greater use of strikes over personnel issues, led to calls for statutory control of industrial relations. Voluntary reform enjoyed undoubted success, although the Labour Court's role under R. J. P. Mortished – its first chairman – attracted criticism, notably in 1950. Both Congresses were dismayed when the Court endorsed the FUE's rejection of a joint agreement for the third pay round. More generally, the CIU complained that the Court was concerned more that judgements conform with national pay trends and the requirements of government economic policy, than with assessing each case on its merits or resolving disputes. According to the Congress, 'a large proportion' of its findings were meeting rejection from trade unionists. Wags began to mutter about 'rigor Mortished': Mortished resigned as chairman in May 1952.[8] Economic conditions gave his successor an easier tenure as, with the exception of the opening months of the fifth pay round in 1955, strike activity remained low for the rest of the decade.

From 1945 to 1950 trade union membership in Éire rose from 172,000 to 285,000, with general unionism the great beneficiary. General unions represented 80,000 members – or 46.7 per cent of all trade unionists – in 1945, and 163,000 members – 57.2 per cent of the total – in 1950. The enterprising ITGWU accounted for the bulk of this growth, swelling to an estimated 120,000 members. By contrast, British-based unions expanded marginally, despite significant advance in the six counties, and their proportion of Éire membership fell from 22.9 per cent to 16.6 per cent. These trends, in their different ways, embarrassed both Congresses, leaving the CIU looking like a

---

6   I am obliged to Donal Nevin for these details.

7   For strike statistics see the *Statistical Abstract of Ireland, 1946–59*.

8   McCarthy, *Trade Unions in Ireland*, pp. 540–3.

shoal of minnows tailing a whale and the, still southern oriented, ITUC with 60 per cent of its membership north of the border. After 1951, trade union growth slowed considerably and in some cases was reversed. Having rocketed from 146,000 in 1945 to 211,00 in 1951, ITUC national affiliation stood at 226,333 in 1958. The respective figures for the overwhelmingly southern-based CIU are even more arresting: 77,500 to 170,601 to 187,969.[9]

'A NEW MACHINE IN NEW TIMES'

Up to 1953 the CIU adopted an implacable opposition to unity overtures from the ITUC. Its more rapid expansion raised hopes that time would see it displace the other congress, and the ITGWU rammed home the point with a militant recruitment drive among road and rail staffs, rattling the British-based Railway Clerks' Association and the NUR.[10] In general, however, CIU unions did not use wage militancy as a strategic weapon, but looked to changes in labour law and closer relations between government and unions to wrong-foot the amalgamateds and thereby weaken the ITUC. The founding manifesto of the CIU had stressed this approach.[11] Trade unions, it argued, must be part of a 'new machine for new times', alive to 'a newer and greater power and status' which they would enjoy through a more productive engage-ment with government. A foreign-controlled congress could not be expected to secure influence over state policy, the more so as legislative reform was likely to undermine further the already 'shaky' legal status of British-based unions. That of course was a prophecy which the CIU intended to fulfil: from the outset it refuted all claims of the ITUC to represent Irish workers, and sought to ensure that labour law would favour Irish unions.

Ideological differences with the ITUC acquired a fresh intensity from the Cold War. Although the Communists – who resurfaced in 1948 as the Irish Workers' League – presented no conceivable danger to anything but them-selves, the international climate exerted an immense impact through two world shrinking developments: the collapse of great power rivalries into a bipolar balance of atomic terror, and the more public pontificate of Pius XII.[12] As the first 'media Pope', and a symbol of the global conflict, Pius brought Irish Catholics into the front line. The arrests of Archbishop Stepinac of

9   Ibid., pp. 302, 622–3, 635.

10 Emmet O'Connor, *A Labour History of Waterford* (Waterford, 1989), pp. 275–6.

11 The manifesto is in D'Arcy and Hannigan, *Workers in Union*, pp. 207–12.

12 For Communist politics see Mike Milotte, *Communism in Modern Ireland: The Pursuit of the Workers' Republic since 1916* (Dublin, 1984), pp. 216–38.

Zagreb and Hungary's Cardinal Mindszenty generated huge popular protest. During the Italian general election of 1948, church gate collections raised nearly £20,000 for the Christian Democrats. Over the next decade, indignation was kept on the boil over the Korean War and the Soviet invasion of Hungary, when union branches and factories collected for the 'Help Hungary' fund and dockers offered to boycott Soviet ships.[13] Exceeding opposition to Communism or anger at Eastern bloc persecution of Catholics, a neurotic fear of Communists per se gripped the public, with infiltration theories giving substance and immediacy to an otherwise remote prospect. As the bulwark against this evil, the Catholic Church enjoyed an unprecedented degree of hegemony. Whereas in the 1930s the Church had courted workers with debate on social action, trade unions now sought clerical protection from the red octopus. Facing no social challenge, contemporary Catholic action focused mainly on direction of thought, devotion, and spirituality. Practical initiatives came in education. In 1946, Professor Alfred O'Rahilly introduced lectures in Catholic social teaching for trade unionists at University College Cork, and, with CIU backing, a similar programme later developed at University College Dublin. The ITUC-backed People's College – a title which aroused suspicions of Eastern European influence – was founded in 1948 to offer courses based on those run in Britain by the Workers' Educational Association. The People's College encountered 'massive opposition', and to forestall the extension of secular adult education, O'Rahilly expanded his programme at Cork into a Diploma in Social and Economic Science, offered extramurally to trade unionists throughout Munster, while the Jesuits founded the Catholic Workers' College, later the College of Industrial Relations, in Dublin in 1951.[14]

Legislative reform, the CIU believed, was key to success, and early pointers were encouraging.[15] In 1945 the High Court rejected a constitutional challenge by the NUR against the crucial Part III of the Trade Union Act (1941). Lemass filled both Irish workers' seats at the 1945 conference of the ILO with CIU delegates. And despite vehement protest from the ITUC, the precedent was continued under the inter-party government. Also, the Industrial Relations Act (1946) precluded worker representatives to the Labour Court being nominated by foreign unions. Lemass told the ITUC plainly that while the cabinet had no plans to force the matter, they should seek unity with the CIU through facilitating the voluntary withdrawal of amalgamated societies. For rather

13   J. H. Whyte, *Church and State in Modern Ireland, 1923–79* (Dublin, 1980), pp. 166–7; O'Connor, *A Labour History of Waterford*, p. 288.

14   Ruaidhrí Roberts, *The Story of the People's College* (Dublin, 1986), p. 21; Whyte, *Church and State in Modern Ireland*, pp. 161–2.

15   A detailed account of Congress politics is found in McCarthy, *Trade Unions in Ireland*, pp. 360–412.

different reasons, his advice was taken seriously by two influential men within the ITUC: the veteran Tom Johnson, recalled to front-line service after the split, and ever the voice of via media, and young Jim Larkin, now maturing as the greatest mind of the post-war movement. Larkin Jr appreciated the merits of CIU analysis. The Larkins had long regarded the British-based unions as hindrance to the development of Labour, and young Jim was keen on a new Labour–state relationship. At the request of its Irish counterpart, the BTUC convened a conference to discuss the options on 15 May 1946, where Johnson proposed that British unions confer autonomy on their Irish sections 'in matters affecting public affairs in general'.[16] However, the BTUC made it clear that it would not direct its affiliates on Irish policy, and for their part the amalgamateds saw no reason to budge. On 4 July 1946, the Supreme Court dropped its bombshell; overturning the High Court decision, it declared Part III of the 1941 Act to be in contravention of a citizen's right of free association. When the ITUC opened its annual congress five days later the amalgamateds had their tails up, and Johnson came under fire for his 'defeatism'. In their eyes, the judicial judgement exposed the brouhaha for what it was: an inter-union conflict, prosecuted by the ITGWU par excellence to dominate the movement.

Still the CIU remained sanguine. Ironically, the demise of the O'Brien–Larkin quarrel entrenched its resolve. On William O'Brien's retirement as ITGWU general secretary in February 1946, the succession had passed to Thomas Kennedy, who tended to invert O'Brien's rationale for the split, placing nationalist differences with the ITUC above trade union reasons. Big Jim's death the following year promised to strengthen his son's voice; and young Jim marked the occasion with a moving appeal for unity. Above all, the CIU believed that developments in law and administration would sustain a tempo for an exclusively Irish trade union centre. It proved to be a complacent assumption. When the CIU demanded both workers' seats on the Labour Court, Lemass circumvented the problem by appointing Cathal O'Shannon, secretary of the CIU, and Johnson, from the ITUC, as nominees of individual unions. When CIU unions refused to make joint submissions to the Labour Court with ITUC colleagues, membership opinion caused the practice to be abandoned. Such procedural problems and the CIU's insistence on dealing with government separately were a nuisance to Lemass. If still pro CIU in principle, he became less sympathetic to its arched stance on unity.

The incongruity of CIU and government interests sharpened in 1947 when Lemass unveiled his plans for a new industrial order. It was an exceptionally difficult year, ushered in with freezing temperatures that caused fuel shortages

16   J. Anthony Gaughan, *Thomas Johnson* (Dublin, 1980), pp. 385–6; Matt Merrigan, *Eagle or Cuckoo? The Story of the ATGWU in Ireland* (Dublin, 1989), pp. 128–9.

and factory closures. Popular unease at the erosion of real wage gains by inflation crystallised in January. Dublin Trade Union Council sponsored a conference to set up a Lower Prices Council, evoking a tremendous response from political, social, and women's groups. Some provincial trades councils followed suit, and the campaign later scored a minor success when the government appointed a Prices Advisory Board in January 1951.[17] One day after the Dublin conference the government imposed bread rationing, and on 22 January 1947 Éamon de Valera announced that a state of emergency still applied, with the possibility of greater hardship ahead. As strikes and price hikes continued, there were conflicting calls for statutory intervention. In May, Lemass prepared to use the Special Powers Act to prevent a strike of flour millers.[18] Against this backdrop, he moved also to replace the tattered Trade Union Act.[19] As the law could not constitutionally circumscribe the right to join a union, Lemass aimed to regulate those unions which a worker might join, through an independent registration authority, empowered to deregister any unions acting in a disruptive manner towards other unions. Workers would be given rights of appeal against unions in cases of inequity, expulsion, or refusal of membership. Only unions conforming to statutory restrictions would receive the protection of the Trades Disputes Act (1906). All new unions would require approval from the authority, and have to be Irish based. The CIU pleaded that the proposals did not go far enough in ensuring native control of the Labour movement, but neither Congress warmed to measures that exceeded the 1941 Act in departing from the voluntary principle, and CIU craft unions were particularly uneasy about workers securing rights of appeal against admission to the trade. The CIU did broach one reform of industrial organisation with Lemass. Owen Hynes, of the Building Workers' Trade Union, outlined a scheme for the creation of industrial groups and joint industrial councils within each industry.[20] The group would convene delegates from craft or occupational sections to act as a negotiating body. The joint council would comprise the workers' industrial group and the employers' industrial group. That Hynes's was the only attempt to apply recommendations of the Commission on Vocational Organisation to industrial relations is indicative of the reactive nature of CIU thinking. Now that the Labour Court had improved the position of private sector unions, the CIU was little less suspicious of structural reform than the hidebound ITUC.

17 Séamus Cody, John O'Dowd and Peter Rigney, *The Parliament of Labour: 100 Years of Dublin Council of Trade Unions* (Dublin, 1986), pp. 190–3.

18 J. J. Lee, *Ireland, 1912–1985: Politics and Society* (Cambridge, 1989), p. 289.

19 For Lemass's legislative proposals and discussions with the Congresses see McCarthy, *Trade Unions in Ireland*, pp. 378–84, 546–9; Paul Bew and Henry Patterson, *Seán Lemass and the Making of Modern Ireland, 1945–66* (Dublin, 1982), p. 46–7.

20 Hynes's scheme is discussed in McCarthy, *Trade Unions in Ireland*, pp. 379–82, 631–2.

Lemass still saw the Labour Court as a step towards a national wages policy, and intended to nudge unions along that road with anything short of compulsion. Alarming price rises in August opened an opportunity. As the ITUC threatened a general strike, Lemass first requested restraint. Then he seized the moment to offer unions a prices and incomes policy, with price control to be introduced through the Industrial Efficiency and Prices Bill, Lemass's blueprint for post-war growth. Primarily the Bill aimed at broadening state intervention to promote efficiency in a protected economy. Joint development councils, involving employers, workers, and others, would be set in each industry to monitor all aspects of production, management, and marketing: a rich prize for trade unions, and bitterly resented by employers. There would also be a commission to regulate prices and deal with restrictive practices, and trade unionists would receive strong representation on a related price advisory committee. Discussions with the Congresses on an incomes policy commenced in October, Lemass's intent being to index link future wage increases with the cost of living. These initiatives lapsed when de Valera decided to forestall the gathering momentum of Clann na Poblachta with a general election. Wages talks continued under the Labour Court, and led to the general agreement of March 1948 that governed the second national pay round. Employer opposition deterred a revival of the Industrial Efficiency and Prices Bill by later administrations.

PUBLIC POLICY: EXPANSION AND REGRESSION

Founded in July 1946 under Seán MacBride, Clann na Poblachta evolved from republican prisoners aid committees and combined nationalism with a programme demanding state-led economic development, repatriation of capital invested abroad, and a break with sterling. To many, the Clann appeared as a revitalised Fianna Fáil of 1932 vintage, brimming with the vigour the elder party had lost. Ninety-three Clann candidates contested the general election. After years of austerity, the mood for change was strong, and other opposition groups looked decidedly feeble in comparison. Despite Fianna Fáil's red scare tactics, Clann na Poblachta won 13.2 per cent of the vote, with Labour taking 8.7 per cent, and National Labour holding 2.6 per cent. The Clann's ten deputies were not the breakthrough it had expected, but enough to stop Fianna Fáil six seats short of a majority.[21] Eyes turned to National Labour,

21 Lee, *Ireland*, pp. 297–8; for details on party strengths and general election results during these years see Michael Gallagher, *Political Parties in the Republic of Ireland* (Manchester, 1985), passim. For the Clann, see Eithne MacDermott, *Clann na Poblachta* (Cork, 1998).

now the political wing of the CIU. A special CIU conference had pledged full support for the National Labour campaign, and the Congress circulated other parties on their attitude towards British-based unionism. As Fianna Fáil alone had replied in favour of 'an Irish self-contained trade union movement', the CIU–National Labour Party Joint Committee instructed its five TDs to re-elect de Valera as Taoiseach. To the Committee's disbelief, the deputies joined the combined opposition to form the first inter-party government, pleading that their constituents put welfare reform before the intricacies of inter-union politics.[22] The incoming cabinet allotted the social portfolios to the left, placing the Labour leader and Tánaiste, William Norton, in Social Welfare; party colleague T. J. Murphy in Local Government, and Dr Noel Browne[23] of Clann na Poblachta in Health.

Loans and grants of £46m from the Marshall Aid programme, most of it earmarked for land reclamation, enabled the government to make strides in tackling infrastructural and social development.[24] The inter-party government could justly claim kudos for redressing neglect of public services. Housing was currently the chief concern of Labour Party members, who lambasted Fianna Fáil's tardiness in reviving the building industry after the Emergency. Though the Department of Local Government estimated the requirement of new dwellings at 110,000 in 1948, a mere 1,602 houses were completed with state aid that year, compared with 14,297 in the year ending 31 March 1938. Murphy's quiet dedication surmounted the problems of skilled labour supply, the lack of speculative construction, and the banks' reluctance to loan capital. After his death in April 1949 the work was continued by Michael Keyes, who boosted the number of dwellings built with state aid to 3,418 in 1949 and 12,305 in 1951. Housing Acts were introduced also to increase grants for private construction, loans for buyers, and the powers of local authorities to deal with housing problems. Social spending doubled over the 1947–51 period, and Norton overcame ideological objections in the cabinet to produce the white paper, *Social Security*, in 1949 and introduce a Social Welfare bill based on the Beveridge report in

22 McCarthy, *Trade Unions in Ireland*, pp. 386–8.

23 Noel Browne (1915–97), born in Waterford, which, unforgivably, meant nothing to him; both his parents died of tuberculosis, probably contracted through his father's work for the National Society for the Prevention of Cruelty to Children; with the help of benefactors, he received an expensive education in England, and qualified as a doctor; after expulsion from Clann na Poblachta he continued as a maverick radical in four more political parties; revered by some, usually contemporaries, for his life-saving fight against tuberculosis, and often criticised by subsequent colleagues as embittered and temperamental. See John Horgan, *Noel Browne: Passionate Outsider* (Dublin, 2000).

24 Lee, *Ireland*, pp. 303–6; Kennedy, Giblin, and McHugh, *The Economic Development of Ireland in the Twentieth Century*, pp. 55–6. For improvements in housing see Lee, *Ireland*, p. 309; *Statistical Abstract of Ireland, 1946–51*.

,o.[25] But the disparate political composition of the cabinet also hampered its ἱility to weather a storm, and in May 1951, the government fell. Its position had been crumbling since late 1950. Devaluation of sterling in 1949 and the Korean War had raised the cost of imports severely, aggravating the balance of payments problem. The 'Mother and Child' scheme delivered the fatal blow.

Browne was a star performer as Minister for Health. The sick were accustomed to blaming themselves and feeling a burden. Through imaginative publicity, laced with an uplifting patriotic tone, Browne propagated the novelty that health was the nation's business, and people had a right to proper medical care. The idea found its supreme expression in his legendary crusade against the dreaded tuberculosis. Initially it appeared that Browne's proposals to provide prenatal and childcare were being delayed by objections from the Irish Medical Association. On 30 March 1951, the ITUC executive, dismayed at the widening gap between social services in Northern Ireland and the Republic, called for the scheme to be implemented urgently. In reality, the crucial hurdle confronting Browne was the Catholic hierarchy, and on 5 April the bishops informed the cabinet of their judgement that the scheme was 'opposed to Catholic social teaching'. The cabinet then refused to back Browne, and he agreed to consider resigning. But when an ITUC lobby urged him to modify his policies instead, Browne let it be known to the press that he was open to suggestions. This merely worsened his relations with the Taoiseach and MacBride. With no alternative, he resigned on 11 April. If Browne's prickliness contributed to his isolation, MacBride's handling of events brought little credit to Clann na Poblachta, and the next election crippled the Clann politically. Embarking on a career as the great 'mugwump' of Irish politics, Browne returned to Dáil Éireann as an Independent and supported a minority Fianna Fáil government, which enacted a modified version of the 'Mother and Child' scheme.[26] Labour dropped from 19 to 16 TDs and the loss of power soured party relations with union leaders. Norton resented ITUC pressure on the government during the 'Mother and Child' affair, and complained that his plans for an 'Irish Beveridge' had been aborted.[27] He had cause for frustration. It fell to Fianna Fáil to lay the basis of the post-war welfare system in the Social Welfare Act (1952), and the 'Fianna Fáil Beveridge' was less considerate than Norton's of Labour's favourite people, notably agricultural workers. The

25 John Curry, *The Irish Social Services* (Dublin, 1980), p. 9.

26 For an account of the 'Mother and Child' controversy see Whyte, *Church and State in Modern Ireland*, pp. 196–302. See also Browne's autobiography *Against The Tide* (Dublin, 1986), and Horgan, *Noel Browne*.

27 Norton's attitude to trade union intervention is referred to in Terence Gerard Cradden, 'Trade unionism and socialism in Northern Ireland, 1939–53' (PhD, QUB, 1988), p. 593.

inter-party government had made substantial progress in health and housing provision, employment levels had reached new heights, emigration was reversed, and the population actually increased! By contrast, the next ten years were a regressive phase for social spending.[28] Betrayal by trade unionists at the ballot box became a theme in Labour Party rhetoric. This was not entirely fair and scarcely sensible. Labour's abiding problem lay in squaring its relations with the unions.

The inter-party government had pursued a more even-handed approach to the Congresses. In any case, Lemass's ineffectual successor in Industry and Commerce ensured that nothing disturbed the routine of Labour–state relations. However, external developments intervened to give the ITUC a buffeting. In September 1948, the Taoiseach confirmed that Éire would become a republic. The British Labour government responded with reassurance to Stormont. These moves intensified support for the Anti-Partition League set up by six-county nationalists in 1945. In January 1949, government and opposition combined to launch an All Party Anti-Partition Committee to seek reunification by peaceful means. The Republic was duly proclaimed on Easter Monday. London reacted with its Ireland Act, guaranteeing the constitutional status of Northern Ireland as long as Stormont so wished. Coming from a Labour government, this was indeed a bombshell. Amalgamateds in the North welcomed the Act and played a big part in pushing the Northern Ireland Labour Party to endorse partition. Humiliatingly, the BTUC disdained to pass on to the British Labour Party an ITUC resolution condemning the Ireland Act.[29] It was all acutely embarrassing for the ITUC.

Because trade union division in the south was not really about nationalism, events failed to rumble the amalgamated membership. But they did seem threatening. In his capacity as ITUC president, Larkin Jr appealed to the fragmented movement for a coordinated response. Though some delegates to the CIU annual congress that year warmed to Larkin's overture, others suspected it as a damage limitation exercise and pointed to attitude of amalgamateds north of the border. With time unfolding CIU logic, the ITGWU reverted briefly to a vintage OBU stance, favouring fraternal appeal before coercion to induce workers out of the amalgamateds, and restating the case for industrial unionism. In November, the National Labour Party proposed that Congress unity talks commence on the understanding that the movement ought to be Irish based. Despite the misgivings of amalgamated unions at this

28 Curry, *The Irish Social Services*, pp. 8–9; for a comparison of Norton's Bill and the 1952 Act see Sophia Carey, *Social Security in Ireland, 1939–1952: The Limits to Solidarity* (Dublin, 2007), pp. 250–2.
29 Cradden, 'Trade unionism and socialism in Northern Ireland', p. 555. The impact of events in Northern Ireland is discussed in chapter 9.

concession, discussions opened in February 1950, only to founder on a poaching wrangle between the ITGWU and the NUR. After parallel moves had succeeded in fusing the two Labour parties in June, the search for a Congress rapprochement began again, with the same result. This time, however, 12 Irish unions within the ITUC signalled their frustration by querying the CIU about shifting Congress allegiance. The coming months brought flickers of hope that the British might go quietly. Since the Trade Union Act (1941), the National Union of Boot and Shoe Operatives' executive had favoured a separate union for its Irish sections. Most members were reluctant to terminate their association with the bigger British body, but the executive saw little future for the union in Ireland. In 1951, members in the Republic balloted to form the Irish Shoe and Leather Workers' Union. Against executive advice, Northern branches insisted on sticking with the National Union. Soon afterwards, the NUR voted to withdraw from Ireland, also against the wishes of Irish members. In this instance, cross-border unity was maintained. Most NUR men joined the successor National Association of Transport Employees. At the 1952 annual ITUC the WUI persisted with a contentious motion that other amalgamateds follow suit. Leading the opposition, Norman Kennedy, one of the ATGWU's most outspoken pro-Unionists, made it very plain that the remnant had every intention of staying put.[30]

It was now patently clear that the CIU offensive had shot its bolt. The Congress had done little to effect the recasting of mentalities it purported to champion – ironically it reinforced anglicisation in replicating the ITUC – and the paucity of CIU thinking was painfully evident in the poor calibre of debate at its annual congresses, and the difficulties it encountered in energising its trades councils.[31] The CIU's tactical ham-handedness played into the amalgamated canard that here was nothing more than inter-union rivalry masquerading as narrow nationalism. Neither was it likely, as economic progress decelerated after 1951, that the CIU would outgrow its rival.

Fianna Fáil suffered a particularly dismal term of office from 1951 to 1954. De Valera's orthodox conservative response to recessionary trends depressed industrial output. Unemployment climbed from 50,000 in 1951 to over 70,000 by 1953. In Dublin, an Unemployed Men's Association caught the public imagination with regular sit-downs on O'Connell Bridge, until the Catholic *Standard* exposed Irish Workers' League involvement.[32] Less exotic but more

30   McCarthy, *Trade Unions in Ireland*, pp. 395–412.

31   See for example Cody, O'Dowd and Rigney, *The Parliament of Labour*, p. 199; and O'Connor, *A Labour History of Waterford*, pp. 280–1, 284.

32   Cody, O'Dowd and Rigney, *The Parliament of Labour*, pp. 199–202. For an account of unemployed protests in Dublin during the 1950s see Evanne Kilmurray, *Fight, Starve, or Emigrate* (Dublin, 1988). On Communist involvement see Milotte, *Communism in Modern Ireland*, p. 228.

troublesome tensions developed over the fourth pay round in 1952. When the CIU's central council recommended a 12s 6d per week ceiling on wage increases, affiliated craft unions expressed strong opposition and opened a liaison with their ITUC counterparts.[33] There was little point in having two British-type congresses at a time of mounting strain. Attitudes were already softening when, in April 1953, Lemass urged Labour to settle its differences or face legislative consequences. And the thaw deepened when another of the old guard, Billy McMullen, retired as general president of the ITGWU in the summer. McMullen clung dourly to the old ideal of Irish-based industrial unionism, and regarded Fianna Fáil as closer to ITGWU interests than Norton. His successor, John Conroy, was more pragmatic. Conroy and young Jim Larkin would be the architects of unity.[34]

UNITY IN ADVERSITY

An inter-Congress correspondence opened on May Day, with the CIU reiterating its demand for a wholly Irish-based, Irish-controlled movement. The ITUC accepted that discussions should be 'very largely concerned with questions relating to the interpretation and application of this principle'. This concession was nothing new, for the crux was how one defined 'Irish control'. But now the CIU chose not to press the point. Both annual Congresses that year encouraged the rapprochement, and in September a joint committee commenced talks on unity. The committee presented a memorandum to conferences of the Congresses in April 1954. Technically, the CIU secured its demands for an all-Ireland, Irish-controlled movement. In practice, the memo endorsed ITUC caveats that any restructuring of organisation must be implemented gradually, and with the consent of members directly concerned. Accepting this compromise in its Irish context, the CIU then turned to what it considered the source of its difficulties, and requested the BTUC to facilitate the withdrawal of amalgamateds from Ireland. Once again, the British put their own interests first, and refused to cooperate. To extricate itself from a highly embarrassing situation, the ITUC sought to deepen the unity process, persuading the CIU that appeals to the British would be more effective from a united trade union authority. In June 1955, a sub-committee met to prepare the way for the formation of the Provisional United Trade Union Organisation (PUO) in January 1956, the umbrella under which both Congresses would later be reconciled.[35]

33 Cody, O'Dowd and Rigney, *The Parliament of Labour*, pp. 197–8.
34 McCarthy, *Trade Unions in Ireland*, pp. 403–4.
35 Ibid., pp. 426–47.

The PUO emerged amidst the troublesome fifth national pay round and a profound economic crisis. The 1954 general election had reduced Fianna Fáil to its lowest ebb since 1932. Fine Gael and Labour almost monopolised the second inter-party government, with Clann na Talmhan holding a solitary cabinet post, and the shrunken Clann na Poblachta supporting from the backbenches. Labour received four portfolios: Norton took Industry and Commerce, James Everett held Justice, Brendan Corish[36] moved into Social Welfare, and Keyes became Minister for Posts and Telegraphs. It was not a happy time for Labour. The old economic policies continued. Rising imports and a fall in cattle exports in 1955 led to another balance of payments crisis. Again the cabinet reacted by deflating the economy, introducing austerity measures in February and July 1956. Then the Suez aggression reversed what had been an encouraging growth in manufacturing exports, plunging the economy deeper into trouble. Between 1955 and 1958 industrial output declined by 11 per cent. By now, state policies were attracting widespread opposition, and trade union criticism of the Labour Party's role included the authoritative voice of backbench deputy Larkin, secretary of the PUO. Up to July 1956, the PUO found itself preoccupied with economic affairs, entering discussions with government and employers on the economy in May, when the preliminary report of the census shocked the nation. Two hundred thousand people had emigrated since 1951, causing a net population drop of 66,000. Ireland, it seemed, was dying. The PUO responded with two special consultative conferences, one in Belfast to discuss the disturbing rise in Northern Ireland's unemployment, and one in Dublin, for which it issued *Planning Full Employment*, a programme demanding the maintenance of existing levels of current public spending, a National Investment Board to plan state investment in capital projects, repatriation of external assets, foreign investment, and a relaxation of the credit squeeze.[37] Within weeks, the initiative passed to the rank and file.

On 12 January 1957, as the live register of unemployed swelled to 95,000, Dublin building workers formed an Unemployed Protest Committee, with *Planning Full Employment* as their platform. Whilst five of the Committee's 12 leaders were members of the Irish Workers' League, a palpable sense of

36   Brendan Corish (1918–90), born in Wexford, educated locally, worked as a clerical officer with Wexford County Council, and succeeded his father as a Labour TD in 1945; parliamentary secretary, 1948–51; minister, 1954–7; Tánaiste, 1973–7; led Labour to the left in the 1960s, and back again after 1969; looked resolute, but lacked steel, and was intimidated by the North and by Labour's fractious 'intellectuals'. For a eulogy, see Brendan Halligan (ed.), *The Brendan Corish Seminar Proceedings* (Dublin, 2006).

37   Michael Gallagher, *The Irish Labour Party in Transition, 1957–82* (Manchester, 1982), pp. 29–30; PUO, *A Trade Union Approach: Planning Full Employment* (Dublin, n.d. [1956]).

historic national failure sufficed to make the movement acutely political. As if to amplify the swansong of old Ireland, the IRA had launched the 'border campaign', officially 'Operation Harvest', its last attempt to fight a 1919–21 type struggle, in December 1956. The ensuant crackdown on republicans pushed Clann na Poblachta into opposition, and the Taoiseach went to the country in February 1957. Labour contested the election with little conviction. Unsure of its policy direction or its attitude to another coalition, the party vote slipped to 9.1 per cent, and the Dáil party to 12 deputies. By contrast, the Unemployed Protest Committee scored a famous victory in getting Jack Murphy[38] returned for Dublin South Central. The incoming Fianna Fáil government promised to tackle unemployment and emigration. De Valera declared that one of its first objectives would be to revive the building industry. Having welcomed de Valera's priorities, it was with some astonishment that the trade union movement learned of his budget in May. Huge cuts were introduced in the housing programme. Public capital spending was to be reduced by one third. The removal of food subsidies led workers to dub it the 'famine budget'. Deputy Murphy and two colleagues responded with a hunger strike. The strike attracted huge publicity but created consternation in the Unemployed Committee. It was called off after four days, following PUO intervention. Agitation continued, and Unemployed Protest Committees were formed in provincial cities, but again the red scare struck. Under pressure from Archbishop John Charles McQuaid, Deputy Murphy dissociated himself from the Dublin Unemployed Committee. Then he announced his intention to retire from agitation and concentrate on Dáil duties. The unemployed movement sank into terminal decline. If Murphy would not work with the movement, he was too conscientious a man to pretend he could do anything without it. He resigned from Dáil Éireann in March 1958 and emigrated to Canada. Trade unions meanwhile took up the running, shying away from protest, but keeping the unemployment question in the public eye. The PUO sponsored a conference on the issue in April, which generated much media coverage, but little else. At this stage, unemployment was falling and the economy stood on the brink of a 15-year period of expansion. Government measures to revive the building industry had already removed a core of activists from the protest movement. Trade union agitation abated as it appeared that the worst was over.

---

38 Jack Murphy (1920–84), born in Dublin, son of an active republican and co-founder of the Irish National Union of Woodworkers, which was launched in 1921 as an alternative to the amalgamated unions; joined Na Fianna and the IRA; interned in the Curragh, 1941–5; attended night classes in Bolton St College of Technology to complete his training in carpentry; returned to Ireland from Canada in 1964 and worked as a carpenter until shortly before his death.

The economic crisis had initially disrupted the PUO's constitutional agenda but also reinforced the desire for unity, encouraging considerable progress to be made after July 1956. Twelve months later a draft constitution was ready, and in September the PUO consolidated its authority in negotiating with employers on a joint agreement for the sixth national pay round. In theory, the proposed constitution affirmed that the new Congress would be an all-Ireland, Irish-controlled body. In practice, there were qualifications. The document made clear the subordination of the Northern Ireland Committee to national policy making structures, but to overcome Northern misgivings the PUO dropped a provision that the national executive appoint the Committee in favour of demands that it be elected by the Northern Ireland Conference. A similar compromise resolved the question of British involvement. Participation in the new Congress was to be confined to Irish-based delegates. Amalgamateds could affiliate only in respect of their Irish memberships. They were to leave purely Irish affairs to their Irish sections and create structures to that end. Ten of the 19 seats on the executive were to be reserved for Irish unions. Thus, with minimum guarantees, some of them cosmetic, the CIU secured the principle of native control, whilst the ITUC defined the terms. Equally, the form and character of trade unionism stayed unaltered. If the CIU carried into the constitution a concern to relate trade unionism to national development and a proclivity for a more interventionist role in industrial relations, it was a slim intellectual dowry. Industrial unionism was indeed dead. On 10 February 1959, separate delegate conferences of both Congresses assembled to vote on the final draft. The jaded CIU scarcely demurred. British spokesmen for the amalgamateds put up strong opposition at the ITUC conference. Irish delegates, however, from whatever quarter, North, south, native or foreign, were near unanimously in favour, and the ITUC approved the constitution by 148–81 votes. On the following day the PUO was replaced with the Irish Congress of Trade Unions (ICTU). The CIU and the ITUC were dissolved at their annual conferences in July.[39]

Philosophically, the ICTU's constitution reflected a social democratic outlook. Clause 6(d) pledged Congress 'to work for such fundamental changes in the social and economic system as will secure for the workers of Ireland adequate and effective participation in the control of the industries and services in which they are employed'; a slightly more moderate phrasing than either of its predecessors had chosen.[40] At all levels of the newly spliced movement, a pervasive wariness discouraged a resumption of the old ties with the Labour Party. A vestigial political instinct remained. The referendum on

39 McCarthy, *Trade Unions in Ireland*, pp. 437–75.
40 Cited in ibid., p. 460.

Proportional Representation in 1959 prompted the ICTU to intervene belatedly in Labour's campaign against the 'straight vote', and in December the Congress appointed a committee to 'study the problem of political organisation'.[41] However tentative, such gestures were eagerly grasped at by Labourites attempting to rebuild a party still shell-shocked from the second inter-party government. In the backwash of the 1957 general election, the left appeared to be at a crossroads. The formation of the 1913 Club, a discussion circle committed to the ideals of independence and social justice, suggested a drift of intellectuals from Labour towards 'progressive unity'. Two of the club's associates – deputies Browne and Jack McQuillan – founded the National Progressive Democrats in 1958.[42] Left-wing frustration within the Labour Party boiled over at the following year's annual conference when Norton received a barracking for an attack on Larkin. A youthful dynamo on assuming the party leadership, Norton had come to personify the stolid, conservative, clientelist style of Labour deputies. Now tired and uninterested in political work outside his constituency, he might yet have held on, but resigned the leadership in February 1960. With the election of Corish to the succession, the long night of the 'Norton years' gave way to a pink hued dawn.[43]

41   Gallagher, *The Irish Labour Party in Transition*, pp. 37–8.

42   The 1913 Club was dissolved in 1963 when Browne joined the Labour Party. See ibid., p. 34.

43   Ibid., pp. 40–1.

NINE

AVOIDING THE ISSUE

Politically the trade union movement in the six counties is a study in paradox.
Andrew Boyd, 1984[1]

—

The primary concern of trade union officials is the organisation they serve. The primary concern of their members is their wages and conditions. While this is true of trade unions anywhere, it is especially so in Northern Ireland, where clinging to core interests has enabled a united, secular Labour movement to function in a confessional society among the very people most divided by sectarianism. Historically, keeping contention out of the unions was in turn made possible by the marginality of nationalism, the self-exclusion of Unionists – as distinct from Protestants – and their management by a self-selecting elite, committed to Labourist values. In fact unions were less concerned about divisions between Catholics and Protestants than the antagonism between Labourism and Unionism. With a mainly Protestant, anti-Unionist leadership and a mainly Protestant, Unionist membership, mutually dependent for their bread and butter, but otherwise at odds, they found themselves walking a tight line between their organisational interests and the politics of their members.

Elite control of the trade unions was made easier by provincialism. The provincial character of Northern Labour was already in place by 1920, when, of some 100,000 trade unionists, about 80 per cent belonged to British, 15 per cent to local, and five per cent to Dublin-based unions.[2] Formally at least, secular and Labourist British values hegemonised the unions, and their wages strategy was usually to track British wage rates. Though the inter-war depression and the establishment of a separate administration after 1920 disrupted the trend towards Northern inclusion in UK level wage agreements, partition

1   Andrew Boyd, *Have the Trade Unions Failed the North?* (Cork, 1984), p. 73.
2   Boyd Black, 'Reassessing Irish industrial relations and labour history: the north-east of Ireland up to 1921', *Historical Studies in Industrial Relations* (autumn 2002), pp. 77–8, 92.

reinforced the underlying orientation towards Britain. To minimise the differences with Britain, the Unionist government decided to follow Westminster legislation 'step by step'. Thus, union members had less incentive to become active when so many key decisions on the economy and industrial relations were taken elsewhere. There was also less pressure on unions to develop a collective voice. The North was relatively industrialised. The 1926 census showed the six counties to have a population of 1.26 million, with only about 25 per cent of the workforce engaged in agriculture. Manufacturing employment was highly aggregated. As late as 1952, after decades of efforts to diversify, shipbuilding and engineering and textiles and clothing still employed 44 per cent of insured male employees in manufacture, and 82 per cent of insured females; with men predominating in the first pair, and women in the second.[3] Aggregation facilitated coordination at industry level, and trade union federations covered shipbuilding and engineering, construction, printing, and, later, teaching and the civil service.[4] At the same time, women and unskilled grades generally were badly organised during the inter-war years. Only with the upsurge of general unionism during the Second World War was consideration given to how unions might forge a collective voice and establish an effective relationship with the government. Over the next 20 years Labour would finally address long-standing questions about its constitutional status.

In politics, the left responded to the divisions of Northern Ireland in two very different ways. One was to try to unite workers around 'bread and butter' policies and avoid divisive issues. The other was to argue that social and constitutional change were inextricably linked. By and large, Protestants preferred the first, and Catholics the second. The first approach was tried in its purest form by the Northern Ireland Labour Party (NILP). The early NILP was mainly Protestant, but drew a mixed vote, and took no position on the constitution until 1949, when anti-partitionists decamped to join the Irish Labour Party (IrLP).

THE HUNGRY DECADES

The post-war slump had a devastating impact on Northern Ireland. In June 1921, out of 260,000 insured workers, 65,500 were idle, and 43,500 were on short time.[5] Conditions improved a little after 1922, but the North shared the

---

3   K. S. Isles and Norman Cuthbert, *An Economic Survey of Northern Ireland* (Belfast, 1957), p. 65.

4   D. W. Bleakley, 'The Northern Ireland trade union movement', *Journal of the Statistical and Social Inquiry Society of Ireland* (1954), p. 162.

5   *Annual Report of the Ministry of Labour for Northern Ireland for the Year 1922* (Belfast), p. 18; *Report of the Ministry of Labour for Northern Ireland for the Years 1923–24* (Belfast), pp. 34–5.

depressed state of the British economy in the inter-war years, with an average unemployment rate among insured workers of 19 per cent from 1923 to 1930, rising to 27 per cent over the next decade. To some extent, this common UK experience camouflaged problems peculiar to the region. Almost 60 per cent of the North's workforce was in declining economic sectors; with the exception of construction, a mere six per cent worked in growth sectors. The overcapacity and oversupply created during the World War continued to affect shipbuilding and agriculture, while changes in clothing and lifestyle were consigning linen to the status of a luxury good. The linen trade dipped into terminal decline after the peak production years of the immediate post-war boom.[6] The underlying crisis was concealed by the generality of recession in 1921, a strong demand from the American market up to 1927, and the Great Depression that followed the Wall Street Crash in 1929. Nearly 20,000 linen workers were idle in Belfast in 1930, when appalling levels of unemployment also afflicted the shipyards and engineering. Shipbuilding employed 2,000 workers in 1933, one tenth of the 1929–30 figure; Workman Clark, Belfast's 'wee yard', closed in 1935. Shipbuilding and engineering began to pull out of recession in the mid 1930s, but linen would never regain its former pre-eminence.[7] Government efforts to diversify the economic base made little headway against the propensity of Britain's growth industries to locate in London and the English midlands. Of 27 firms operating under new industries acts in 1939, only the Short and Harland aircraft factory, established in 1937, made a significant contribution to job creation. Nonetheless, the workforce grew by about 12 per cent between the wars, with additional jobs coming mainly in distribution, services, public employment, and construction. Incomes rose by 10–15 per cent, compared with a British average of about 25 per cent, leaving per capita income at 58 per cent of the UK average in 1939 compared with 61 per cent in 1924.[8]

For political reasons, the onset of the slump was made exceptionally traumatic for Labour. The pockets of, mainly Protestant, Labour representation that flourished in mid and east Ulster after 1917 generally sought to evade the national question through 'bread and butter' politics. However, almost all Labour councillors opposed partition, and Unionist leaders detected here a trojan horse of 'Sinn Féin Bolshevism'. In particular, Labour successes in the

6   D. S. Johnson, 'The Northern Ireland economy, 1914–39', in Liam Kennedy and Philip Ollerenshaw (eds), *An Economic History of Ulster, 1820–1939* (Manchester, 1985), pp. 184–223.

7   W. Black, 'Industrial change in the twentieth century', in J. C. Beckett and R. E. Glasscock (eds), *Belfast: The Origins and Growth of an Industrial City* (London, 1967), pp. 157–68; Johnson, 'The Northern Ireland economy', pp. 192–3.

8   Patrick Buckland, *A History of Northern Ireland* (Dublin, 1981), p. 74; Johnson, 'The Northern Ireland economy', pp. 201–2; Isles and Cuthbert, *An Economic Survey of Northern Ireland*, p. 457.

1920 local elections were seen to weaken the case for six-county exclusion.[9] Sir Edward Carson declared on 12 July:

> The more insidious method is tacking on the Sinn Féin question and the Irish Republican question to the Labour question. (A voice – 'Ireland is the most Labour centre in the United Kingdom'). I know that. What I say is this – these men who come forward posing as friends of Labour care no more about Labour than does the man in the moon. Their real object and the real insidious nature of their propaganda is that they may mislead and bring about disunity amongst our own people . . .[10]

Both Carson and James Craig applauded what followed. On 21 July, the Belfast Protestant Association instigated workplace expulsions in the shipyards. Next day, the terror spread. Three distinct justifications were offered: Britain's failure to stop the advance of republicanism, Sinn Féin infiltration of Labour, and claims that men from 'the south and west' had taken the jobs of Loyalists who had enlisted during the world war. Over 7,400 men and women – one quarter of them Protestants – were forced out of their jobs by the end of the year. Others deemed it wise to leave of their own volition. The Protestant victims were likely to be Labour activists. 'Every man who was prominently known as an ILP'er was expelled from his work just the same as the rebel Sinn Féiners', James Baird[11] told the BTUC.[12] D. R. Campbell and Baird, who was dubbed 'Dungaree Baird' for wearing his working clothes in the splendid City Hall and particularly loathed by Loyalists, called a meeting of the Corporation. With Loyalists packing the gallery, they were the only members of the 12-

---

9　Studies of Labour in Ulster remain concentrated on Belfast, but see Jim Quinn, 'Labouring on the margins; trade union activity in Enniskillen, 1917–23', *Saothar* 15 (1990), pp. 57–64. For events in Belfast and the workplace expulsions see Henry Patterson, *Class Conflict and Sectarianism: The Protestant Working Class and the Belfast Labour Movement, 1868–1920* (Belfast, 1980), pp. 115–42; Austen Morgan, *Labour and Partition: The Belfast Working Class, 1905–23* (London, 1991), pp. 250–312; Christopher Norton, 'Unionist politics, the Belfast shipyards, and the Labour movement in the inter-war period' (D.Phil, University of Ulster, Jordanstown, 1987); and G. B. McKenna, *Facts and Figures: The Belfast Pogroms, 1920–22* (Dublin, 1922).

10　*Belfast News Letter*, 13 July 1920.

11　James Baird (–*d.*1948), a boilermaker and 'a pronounced Home Ruler and socialist since 1893'; active on Belfast trades council from 1903; joined the ILP and was elected to Belfast Corporation for Ormeau in 1920; expelled from Harland and Wolff in July 1920; later an ITGWU organiser and a firebrand in the Waterford farm strike, 1923; polled well as a Labour candidate for Waterford in 1923; emigrated to Australia in 1924, and died in Brisbane.

12　Morgan, *Labour and Partition*, pp. 265, 270.

strong Labour group to protest against the expulsions. By 35–5 votes, the Corporation agreed to take no action.

Baird meanwhile helped to form an Expelled Workers' Relief Committee, which turned for aid to Congress and the BTUC. Neither was particularly forthcoming. Arguing that the key lay with the unions concerned, the ITUC did nothing to pressure the British. British officials urged their Belfast committees to work with expelled members, but buckled under a negative response. Only the Amalgamated Society of Carpenters and Joiners took resolute action, going so far as to strike companies which refused to reinstate expelled members. Of its 4,000 members in Belfast, up to 3,000 ignored the strike call and had their union cards withdrawn. In early September, the BTUC annual conference had accepted a motion from an expelled workers' delegation calling on the parliamentary committee to summon a meeting of the executives of the unions concerned to pursue a 'common line of action'. The parliamentary committee then appointed a three-man commission of enquiry which finally crossed the water to Belfast in December. Adding insult to injury, their report deplored the expulsions as one more expression of the Irish tragedy; reason, it was hoped, would prevail. With Belfast sliding into communal violence that would claim 500 lives and 2,000 injuries between July 1920 and July 1922, the eyes of the BTUC glazed over. It now became more anxious about the dispute within the Carpenters and Joiners, would eventually be resolved in favour of the renegades.

Most of the assistance given the expelled workers came from Catholic, nationalist, and Sinn Féin sources. Southern Ireland expressed solidarity through the 'Belfast boycott'.[13] Already, there had been talk of an economic embargo to scuttle 'Carsonia', and a spontaneous boycott evolved in August 1920, before coming under Dáil direction. Congress assisted in its enforcement, and the Expelled Workers' Committee vainly urged the British Labour Party to effect a similar action in Britain, where it might have had a real impact. In January 1922, the boycott was suspended as part of the Craig–Collins pact, in return for Craig's promise to endeavour to get the expelled workers reinstated. When the deal went unfulfilled – Collins repudiated but could not unmake the boycott, while Craig cited the boundary commission as the latest source of Loyalist insecurity – a second pact in March included a British grant of £500,000 for relief works in the Belfast area, one third of which was to be earmarked for Catholics, with preference in employment being given to expelled workers.

---

13   D. S. Johnson, 'The Belfast Boycott, 1920–22', in J. M. Goldstrom and L. A. Clarkson (eds), *Irish Population, Economy, and Society: Essays in Honour of the Late K. H. Connell* (Oxford, 1981), pp. 287–307.

Unionism threatened a permanent anti-Labour mobilisation. Vigilance committees were set up to confirm the new sectarian realities on the shop floor, their leading figures drawn from the UULA. In politics, the British Empire Union and the Ex-Servicemen's Association performed a similar directive role in hounding Labour during the 1921 Northern Ireland elections. The Belfast Labour Party had largely gone to ground after July 1920, but Baird, John Hanna, and Harry Midgley[14] stood with covert funding from Sinn Féin. 'We are completely against partition,' declared their manifesto, 'It is an unworkable stupidity . . . the interests of the workers of Ireland are politically and economically one'.[15] When Loyalists prevented them from holding a rally in the Ulster Hall they folded their campaign. All three lost their deposits, as did a fourth independent socialist – Reverend Bruce Wallace.[16] Nonetheless, reaction could build no enduring alternatives to Labourism. The Ulster Workers' Trade Union, which had been established in 1918 as a loyalist union, operated mainly outside Belfast before the expulsions. Its entry into the shipyards was resisted effectively by other unions, which regarded it as 'yellow'.[17] Even the Unionist Party found its obsequious UULA to be quite useless. As the crisis receded, most of the five UULA MPs elected in 1921 faded from politics.[18] Northern ties with Congress withered in the 1920s, but no serious demand arose for an 'Ulster TUC'. British unions with a substantial cross-border membership continued to locate their Irish offices in Dublin, and Loyalist aggression made officialdom more inclined to maintain lifelines to London and Dublin.

The expulsions had a selective and short-term impact on trade union efficiency. The general assault on wage levels was in full swing in 1921, with 23 of the 27 wage strikes that year being directed against reductions. Though

14   Henry Cassidy Midgley (1893–1957), born in north Belfast; a joiner in the shipyards; served in the 36th (Ulster) Division and published a volume of poetry, *Thoughts From Flanders* (1924); elected to Belfast Corporation in 1920; Connollyite, but moved steadily to pro-Unionism; embittered against Catholicism over Spain; left the NILP in 1942 to found the Commonwealth Labour Party; joined the Unionist government in 1943, and then the Unionist Party and the Orange Order. See Graham Walker, *The Politics of Frustration: Harry Midgley and the Failure of Labour in Northern Ireland* (Manchester, 1985).

15   *Irish News*, 21 May 1921.

16   Morgan, *Labour and Partition*, pp. 260–2.

17   Norton, 'Unionist politics, the Belfast shipyards, and the Labour movement in the inter-war period', pp. 46–7.

18   E. Rumpf and A. C. Hepburn, *Nationalism and Socialism in Twentieth Century Ireland* (Liverpool, 1977), p. 179.

19   Morgan, *Labour and Partition*, p. 283; Emmet O'Connor, *Syndicalism in Ireland, 1917–23* (Cork, 1988), pp. 100–1.

shipbuilding workers opted out of UK stoppages against pay cuts in 1920 and 1922, engineers and printers joined UK strikes in 1922, and local disputes occurred in construction and divers smaller occupations. High unemployment in the staple industries forestalled a resurgence in 1923; but when the decline in living costs bottomed out the following year, militants managed to restore 1922 conditions.[19] Wages fell steadily over the next ten years, before recovering their 1924 levels by 1937. However, the rate of decline was almost exactly the same as in Britain, and wages for craftsmen in Northern Ireland generally stayed above the UK average during the inter-war years. Reflecting the relative scarcity of skilled and abundance of unskilled labour in the region, it was the latter who fared worst, with rates well below the UK average. Equally, the drop in union membership, to a nadir of 60,000 in 1933, conceals a major disparity in performance between skilled and general unions. Excluding agriculture, where trade unionism collapsed in 1920, the proportion of male insured workers in trade unions in 1931 was 40 per cent, little less than the UK figure; in contrast – with women making up 40 per cent of the employed industrial workforce – a mere seven per cent of insured female workers were unionised, compared with 21 per cent in the UK as a whole.[20]

The difficulties facing low paid workers in arresting the erosion of pay levels were demonstrated in the major dispute of these years – the 1933 rail strike. The NUR had conceded a four per cent pay cut in 1931, and was dismayed to find the railway companies seeking a further ten per cent reduction 12 months later. When the companies refused to meet the union half way, the executive reluctantly decided to make a stand. An all-out strike on Northern-based systems began on 30 January 1933. Of 3,478 members called out, 2,765 responded, along with 1,037 'nons'; crucially, the recalcitrants were mainly busworkers. Strike breaking by busmen and railway clerks provoked a violent reaction. A train was derailed, killing two blacklegs. Then the IRA started to bomb transport installations. On 6 April, the NUR executive caved in, unilaterally accepting most of the companies' terms, including the retention of strike-breakers, over the heads of its members. Six months later, there were still 599 NUR men awaiting re-employment.[21] As industry climbed out of the worst of

20 Boyd Black, 'Against the trend; trade union growth in Northern Ireland', *Industrial Relations Journal* 17:1 (1986), pp. 71–80; Bleakley, 'The Northern Ireland trade union movement', p. 158, cites a figure of 56,000 members in UK registered unions in Northern Ireland in 1933. To this must be added about 4,000 members of Dublin based unions; Isles and Cuthbert, *An Economic Survey of Northern Ireland*, pp. 211–21, 613.

21 Philip S. Bagwell, *The Railwaymen: The History of the National Union of Railwaymen* (London, 1963), pp. 523–7; Mike Milotte, *Communism in Modern Ireland: The Pursuit of the Workers' Republic since 1916* (Dublin, 1984), pp. 138–9.

the depression, union membership recovered. By 1937, shortly before another sharp rise in unemployment, there were about 70 trade unions in Northern Ireland, representing approximately 80,000 out of 300,000 insured workers.[22]

The misleading perception of inter-war trade unionism in Northern Ireland as timid and crippled by sectarianism is due largely to its policy failures – for which Congress cannot be exculpated – to confront sectarianism, to transcend sectionalism, to address the problem of building a bargaining power for the lower paid, and to unite as a movement in challenging public policy. Labour–state relations functioned in a haphazard, low-key fashion up to the 1960s. Craig, who was ennobled in 1927 as Viscount Craigavon, liked a personal approach to government, and once described his role as 'distributing bones' to his supporters.[23] Unionists would listen to workers through patronage channels – the Minister of Labour from 1921 to 1937, J. M. Andrews, chaired the UULA – but an open relationship with an independent labour movement was not on. As a linen manufacturer, landowner, and railway director, Andrews was a typical Unionist MP, 85 per cent of whom usually came from the business, professional or large farming classes.[24] Fortunately for the electors, their conservative instincts were circumscribed by the lodestar principle of 'step by step' and an awareness that it was politically desirable to keep social services on a par with British levels. The Treasury, they argued, should cover the financial burden of coping with Northern Ireland's greater housing, health, and unemployment problems. The result was a xeroxing of Westminster policy, with pennies pinched where possible. Civil service unions fought a long campaign before the Whitley process was finally extended to the North in 1945.[25] Whitleyism was also pruned out of trade board legislation in 1923, and the government acceded to employer demands for the abolition of the big flax and hemp trade board. Due largely to this move, the number of workers covered by trade boards was slashed from 115,000 to 51,000, over 80 per cent of whom were in the textile and clothing industries. Stormont showed no desire to keep pace with Britain in extending the system, rejecting a plea for a trade board for linen weavers, in response to a proposed 20 per cent wage cut in 1931, and a similar request from catering staffs, following the defeat of the Belfast hotel strike in 1936. Only one new board was approved in Northern Ireland between 1923 and 1945, on foot of a

---

22   *Ulster Year Book, 1938* (Belfast), p. 163 cites a figure of 75,345 members of UK unions. To this must be added members of Éire based unions. Terence Gerard Cradden, 'Trade unionism and socialism in Northern Ireland, 1939–53' (PhD, QUB, 1988), p. 201 cites a figure of 300,000 workers.

23   Buckland, *A History of Northern Ireland*, p. 81.

24   Rumpf and Hepburn, *Nationalism and Socialism in Twentieth Century Ireland*, pp. 177–9; Brendan Mark Browne, 'Trade boards in Northern Ireland, 1909–45' (PhD, QUB, 1989), p. 227.

25   Edna Donnelly, 'The struggle for Whitleyism in the Northern Ireland civil service', *Saothar* 10 (1984), pp. 12–18.

joint appeal from the baking industry in 1938. Trade board minimum rates, which offered no more than a subsistence income approximate to the local average wage for unskilled labour, fell steadily from 1924 to 1936, and did not recover their old levels until 1940. By then, employees covered by trade board had fallen well astern of the average wage earner, and their counterparts cross-channel, with women faring worse than men. Stormont also declined to follow England or the Free State in reintroducing an Agricultural Wages Board, with the result that when the North's 19,000 farm labourers were brought under the Insurance Acts in 1936 they were almost as well off on the dole.[26] One area where the government was happy to emulate Westminster was in copying the Trade Disputes and Trade Union Act (1927). Aside from some spontaneous blacking by dockers, Northern Ireland played no part in the British general strike which prompted the Act, and unions regarded the introduction of the Act as vindictive. The Act changed the procedure in paying trade union political levies from 'contracting out' to 'contracting in'; thus placing the onus on the individual member to choose to pay. Political strikes were outlawed, and public employees debarred from membership of Congress, compelling the Union of Post Office Workers to disaffiliate.[27] Repealed at Westminster in 1945, and amended in Northern Ireland in 1958, the 'contracting in' stipulation remained on the six-county statute book.

THE LEFT

After its hammering in 1920–1, the Belfast Labour Party regrouped in 1923, with Midgley as secretary. Elated with Midgley's excellent showing in the Belfast West Westminster constituency in December, the party met with delegates of the Confederation of Engineering and Shipbuilding Unions and country groups on 8 March 1924 to found the NILP.[28] Officially, the initiative was taken without reference to the ILPTUC, from which the NILP was, technically, a breakaway. Covertly, Congress officers may have nodded their approval. Luke Duffy and Tom Johnson, as chairman and secretary of Congress, had visited Belfast in February to discuss various issues, including the creation

---

26 Browne, 'Trade boards in Northern Ireland', pp. 221–97; Sabine Wichert, *Northern Ireland since 1945* (London, 1991), p. 22; Isles and Cuthbert, *An Economic Survey of Northern Ireland*, p. 61.

27 Charles McCarthy, *Trade Unions in Ireland, 1894–1960* (Dublin, 1977), p. 80–1; Milotte, *Communism in Modern Ireland*, p. 124.

28 Graham Walker, 'The Northern Ireland Labour Party in the 1920s', *Saothar* 10 (1984), pp. 19–29. Originally the 'Labour Party (Northern Ireland)', the more familiar name came into widespread use in the late 1920s and was later adopted formally. To avoid confusion and minimise the acronymic alphabet soup, it will be used here throughout.

of party for the six counties. In a 'disingenuous' report, they indicated veiled assent to the partition of Labour, noting 'that the trend of [social] legislation' in the Free State and the UK 'would be a powerful influence against national unification'.[29] The NILP's constitution ignored partition. Party strategy was to let members hold their own opinions on the national question, backwater 'non-essential' – ie. constitutional – issues and unite workers around social democratic policies borrowed from British Labourism. In part, this reflected the fact that the problems of cultural identity so dismissed by the party were not exclusively external: the NILP embraced a medley of Connollyites, leftish nationalists, neo-Walkerites, and variations in between. Party unity demanded that the central questions in Northern politics were rarely confronted, and activists became adept at tailoring their message to the religious geography of the occasion. Labour ambivalence was deepened by the introduction of the 'straight vote', in local elections from 1922 and provincial elections from 1929. As Craigavon intended, the system created a grid of 'Catholic' and 'Protestant' constituencies and reinforced the polarisation of politics around the border question.

The abolition of Proportional Representation was directed primarily against the NILP and other elements which threatened to splinter the 'Protestant' vote. Against a background of widespread unemployed protest, Labour took three of the 52 seats in the Northern Ireland parliament in 1925. Independent Unionists too were returned on social issue platforms, and Joe Devlin led the National League out of its parliamentary boycott.[30] It looked as if parliament might become something more than a rubber stamp for Westminster legislation, until Craigavon changed the electoral rules. With two brief exceptions, the NILP was reduced to one or two MPs for the next 20 years, and none at all from 1949 to 1958. It would remain also a Belfast-centred party. Only once did it capture a Stormont seat outside Belfast: South Armagh in 1938, won by default, when the Nationalists abstained. Within Belfast, it variously represented five constituencies from 1929 to 1958; Pottinger, Dock, Willowfield, Oldpark, and Central, none of which could be called 'safe'. Pottinger alone was held in consecutive elections, and then by the maverick Jack Beattie,[31] who flitted in

---

29 UUMC, ILPTUC, *Report* (1925), pp. 104–5; J. Anthony Gaughan, *Thomas Johnson* (Dublin, 1980), p. 278 describes their report as 'disingenuous'.

30 For nationalist politics see Michael Farrell, *Northern Ireland: The Orange State* (London, 1990), pp. 98–120.

31 Jack Beattie (1886–1960), Protestant and Freemason, teacher and union official; 1925, MP for East Belfast; 1929, MP for Pottinger; 1934, expelled from the NILP; 1942, re-admitted to the NILP; 1943, won a bye-election in West Belfast, and resigned from the NILP; 1945, held West Belfast, founded the Federation of Labour (Ireland), took the Labour whip at Westminster, but was expelled from the British Labour Party, ostensibly for being a Northern Ireland resident; 1949, supported the Anti-Partition League and joined the IrLP; 1950, lost West Belfast; 1951, regained West Belfast, losing it again in 1955.

and out of the party. Vital to NILP success in Belfast was the ghetto mentality of the Nationalists. The National League adopted a fairly radical social programme, and Devlin welcomed an alliance with Labour in the 1925–9 parliament. As 'wee Joe' saw it, Nationalists should dominate majority Catholic areas and Labour could have a go at the Unionists elsewhere. This formula gave the NILP the space to win mixed constituencies like Dock, Oldpark, and Pottinger, with a combination of blanket Catholic and radical Protestant support. After Devlin's death in 1934 the Nationalist machine atrophied in Belfast, making life easier for Labour. Important too was Belfast's status as the regional hub of trade union officialdom, from which the NILP drew its MPs; just three of the 13 MPs in its history were Catholics.[32] Crucial as the union input was, it did not guarantee a sound financial or electoral footing. Political dues normally went to London, returning in the form of grants to members contesting elections. Proposals to the British Labour Party for a clawback arrangement were never resolved satisfactorily. The NILP received subventions from Congress in 1925, 1927, and 1928, but otherwise had to rely on unions making special provision for local dues.[33] In the circumstances, it was an achievement for the party to secure the affiliation of about 20 unions initially, and this figure declined in the years ahead.[34]

Up to 1945, the NILP leadership was identified with a series of individualist union officials. Midgley worked for the Linenlappers and then the National Union of Distributive and Allied Workers. Sam Kyle, of the Workers' Union and later the ATGWU, William McMullen, ITGWU, and Jack Beattie, of the Blacksmiths' Society, made up its parliamentary party from 1925 to 1929. Kyle and McMullen took up union jobs in Dublin in 1932, leaving the mutually antagonistic Beattie and Midgley to jostle for control in Belfast. Midgley had become party chairman months earlier. He entered Stormont as MP for Dock in 1933, and saw the expulsion of Beattie, for collusion with the Nationalists, in 1934. Just as Beattie was going green, coincidentally with becoming an official of the Irish National Teachers' Organisation, Midgley was moving in the other direction. Difficult to work with, but a fine speaker and forceful personality, he nudged the NILP closer to the British Labour Party, which was represented at an NILP conference for the first time in 1932.[35]

32   Rumpf and Hepburn, *Nationalism and Socialism in Twentieth Century Ireland*, p. 196; John Fitzsimons Harbinson, 'A history of the Northern Ireland Labour Party, 1891–1949' (M.Sc.Econ, QUB, 1966), p. 295; Cradden, 'Trade unionism and socialism in Northern Ireland', p. 441.

33   UUMC, ILPTUC, *Report* (1925), p. 25; Harbinson, 'A history of the Northern Ireland Labour Party', pp. 49, 55; Walker, *The Politics of Frustration*, pp. 86–7; Arthur Mitchell, *Labour in Irish Politics, 1890–1930: The Irish Labour Movement in an Age of Revolution* (Dublin, 1974), p. 221.

34   Harbinson, 'A history of the Northern Ireland Labour Party', p. 264.

Efforts of anti-partitionists to ensure that external links gravitated instead towards Irish Labour could not offset the mesmeric lure of mighty Britannia; the more so as southerners showed little concern for the NILP per se, and treated it as a subset of wider positions on the North. Some delegates to the 1924 ITUC demurred at the idea of a separate Northern party, and left it at that.[36] In the wake of the boundary commission debacle, Congress was in a more anti-partitionist mood. A policy of non-cooperation was adopted in 1926 until the NILP affiliated to Congress in 1927. Following the separation of the Labour Party and Congress in 1930, a joint IrLP–NILP council was set up; the council was supposed to convene biannually and publish annual reports, but meetings were few and discussions confined to general exchanges of views.[37]

Up to 1930, the NILP monopolised radical politics in Northern Ireland. The Republican movement shared little of the socialism that permeated its southern wing after 1925.[38] An ILP branch existed in Belfast until 1932, when the ILP disaffiliated from the British Labour Party. The branch then reformed as the Socialist Party (Northern Ireland), but continued its role as a ginger group within the NILP. Ironically, in view of their own history, Socialist Party members were mainly Connollyite, and hostile to links with the British Labour Party.[39] A challenge from the far left materialised in 1930 with the formation of a Belfast section of the Workers' Revolutionary Party, soon to become the RWG. As capitalism faltered throughout the western world, Communist agitation on unemployment attracted hundreds of people, especially after the collapse of the MacDonald government in Britain. Revolutionary groups were formed in Ballymena and Ballymoney, and weekly sales of the RWG paper – *Workers' Voice* – topped 1,200 copies in Belfast. Much of this support was ephemeral, narrowly based on unemployed protest, and conditional on constant street politics, which the Ulster Protestant League and heavy policing made an onerous strategy for an organisation with a core of about 50 cadres. Moreover, this was Northern Ireland, a state on permanent alert for subversion. In September 1930, the first of many Communists was jailed for sedition under the Special Powers Act.[40]

---

35 Rumpf and Hepburn, *Nationalism and Socialism in Twentieth Century Ireland*, pp. 198–200.

36 McCarthy, *Trade Unions in Ireland*, p. 69.

37 Michael Gallagher, *The Irish Labour Party in Transition, 1957–82* (Manchester, 1982), pp. 131–2; Harbinson, 'A history of the Northern Ireland Labour Party', p. 54.

38 Milotte, *Communism in Modern Ireland*, p. 126.

39 Walker, *The Politics of Frustration*, p. 60; Cradden, 'Trade unionism and socialism in Northern Ireland', p. 104.

40 Milotte, *Communism in Modern Ireland*, pp. 125–8.

The Ulster Protestant League was founded in 1931 to combat class politics with a 'jobs for Protestants' appeal. This standard Loyalist response to recession was largely successful. Membership of the Orange Order expanded during the slump.[41] Even so, rising levels of long-term unemployment, adverse changes in the payment of benefit in 1931, and the example of violent protest in Britain against the changes, induced an attitudinal shift which caught Unionists napping. Roughly 100,000 people were idle in Northern Ireland at this time, half of them in Belfast. Of the total, about 43,000 were on benefit, 19,000 received transitional benefit, and 14,000 were eligible for the lowest form of assistance, outdoor relief.[42] Outdoor relief existed for married men only, and was administered by miserly Boards of Guardians under the Poor Law. Cash payments were given to men on public works; others received food parcels. The Poor Law reeked of pauperism, and the introduction of a means test in 1931 for those on transitional benefit suddenly increased the number of people under its wretched care. A system geared to squeezing the pips from improvident Catholics now faced humiliating many of its own as well. As the NILP and Belfast trades council thrashed about with resolutions, deputations, and parliamentary questions, the RWG demanded direct action. In July 1932, the Communists helped set up an Outdoor Relief Workers' Committee to seek better pay and condition, abolition of payment in kind, and relief for single people. After months of campaigning, the 2,000 men on Belfast relief works struck on 3 October. That evening, 20,000 people marched through the city in support. Mass meetings culminated in serious disturbances on 11 October when the Royal Ulster Constabulary (RUC) tried to prevent a banned march. Catholic and Protestant workers united in battles with the RUC, who replied with gunfire, leaving two dead, 15 wounded, and at least 19 suffering other injuries. Belatedly, the government had begun to heed the tocsin sounded by Protestant clergy and businessmen. The Belfast Guardians were pressured to improve rates immediately. On 14 October, the Outdoor Relief Workers' Committee hailed a 'glorious victory'.

The outdoor relief strike marked the zenith of Communist influence. The RWG's techy relations with mainstream Labour were further strained by recriminations over the October events. From the right, Midgley charged the RWG with making workers suffer for irresponsible politics; from the left, the settlement was criticised for not including an extension of relief to single persons. Belfast trades council launched a moderate unemployed workers'

41   Ibid., p. 135.

42   The following account of the outdoor relief strike is based on ibid., pp. 128–38; Walker, *The Politics of Frustration*, pp. 61–7; and Paddy Devlin, *Yes We Have No Bananas: Outdoor Relief in Belfast, 1920–39* (Belfast, 1981), pp. 116–45.

movement, and the Ulster Protestant League redoubled its efforts. At the next elections for the Board of Guardians, in June 1933, the NILP won a solitary seat, compared with 29 for the Unionists. It was among dissidents that the class unity achieved in the outdoor relief agitation had some positive effect, as is evident in IRA intervention in the 1933 rail strike, and in the formation of Republican Congress clubs in the Protestant Shankill and Newtownards Road districts of Belfast; there was even a Shankill contingent at the annual Wolfe Tone commemoration at Bodenstown in 1934. Thirty Northern delegates attended the Republican Congress that year, including members of the CPI, the ITGWU, and the Socialist Party.[43] Communist trade unionists won representation on Belfast trades council, and the CPI, as the RWG had now become, continued to unite Catholics and Protestants through agitation on unemployment and housing rents.[44]

Leading Unionists hit back by endorsing the message of the Ulster Protestant League, and the League itself embarked on an escalating anti-left campaign, made more paranoid by the CPI's adoption of a 'united front' line. Both the NILP and the CPI headquarters in Belfast were attacked by Protestants in June 1935. Midgley's election agent complained of the impossibility of holding public meetings since the start of the Royal Silver Jubilee celebrations in early May.[45] When unknown gunmen fired on Belfast's 12 July parade, the powder keg exploded. Three weeks later there were 13 dead, dozens injured, and hundreds homeless. Midgley's own Dock constituency bore the brunt of the trouble, and his restrained and 'balanced' condemnation of events, possibly to avoid antagonising his Protestant electors, alienated Catholics, who were the main victims of the unrest. Midgley's more outspoken defence of the Spanish Republic deepened the rift and cost him the Dock seat in 1938.[46]

The Spanish Civil War embarrassed sections of the Northern left; Beattie, with an eye on his union job and the Catholic component of his vote, kept a low profile. For others, it offered an ideal rallying point. Here at last was an issue on which they could hardly be accused of being anti-Protestant. Unionists took a non-interventionist view of Spain; naturally they had no

43 Milotte, *Communism in Modern Ireland*, pp. 150–7; Seán Cronin, *Frank Ryan: The Search for the Republic* (Dublin, 1980), pp. 56–8; and Macdara Doyle, 'The Republican Congress (a study in Irish radicalism)' (MA, UCD, 1988).

44 Milotte, *Communism in Modern Ireland*, p. 162–6.

45 Ibid., pp. 162–6; Walker, *The Politics of Frustration*, pp. 75–6; Devlin, *Yes We Have No Bananas*, p. 144.

46 For Midgley's attitude to the riots and Spain see Walker, *The Politics of Frustration*, pp. 76–110. Others take a less apologetic view of Midgley. See for example Devlin, *Yes We have No Bananas*, p. 143; and Jack Macgougan, 'Letting Labour lead: Jack Macgougan and the pursuit of unity, 1913–58', *Saothar* 14 (1989), p. 114.

sympathy with Spanish Catholic politics. For the first time, the political climate seemed more tolerant north of the border. Midgley warmed to this novelty and polemicised against clerical apologists for Franco. Belfast Communists gradually swapped anti-partitionism for advocacy of a progressive opposition at Stormont. Munich, and concern at British appeasement of Hitler, gave the anglo-centric left an agreeably non-nationalist agenda at last. Midgley beavered away at projecting the British Commonwealth as a haven of liberalism in a world descending into totalitarianism, much to the irritation of his nationally-minded colleagues.[47] Their first formal challenge to the NILP's 'non-committal' stance on partition surfaced at the party's 1937 annual conference. It was defeated comfortably by a motion on 'internationalism', and Midgley consolidated his position in 1938 with a promise of financial assistance from the British Labour Party to fight the Westminster seats.[48] Sensitive to red scare tactics and gung-ho behind the Economic War, the IrLP also bridled at these developments. Executives of the two Labour parties met in 1936 to review an item in the NILP's annual report dealing with a united front with the CPI. As Midgley was no less anti-communist than William Norton, the problem wasn't insur-mountable. The national question was not so easily dealt with. Though the IrLP's 1936 constitution confirmed the NILP as its fraternal equivalent in the six counties, Norton snubbed the NILP's annual conference in 1938 because of its attitude towards partition and links with British Labour. When informed that the conference had called for greater cross-border trade, the IrLP replied that political unity must precede any economic cooperation with the six counties. Against Norton's advice, Labour's annual conference voted heavily for renewed liaison in 1939, but when the NILP pledged support for the war, contact ceased for the duration.[49]

FORWARD WITH BRITAIN

Northern Ireland had a good war. There were teething problems, and a feeling that the region was not pulling its weight initially. Certainly, the economy's full potential was not exploited under Craigavon and his hapless

---

47 Milotte, *Communism in Modern Ireland*, pp. 169–81; Cronin, *Frank Ryan*, p. 104; Walker, *The Politics of Frustration*, pp. 101–18.

48 Harbinson, 'A history of the Northern Ireland Labour Party', pp. 84–6; Walker, *The Politics of Frustration*, p. 115.

49 Harbinson, 'A history of the Northern Ireland Labour Party', p. 105; Gallagher, *The Irish Labour Party in Transition*, pp. 131–2.

successor, Andrews; 60,000 workers had migrated to Britain by 1945.[50] But war production eventually boosted industrial employment by 20 per cent, virtually eliminating unemployment in 1944. Government subsidies kept prices in check, so that from 1939 to 1944 the cost of living rose by 29 per cent, whereas wages increased by 35 to 70 per cent, with lower paid workers catching up on skilled grades. The gap in living standards with Britain narrowed. Income per capita in Northern Ireland stood at 71 per cent of the UK average in 1946.[51] Attitudes towards social services changed, notably after the publication of the Beveridge Report. London eased the adjustment by approving the principle of parity in social services between Northern Ireland and Britain.[52] At home, the greatest single tragedy of the war, the Belfast Blitz of 1941, created an evacuee problem which confronted middle class people with the shocking conditions of working-class life.[53] Increased contact with London smartened up the slack Stormont administration. Research for post-war reconstruction revealed the extent of public health problems and the magnitude of housing neglect during the inter-war years, estimating the housing requirement at 100,000 new dwellings, or twice that if slums and overcrowding were to be eliminated. In response, a Ministry of Health and Local Government was established in 1944.[54] Public opinion was liberalised also by the war agenda; at this level at least, it was possible to believe that local political values were converging with those of the wider world. Fortuitously, sectarian tensions were eased by the suspension of Orange parades for the duration, and intermittent IRA action and the internment of hundreds of republicans did not discourage Catholic participation in the war effort. On the declaration of the war, Catholics were expelled from the shipyard and textile mills, and Protestants leaving Mackie's foundry in west Belfast were given police escorts. Two years later, Malachy Gray, a 'Falls Road red', was spearheading the shopstewards' movement in Harland and Wolff.[55]

The war brought an immediate extension of state control over labour. Defence Regulation 55 allowed London to direct production, distribution and

50   Walker, *The Politics of Frustration*, p. 121. The official history of the period is John W. Blake, *Northern Ireland in the Second World War* (Belfast, 1956). See also Robert Fisk, *In Time of War: Ireland, Ulster, and the Price of Neutrality, 1939–45* (London, 1985).

51   McCarthy, *Trade Unions In Ireland*, pp. 260–1; Isles and Cuthbert, *An Economic Survey of Northern Ireland* pp. 213–16, 457.

52   Buckland, *A History of Northern Ireland*, p. 83; Wichert, *Northern Ireland since 1945*, p. 41.

53   See Brian Barton, *The Blitz: Belfast and the War Years* (Belfast, 1989).

54   Wichert, *Northern Ireland since 1945*, pp. 41, 47–9.

55   Henry Patterson, *Ireland since 1939: The Persistence of Conflict* (Dublin, 2006), p. 32; Malachy Gray, 'A shop steward remembers: Malachy Gray', *Saothar* 11 (1986), pp. 109–15.

prices throughout the UK. Normal union trade practices were suspended for the duration, strikes were made illegal, and disputes were to be referred to compulsory arbitration. A further imposition was introduced in 1942 with the Restrictions of Employment Order, which regulated the movement of workers between industries.[56] In contrast with the situation in Éire, trade unions cooperated quite happily with the new arrangements, and their block vote also kept the NILP from adopting a policy of non-collaboration with Stormont on defence and campaigning against the Special Powers Act.[57] Eager to push for parity with British wage rates, union members were less compliant and a strong shopstewards' movement evolved to fill the resultant leadership vacuum. Between 1941 and 1945, Northern Ireland recorded 523 strike days per 1,000 employees, compared with a UK average of 153.[58] The biggest wartime action began on 24 February 1944, when 1,200 shipyard engineers struck for a pay rise. By 24 March, the strike had spread to 20,000 men. When the five shopstewards leading the strike were imprisoned, dockers struck in sympathy. As the city near ground to a halt, Belfast trades council persuaded the five to accept bail. Employers then granted a wage increase and the jail sentences were lifted on appeal.[59] Union officialdom recovered its authority with the dismantling of wartime controls, and trade unions could reflect on a satisfactory record of membership growth, from about 114,000 in 1941 to 147,000 by 1945.[60] They were also able to check shop-floor Loyalism. The Ulster Association of Loyalist Workers, founded in the yard in 1942, did not last long. Similar bodies existed in the aircraft and shipbuilding industries in the 1950s and 1960s without attracting much interest.[61]

Membership expansion, the debility of shop-floor Loyalism, and the novel experience of collaboration with the state encouraged Labour to create a regional trade union centre. Northern Ireland had made little input into Congress until the mid 1930s, when tensions between Irish and amalgamated unions spurred the latter to maximise their voting strength. Northern attendance at Congress grew rapidly after 1942 as union membership increased. Timely criticism from Beattie of the ITUC's silence on six-county affairs

56   McCarthy, *Trade Unions in Ireland*, pp. 260–1; Wichert, *Northern Ireland since 1945*, p. 39.

57   Walker, *The Politics of Frustration*, p. 122.

58   J. Boyd H. Black, 'Industrial relations', in R. I. D. Harris, C. W. Jefferson, and J. E. Spencer (eds), *The Northern Ireland Economy: A Comparative Study in the Economic Development of a Peripheral Region* (London, 1990), p. 218.

59   Milotte, *Communism in Modern Ireland*, p. 205; Harbinson, 'A history of the Northern Ireland Labour Party', pp. 165–8.

60   Bleakley, 'The Northern Ireland trade union movement', p. 158; 5,000 has been added to Bleakley's figures to cover members of Éire based unions.

61   Denis P. Barritt and Charles F. Carter, *The Northern Ireland Problem: A Study in Group Relations* (Oxford, 1962), pp. 141–2.

inspired the executive to appoint a special committee on the matter in 1943.[62] One year later, the executive announced the establishment of a sub-committee on Northern Ireland. From the outset, there was evident anxiety to keep the initiative under wraps. Not that Irish unions had any objections to separate machinery for the six counties; the fear was of rank and file Loyalism. The Northern Ireland Committee (NIC), as it became known, was to have six members appointed by the executive, and to be advisory and consultative only. To forestall a debate on its significance, the executive presented the package to the 1944 Congress as a fait accompli. In a rare display of unity at this time, both the ITGWU and the ATGWU opposed a motion that the NIC be elected. However the split in Congress instantly magnified the North's importance within the ITUC. With the CIU having no more than a toehold over the border, the NIC was now exclusively an ITUC concern. The executive soon agreed to raise its complement to 13, comprising the president, vice-president, and secretary of Congress, and ten nominees of an annual conference of Northern affiliates. While it remained technically a sub-committee 'empowered to act for the National Executive in matters peculiar to the Six County area', the NIC gradually assumed a de facto autonomy. Its democratic basis continued to be circumscribed; motions at its annual conference were devised by the NIC itself, and ratified by the ITUC executive, while the absence of a full-time staff restricted its capacity.

The war probed the deficiencies of the Unionist leadership. Craigavon's declining health had already reduced the cabinet to the same perfunctory role as the Stormont parliament. Morale sagged noticeably under the lacklustre Andrews, who succeeded him in November 1940.[63] In 1941, Midgley, standing on a 'let's win the war' platform, and liberally side-swiping neutral Éire, returned to Stormont as MP for Willowfield in a bye-election upset which trumpeted the depth of disgruntlement with the Andrews' government.[64] In 1942, two Nationalist councillors on Belfast Corporation defected to the NILP and Beattie rejoined the fold after eight years as an Independent MP. Midgley's mounting impatience for the party to declare openly for the Union resuscitated old frictions with Beattie. When Beattie was elected party leader in December 1942, Midgley resigned, launched the Commonwealth Labour Party, and later entered the 'coalition' cabinet of Andrews' successor, Basil Brooke. The 'coalition' – Midgley was the only non-Unionist minister – was a simulacrum of Britain's national government, designed to cosmetise Stormont's image at

62   McCarthy, *Trade Unions in Ireland*, pp. 261–4, 316–17.

63   Buckland, *A History of Northern Ireland*, pp. 81–3.

64   For the 'Midgley affair' and the NILP at this time see Harbinson, 'A history of the Northern Ireland Labour Party', pp. 105–31. Walker, *The Politics of Frustration*, p. 123ff discusses Midgley's path to the Unionist Party.

Westminster. Now perceived by many as self-centred and anti-Catholic, Midgley carried few of his old comrades with him into Commonwealth Labour.[65] Beattie too would soon quit the party, again edged out for collusion with the Nationalists. He then convened the Federation of Labour (Ireland), a loose assemblage committed to Irish unity and socialism. Coevally, Harry Diamond founded the Socialist Republican Party, with former Nationalists, IRA men, and west Belfast Protestants associated with Victor Halley.[66] None of this shuffling in the anti-partitionist undergrowth seemed significant at the time. The NILP continued to broaden its appeal, extending its branch network west of the Bann, and boosting the number of trade unions affiliated from 11 in 1941, to 17 in 1945.[67]

The CPI offers the most extraordinary example of the way in which the war conjured a vicarious political culture on the left. Having suffered arrests and suppression of its publications for opposition to the war after the Hitler–Stalin pact, the CPI promptly turned enthusiastically pro-war when Germany invaded the Soviet Union.[68] It also became more partitionist than the NILP, and in this respect matters were simplified by the dissolution of the party in Éire, which left the CPI a Northern Ireland party for nearly 30 years. Throwing everything into their 'second front' campaign, Communists called on the NILP to enter a coalition government with the Unionists, denounced strikes in war industries, and applied, unsuccessfully, to affiliate to the NILP in 1943. Membership of the now respectable CPI had mushroomed to 1,000, little less than the individual muster of the NILP.[69] Most of this support evaporated just as quickly, and the Cold War brought cold times. The party stuck to its partitionist line until the early 1960s, when polemics from the London-based Connolly Association and Desmond Greaves[70] induced a revision. One

65   Macgougan, 'Letting Labour lead', p. 115.

66   Victor Halley (–*d*.1966), a Presbyterian from the Shankill; joined the ILP when it disaffiliated from the British Labour Party in 1931, and helped turn the Belfast branch into the Socialist Party, which was largely Protestant, anti-partition, and anti-IRA; represented the party on the editorial board of the *Irish Democrat* in 1937; clashed with the board over its denunciation of the Partido Obrero de Unificación Marxista (POUM) and sympathy for the IRA; stood, unsuccessfully, for the Socialist Republican Party in a bye-election in 1946; prominent subsequently in the ATGWU; remembered for the aphorism: 'a text out of context is a pretext'. Cradden, 'Trade unionism and socialism in Northern Ireland', p. 165; Harbinson, 'A history of the Northern Ireland Labour Party', p. 179; Farrell, *Northern Ireland*, p. 178, 377n.

67   Cradden, 'Trade unionism and socialism in Northern Ireland', p. 158.

68   For the CPI in the war years and after see Milotte, *Communism in Modern Ireland*, p. 200ff.

69   Ibid., p. 209; Cradden, 'Trade unionism and socialism in Northern Ireland', p. 159.

70   Charles Desmond Greaves (1913–88), born in Birkenhead into a middle-class Protestant Irish–Welsh family; graduated in botany, chemistry and geography at Liverpool University in 1936; joined the CPGB in 1934 and the Connolly Club, later Connolly Association, in London in 1941;

long-term legacy of the war years for Communists was the prominence they acquired in the trade union movement, notably on Belfast trades council and in the Amalgamated Engineering Union.

Socialists held high hopes of the first post-war elections. Figures for Belfast were impressive: the left aggregated nearly 45 per cent of votes cast. Outside the city the NILP won an average 30 per cent of the poll in the seven constituencies it contested. These results translated into a disappointing two seats for the NILP, together with victories for Midgley, Beattie, and Diamond. The Westminster elections three weeks later more or less confirmed the left-wing vote in Belfast, where Beattie won the West constituency; elsewhere the NILP recorded a poor turnout in Antrim and Derry. However, the NILP clocked up a good performance in the local elections in September, winning eight seats on Belfast Corporation, control of Newry and Warrenpoint urban councils, and increased representation elsewhere.[71] Ironically, in contests which the non-nationalist left fought on a 'Forward with British Labour' platform, convinced that the Union would now be transformed into a conduit of progressive values, Diamond's breakthrough in the Falls proved to be the real portend. After 1945, the Nationalist Party decided that Belfast Catholics were too proletarian for its taste, and abandoned the city to a fractious assortment of leftists. In the long run, the Nationalist retreat made way for a new current of left-nationalism in Belfast, and the electoral bear-pits of Falls, Central, and Dock produced tough, self-made political bosses like Gerry Fitt[72] and Paddy Devlin[73] who would spearhead change in the 1960s.

edited the Association's paper, the *Irish Democrat*, from 1948; devoted himself full time to politics from 1951; anticipated and encouraged the civil rights campaign in Northern Ireland; wrote widely on science and aesthetics, and was a pillar of the Connolly school of history. See Anthony Coughlan, *C. Desmond Greaves, 1913–1988: An Obituary Essay* (Dublin, 1994).

71 For contrasting interpretations of the results see Rumpf and Hepburn, *Nationalism and Socialism in Twentieth Century Ireland*, p. 201; Cradden, 'Trade unionism and socialism in Northern Ireland', pp. 165–85.

72 Gerard Fitt (1926–2005), born in Belfast; left school at 14 and served in the British merchant navy, 1941–53; elected to Belfast Corporation, 1958; IrLP MP at Stormont, 1962; Westminster MP for West Belfast, 1966–83; exceptionally important in raising British interest in civil rights; leader of the SDLP, 1970–9; resigned from the SDLP, claiming it had abandoned socialism; attacked the hunger strikers in 1980–1; lost his Westminster seat to Gerry Adams and accepted a peerage in 1983 after his Belfast home was burned by nationalists. See Michael A. Murphy, *Gerry Fitt: A Political Chameleon* (Cork, 2007).

73 Paddy Devlin (1925–99), born off the Falls Road, Belfast; imprisoned for IRA membership in 1942; worked in the car industry in Coventry, where he became interested in Labour politics; back in Belfast he joined the IrLP in 1950, the NILP in the 1960s, and co-founded the SDLP; Minister of Health and Social Services, 1974; appointed Northern organiser of the ITGWU in 1975; expelled from the SDLP in 1977, after attacking it for 'losing its socialist content'; tried to revive Labour politics; made a Commander of the Order of the British Empire in 1999. See *Straight Left: An Autobiography* (Belfast, 1993).

The post-war welfare state brought structural rather than political progress. Unionists were shocked by the British Labour landslide in 1945.[74] With some apprehension about granting the first majority Labour government more control over its purse strings, and talk of opting for dominion status instead, Stormont decided to stick with 'step by step'. The greater peril, Unionists concluded, lay in sinking below Éire levels of public spending. Backed by a guaranteed British subvention, social services improved steadily. The National Insurance Act (1946) and the Health Service Act (1948) provided for social insurance and health care at par with British levels. The cabinet also agreed that wage machinery for low paid workers should be treated 'as part of the social security code', and extended the Wages Councils Act (1945) to Northern Ireland. The Education Act (1947) – modelled on the British Education Act (1944) – introduced universal free secondary education and increased access to tertiary education. The annual rate of housing construction was doubled, enabling the target of 100,000 new dwellings to be met by 1965. But Stormont did not follow Westminster in assimilating the local and parliamentary franchises.[75] In local government, security legislation, and the application of regional policy, the Orange state remained intact. More houses and new industries meant more discrimination.

INDUSTRIAL UNITY

During the 1950s, the population of Northern Ireland increased from 1.37 million to 1.43 million. Economic growth exceeded UK levels. Stormont created 3,000 new jobs each year through external investment in new industries, and the number of insured workers rose from 438,000 to 450,000. But the gap with British income per capita had widened slightly by 1960, and the narrow manufacturing base presented recurring troubles. As the immediate post-war consumer demand abated, the underlying problems of obsolescence or lack of competitiveness re-emerged in the staples. Textile employment fell by 28 per cent over the decade, and shipbuilding, repair, and marine engineering by 16 per cent.[76] With a continuing flight from the land, unemployment climbed to 6.8% in 1955, and 9.3% in 1959. Difficulties multiplied over the next five years. One third of linen plants shut down between 1958 and 1964, with the loss of

74 Russell Rees, *Labour and the Northern Ireland Problem, 1945–51: The Missed Opportunity* (Dublin, 2009), pp. 33–4.

75 Browne, 'Trade boards in Northern Ireland' p. 299; James Loughlin, *The Ulster Question since 1945* (London, 2004), pp. 30–1.

76 Wichert, *Northern Ireland since 1945*, pp. 58–60.

27,000 jobs. In shipbuilding and allied sectors, 11,500 jobs were lost between 1960 and 1964.[77] The impact on the Protestant working class led to the NILP's most serious challenge to the Unionist Party. Though confidently ahead of the Republic in living standards and social services, the electorate were beginning to expect parity with Britain, the more so as, unlike the inter-war years, Northern Ireland was no longer one of a number of depressed pockets of the UK; it was the only region suffering high unemployment. In parity lay an argument that would prove to be the regime's undoing.

Trade union membership continued to consolidate after 1945, reaching 200,000 by 1953. Strike activity declined in the 1945–51 period, but remained well above the UK average.[78] The composition of the movement was still predominantly male – 80 per cent – manual, and manufacturing, though the proportion of insured women workers was double the pre-war figure at 20 per cent, and white-collar unionism was growing with the health and education services. Reflecting the rapid strides of general unionism over the previous decade, the ATGWU made up 73,000 of the 1953 total. The sizable craft sector included 30 unions with 52,000 members, the largest being the Amalgamated Engineering Union. Out of 92 unions in all, 18 were local, with 27,000 members; for a variety of reasons – size, insularity, politics, or legal restrictions in the case of civil service associations – they took little interest in the wider movement. A mere five unions, with 8,700 members, were Dublin based.[79] The NIC's inaugural conference in November 1945 convened 41 delegates from 19 unions and Belfast trades council.[80] Three functions were adopted for its remit; to discuss industrial and economic questions, excluding politics, except in so far as it affected trade unionists; to promote trades councils; and to obtain a formal recognition from the government of its status as the 'representative organ of the trade unions operating in Northern Ireland'. Its immediate task however, was to secure recognition from local branches of the trade union federations, the pillars of the hitherto disparate Northern movement, and in this it encountered surprisingly little resistance. Equally, it persuaded most unions to affiliate to the ITUC – 90 per cent of members were in affiliation with the Congresses in 1953 – the only active resistance coming

77   Buckland, *A History of Northern Ireland*, p. 94.

78   Bleakley, 'The Northern Ireland trade union movement', p. 158; Black, 'Industrial relations', p. 220.

79   Bleakley, 'The Northern Ireland trade union movement', pp. 158–64; Isles and Cuthbert, *An Economic Survey of Northern Ireland*, pp. 211–12.

80   For the NIC and its relations with Stormont see McCarthy, *Trade Unions in Ireland*, pp. 320–49; Cradden, 'Trade unionism and socialism in Northern Ireland', pp. 423–89; and Boyd, *Have the Trade Unions Failed the North?* for a more sceptical view.

from two 'Ulster' societies, the Ulster Teachers' Union and the Ulster Transport and Allied Operatives' Union. Further successes were scored in building up Labour's profile beyond its traditional Belfast stomping ground. The number of trades councils in Northern Ireland rose from two in 1945 to 11 in 1955, including one in Ballymena which declined to affiliate to the NIC on the ground that it answered to a foreign congress.[81]

How did they do it, at a time when the national question was dividing the two Congresses and the NILP, and Stormont was refusing to recognise the NIC and calling for an 'Ulster TUC'? The hegemony of the amalgamateds and their interest in maintaining a presence in Éire, scepticism about 'Ulster' trade unionism and fear of shop-floor Loyalism, and southern reluctance to engage with the North, all combined to ballast the status quo. The contentions actually reinforced the equilibrium. The heave against the ITUC in Éire strengthened Northern commitment to the cross-border link, Stormont backing was a kiss of death for an 'Ulster TUC', and nationalists found that they had bitten off more than they could chew. The difficulty of rocking the boat is illustrated by the two most disruptive developments during these years. Formed in 1945 by busworkers unhappy with the ATGWU, the Ulster Transport and Allied Operatives' Union was an assertion of rank and file democracy with a Loyalist undertow, and led by Hugh Geddis, sometime Unionist councillor in Newtownabbey. Much to the concern of the NIC, it grew to 8,000 members, mainly in public transport. But other unions isolated it, ostensibly for poaching; in one instance they boycotted a national insurance court of referees because an Ulster Transport member sat on the bench. In 1954, Geddis merged his union and took a job with the National Union of General and Municipal Workers.[82] The limits of nationalist Labourism were exposed in a Derry shirt tale. Frustrated with the National Union of Tailors and Garment Workers, the Derry branch secretary, Stephen McGonagle,[83] launched the Clothing Workers' Union in 1952. About 3,500 workers joined up. One year later the Clothing Workers' Union merged with the ITGWU.

81   Bleakley, 'The Northern Ireland trade union movement', p. 163; Cradden, 'Trade unionism and socialism in Northern Ireland', p. 432.

82   Cradden, 'Trade unionism and socialism in Northern Ireland', pp. 154, 208, 433; Bleakley, 'The Northern Ireland trade union movement', p. 160.

83   Stephen McGonagle (1914–2002), born in Derry, son of an activist in the Plumbing Trades Union; followed his father into the trade; appointed an official of the National Union of Tailors and Garment Makers in 1947, and the ITGWU in 1954; declined to join the civil rights movement, and served on the NIC and in several public roles, notably as Ombudsman, 1974–9, and in Seanad Éireann, 1983–7; variously remembered as a nationalist splittist, an 'Uncle Tom', or a constructive moderate, he refused an OBE. See Stephen McGonagle, 'Navigating a lone channel: Stephen McGonagle, trade unionism and Labour politics in Derry, 1914–97', *Saothar* 22 (1997), pp. 139–52.

Protestant women who had defected to the Clothing Workers' reverted to the National Union of Tailors and Garment Makers, and ensuant inter-union friction had an unavoidably sectarian flavour. McGonagle came to doubt his once ardent Irish Labourism. The ITGWU made little of what amounted to the biggest transfer of members from a British to an Irish union in the history of Northern Ireland, and the chance to lead Labour in the North's second city; and McGonagle's experience of the CIU led him to the conclusion that it had no practical policy for what it termed 'The Occupied Area' and lacked the ITUC's 'sophistication' on the North. He left the IrLP, and resolved to concentrate on union work and 'make Northern Ireland a viable proposition' in the belief that it was the only way to avoid a sectarian divide in trade unionism.[84]

The 'foreign congress' argument became the great stumbling block for the NIC in its attempts to nurse a working relationship with Stormont. Sensitive of Unionist mistrust of Labour, the NIC opted to pursue recognition on an ad hoc basis. Early signals were mixed: some queries were responded to, and contacts remained friendly, but in 1947 the Minister of Labour advised the NIC to create a Northern Ireland congress. By 1948, only the Health Ministry gave any indication of acknowledging the NIC's status. The crunch came in 1950 when the Minister of Labour – now Major Ivan Neill – rebuffed appeals for consultation on the Employment and Training Bill. Neill was happy to deal with UK trade unions, but not with a body headquartered in a foreign country. The ITUC rallied the trade union federations to pledge non-cooperation with schemes set up under the Employment and Training Act, and Neill swung the cabinet behind him. By February 1951, the skirmishing had escalated into an open stand off. Again the ITUC sought to intensify trade union non-cooperation: this time the unions said no. Yet despite a reluctance to confront the government, affiliates stood squarely behind the NIC in a selective boycott of the administration. Perversely, the government infuriated the unions in refusing to follow Westminster in repealing the Trade Disputes and Trade Union Act (1927). The imperative of cultivating efficient Labour–state relations against a background of rising unemployment and a dawning realisation of the need to modernise Northern Ireland's ageing industrial base gradually isolated the government. The cabinet's obduracy was highlighted in 1955 when it established an Industrial Development Council – the Chandos Council – without consulting the NIC, and the NIC kept up the pressure by convening a major conference on the economy the following year. By the end of the decade, both the Protestant churches and the business community were urging a compromise.

---

84 Eithne McLaughlin, 'Women and work in Derry City: a survey', *Saothar* 14 (1989), p. 39; Andrew Finlay, 'Trade unionism and sectarianism among Derry shirt workers' (PhD, University of London, 1989); McGonagle, 'Navigating a lone channel', pp. 139–52.

Congress unity moves in the Republic complicated the NIC's position. However, Unionist hopes that the process would provoke an 'Ulster TUC' never looked like being fulfilled. Northern participation in the ITUC increased in the 1950s. A Belfast-based president was elected in 1953, Northern business featured more on the agenda of annual congresses, and the jealousies that plagued cross-border debate during the Emergency yielded to a pointed amity. Labour leaders were keen to carry the North with them into the new dispensation, as well they might be since it accounted for 60 per cent of the ITUC affiliation.[85] In February 1956 the newly inaugurated PUO briefed union officials, the NIC, and the federations in Belfast. The NIC received a full-time official in 1957, and the PUO later acceded to demands that the ICTU constitution allow the NIC to be elected. Of course the constitution's provisions for guaranteed Irish control of Congress did not pass without criticism, notably from the Amalgamated Engineering Union, and they reinforced Unionist antipathy to the NIC. With the formation of the ICTU, Northern affiliates were more firmly embedded in an all-Ireland framework, while southerners accepted Northern realities.

Thus, between 1944 and 1959, trade unions finally settled long-standing contentions about Irish–British and North–south relations. The one missing piece of the constitutional jigsaw was recognition from Stormont. Terence O'Neill continued Brooke's policy initially. In 1963 Unionists launched the Ulster Trade Union Alliance. Within months the Alliance had 1,200 members, and planned to create an Ulster Workers' Union, which would affiliate to the BTUC, and pursue moderation in industrial relations. The UULA was also revitalised. With an eye on the growth of the NILP, O'Neill presented a 'workers' charter' in his first Queen's speech. Once again, Labour Unionism faltered. O'Neill's modernisation project gave the NIC its chance. One of the engines of modernisation was to be the Northern Ireland Economic Council, a tripartite committee of government, employer, and worker representatives to replace the embarrassingly ineffective Chandos Council. When the government rejected an NIC nominee, trade unions boycotted the Council. Under pressure from employers, and apprehensive about the consequences of a Labour victory in the upcoming general election in Britain, the parliamentary Unionist Party assented to recognition in June 1964.[86] It seemed that if unions could not challenge Unionism politically, Unionists could not best trade unions in the industrial field.

85   Bleakley, 'The Northern Ireland trade union movement', p. 163.

86   Marc Mulholland, *Northern Ireland at the Crossroads: Ulster Unionism in the O'Neill Years, 1960–9* (London, 2000), pp. 43–4.

POLITICAL DIVISION

Jubilant at the election of a Labour government at Westminster, the NILP entered the post-war era in good heart. The Labour triumph encouraged it to extend the 'forward with Britain' line to emphasis on the anomalies of the Unionist state.[87] In addition to its perennial concern with bread and butter issues, the party enlisted NIC support to solicit the British Home Secretary to repeal the Special Powers Act, the Trade Unions and Trade Disputes Act, and the Franchise Act. The NILP's concern with civil rights reached a peak at its 1947 annual conference, which called for the disbandment of the B Specials. Clement Attlee's government, of course, upheld the 'Speaker's convention' that the use of powers devolved to Northern Ireland should not be discussed at Westminster. The limits of anglo-centrism were exposed too, in a rather different way, by the Friends of Ireland – a caucus of some 30 Labour MPs – formed in 1945 to raise six-county grievances and marshal Labour parties in all three jurisdictions behind a united Ireland policy. Initially, the Friends attached some importance to the NILP. Speakers from the caucus persuaded British Labour to assist the NILP in the County Down Westminster bye-election in 1946. This rapport was soon overshadowed by an alliance between the Friends and the Anti-Partition League. Given the legacy of the war years, the widening gap in welfare provision and living standards between Northern Ireland and Éire, and the split in Congress, there could hardly have been a less propitious time to launch an anti-partition campaign, and Labourites in all jurisdictions were prone to the same counterproductive policies as the League. The Friends merely uncovered pro-Union sentiment in both the NILP and the British government, where some senior figures, notably Herbert Morrison, nursed bitter memories of Irish neutrality.[88]

Once the association of the Friends with the League became more prominent, pro-Union elements in the NILP objected. They had their own bandwaggon already rolling. Affiliated unions were particularly anxious to lock the North within the UK in view of anti-amalgamated feeling in Éire. Anti-partitionists tried to halt the momentum. Under the chairmanship of

87 For the pro-Union perspective see Aaron Edwards, *A History of the Northern Ireland Labour Party: Democratic Socialism and Sectarianism* (Manchester, 2009).

88 For the events that led to the NILP split see also Bob Purdie, 'The Friends of Ireland; British Labour and Irish nationalism, 1945–9', in Tom Gallagher and James O'Connell (eds), *Contemporary Irish Studies* (Manchester, 1983), pp. 81–94; Harbinson, 'A history of the Northern Ireland Labour Party', pp. 190–235, and Cradden, 'Trade unionism and socialism in Northern Ireland', pp. 439–43; 510–42.

Jack Macgougan,[89] the NILP opened relations with the ITUC and activated the 'Waterford agreement', a joint machinery constructed with the IrLP in 1939. This was soon balanced by financial aid and the secondment of a full-time agent from the British Labour Party in mid 1948. Macgougan reflected the frustration of the anti-partitionists: '[He] got off the Heysham boat at eight o'clock that morning and said that "In the time I've been here I can see no difference between [Belfast] and Yorkshire except the policemen carry guns". So far as I was concerned he was a bit of a nit from then on'.[90] For a time it seemed as if the centre might hold. The Irish government's proposed declaration of a republic was countered by Attlee's assurance 'that no change should be made in the constitutional status of Northern Ireland without Northern Ireland's full consent'. Those in the NILP who favoured the 'non-committal' status quo were relieved to receive a new political formula with the imprimatur of British Labour. But Attlee had encouraged partitionists in the belief that his party would look favourably on a merger with the NILP. They turned up the heat at the party conference in November. The ATGWU and the Union of Shop, Distributive and Allied Workers proposed a motion hostile to the Friends of Ireland, which was passed by 183–96 votes. When the West Belfast branch convened a conference in protest, it was expelled forthwith. On 28 November, the executive tried to sidestep the nearing storm by approving an approach to the British Labour Party for affiliation as a regional council. As it had done before, and would again, London refused the request. The debacle threatened to alienate the 'non-committals' as well as the anti-partitionists.

Events moved briskly in January. Early in the month the NILP unveiled plans for a new party structure involving closer ties with British Labour. Fortified with a cast-iron constitutional guarantee from Attlee, Brooke announced a general election on 21 January, to be fought, naturally, on the constitution. On 24 January, the IrLP met dissident Northern Labourites and agreed to embrace them in a 32-county structure. It had earlier warned the NILP that links with British Labour would force this eventuality. Three days later the first meeting of the All-Party Anti-Partition Committee called for a church gate collection for anti-partition candidates, including five Belfast Labour men, in the six counties. The NILP then issued a pro-partition statement.

---

89 Jack Macgougan (1913–98), born in Belfast, son of an official of the Amalgamated Engineering Union and NILP activist; Irish organiser of the National Union of Tailors and Garment Makers from 1945; argued for a civil rights agenda and cross-border economic cooperation within the NILP; elected to Belfast Corporation for the IrLP in 1950; concentrated on union work in the 1960s; president of the ICTU, 1963; general secretary of the NUTGW, 1968–79; the first Irish-based official to lead a British union. See Macgougan, 'Letting Labour lead', pp. 113–24.

90 Ibid., p. 117.

The 'chapel gates' election was a bruising experience for Labourites of all hues. Beattie campaigned in a steel helmet and got 200 British Labour MPs to demand that the contest be postponed until the passions subsided. The result was a disaster for the NILP, despite a vigorous, unambiguously pro-Union campaign. The left at Stormont now comprised two anti-partitionists, Diamond and Frank Hanna, and, for the first time, all opposition MPs were Catholic.

After the hustings, anti-partitionists forged ahead with the extension of the IrLP to the six counties.[91] Backing came chiefly from the Socialist Republican Party, ex-NILP branches grouped in the Irish Labour Association, other adherents from the NILP, and Beattie's following. Clearly, a sectarian geography mapped out the Labour split, but the IrLP attracted prominent Protestant activists and contested Protestant constituencies. Prospects looked deceptively good. The IrLP appeared to have a united and talented leadership. With Diamond, Hanna, and Beattie, it enjoyed the unique position of being represented in the Irish government, Stormont, and Westminster. At the base, it gained strongholds in west Belfast, Derry, south Armagh, and south Down. In the 1949 local elections, the IrLP swept all seven seats in the Falls and Smithfield wards of Belfast – the NILP and Nationalists were reduced to one councillor each on Belfast Corporation – and won control of Newry and Warrenpoint councils, and seats in Armagh and Dungannon. But there were structural weaknesses. The top-heavy leadership was not ballasted by the unions or stabilised by assistance from Britain or the Republic. The ITUC took a detached stand on the schism from the outset. Pressure from southern delegates to snub the NILP for its partitionism was checked with an appeal for unity in the industrial field.[92] The Congress had no wish to fuel demands for an 'Ulster TUC'. The IrLP's wider goal of weaning support for Irish unity within the British movement failed disastrously. The Friends of Ireland divided in their response to the Ireland Bill, which passed through Westminster with much less opposition from Labour MPs than anyone expected. Internal cracks appeared in west Belfast in 1951, where the IrLP included 'the greatest crowd of mavericks that you could ever imagine', according to McGonagle.[93] Diamond objected to criticism of the Catholic Church in the wake of the 'Mother and Child' controversy and denounced the IrLP as Communist. Hanna decamped to form a more explicitly Catholic Independent Labour group, which cleaned the IrLP out of Belfast Corporation in 1958. Thereafter, the Northern IrLP shrivelled to Fitt's machine in Dock and 'lingering limbs'

91 See Christopher Norton, 'The Irish Labour Party in Northern Ireland, 1949–58', *Saothar* 21 (1996), pp. 47–59.

92 McCarthy, *Trade Unions in Ireland*, p. 328.

93 McGonagle, 'Navigating a lone channel', p. 144.

in Newry and Warrenpoint.[94] A headquarters enquiry into this reverse never managed to cross the border.

The NILP pledged itself formally to uphold the Union with Britain in April 1949. The card votes of the unions mustered 20,000 for the resolution; 700 votes were cast against.[95] As the anti-partitionists had already departed, the major immediate repercussion was a hostile reaction within the ATGWU, which was reputed to have an even balance of Catholic and Protestant members. To end the controversy, the union disaffiliated. This still left the NILP with some 22 union affiliates and about 17,000 corporate members.[96] Slowly but surely, the partitionist line took its toll. The British Labour Party withdrew its agent in 1952, offering instead an annual subvention of £300 for three years. With about 300 members, the party still found itself in difficulties. After another disappointment in the 1953 Stormont elections, it chose to place greater emphasis on its loyalty to the constitution;[97] not that an impartial observer could seriously doubt its existing loyalty. In London the NILP sponsored an Ulster Labour Group to counter the 'misleading and dishonest propaganda of the Anti-Partition League'. The Group's president, David Bleakley,[98] favoured an 'Ulster TUC', and many of his colleagues were uncomfortable about the creation of the ICTU. Indeed, the NILP became as fond of disparaging the 'backward south' as the Unionist Party.[99] Unionism was arraigned for incompetence rather than sectarianism. The party no longer contested nationalist constituencies, and canvassers were advised to support the B Specials and the Special Powers Act; 'guarded criticism' of discrimination in housing and employment, and gerrymandering was permissible only in response to 'pointed questions'.[100] Inevitably, it came to be perceived as Protestant, though Catholics were said to form some 30 per cent of individual membership.[101]

94   Farrell, *Northern Ireland*, pp. 223–4; Rumpf and Hepburn, *Nationalism and Socialism in Twentieth Century Ireland*, pp. 191–2; Gallagher, *The Irish Labour Party in Transition*, pp. 133–5.

95   Harbinson, 'A history of the Northern Ireland Labour Party', pp. 220–35.

96   Bleakley, 'The Northern Ireland trade union movement', pp. 163–7.

97   Cradden, 'Trade unionism and socialism in Northern Ireland', pp. 606–8.

98   David Bleakley (1925–), born in Belfast; an electrician in Harland and Wolff; studied at Ruskin College; joined the NILP in 1949 and was its last elected representative in the 1970s; made an Officer of the Order of the British Empire in 1984; served on various quangos, joined the Alliance Party in 1992, and the Labour Party of Northern Ireland in 1998; an Anglican lay-preacher and friend of C. S. Lewis; for some he typified the sanctimoniousness and crypto-Unionism of the NILP.

99   Andrew Boyd, *Northern Ireland: Who is to Blame?* (Cork, 1984), pp. 86–92; Bleakley, 'The Northern Ireland trade union movement', p. 168.

100 Cradden, 'Trade unionism and socialism in Northern Ireland', p. 667.

101 Harbinson, 'A history of the Northern Ireland Labour Party', p. 280.

The crescendo of Protestant job losses at the turn of the decade finally paid dividends for the NILP. In 1958 the party won four Stormont seats, and held them with bigger majorities in 1962. With trade unions more united than ever and the NIC edging closer to the NILP, the IRA's border campaign defeated, the Nationalists intellectually exhausted, and sectarian tensions abating, the future looked promising.

TEN

MODERNISM 1960-87

It is not a populist plan for a return to a Tír na nÓg village society, peopled by casual
handymen and weatherproof farm labourers. It is not a plan for any kind of Éire Nua
with its seedy echoes of an old and unlamented Ireland. This book sets forth a plan for
the construction of a modern urban society.
SFWP, *The Irish Industrial Revolution* (1977), p. 13.

What passes for economics and politics in this country is a cargo cult.
Michael D. Higgins, 1979

——

No development in Irish economic history has been as acclaimed as the switch
from protectionism to free trade. Was the decision so imaginative or so brave?
The creation of the European Economic Community (EEC) in 1957 and the
European Free Trade Agreement in 1959 left no doubt as to the direction of
economic thinking, and if free trade involved a historic u-turn in Fianna Fáil
policy, it encountered little opposition. The depressing thing about the 1950s
was not just that Ireland was doing badly as that its neighbours were doing far
better. Free trade was seen as a chance to catch up with modernity. The
demise of national capitalism entailed a shift to modernism in social and
cultural values, and laid the basis for the eventual hegemony of liberalism.

Fianna Fáil returned to power for another 16-year stretch in 1957, with Seán
Lemass succeeding Éamon de Valera as Taoiseach in 1959. Lemass adopted an
'open-door' policy towards foreign investment, endorsing 'freer trade', applying
for Ireland to join the EEC in 1961, and signing the Anglo-Irish Free Trade
Area Agreement in 1965. The free trade/open door strategy transformed the
economy. Between 1958 and 1973, industrial output rose by over 250 per cent.
Manufacturing exports increased from one quarter of, to near parity with,
agricultural exports. By 1972, 30 per cent of the labour force were engaged in
industrial employment, compared with about 25 per cent in agriculture. The
economy was now highly export oriented, with 30 per cent of total manufacture
being exported, compared with five per cent in 1962. Economic recovery was
due less to indigenous industrial activity than interaction with international
capitalism during the greatest boom in history. The open door strategy left

Ireland highly vulnerable to international instability. Once the western world's economy began to slow down towards the late 1960s, inflation, unemployment, and the cost of job creation increased. If the 1960s produced no economically disruptive crises comparable with the Korean War or Suez, the next decade would not be so favourable.[1]

In social and political terms, the 1960s echoed the 1930s: a time of industrial expansion and strike waves; of political idealism, social reform, radical experiments, and passionate concern with international affairs; of fresh popular consumerism, novel entertainments for the masses, and a lessening of habits of obedience and conformity. After a decade of regression, social services again began to expand from 1963, and there were major structural improvements in education, housing, and health. The first comprehensive report on the education system, *Investment in Education*, was published in 1965. Free secondary education, community schools, regional technical colleges, and higher education grants came on-stream in the late 1960s. Housing construction was revived, with a greater emphasis on the private sector, and the Housing Act (1966) encouraged tenant-purchase schemes.[2] The Health Act (1970) established regional health boards and replaced the free general practitioner service for the poor established in 1851 with a general medical service and a choice of doctor scheme.[3]

The long-term differences between the 1930s and the 1960s related to the Catholic Church, social liberation and the status of women, and economic policy. Whereas the church consolidated a political hegemony in the 1930s, flaunting its power in symbolic victories over left republicanism and Communism, the Second Vatican Council in 1962 initiated a relaxation of clericalism. The public pieties of the 1950s evaporated in the dry heat of liberalism. Prayers ended at trade union meetings, and icons were removed from union halls. And whereas the liberalism of the 1960s was often justified with references to the reforming pontificate of John XXIII, the 1970s saw the growth of secularism, and the demands for reform of legislation on sexuality, public morality, and control of education: a socio-political force which the media labelled 'the liberal agenda'. A second and related phenomenon was the emergence of the feminist movement and changes in attitudes to the role of women in society. Little over five per cent of married women were classed as

---

1   On the economy and industrial relations see Kieran A. Kennedy, Thomas Giblin and Deirdre McHugh, *The Economic Development of Ireland in the Twentieth Century* (London, 1988), pp. 65–74; and T. V. Murphy and W. K. Roche (eds), *Irish Industrial Relations in Practice* (Dublin, 1994).

2   Barry Brunt, *The Republic of Ireland* (London, 1988), pp. 38–9.

3   John Curry, *The Irish Social Services* (Dublin, 1980), p. 10.

economically active in 1961; the proportion tripled in the 1970s, and rose to 36.6 per cent by 1995.[4] The Catholic hierarchy won some tactical battles against the liberal agenda in the 1970s, and pyrrhic victories in the early 1980s, but it was patently losing the war. As if still smarting from the 1930s, the left marked the secular turn with memorials – 14 between 1984 and 2008 – to men of the Connolly Column, who became re-imagined as prophetic forerunners of modern, pluralist Ireland.[5] The third major difference was that there would be no going back on economic policy. Despite, the return to high unemployment and emigration in the 1970s and 1980s, the pursuit of industrialisation through foreign investment continued.

The 1970s and 1980s brought crushing disappointments for the left. The aggregate radical vote in general elections between 1948 and 1969 averaged 17.2 per cent: between 1973 and 1987 it averaged 13.5 per cent.[6] It had been expected that modernisation would lead to radicalisation and inevitably realign politics along a conventional right–left cleavage. This assumption was not confined to the left: in 1968, Fine Gael's 'young tigers' suggested the party solve its endemic identity problem by merging with Labour as a social democratic party.[7] After 1969, it was Labour that drifted into the orbit of Fine Gael. The national question, which modernists liked to think of as passé in the Republic, was influential in reversing Labour's stance on coalition. With no tradition of an independent line on Northern Ireland, most Labourites were bemused by the Troubles, and the experience of dealing with paramilitarism bonded the Labour and Fine Gael parliamentary parties during their term in government, with consequences for policy on a second old thorn in Labour's side: the trade unions. Labour matched Fianna Fáil in competing for union support up to 1979. If it failed – as it always had done – to offer a lead on industrial relations reform, neither did it alienate trade unionists. Between 1973 and 1977, the National Coalition government continued the industrial relations policy of its predecessor with a slightly more pro-union stance. The Pay As You Earn (PAYE) revolt in 1979 was a watershed. Labour declined to identify with the tax protests, and then joined a Fine Gael-led government that was determined to reduce union influence on public policy.

4   Henry Patterson, *Ireland since 1939: The Persistence of Conflict* (Dublin, 2006), p. 290.

5   Emmet O'Connor, 'Identity and self-representation in Irish communism: the Connolly Column and the Spanish Civil War', *Socialist History* 34 (2009), pp. 36–51.

6   'Radical' includes the Labour Party, National Labour, Clann na Poblachta, the National Progressive Democrats, SFWP and the WP, Sinn Féin, H Blocks candidates, the Greens, and the Democratic Socialist Party. The figures do not include independents.

INDUSTRIAL RELATIONS: PLANNING, PAY, AND REFORM

Preparing a highly protected economy for free trade prompted state initiatives in four areas: the adoption of an outline form of planning in programmes for economic expansion; the creation of tripartite consultative bodies on productivity and planning; reform of pay determination; and reform of industrial relations.[8] Lemass was keen to foster a consensus on change in economic policy, and willing to involve the trade unions in tripartism on productivity and planning. The unions were not so enthusiastic about Lemass's other aims: a consensus on pay restraint through bipartite centralised bargaining, and reform of industrial relations; objectives he saw as interconnected. He had long held that free collective bargaining by a multiplicity of unions encouraged wage militancy, and that the answer lay in centralising authority, within unions, and within the industrial relations system: 'one of the main weaknesses in our present situation is the lack of cohesion and authority in the Trade Union movement', he told Jack Lynch, his successor as Taoiseach.[9]

The First Programme for Economic Expansion, launched in 1958, aimed to channel investment from social to productive employment and raise national income by two per cent per annum between 1959 and 1963. In fact, real incomes rose by four per cent annually under the programme. Unemployment continued to fall and, for the first time in the history of the state, non-agricultural unemployment fell below five per cent in 1964. Involuntary emigration virtually ended, allowing the population to grow by a half per cent per annum from an all time low of 2.8 million in 1961. On the assumption that Ireland would accede to the EEC by 1970, a more ambitious Second Programme set out economic objectives for 1964–70. Tripartism was initiated in 1961, with the appointment of the Committee on Industrial Organisation, with members drawn from the Confederation of Irish Industry and the civil service to study the preparedness of industry for free trade. No one thought of including the unions, but there were no difficulties about accepting the ICTU's request for admission.[10] The Committee discussed rationalisation with employer Adaptation Councils and

---

7 Patterson, *Ireland since 1939*, pp. 264–5.

8 In contrast with the earlier years, the post-1958 period is reasonably well covered in industrial relations studies. See especially W. K. Roche, 'Pay determination and the politics of industrial relations', in Murphy and Roche, *Irish Industrial Relations in Practice*, pp. 126–205; W. K. Roche, 'Industrial relations', in Donal Nevin, *Trade Union Century* (Cork, 1996), pp. 133–46; Niamh Hardiman, *Pay, Politics and Economic Performance in Ireland, 1970–1987* (Oxford, 1988); and Niamh Hardiman, 'Pay bargaining: confrontation and consensus', in Nevin, *Trade Union Century*, pp. 147–58.

9 John Horgan, *Seán Lemass: The Enigmatic Patriot* (Dublin, 1997), p. 229.

10 Garret FitzGerald, *All in a Life: An Autobiography* (Dublin, 1991), pp. 58–9.

Trade Union Advisory Boards, the latter subvented by the government.[11] Two years later, the National Industrial Economic Council brought unions, employers, and government representatives together to discuss the broad direction of economic policy.

Lemass's hopes of pay restraint as a quid pro quo for tripartism showed some signs of bearing fruit. The FUE became openly favourable, and Congress leaders more sympathetic to centralised bargaining, and the National Industrial Economic Council discussed linking economic planning and pay regulation. The unions' traditional suspicion of class collaboration began to soften. In 1960, Jim Larkin Jr, bemoaned the narrowness of the prevailing wage militant mentality.

> But what do we do about our backward economy? Get more wages! What do we do about the insecurity of jobs, and about unemployment and the underemployed? Get more wages! . . . We can go on with rounds of wages increases [but] we will still have . . . all these problems . . .[12]

Three years later he could tell the WUI's annual conference:

> I recall that some years ago if you mentioned the question of increased productivity in a trade union meeting, you would probably be expelled out of the union. Now we have not merely Productivity Committees but we have got the trade unions demanding the right to be represented on Productivity Committees, because the feeling has been developed at least on a limited scale that the efficient running of industry is not just the concern of the employer, or solely his responsibility.[13]

Larkin was careful to balance industrial collaboration with the affiliation of the WUI to the Labour Party in 1964. For most trade unionists, bipartism stopped short at centralised wage bargaining, which they continued to see as synonymous with pay restraint. When the 1963 white paper – *Closing the Gap* – called for pay restraint, the ICTU withdrew from the recently formed Employer–Labour Conference.

Another setback for tripartism arose from Lynch's gradual discontinuation of planning. A mild recession in 1966, and the realisation that its targets would be realised, provided the excuse for shelving the Second Programme for Economic Expansion in 1967.[14] A less detailed Third Programme followed to

11   Kieran Allen, *Fianna Fáil and Irish Labour: 1926 to the Present* (London, 1997), pp. 115–16.

12   Manus O'Riordan, 'James Larkin Junior and the forging of a thinking intelligent movement', *Saothar* 19 (1994), p. 60.

13   Ibid., pp. 62–3.

cover 1969–72, but the shortfall in job creation was so great that it too was soon abandoned. Arguably, the Third Programme was no more than window dressing for the government's view that an open economy could not be planned, even in the limited sense in which the term was used, and that given Ireland's reliance on investment from transnational corporations, for whom the idea had negative connotations, attempts at planning could only be counter-productive. Lynch took the lazier option of prioritising foreign private investment, and stimulating domestic capitalism through the building industry. A more powerful Industrial Development Authority (IDA) now became the main state instrument of economic development, and a toxic chemistry evolved between Fianna Fáil and property developers through Fianna Fáil's fund-raising agency, Taca.[15]

Lynch had a poor record in coping with the escalation of industrial unrest as Minister for Industry and Commerce from 1959 to 1965, and he faced greater difficulties as Taoiseach. Labour costs were high by European standards due to low productivity rather than high wages, and many sectors had yet to recoup the fall in real wages during the Emergency. Nearly 60 per cent of industrial workers earned under £10 per week in 1960, compared with less than eight per cent in Britain.[16] Economic growth provided an opportunity for recovery, and the Republic near topped the European strike league in the mid to late 1960s.

Table 10.1: *The number of strikes, strikers, and strike days in the Republic, 1964–70*

	1964	1965	1966	1967	1968	1969	1970
Strikes	87	89	112	79	126	134	134
Strikers (000s)	25.2	38.9	52.2	20.9	38.9	61.8	28.8
Strike days (000s)	545.4	552.4	783.6	182.7	405.7	953.9	1,007.7

Source: *Statistical Abstract of Ireland, 1964–70*

Most disputes were selective and brief, as is usual in prosperous times. A nine-week building strike in Dublin accounted for 75 per cent of strike days in 1964. Three disputes were responsible for 80 per cent of strike days in 1965. Almost 70 per cent of strike days in 1969 were due to the maintenance men's dispute, while 1970 saw a six-month bank strike. Indeed 1966, dubbed the 'year of the striker' (after John B. Keane's latest play *The Year of the Hiker*), was the only

14   FitzGerald, *All in a Life*, p. 59.

15   Dermot Keogh, *Jack Lynch: A Biography* (Dublin, 2008), p. 126.

16   Brian Girvin, 'Industrialisation and the Irish working class since 1922', *Saothar* 10 (1984), p. 35.

time when conflict could be described as general. Nonetheless, the incidence of one or two major struggles each year, and the recurrence of high profile disruption in public services like Córas Iompar Éireann or the Electricity Supply Board, sustained a hue and cry over strikes.

The government responded with a mixture of carrot and stick. In April 1966 it proposed to make Labour Court recommendations binding in law and remove legal protection from unofficial strikes. In not consulting Congress beforehand, it left union leaders with little option but to reaffirm their conviction in the voluntary principle. Fianna Fáil blundered on and, during a power crisis in June, enacted the Electricity (Special Provisions) Bill, to make strikes illegal in the Electricity Supply Board in certain circumstances. The Act aroused considerable resentment and would later be proved inoperable. In this atmosphere, the creation of the Department of Labour in July was regarded by unions with some suspicion, though they had long advocated steps in this direction. Over the next two years the diplomatic war persisted, with the government seeking to orchestrate public opinion in its bid for statutory control of strikes and wages, and Congress trying to mollify criticism on the one side, and restrain its members on the other.

Threats of a statutory incomes policy, and legislation to restrict strikes, failed to deliver substantial reform until the maintenance men's dispute in 1969. This six-week stoppage of some 3,000 industrial craftsmen in 18 unions led to widespread closures. In Waterford alone, 15 firms shut down, laying off 3,000 workers.[17] A confused and inconsistent application of picketing caused considerable friction between the striking unions and others. The Congress executive responded by proposing a two-tier picketing system, one which applied to workers directly affected and which might be placed at the discretion of the union concerned, and an 'all-out' picket which could be mounted only with Congress approval. The idea that a picket – the hinge of solidarity since Big Jim Larkin's heyday – might legitimately be passed generated considerable soul-searching. A conference in May 1970 accepted the recommendation by 173–123 votes. The second consequence of the maintenance strike derived from its success in securing a 20 per cent pay rise, inviting comparable claims from other workers. The National Industrial Economic Council now took the view that the 'round' system, wherein pay increases had a 'knock-on' effect, was inherently unmanageable. In 1970 it recommended a bipartite body to set guidelines for wage determination. The government reconvened the Employer–Labour Conference and, when the ICTU annual conference rejected centralised

---

17   Emmet O'Connor, *A Labour History of Waterford* (Waterford, 1989), pp. 317–19; for an account of the strike and its consequences see Charles McCarthy, *The Decade of Upheaval: Irish Trade Unions in the Nineteen Sixties* (Dublin, 1973), pp. 99–149, 179–81.

bargaining, introduced a bill for a statutory incomes policy. Congress then backed down and concluded the first National Wage Agreement (NWA). In return, the government offered some concessions and withdrew its bill.

Numerically, trade unions were doing well. The challenge of increased reliance on multinationals, some of them implacably non-union at home, was met with 'sweetheart deals' with incoming employers, who were advised by the IDA that a deal with one union was preferable to having shopfloor militants form multiple unions. In most instances the IDA recommended 'the large and responsible' ITGWU. Militants pilloried the ITGWU for the deals, but Matt Merrigan[18] was bitter at the ATGWU being offered so few, and it was militancy that made them advisable.[19] The ITGWU drew a line in the sand at EI, a subsidiary of General Electric, at Shannon. After EI refused to talk with the union, a strike was called in March 1968. When EI recruited strike-breakers, buses transporting them to Shannon were burned or disabled. The threat of a national strike persuaded the government to pressure EI into recognising the union. In 1971 the government confirmed that IDA grants would not be awarded to companies that refused to negotiate with trade unions.[20]

Aggregate union membership expanded from 310,000 to 410,000 between 1960 and 1972, and density rose from 45 to 52 per cent.[21] Liberty Hall, rebuilt as Dublin's first skyscraper in 1966, symbolised the assured place of trade union-ism in modern Ireland. The record on public policy was not so impressive. The government set the agenda on change in economic strategy. Tripartism merely offered unions some limited opportunity to mitigate the consequences. While unions had grown increasingly uneasy about the impact of free trade on jobs, they failed to develop an alternative. A special ICTU conference in January 1972 voted to oppose entry into the EEC, but few Congress leaders joined the referendum campaign with conviction.[22] One can detect a similar dissonance

---

18 Matt Merrigan (1921–2000), born in Dublin; his father, a builder's labourer, died when he was six; went to work in a factory at 14; joined the Labour Party in 1941; associated with Trotskyists from the 1940s; appointed ATGWU branch secretary in 1957 and Irish district secretary in 1960, becoming synonymous with opposition to centralised bargaining and Labour's coalition policy. See his *Eagle or Cuckoo? The Story of the ATGWU in Ireland* (Dublin, 1989), the title reflecting his self-consciousness about being 'an amalgamated man' and a republican.

19 O'Connor, *A Labour History of Waterford*, p. 341.

20 'The facts about the Shannon dispute', *Liberty Magazine* (May, 1968), pp. 2–7; Francis Devine, *Organising History: A Centenary of SIPTU, 1909–2009* (Dublin, 2009), pp. 531–2; Allen, *Fianna Fáil and Irish Labour*, pp. 129–31.

21 W. K. Roche and Joe Larragy, 'The trend of unionisation in the Irish Republic', in UCD, *Industrial Relations in Ireland: Contemporary Issues and Developments* (Dublin, 1987), pp. 21–37.

22 Merrigan, *Eagle or Cuckoo?*, p. 234.

between unions and the Congress executive on the old chestnut of rationalisation. The ICTU appointed a Committee on Trade Union Organisation in
1963, and its findings were the subject of regular and ineffectual debate.
Another round of talks on a merger between the ITGWU and WUI opened
in 1967, and closed in 1975. With Congress approval, the Industrial Relations
Act (1971) discouraged breakaway unions by raising the deposit and membership
required to obtain a negotiating licence.[23] Denis Larkin rattled an old skeleton
in his presidential address to Congress in 1974, asking the British unions to
'cut the apron strings'.[24] The only response was a collective intake of breath.
Few wished to disturb the consensus that the issue was buried. That same year
the ILO was invited to address rationalisation. Its report noted that: 'this gap
between, on the one hand, the expression of a general desire for change and,
on the other hand, an apparent inability or unwillingness to translate this
desire into practice, has become a matter of serious concern to many Irish
trade unionists'. It also observed that 'there seems to be a consensus among
Irish trade unionists that any new structure of the trade union movement
should be on an industrial basis'.[25] The 'apparent inability' persisted up to the
1980s, when unions were gripped by a merger mania, one not led by the old
ideal of industrial unionism, but driven by adverse market forces.

NEW REPUBLIC, OLD REPUBLIC

In 1966 Lemass famously taunted Labour TDs as 'the most conservative
element in our community . . . a nice, respectable, docile, harmless body of
men . . .'.[26] It was an image the party was beginning to resent as it scrambled to
catch the mood of the times. Young – relatively, at 42 – sanguine, and collegial,
Brendan Corish had the appeal of being a refreshing change from the veteran
William Norton in 1960. Equally, he lacked his predecessor's astuteness and
capacity for command, and tended to defer to more forceful personalities,

23   Gary Murphy and John Hogan, 'Fianna Fáil, the trade union movement and the politics of
macroeconomic crises, 1970–82', *Irish Political Studies* 23: 4 (2008), p. 586.

24   Denis Larkin (1908–87), born Rostrevor, County Down, the second son of Big Jim and Elizabeth;
educated at Pearse's Scoil Éanna; worked in London and became an organiser for the WUI in 1928; a
councillor on Dublin Corporation, 1948–69; Labour TD, 1954–61, 1965–9; served on the executive of
the ITUC, 1956–9, and the ICTU, 1969–76; regarded as a moderate, and favoured Ireland's accession
to the EEC; see Charles Callan and Barry Desmond, *Irish Labour Lives: A Biographical Dictionary of
Irish Labour Party Deputies, Senators, MPs and MEPs* (Dublin, 2010), pp. 146–7; NLI, ICTU, *Annual
Report* (1974), p. 393.

25   Ibid (1975), pp. 364–5.

26   Seán Lemass, Parliamentary Debates, Dáil Éireann, vol. 223, cols 2550–1, 8 July 1966.

including Norton up to his death in 1963.[27] Though not associated with any particular outlook, Corish did the obvious thing in pointing Labour towards the left, calling for 'unity of progressive forces' with the National Progressive Democrats and Clann na Poblachta. The 1961 general election enabled Labour to reclaim it pre-eminence on the left, and over the next four years its standing was augmented by the absorption of the National Progressive Democrats and independents, and the affiliation of the WUI. The ITGWU re-affiliated in 1968, and the ATGWU in 1969. When Labour returned 22 deputies in 1965, equalling its best previous performance in 1927, it seemed as if it was teed up for a great leap forward. The 1965 election was deceptive in that all three major parties had increased their share of the poll, at the expense of the smaller parties and independents, and parliamentary representation was tidied into a 'two and a half party' system. Whilst a major advance – of 8.4 per cent to 18.5 per cent – was won in Dublin, on aggregate Labour had not done much more than reclaim the radical vote that had been fragmented since the 1940s. Labour experienced a clearer warning in the 1967 local elections, when its vote rose in Dublin and fell in the provinces. Party leaders shrugged off the setback as a symptom of organisational difficulties, convinced that modernisation was on their side. Internally at least, modernisation was afoot. The number of branches rose from 248 in 1964 to 501 in 1969, with Dublin branches, which usually contained a higher proportion of ideologically committed activists, increasing from 29 to 83 over the same period.[28] University students and professionals, hitherto regarded by Labour with some suspicion, joined in numbers. In 1965, Corish nominated parliamentary spokesmen on specific policy areas, and, in 1966, a personal political adviser, Brendan Halligan.[29] Halligan consolidated his influence on strategy in 1967 when he was appointed to a revised general secretaryship, a post which formerly had had a largely administrative remit.[30] Labour affiliated to the Socialist International that same year.[31]

27 Barry Desmond, *Finally and in Conclusion: A Political Memoir* (Dublin, 2000), p. 32.

28 Michael Gallagher, *The Irish Labour Party in Transition, 1957–82* (Manchester, 1982), pp. 63, 75, 303.

29 Brendan Halligan (1936–), born in Dublin; educated at Kevin St, College of Technology; an economist with Irish Sugar until 1967; Labour Party general secretary, 1967–80; a guiding influence on Corish; appointed to the Seanad, 1973; elected a TD in a bye-election in 1976, but failed to secure re-election in 1977, 1981 and 1982; strongly communautaire, and an MEP, by nomination, 1983–4; subsequently developed a career in consultancy; a modernist and moderate who found himself on Labour's left under Dick Spring.

30 John Horgan, *Labour: The Price of Power* (Dublin, 1986), pp. 81–2; Niamh Puirséil, *The Irish Labour Party, 1922–73* (Dublin, 2007), p. 246.

31 Michael Holmes, 'The Irish Labour Party: the advantages, disadvantages and irrelevance of Europeanisation?', *Irish Political Studies* 24: 4 (2009), p. 535.

The ideological transformation was unmistakable in 1967. In 1960, Corish evaded questions on whether Labour was socialist, conceding eventually its values could be deemed 'a form of Christian Socialism'.[32] Not until 1964 did he describe Labour as socialist, and the 1965 election manifesto avoided the word. However, Labour's programme for the 1967 local elections contained many references to 'socialism', and the term seemed to have an intrinsic power for delegates to that year's annual conference. Amidst tremendous enthusiasm, Corish delivered his 'Let's Build the New Republic' address, which began with the memorable hostage to fortune: 'The seventies will be Socialist.'[33] Speeches from the floor invoked 'socialism', like a mantra, at almost every opportunity. The conference made opposition to coalition a matter of policy, and Labour declined to work with Fine Gael in opposing the 1968 referendum on changing the electoral system.[34] Corish delighted the 1969 annual conference in pledging that if Labour rescinded its anti-coalition stance, his 'continued fight for socialism [would] be from the backbenches'.[35]

The more tolerant climate also enabled the far left to emerge from the shadows for the first time since the 1930s. The IRA called off its border campaign in 1962, and republicans turned towards Marxism and electoral politics.[36] Agitation against foreign-owned ranches, and the 'fish-ins' of the National Waterways Restoration League, in protest at the residual control of waterways by British aristocrats, were a step towards more secular agitation in groups like the Dublin Housing Action Committee. Communists renamed the Irish Workers' League as the Irish Workers' Party in 1962 and engaged with several single-issue campaigns, notably nuclear disarmament, Vietnam, and housing. The Irish Workers' Party merged with the Communist Party in Northern Ireland to become the third CPI in 1970. It claimed a membership of 600.[37] This period also saw the rise of a new left, challenging the traditional dominance of revolutionism by the Communists and republicans. Some groups, like Students for Democratic Action and the Irish Christian Left, were ephemeral echoes of international fashions. Maoism sustained a presence from 1965 in the Internationalists and the CPI (Marxist–Leninist), which

32 Gallagher, *The Irish Labour Party in Transition*, p. 44.

33 The Labour Party, *The New Republic: Complete Text of 'The New Republic' Address by Brendan Corish, TD, Leader of the Labour Party* (Dublin, 1968), p. 1.

34 Puirséil, *The Irish Labour Party*, pp. 253–4.

35 Allen, *Fianna Fáil and Irish Labour*, p. 141.

36 For an excellent account of the Officials, SFWP and the WP, see Brian Hanley and Scott Millar, *The Lost Revolution: The Story of the Official IRA and the Workers' Party* (Dublin, 2009).

37 Mike Milotte, *Communism in Modern Ireland: The Pursuit of the Workers' Republic since 1916* (Dublin, 1984), pp. 241, 292.

sided with Enver Hoxha after the Sino–Albanian split of 1978. The most ubiquitous tendency was Trotskyism. A flickering candle from the late 1930s, Irish Trotskyism was transformed by the flowering of interest in libertarian socialism in Europe. Up to a dozen Trotskyist groups were created in the decade after 1968. A few would make an impact: the People's Democracy (PD) in the North, the Socialist Workers' Movement on the shopfloor – the floor being mainly in Waterford Glass – and the entryist Militant tendency in the Labour Party. Most Irish Trotskyist factions were satellites of parent bodies in England, and were slow to develop indigenous thinking.[38] The Socialist Workers' Movement specialised in single-issue campaigns. Militant were like a millenarian cult, prophesying the downfall of capitalism within ten to 15 years; it was always ten to 15 years, they had a rolling horizon.

The 1969 annual conference marked the zenith of Labour leftism. Labour's socialism, which up to now had been fairly vague and moderate in specifics, was substantiated with a detailed 150-page policy document; itself a phenomenon in a culture where political parties rarely bothered with manifestos. The document called for more democratic control of industry and education, a stronger role for the state in planning and economic development, and a capital gains tax and the extension of income tax to farmers. Its proposals for nationalisation were confined to building land, the building industry, and building societies. Again, the conference mood was ecstatic, with many speakers referring to what 'the Labour government' would do following the general election which everyone expected that year. Few Labour deputies shared this brash optimism. One had resigned from the party in December 1968 in protest at its alleged takeover by 'a small but vocal group of ambitious fellow-travellers'.[39] Others could not resist playing to the socialist gallery themselves. Most, if uncomfortable with these developments, offered little dissent beyond occasional warnings of an electoral backlash. One commentator observed that Labour had become two parties: a right-wing parliamentary group, and 'a fire-breathing party congress, whose ideological purity is in inverse ratio to its political realism'.[40] Having expected a substantial increase in its Dáil representation, the results of the June 1969 general election were a crushing disappointment. The vote in Dublin had again jumped – to 28.3 per cent – but only 18 TDs were returned. In the immediate aftermath, Labour blamed the red scare generated by Fianna Fáil, and to a

38 Ciarán Crossey and James Monaghan, 'The origins of Trotskyism in Ireland', in *Revolutionary History* 6: 2/3 (summer, 1996), pp. 4–57; John Goodwillie, 'Lesser Marxist movements in Ireland: a bibliography, 1934–1984', *Saothar* 11 (1986), pp. 116–36.

39 Gallagher, *The Irish Labour Party in Transition*, p. 71.

40 Ibid., p. 76.

lesser extent Fine Gael and the provincial press, who denounced the party as communist and its new intellectuals as anti-clerical.[41] Lynch made the point in his genteel manner with an egregious tour of convents. On reflection, the Labour leadership concluded that its policies were too radical and its tactics unrealistic. Retreat turned assets into ashes. The general election had returned a talented parliamentary party, but Corish's failure to dominate 'the doctors' – his TDs included three academics and two physicians – eroded his standing. Events in Northern Ireland presented a similar choice of radical advance or radical retreat, and the Yellowbelly had no stomach for the national question.

Fear of the Northern violence destabilising the state gave the back-sliders their chance. Labour had been diffident about the Northern civil rights movement, and then surfed the surge of anti-Unionist feeling in the Republic in 1969. The outbreak of serious violence in August 1969 caused the party leadership to resile. Labour struggled to formulate a Northern policy in the context of open friction between, on the one side, a combination of old guard anti-partitionist TDs and rank and file radicals, and, on the other, those for whom violence confirmed their endemic suspicion of nationalism and the North. Chief among the latter was Labour's new Northern and foreign affairs spokesman, Conor Cruise O'Brien. An internationally celebrated critic of colonialism in the 1960s, O'Brien had moved to a Burkean view of revolution, and the North was a catalyst. O'Brien's trenchant opposition to the use of force in pursuit of Irish unity became party policy in 1971. Nominally, Labour remained committed to a 'socialist, non-sectarian, and united Ireland'.[42] In reality, its key TDs admired O'Brien's increasingly critical view of nationalism. Within a week of the 'Arms crisis' of May 1970, when Lynch sacked two ministers – Neil Blaney and Charles J. Haughey – for complicity in an attempt to import arms for Northern nationalists, O'Brien had called for a coalition with Fine Gael. Bizarrely, Labour leaders discussed the possibility of Fianna Fáil hawks staging a military coup. Corish decided that the 'New Republic' would have to be sacrificed to save the old Republic. The ban on coalition was dropped at a special conference in Cork in December 1970.[43] Coalition would become the most divisive issue in the party for the next two decades, and the defining marker between right and left. It was not a constructive debate. Some on the left were willing to put a price on coalition, but for most, coalition itself was the crime. Corish was unequal to the task of carrying the idealists with him. The leadership relied increasingly on suppressing dissent and on the parliamentary party's capacity to pack conferences.

41　Horgan, *Labour*, p. 83.

42　Puirséil, *The Irish Labour Party*, p. 293.

43　Charlie McGuire, *Roddy Connolly and the Struggle for Socialism in Ireland* (Cork, 2008), pp. 218–19.

The referendum on EEC accession was Labour's last indulgence of contemporary radicalism. The right claimed the EEC would bring modernisation, a bonanza to agriculture, and more foreign investment. The left said it would mean less democracy, higher food prices, and severe job losses in home industries. Both were correct. With the country conditioned for accession by a decade of state policy and the enthusiasm of the major parties and farmers' groups, a big 'yes' vote was taken for granted. Rather like the ICTU, Labour formally opposed, rejecting the terms of entry rather than the principle, with, as David Thornley put it, 'all the enthusiasm of a dog for a bath'. Corish allowed Justin Keating[44] to shoulder the brunt of the party's campaign, and then considered the matter closed.

NATIONAL COALITION, NATIONAL AGREEMENTS, AND NATIONAL MISUNDERSTANDINGS

Ireland joined the EEC on 1 January 1973. Nine months later, the Arab-Israeli War sent oil prices soaring and western Europe into its first post-1945 recession. The mismanaged consequences would haunt government policy for the next 20 years. Lynch called a general election in February 1973, buoyed up by a generous budget in 1972, 21 per cent pay hikes in the last NWA, public confidence in his approach to the North, and lack of progress in talks between Labour and Fine Gael, under way since October.[45] His hopes of dishing a divided opposition were dashed by their prompt agreement on a programme for a 'National Coalition', both parties being anxious to avoid 'inter-party', with its echoes of the 1950s recessions. The 14-point programme offered something for everyone. Its promises to cut domestic rates, abolish death duties, and boost public spending tickled the electorate with a new political gimmick: auction politics. There were also three secret points, providing for the introduction of a wealth tax, the inclusion of farmers in the tax net, and a promise that Labour would not seek the repeal of the Offences Against the State Act (1972).[46] The election saw a 0.5 per cent rise in Fianna Fáil first preferences trumped by a greater increase in the Fine Gael tally and the very

44 Justin Keating (1930–2009) was born in Dublin, son of the painter Seán Keating; educated at UCD; university lecturer, veterinary surgeon, farmer, and television presenter; a member of the Irish Workers' League in the 1950s; Labour TD, 1969–77, senator, 1977–81, and MEP in 1973 and 1984; president of the Irish Humanist Association in the 1990s; see Callan and Desmond, *Irish Labour Lives*, pp. 130–1.

45 J. J. Lee, *Ireland, 1912–1985: Politics and Society* (Cambridge, 1989), pp. 464–9.

46 Gallagher, *The Irish Labour Party in Transition*, pp. 190–1.

high level of transfers between Fine Gael and Labour. Labour slipped to 13.7 per cent of the poll, but won an extra seat, and secured five portfolios in Liam Cosgrave's cabinet: Corish took Health and Social Welfare, and allocated Local Government to James Tully, Labour to Michael O'Leary,[47] Posts and Telegraphs to O'Brien, and, in a gesture to the left, Industry and Commerce to Keating. Labour's concern was to sustain the growth of welfare benefits, employment, and living standards, and the prevailing climate was sympathetic. Having whipped up expectations of a 'Euro-bonanza', neither Fianna Fáil nor Fine Gael were geared psychologically for retrenchment, and the National Coalition was anxious to nail the Fianna Fáil canard that recessions coincided with coalitions.

Tully was a dynamo on housing. Over 100,000 houses were built between 1973 and 1977, doubling the previous rate of construction. The most influential of the old right-wing Labour TDs, Tully also flaunted a swaggering indifference to environmental planning, and cultivated financial links between Labour and a new breed of small builders. Corish had mixed fortunes. Spending on welfare rose from 6.5 per cent of gross national product to 10.5 per cent, big improvements were made in the real value of benefits, new allowances were introduced, and Frank Cluskey[48] – parliamentary secretary at Social Welfare – originated the EEC's Combat Poverty programme. But the pace of structural advance since the 1960s was not sustained. A plan to create a universal health system was frustrated by hospital consultants. Another embarrassment arose from the defeat of a government bill to legalise the sale of contraceptives. To the cabinet's astonishment, those voting against included the Taoiseach. O'Leary generated an impressive quantity of labour law, including: legislation to encourage trade union mergers, provide protection against unfair dismissal, improve conditions for agricultural workers, introduce worker directors on semi-state bodies, and end gender discrimination in pay, albeit in the wake of an EEC directive on equal pay. Labour's main disappointments came in its

47 Michael O'Leary (1936–2006), born in Cork, son of a publican; studied law at university and worked as an education officer for the ITGWU; elected TD for Dublin North Central in 1965; strongly anti-coalition up to 1969; Labour Party leader, 1981–2; Tánaiste and Minister for Energy, 1981–2; joined Fine Gael in 1982, with the encouragement of Garret FitzGerald; elected a TD for Fine Gael in 1982; returned to Cork to work as a barrister in 1987; appointed a district judge in 1997; remembered in the Labour Party as a gifted personality, flawed by indiscipline and fickleness.

48 Frank Cluskey (1930–89), born in Dublin; worked as a butcher and became a WUI branch secretary; a TD 1965–81, and Lord Mayor of Dublin, 1968–9; MEP, by appointment, 1981–2; returned to Dáil Éireann in 1982; Minister for Trade, Commerce and Tourism, 1982–3; resigned from the government, ostensibly over its failure to nationalise Dublin Gas; a witty and effective parliamentarian, respected for his integrity, but seen by the media as gruff and lacklustre.

inability to adjust economic policy. Keating never forgot being branded 'Mr Prices'.[49] Prices almost doubled, inflation topped 20 per cent, and unemployment climbed from 7.9 per cent to 12.5 per cent between 1973 and 1977. New taxes were applied to farmers, wealth, and the mining of natural resources, but hopes for a stronger role for public enterprise through a National Development Corporation and other state agencies were not realised.[50] O'Brien exploited his ministerial control over public broadcasting to pursue his obsession with revising popular nationalism. If the relentless Northern violence, and more occasional, but serious, paramilitary actions in the Republic caused many to agree with him, his abrasive style and calls for more severe censorship and curbs on civil liberties stoked intense resentment among liberals.

While more cohesive than the inter-party governments, the Coalition repeated their ineptitude with public relations. Fine Gael crawled into the Cumann na nGaedheal womb to flaunt a Cosgravian relish for law and order, austerity, and croneyism. Labour dismayed its rank and file in demanding its own ration of jobbery, and Tully ensured that the updating of constituency boundaries for the next election amounted to a crass gerrymander. Typically, the growing perception of the government as arrogant persuaded the cabinet of its electoral invincibility. But Lynch was determined not to repeat his 1973 mistake of taking the electorate for granted. Fianna Fáil's 1977 manifesto dazzled the voters with an alluring array of tax cuts and increased public spending. Lynch swept back to power with a thumping majority, and Labour was reduced to 11.6 per cent of the poll.

The 1970s were a decade of centralised bargaining. Seven NWAs were concluded through the Employer–Labour Conference between 1970 and 1978. Unlike previous national agreements, which merely set guidelines for decentralised bargaining, the NWAs marked a real departure. While the first five were bipartite, those concluded in 1977 – before the general election – and 1978, were tripartite. Even before 1977, the distinction between bipartism and tripartism was blurred by the National Coalition's willingness to use budgetary inducements to secure the agreements. The National Industrial Economic Council was replaced with a National Economic and Social Council (NESC) in 1973, and by the mid 1970s, the NWAs were generating a momentum towards what was coming to be called 'social partnership'.[51] Employers were strongly favourable to central agreements, and both Congress and government sought to surmount trade union dissent through intensifying tripartism. Initially, the NWAs reduced the level of industrial conflict. By the mid 1970s,

49 Brendan Halligan (ed.), *The Brendan Corish Seminar Proceedings* (Dublin, 2006), p. 24.
50 Gallagher, *The Irish Labour Party in Transition*, pp. 197–223.
51 Roche, 'Pay determination and the politics of industrial relations', p. 183.

the agreements were coming under pressure as inflation accelerated and employers pressed for wage restraint, at a time when real incomes per capita were rising by just one per cent per annum. There was a fourfold increase in cases referred to the Labour Court under the NWAs, and demands for action in breach of the agreements. Between 1973 and 1978, unofficial disputes accounted for almost two thirds of strikers, over two thirds of strikes, and over one third of strike days.[52]

Table 10.2: **The number of strikes, strikers, and strike days in the Republic, 1971–80**

	1971	1972	1973	1974	1975	1976	1977	1978	1979	1980
Strikes	133	131	182	219	151	134	175	152	140	130
Strikers										
(000s)	43.8	22.3	31.8	43.5	29.1	42.3	33.8	32.6	49.6	30.9
Strike days										
(000s)	273.8	207.0	206.7	551.8	295.7	776.9	442.1	634.3	1,465.0	412.0

Source: Statistical Abstract of Ireland, 1971–80

Pay restraint was integral to Fianna Fáil's ambitious programme of economic expansion in 1977, and the government overcame mounting trade union misgivings about the NWAs by acceding to union calls for a deepening of social partnership.[53] The twentieth wage round was incorporated into a 'National Understanding for Social and Economic Development'. The two National Understandings of 1979 and 1980 were novel in being two-tier agreements, the first relating to pay, and the second to specific objectives in policy on taxation, education, health, and housing. The 1979 deal was initially rejected by the ICTU, and neither Understanding brought industrial peace: 1979 opened with a two-week national bus strike, followed by a four-month national postal strike, and saw the greatest ever level of industrial conflict in the history of the state.[54] Lynch's hopes of buying industrial peace in return for job creation also ran into financial difficulties. Employment grew at one per cent per annum in the 1970s, creating an extra 97,000 jobs between 1971 and 1981. However, the labour force grew by 126,000 over the same period. About half the additional jobs created were in the public sector, and the state's contribution to national

52   Aidan Kelly and Teresa Brannick, 'Strikes in Ireland: measurement, incidence and trends', in UCD, *Industrial Relations in Ireland*, pp. 121–32.

53   Paul Bew, Ellen Hazelkorn and Henry Patterson, *The Dynamics of Irish Politics* (London, 1989), p. 173.

54   Keogh, *Jack Lynch*, p. 415.

output rose from 43 to 63 per cent. The difficulties in generating jobs through or taxation from the private sector required that expansion of the public finances be subvented by heavy government borrowing, accumulating a state debt serviced by higher taxes on labour, and resulting in a tax revolt.[55]

Between 1970 and 1981, the contribution of the PAYE and Pay Related Social Insurance schemes to the total tax take rose from 30 to 45 per cent; partly because of an absolute increase in taxation, and partly because taxes on property and capital were reduced. Eighty-seven per cent of income tax in 1978 came from PAYE, and there was particular resentment at the fact that farmers paid little tax, although real per capita income in agriculture had risen by 72 per cent between 1970 and 1978 without a commensurate improvement in farm output. When the government yielded to pressure from the Irish Farmers' Association to drop a two per cent levy on farmers in the 1979 budget, unofficial strike action erupted. An uncomfortable ICTU allowed trades councils to become focal points of the discontent. Fifty thousand people marched through Dublin for tax equity on 11 March 1979, and 150,000 on 20 March. The Congress executive then appointed a committee to lead a less disruptive and largely ineffective campaign. A one-day general strike was called on 22 January 1980: 700,000 took part in nationwide demonstrations.[56] In 1982, in what was widely interpreted as a rebuke, the ICTU restricted the voting rights of trades councils at annual conferences.

ERIN GUBU

The Labour Party shared the ICTU's misgivings about street protest. Corish had resigned as leader on the defeat of the National Coalition, handing over to Cluskey, who had narrowly beat O'Leary after a tied vote on the first ballot. It was not an auspicious start to Cluskey's command, as he and O'Leary were barely on speaking terms.[57] Cluskey sounded like the archetypal Labour man. Tellingly, he was the party's first leader to be a Dubliner and a TD for Dublin. Working-class credentials notwithstanding, he sought to position the party as mildly social democratic. The 1977 defeat did not generate the same degree of disillusionment with coalition as the 1951 and 1957 elections. Fine Gael had taken the bigger hit in 1977, and Labour got lucky in the first direct elections to the European Parliament in 1979, when it won four of the 15 seats, with 14.5

55 Kennedy, Giblin and McHugh, *The Economic Development of Ireland in the Twentieth Century*, pp. 85–6; L. M. Cullen, *An Economic History of Ireland since 1660* (London, 1987), pp. 188–90.

56 Allen, *Fianna Fáil and Irish Labour*, pp. 154–6.

57 Tim Ryan, *Dick Spring: A Safe Pair of Hands* (Dublin, 1993), p. 21.

per cent of the vote. Ostensibly, Labour's 1979 annual conference adopted a conditional stance on coalition, deciding that any such arrangement would have to be approved by a post-election special conference. Privately, Cluskey was set on another coalition with Fine Gael's energetic and personable new leader, Garret FitzGerald. Cluskey liaised closely with FitzGerald in Dáil Éireann. The collusion deepened after December 1979, when Haughey, perceived as a nationalist hawk since the Arms Trial, shocked the bien pensants by winning the ballot to succeed Lynch as Taoiseach. Both Cluskey and O'Leary were firm O'Brienites on the North.[58] Cluskey favoured an internal settlement, and moved Labour to a more partitionist stance as FitzGerald was taking Fine Gael closer to the Social Democratic and Labour Party (SDLP). Cluskey also distanced Labour from radical protest. Labour ignored the PAYE revolt; some TDs were appalled at its syndicalist undertones.[59] More predictably, Labour steered clear of trades council and rank file trade union involvement with the H Blocks campaign and the hunger strikes of 1980–1.

If Cluskey was a doughty opponent of Haughey in Dáil Éireann, Labour was unable to match Haughey's gritty survival skills. Even in adversity, Fianna Fáil could still keep onside with the unions. The Coalition had borrowed heavily in 1974–5 to counter adverse terms of trade, but reduced net foreign borrowing and the budget deficit in 1976–7. Fianna Fáil's gamble for growth doubled the budget deficit in 1978. Hopes that borrowing would prime private sector economic activity, dented by the oil crisis of 1973, were crushed by the recession that followed the second oil crisis in 1979. On becoming Taoiseach, Haughey told the nation in solemn cadences: 'we have been living way beyond our means'.[60] But retrenchment in the run up to an election was not politic, and state borrowing assumed alarming proportions in 1980–1. To employer dismay, Haughey bowed to pressure from the unions for a second National Understanding, albeit one less ambitious in its social scope. His various vote-buying strokes at this time included a deal with redundant workers occupying the Talbot car assembly plant, located coincidentally in his constituency. After the company injuncted the Congress executive, Haughey defused the crisis by guaranteeing the workers a replacement industry, or full pay pending the provision of jobs in the public sector. As Merrigan observed, 'It was a unique Agreement'.[61] Haughey went to the country during the 1981 hunger strike, hoping to divert attention from the economy by playing the green card. He was, nonetheless, careful to promise more spending. The outcome was a

58   Horgan, *Labour*, p. 56.
59   Allen, *Fianna Fáil and Irish Labour*, pp. 155–6.
60   Patterson, *Ireland since 1939*, p. 277.
61   Merrigan, *Eagle or Cuckoo?*, pp. 267–8.

victory, chiefly, for FitzGerald, who attacked Haughey as irresponsible, and was equally eager to promise big cuts in income tax. The Labour vote slipped further, to 9.9 per cent, and Cluskey became the first Labour leader to be unseated since T. J. O'Connell in 1932.

Labour's dismal performance at a time of high unemployment and seething anger at tax inequity, opened opportunities on the far left. In September 1977 Labour had expelled Merrigan and Noel Browne, who had been returned as an independent socialist TD, leaders of the principal anti-coalition faction, the Liaison Committee of the Labour Left. With the backing of other Liaison supporters, both formed the Socialist Labour Party. The Socialist Labour Party was doomed. Moody and subjective, Browne was an unreliable spokesman, unwilling to uphold the party's anti-imperialist line on the North, and openly contemptuous of the Trotskyist groups that were allowed to enter the party as 'tendencies'.[62] Most of the tendencies disaffiliated in 1979 and 1980, and the shrunken little party was dissolved in 1982.

A more sinewy challenge to Labour was at hand. After the republican movement split in 1969–70 between Official and Provisional wings, the Official IRA called a ceasefire in 1972, and Official Sinn Féin evolved into Sinn Féin/the Workers' Party (SFWP) in 1977, or Republican Clubs/the Workers' Party in Northern Ireland. The trajectory was determined by the 'push' of their internecine war with the Provisionals and the 'pull' of becoming a vanguard party on the Leninist model. Despite opposition from the unwaveringly republican CPI, SFWP gradually established links with a range of Communist states and liberation fronts in Palestine, Namibia, and Rhodesia.[63] The theoretical rationale was set out by Eamon Smullen and Eoghan Harris in *The Irish Industrial Revolution* – adopted as SFWP's 'bible' in 1977. In sledgehammer style, the 151-page polemic rubbished the 'fable' that British imperialism had retarded the Irish economy, and blamed underdevelopment on lazy, parasitic native capitalists and farmers.[64] Beneath the superficial Marxism lurked a fanatical modernism. The priest and the patriot, it was argued, had both encouraged native elites to be so unproductive with their capital, and enabled them to hoodwink the people by blaming the British; progress was coming through secularisation and industrialisation. In the North, the Republican Clubs dwindled to insignificance as their Marxism degenerated into the use of 'class politics' as a shibboleth against the Provisionals. But in the Republic, modernism had its attractions for those losing faith in priests and patriots, and SFWP recruited a few leaders of opinion in public life, especially in the

---

62 Gallagher, *The Irish Labour Party in Transition*, p. 235.

63 Hanley and Millar, *The Lost Revolution*, pp. 334–5.

64 SFWP, *The Irish Industrial Revolution* (Dublin, 1977), p. 3.

Dublin media. Notoriously, the party acquired a major influence in RTÉ's current affairs division, where the authorities were happy to see it police a censorious line on all things nationalist. No questions were raised about what happened to the Official IRA. Initially the Officials had sought to broaden their 1960s strategy of developing single-issue campaigns through fronts like the National Income Tax Reform Organisation. Popular resentment against the farmers dovetailed neatly with the thinking behind *The Irish Industrial Revolution,* and SFWP cadres were instrumental in kick-starting the tax protests. More generally, as Labour Party branches started to wither, SFWP discarded protest politics for intensive constituency work. Housing complaints from public authority tenants, the staple fare of left-wing clientelism, and identification with local issues, became the bread and butter of aspiring SFWP candidates. In 1981, the party elected its first TD, Joe Sherlock, in the largely rural constituency of Cork East.[65]

The 1981 general election led to 18 months of political instability, and further confusion on the left. Eight independent TDs held the balance of power, two of them prisoners in the H Blocks. O'Leary was the unanimous choice to replace Cluskey, and a special party conference voted Labour into a fourth coalition with Fine Gael. Labour held four cabinet posts, with O'Leary as Tánaiste and Minister for Energy, Liam Kavanagh as Minister for Labour, Eileen Desmond as Minister for Health and Social Welfare, and Tully as Minister for Defence. FitzGerald was not impressed with O'Leary's choice of portfolios.[66] Defence was essentially a 'non-political' ministry, and Desmond was unlikely to have the steel to protect her budget. The coalition relied on the support or neutrality of three left-wing TDs averse to Haughey: Browne, Sherlock, and Jim Kemmy.[67] Once in office, FitzGerald declared the state of the public finances to be worse than Haughey had admitted, and introduced a tough budget in July. A harsher budget in February 1982 was defeated. Taxing children's shoes was too much for Kemmy, who voted against. FitzGerald's plea that exempting small shoes would create a tax loophole for women with small feet encapsulated his unfortunate tendency to get lost in detail. The ensuant election saw Labour's vote dip to 9.1 per cent, though it held its 15 seats. Five other left-wing TDs were returned: Kemmy, Tony Gregory,[68] and

65   Hanley and Millar, *The Lost Revolution*, pp. 336–76.

66   FitzGerald, *All in a Life*, p. 362.

67   James Kemmy (1936–97), born in Limerick; a stonemason and bricklayer; joined the Labour Party in 1963 on returning from England; clashed with Limerick's right-wing Labour TD in 1972 and formed the breakaway Limerick Socialist Organisation; led the Democratic Socialist Party into a merger with Labour in 1990; chairman of the Labour Party, 1993; Mayor of Limerick, 1991–2 and 1995–6; a local historian and enthusiast and, eventually, a favoured son of his native city.

68   Tony Gregory (1947–2009), born in Dublin; educated at UCD; teacher; a member of Official

three SFWP men. Kemmy backed FitzGerald for Taoiseach, citing Haughey's position on Northern Ireland in justification. Later that year his Limerick Socialist Organisation joined with the Socialist Party of Ireland – which had splintered from Official Sinn Féin in 1971 and was based mainly in Ballymun – and elements of the British and Irish Communist Organisation to form the Democratic Socialist Party.[69] Like Kemmy himself, the party would be distinguished by its secularism and 'two-nations' view of the national question. Haughey bought the other left-wing votes with trademark strokes. SFWP's support caused surprise, given Haughey's reputation on the national question. In return, Haughey agreed not to endorse SDLP opposition to a new assembly in Northern Ireland, to guarantee the jobs of workers in Clondalkin Paper Mills and welfare benefits for workers laid-off at Clover Meats, and publish an economic and social plan which would not include privatisation. His stroke of strokes was the 'Gregory deal', the promise of a IR£150 million investment package for Gregory's drug-ridden inner-city constituency and other projects in Dublin.[70] There followed the hapless GUBU government – so-called after O'Brien satirised Haughey's description of one of its serial misfortunes as 'grotesque, unbelievable, bizarre, and unprecedented'. For many, the acronym summed up the politics of the period. In October, O'Leary failed to persuade a Labour conference to allow the parliamentary party and the administrative council to decide on whether or not to enter a coalition. The conference instead approved Cluskey's proposal that the decision rest with a post-election delegate convention.[71] O'Leary promptly decamped to Fine Gael. Fianna Fáil switched tack towards austerity when it finally published its economic plan – *The Way Forward*. The Workers' Party (WP), having dropped the 'Sinn Féin' prefix at its Árd Fheis in April, pulled the plug, and the government fell in November.[72]

Labour fought the second election of 1982 under Dick Spring,[73] who had easily defeated the parliamentary party's eloquent anti-coalitionist, Michael

Sinn Féin and the Irish Republican Socialist Party before becoming independent TD for Dublin Central, 1982–2009; after the 'Gregory deal' he remained prominent in campaigns against drugs and neglect of inner-city Dublin.

69 Hanley and Millar, *The Lost Revolution*, pp. 241, 437.

70 FitzGerald, *All in a Life*, p. 404.

71 Stephen Collins, *Spring and the Labour Story* (Dublin, 1993), pp. 89–91.

72 Patterson, *Ireland since 1939*, pp. 280–2.

73 Dick Spring (1950–), born in Tralee, son of Labour TD Dan Spring; an unusual Kerryman, reflective of the new Ireland; educated at boarding school, Trinity, and the King's Inns, and a rugby international; Labour TD, 1981–2002; party leader 1982–97; minister for the Environment, 1982–3, Energy, 1983–7, and Foreign Affairs, 1993–7; prickly, but increasingly media savvy; led Labour to the right and to surf the 'spring tide' as a champion of liberalism in 1993; retired from politics to various directorships in 2002. See Collins, *Spring and the Labour Story*.

D. Higgins. Rather like Corish in 1960, Spring had the attraction of being young, liberal but not radical, and universally liked, or not long enough in Leinster House to be widely disliked. Labour marginally increased its vote, to 9.4 per cent, and won an extra seat. The WP vote rose again, but it lost a seat. Fine Gael secured a historic peak of 70 seats and formed its fifth coalition with Labour. Labour held four ministries: Spring took the Environment, reappointed Kavanagh to Labour, and appointed Cluskey to Trade, Commerce, and Tourism, and Barry Desmond to Health and Social Welfare. It was a better selection than O'Leary's in 1981, but it faced more daunting adversity, and appeared less radical than the Fine Gael team. Right-wing economic radicalism was in vogue as 1970s neo-Keynesianism yielded to 1980s monetarism. Finance minister Alan Dukes favoured shock therapy to slash inflation and borrowing. Labour's role became one of restraint, as Spring persuaded FitzGerald to stagger cuts in spending. The left was not appeased and others saw the party as a deadweight on the required corrective action. Labour did have positive ideas, but its proposal for state-led job creation through a National Development Corporation ran foul of the zeitgeist and fierce opposition from the Fine Gael right, led by Dukes and John Bruton. The anaemic National Development Corporation to which Fine Gael eventually assented achieved little.[74]

With the cabinet patently at odds, national morale sank to 1950s levels. The gloom seemed endless – between 1981 and 1987, employment fell by seven per cent, unemployment climbed to over 19 per cent, real take-home pay declined by seven per cent, and net emigration reached 15,000 per annum – and the sacrifices futile. While inflation and borrowing fell dramatically, the national debt rose relentlessly, from IR£12 billion to IR£24 billion, or almost 150 per cent of gross national product.[75] The talk of national insolvency was not unfounded. It was a similar story on the liberal agenda: Labour was at once overshadowed by Fine Gael and tarnished by the cabinet's incompetence. Popular opinion was just about tilting in favour of the agenda. FitzGerald proclaimed a 'crusade' to remove 'sectarianism' from the constitution. Then he bowed to Catholic

74   Lee, *Ireland*, pp. 538–9; Fergus Finlay, *Snakes and Ladders* (Dublin, 1998), p. 23.

75   Rory O'Donnell and Damian Thomas, 'Ireland in the 1990s: policy concertation triumphant', in Stefan Berger and Hugh Compston (eds), *Policy Concertation and Social Partnership in Western Europe: Lessons for the 21st Century* (Oxford, 2002), p. 171; Rory O'Donnell and Colm O'Reardon, 'Social partnership in Ireland's economic transformation', in Giuseppe Fajertag and Philippe Pochet (eds), *Social Pacts in Europe: New Dynamics* (Brussels, 2000), pp. 237–56; Patterson, *Ireland since 1939*, p. 285; Tim Hastings, Brian Sheehan and Padraig Yeates, *Saving the Future: How Social Partnership Shaped Ireland's Economic Success* (Dublin, 2007), p. 2; Richard Breen, Damian F. Hannan, David B. Rottman and Christopher T. Whelan, *Understanding Contemporary Ireland: State, Class and Development in the Republic of Ireland* (Dublin, 1990), p. 147.

pressure groups and held a referendum on the prohibition of abortion in 1983. His 'crusade' suffered another setback when the government failed to carry a referendum to legalise divorce in 1986. Barry Desmond had more success in liberalising access to contraception in the Health (Family Planning) Act (1985). It was symptomatic of the time that even success boomeranged against Labour. Desmond O'Malley's refusal to oppose the Act led to his expulsion from Fianna Fáil and the formation of the Progressive Democrats (PDs), who would push public policy to the right over the next 20 years.[76] Northern Ireland provided the one bright light in the darkness. To stem the rise of Sinn Féin after the hunger strikes, FitzGerald set a dazzling pace, convincing sceptical cabinet colleagues of the need to throw a lifeline to the SDLP. Spring was malleable on the North, and disgruntled O'Brienites like Cluskey suffered in silence.[77] The upshot was the Anglo-Irish Agreement of 1985, a diplomatic triumph which caused Labour's internal settlement policy to die of embarrassment.

Labour's ties with the trade unions strained to near breaking point. FitzGerald had come to regard unions as a malign factor in policymaking, and there was a marked decline in ICTU influence on government policy under the coalition. Congress was particularly unhappy with welfare cuts and additional taxation on the PAYE sector.[78] When talks on a third National Understanding reached an impasse on the pay element, the government did not intervene. None of the social partners were happy with the results of centralised bargaining, which had not brought lower inflation, industrial peace, wage moderation, or tax equity. Free collective bargaining in recessionary conditions did not restore the 'round' system in anything but name, and generally worked to the advantage of employers. Industrial unrest, both official and unofficial, declined. Aggregate union membership, which had climbed from 407,000 in 1970 to 526,000 in 1980, had fallen back to 485,000 by 1984, and there was a worrying growth of non-union companies, especially in the expanding electronics industry.[79] Industrial relations theory was itself changing as the pluralist model, accepting the inevitability of employer–labour differences, was challenged by

76   Brian Girvin, 'Contraception, moral panic, and social change in Ireland, 1969–79', *Irish Political Studies* 23: 4 (2008), pp. 555–76.

77   FitzGerald, *All in a Life*, p. 606.

78   Murphy and Hogan, 'Fianna Fáil, the trade union movement, and the politics of macroeconomic crises, 1970–82', pp. 594–5.

79   Brian J. Hillery, 'An overview of the Irish industrial relations system', in UCD, *Industrial Relations in Ireland*, pp. 2, 8–9; Roche and Larragy, 'The trend of unionisation in the Irish Republic', p. 20; Joseph Wallace, Patrick Gunnigle and Gerard McMahon, *Industrial Relations in Ireland* (Dublin, 2004), p. 146.

human resource management, which aimed to convince 'colleagues' that they and management had identical interests. Fourteen unions were affiliated to the Labour Party, and by 1984 there were regular calls for disaffiliation in the big three – the ITGWU, the ATGWU, and the Federated WUI (FWUI), as it was since a merger with the Federation of Rural Workers in 1979.[80] Spring's apparent 'nonchalance' towards the possible loss of the unions was a consideration in the formation of Labour Left in 1983.[81]

Relations with union leaders had been deteriorating since 1969. Michael Mullen[82] rounded openly on O'Brien's Northern policy. Mullen regarded Cluskey, a WUI man to boot, as no better than O'Brien, and took the ITGWU close to Haughey. Fianna Fáil's Árd Fheis in 1980 opened to the strains of the ITGWU band. Haughey was made an honorary member of the union, and Mullen brokered his deal with Gregory. Republicanism was also a factor in an initiative by John Mitchell, maverick general secretary of the traditionally conservative Irish Distributive and Administrative Trade Union, to canvass colleagues on the formation of a new radical party in 1985–6. John Carroll, ITGWU president, and William Attley, FWUI general secretary, threatened to break with the party on economic issues, though both favoured the link and opposed rank and file initiatives to sever it. One reason for the ITGWU's reluctance to throw its political ties into the melting pot was anxiety about the conspiratorial WP's influence within the union. In the run-up to the 1987 general election, Liberty Hall decreed that TDs would no longer be allowed to hold union jobs, a decision directed against four officials who were likely to be WP candidates.[83] Big Jim Larkin had tried to shaft William O'Brien in similar fashion in June 1923. Financially, Labour was becoming less dependent on the unions – their contribution to party income fell from 27.5 per cent in 1970 to 11.2 per cent in 1982 – and they no longer wielded the same clout in the parliamentary party.[84] Spring was bemused by the unions, frustrated by their

80 Sam Nolan, 'Labour and the unions: the rift widens', *Labour Left* 6 (Jan./Mar. 1985), p. 8; Horgan, *Labour*, p. 122.

81 Brian Trench, 'Labour and the unions: one big movement?', *Labour Left* 6 (Jan./Mar. 1985), pp. 8–9.

82 Michael Mullen (1919–82), born in Dublin, son of a glass-blower and Labour man; graduated from Na Fianna to the IRA, leaving in 1945 to join the Labour Party; rose through the ranks in the ITGWU from shop steward to branch secretary in 1950, national group secretary in 1964, and general secretary from 1969 to his death; Labour TD for Dublin North West, 1961–9; identified with various republican causes after 1969; gregarious, independent-minded, and widely regarded as an old style union boss. See Devine, *Organising* History, pp. 967–8.

83 Horgan, *Labour*, pp. 124–32; Hanley and Millar, *The Lost Revolution*, p. 477.

84 Horgan, *Labour*, p. 133.

ingratitude for his grinding attrition of Fine Gael demands, and irritated by their readiness to criticise Labour without delivering for it in the polling booths. His deputy, Barry Desmond, a former ITGWU official wedded to Fine Gael by his Dún Laoghaire electors and Northern events, viscerally resented union affinities with Fianna Fáil.[85] Peevish and bombastic, respectively, neither were the most tactful in handling union pressure. Before the government had run its course, the party and union leaderships were barely on speaking terms.

In January 1987, Spring pulled Labour out of the government rather than approve health cuts in another hair-shirt budget. It was too little, too late. In the general election, the Labour vote slumped to 6.4 per cent.

---

85 See his memoirs: Barry Desmond, *No Workers' Republic! Reflections on Labour and Ireland, 1913–1967* (Dublin, 2009), and *Finally and in Conclusion*.

ELEVEN

LIBERALISM AND NEO-LIBERALISM
1987–2000

A frequently heard criticism of the [Labour] party is that while it has a clear programme
on the liberal agenda . . . it has no clear programme on the economy . . .
Stephen Collins, 1993[1]

—

On returning to power with a minority government in February 1987, Charles J. Haughey responded to the economic crisis with policies in which social partnership was, as he put it, 'a pearl of great price'. In October, the government, the ICTU, farmers' organisations, and employer and business bodies, concluded the first partnership agreement – the Programme for National Recovery (PNR). The success of the PNR led to a series of similar agreements and over two decades of unbroken, and ever deepening, social partnership. Within seven years of the PNR, the 'Celtic tiger' was born, and Ireland moved from being 'the poorest of the rich' to one of the wealthiest countries in the European Union (EU). Partnership was the culmination of a corporatist theme in Irish history stretching back to the first Dáil, and of a special relationship between Fianna Fáil and the trade unions. It was also a product of fear within the unions of the marginalisation which overtook their counterparts in Britain after 1979. Economic recovery did not lessen the pressure. The 'fall of the wall' in 1989 raised the stakes to a choice of 'Celtic tiger' or 'Celtic Thatcher'. The Communist regimes were deemed to have failed because of their command economies; and, ergo, if the command economy didn't work, all socialist ideas were dysfunctional ghosts in the machine of the free market. The 1980s reaction to Keynesianism escalated into unapologetic neo-liberalism. Ideology was passé. Right and left would be replaced with right and wrong. Proponents of partnership argued that if it was a form of corporatism, it was too a means of modifying neo-liberalism with a measure of social solidarity.

Politically, neo-liberalism made a dramatic imprint in the 1987 general election, when the PDs won 11.9 per cent of the vote and 14 seats, beating

1   Stephen Collins, *Spring and the Labour Story* (Dublin, 1993), p. 216.

Labour into fourth place. Though their vote fell to four or five per cent thereafter, they would colour coalitions with Fianna Fáil like a drop of ink in a glass of water. In 1989, the pendulum swung to the left, and the WP won seven seats, entitling a Marxist party to formal recognition as a group in Dáil Éireann for the first time. At 17.8 per cent, the combined left vote was the highest since Clann na Poblachta shot its bolt in 1948. It was indeed a watershed. In subsequent general elections the left vote rose even higher, and averaged 21.5 per cent between 1989 and 2007. However, the post-1989 years would also see a dilution of conventional radicalism by liberalism, and the emergence of alternative radicalism in the Greens, republicanism, and Trotskyism.

Three main forces lay behind the ascent of liberalism. By the 1990s the socialist dream of modernisation transforming the class structure was realised, but not in the form anticipated by those envisaging a massed proletariat in smoke-stack industries. A second wave of economic modernisation was underway, driven by services rather than industry. In 1966, industry accounted for a peak 35 per cent of employment, services for 34 per cent, and agriculture for 31 per cent; in 1992, the proportions were 28 per cent, 59 per cent, and 13 per cent.[2] The flight from the land had made the workforce less proprietorial. Between 1961 and 1985, the proportion of working males classed as employers or self-employed fell from 44 to 30 per cent. But the service sector was consolidating a new, suburban, bourgeoisie. Over the 1961 to 1985 period, the proportion of professionals and managers among working males had risen from eight per cent to 17 per cent, and lower middle-class employees had risen from 16 per cent to 22 per cent. The two blue-collar grades had swapped positions. Skilled manual workers had risen from 12 per cent to 20 per cent of the male workforce, and semi and unskilled workers had fallen from 21 per cent to 12 per cent.[3] Possessive individualism was also encouraged by housing Acts that gave Ireland the highest rate of private home-ownership in Europe – over 70 per cent of units – by the mid 1980s.[4] Secondly, these years saw the continued advance of the liberal agenda. If the pace of secularisation was slower than elsewhere in western Europe, the trajectory was unmistakable. The sex scandals that disgraced the Catholic clergy from 1992 merely accelerated the trend. Referendums in 1992 legalised rights to leave the state for and obtain information on abortion, and rejected a proposal to restrict abortion. The legalisation

2   Cormac Ó Gráda, *A Rocky Road: The Irish Economy since the 1920s* (Manchester, 1997), p. 170.

3   Richard Breen, Damian F. Hannan, David B. Rottman and Christopher T. Whelan, *Understanding Contemporary Ireland: State, Class and Development in the Republic of Ireland* (Dublin, 1990), pp. 56–9.

4   Barry Brunt, *The Republic of Ireland* (London, 1988), pp. 38–9.

of divorce in 1995 heralded the hegemony of the liberal agenda. Though approved in a referendum by a narrow margin, no party in Dáil Éireann dared to oppose it. The Labour Party especially, was the beneficiary of the liberal agenda, and Dick Spring virtually repackaged Labour as a liberal party. Thirdly, the 'fall of the wall' affected the left in Ireland, as elsewhere. The WP split and withered, and its 'post-Marxist' offshoot – Democratic Left (DL) – struggled to find a role before retreating into the Labour Party.

Disparate factors lay behind the rise of other groups on the left. The drift of the bigger left parties to the centre created space for alternatives, most obviously so for Trotskyist groups. Sinn Féin also made a strong appeal to marginalised sectors and anti-establishment feeling. The Greens were at once a reflection of Europeanisation and Euro-sceptic, playing a leading role in opposition to EU integration up to 2008. The seven referendums on the EU treaties between 1987 and 2009 differentiated the old from the new left, and provided a rallying point for alternative radicals.

<h2 style="text-align:center">SOCIAL PARTNERSHIP</h2>

The impetus for social partnership came from the NESC paper – *A Strategy for Development, 1986–90* (1986). The social partners themselves, or their representatives on the NESC, had reached a consensus on macroeconomic issues, based on the need for Ireland to meet the criteria of the European Exchange Rate Mechanism, as a preliminary to joining the European Monetary Union. Implicitly, *A Strategy for Development* suggested that adversarial politics could not create the consensus necessary for tough decisions. So it seemed. Haughey was being ruthlessly critical of the Fine Gael–Labour government's efforts to prune public spending. 'Health cuts hurt the old, the sick, and the handicapped,' was Fianna Fáil's best-known campaign slogan in 1987. Haughey was also exploiting union alienation from the government. A Fianna Fáil Trade Union Committee was established in 1986 and Bertie Ahern convened meetings of senior party and Congress leaders. The PNR was another example of Fianna Fáil compromising with trade unionism to cover an electoral flank. It would muzzle the unions, embarrass the Labour Party, and neutralise opposition to the spending cuts being introduced by the government. Support from public service unions, the ITGWU, and the FWUI ensured its approval by Congress. Facing the prospect of swingeing cuts and a public sector pay freeze, the Public Services Committee of Congress had been instrumental in encouraging an accord. In the private sector, general unions were struggling to hold their own in free collective bargaining. And all unions were feeling snubbed by the Labour Party, and glancing nervously at Thatcherism in Britain and politics at home.[5] The 1987 election had amounted to a landslide for the right. In March, Garret FitzGerald told Haughey that Fine Gael would not oppose 'necessary' fiscal correction, and in September his successor, Alan Dukes, made a similar commitment in a speech to Tallaght Chamber of Commerce. The 'Tallaght strategy', as it came to be called, delighted employers.[6] Their misgivings about the wisdom of a pay deal were overcome by Haughey's assurance that they would be compensated by macroeconomic stability. Haughey was having it both ways. His courtship of the unions continued, and 300 delegates attended Fianna Fáil's first trade union conference in 1989. Prior to the general election that year, John Carroll stated that none of the parties could deal with the unions as well as Fianna Fáil. Not since the 1940s, had the ITGWU been so openly sympathetic to Fianna Fáil.[7]

The PNR raised Irish corporatism to a new level. Whereas the National Understandings amounted to two-tier trade-offs on pay and specific policies, the PNR integrated a pay deal into a comprehensive framework. Covering 1987 to 1990, it set out macroeconomic goals dictated by requirements of European monetary convergence, and social concessions to the ICTU, notably the maintenance of the value of social welfare benefits, and, if feasible, tax reform and job creation. The crucial pay element, the meat in the sandwich, provided for wage increases of 7.5 per cent over three years. The PNR also created a Central Review Committee to monitor the programme and act as a forum for the resolution of difficulties of implementation. As such, the Committee gave the ICTU an unprecedented institutional access to government ministers and civil servants.[8] Fianna Fáil, meanwhile, slashed public spending by IR£900 million. Luckily, the restoration of fiscal stability boosted investor confidence in time for an upswing in the international economy in 1989. Gross national product rose by one third between 1987 and 1993. Annual growth rates exceeded eight per cent from 1994 to 1999. Social partnership has been cited as one of the four sires of the 'tiger', the others being the low rate of corporation tax and the IDA's success in attracting high-technology investment, a plentiful supply of well-educated, anglophone employees, and the kick-starts provided by the

---

5   Tim Hastings, Brian Sheehan and Padraig Yeates, *Saving the Future: How Social Partnership Shaped Ireland's Economic Success* (Dublin, 2007), pp. 8–13; Martin Maguire, *Servants to the Public: A History of the Local Government and Public Services Union, 1901–1990* (Dublin, 1998), pp. 260–2.

6   Con Power, *Metamorphosis: Lessons from the Formative Years of the Celtic Tiger* (Cork, 2009), p. 64, which offers the employers' perspective.

7   Kieran Allen, *Fianna Fáil and Irish Labour: 1926 to the Present* (London, 1997), pp. 170–1.

8   Rory O'Donnell and Damian Thomas, 'Ireland in the 1990s: policy concertation triumphant', in Stefan Berger and Hugh Compston (eds), *Policy Concertation and Social Partnership in Western Europe: Lessons for the 21st Century* (Oxford, 2002), p. 173.

devaluation of 1993 and IR£6 billion received in European Union structural and cohesion funds to help Ireland adjust to the Single European Market.[9]

Subsequent partnership agreements were emended to take account of evolving circumstances. Workers' frustration at being unable to exploit the profits boom in 1989–90 led the Programme for Economic and Social Progress (PESP), 1991–4, to allow for a measure of local bargaining. Continuing high unemployment and 'jobless growth' enabled unions to secure a higher priority for job creation in the Programme for Competitiveness and Work, 1994–6. Between 1994 and 1998, the unemployment rate tumbled from 15.6 per cent to 7.8 per cent.[10] Partnership 2000: Employment, Competitiveness, and Inclusion, 1997–2000, incorporated voluntary organisations concerned with social cohesion in a 'social pillar', in response to criticism that the partnership deals were not doing enough for people unable to work. Succeeding deals, the Programme for Prosperity and Fairness, 2000–2, Sustaining Progress, 2003–5, and Towards 2016 began to address the unfamiliar problems of abundance, such as soaring property prices and traffic gridlock. The process also involved the creation of an increasingly elaborate institutional framework to monitor and foster partnership, and acquired an ever-widening remit. In 1993, the Oireachtas Standing Committee on Employment was supplanted by the National Economic and Social Forum, which brought together the original social partners, the social pillar, and political parties to develop consensual policy initiatives.[11]

The ICTU championed partnership as the bearer of higher gains in real wages, greater improvements for lower paid workers, a big increase in employment, influence over public policy, and greater institutional support and legitimacy for trade unionism. The British-based unions maintained their ancient opposition to centralised bargaining; others took a more a la carte approach. Craft unions, being better placed for wage militancy, frequently voted against the deals, but in some cases became more supportive. General and public sector unions were supportive of the early agreements, but become more hostile in the 2000s. Within the unions, the most trenchant opponents of the process were shopstewards, whose traditional role as the corporals of the Labour movement was undermined by centralised bargaining. There were valid complaints about the deals not doing enough to raise the 'wage floor', to

9   Henry Patterson, *Ireland since 1939: The Persistence of Conflict* (Dublin, 2006), pp. 287–8; Rory O'Donnell and Colm O'Reardon, 'Social partnership in Ireland's economic transformation', in Giuseppe Fajertag and Philippe Pochet (eds), *Social Pacts in Europe: New Dynamics* (Brussels, 2000), p. 241.

10   O'Donnell and O'Reardon, 'Social partnership in Ireland's economic transformation', p. 240.

11   O'Donnell and Thomas, 'Ireland in the 1990s', p. 170.

address the issue of non-recognition of unions, and to translate partnership at national level to company level. Partnership 2000 involved significant measures to diffuse partnership, as progress in the private sector lagged behind that in the public sector. Without opposing the programmes in principle, the social pillar protested that income inequality and relative poverty increased in the 1990s.[12]

The left divided on the merits of partnership. Spring was furious with the unions for cosying up to Haughey. Barry Desmond advised him to oppose the PNR. Labour's relations with the unions improved after Desmond departed for the European Parliament in 1989 and was replaced as deputy leader by Ruairi Quinn,[13] who told his colleagues to ask 'why [they] had not been able to persuade the unions, instead of giving out about them'.[14] The WP endorsed the principle of centralised bargaining, as a means of encouraging solidarity, and welcomed the PNR as a check on neo-liberalism. Leading members helped to negotiate the PESP, though the WP voted against it in Dáil Éireann.[15] The eternal oppositionists of Trotskyism contended that partnership was merely coincidental with the boom, prevented workers from taking full advantage of it, locked unions into a neo-liberal agenda, and eroded democracy within the unions. From the right, the deals were arraigned by economists, the feisty Irish Small and Medium Enterprise employer body, and some Fine Gaelers and PDs, for creating rigidities in the labour market, propping up the unions, and shifting decision-making from the Oireachtas to non-elected interests.[16]

The 1980s introduced other important changes in the structural context of industrial relations. The IDA ceased to press clients for union recognition. One survey of 32 companies incoming in 1995–6 found that only two

---

12   O'Donnell and O'Reardon, 'Social partnership in Ireland's economic transformation', pp. 246–8.

13   Ruairi Quinn (1946–), born in Dublin, of a prosperous republican family originally from south Down; studied architecture at UCD; active in UCD's 'gentle revolution'; joined the Labour Party in 1965, and decided on a political career in 1972; elected TD for Dublin South East, 1977; Minister for Labour, 1983–7, for Enterprise and Employment, 1993–4, and for Finance, 1994–7; Labour Party leader, 1997–2002; a conviction social democrat, strongly pro-EU; seen as the archetypal 'Dublin 4' liberal, but relatively sympathetic to the trade unions, Fianna Fáil and the SDLP. See his autobiography, *Straight Left: A Journey in Politics* (Dublin, 2005).

14   Ibid., pp. 246–7; see also Tim Hastings, Brian Sheehan and Padraig Yeates, *Saving the Future: How Social Partnership Shaped Ireland's Economic Success* (Dublin, 2007), p. 29.

15   Brian Hanley and Scott Millar, *The Lost Revolution: The Story of the Official IRA and the Workers' Party* (Dublin, 2009), pp. 481, 568.

16   O'Donnell and Thomas, 'Ireland in the 1990s', pp. 177–81; for a more detailed review of the debate see Nicola Jo-Anne Smith, *Showcasing Globalisation? The Political Economy of the Irish Republic* (Manchester, 2005),

recognised unions.[17] The Trades Disputes Act (1906) was replaced with the more restrictive Industrial Relations Act (1990). Secret ballots became mandatory for strike action, rights to picketing and sympathetic action were limited, and political strikes were no longer to be regarded as trade disputes. Unions tried to move with the times. Mergers accelerated. The number of unions fell from 95 in 1970 to 68 in 1990, the year the ITGWU and the FWUI were finally united as the Services, Industrial, Professional, and Technical Union (SIPTU), with over 160,000 members, or 24 per cent of Congress affilia-tion. Subvented by a grant of IR£700,000 from the Department of Labour, the merger encouraged others, and by 1995 there were 46 unions.[18] Increasingly, unions shifted from an organising to a service model of operations, enticing members with benefits like discounts on travel, consumer goods, or credit cards. New attitudes took root, along with a new language of commitment to 'total quality management' and 'world class trade unionism'. The ICTU gave a guard-ed welcome to privatisation in *Public Enterprise and Economic Development*, and to innovation in *Managing Change: Review of Union Involvement in Company Restructuring*.[19] Trotskyists blamed the changes on social partnership; others argued that reform of industrial relations was to be expected from the advance of human resource management, and the global retreat of socialism. In Britain, for example, the BTUC created a Partnership Institute and pleaded for a form of partnership that would be considered feeble by Irish standards.[20]

By the 2000s, Irish unions were recoiling from neo-liberalism. High profile instances of Irish employer militancy encouraged by the Industrial Relations Act (1990) caused the ICTU to compel the introduction of amend-ing Acts in 2000, 2003, and 2004 to provide greater protection for workers seeking union recognition. SIPTU again sought to become an 'organising' rather than a 'service' union.[21] Congress was again calling for an end to privatisation in 2003.[22]

It is difficult to be definitive on the impact of partnership on militancy. The annual average of strike days dropped from 719,000 between 1975 and 1979, to

17   Hastings, Sheehan and Yeates, *Saving the Future*, p. 91.

18   Allen, *Fianna Fáil and Irish Labour*, pp. 171–2; Francis Devine, *Organising History: A Centenary of SIPTU, 1909–2009* (Dublin, 2009), pp. 800, 804; Joseph Wallace, Patrick Gunnigle, and Gerard McMahon, *Industrial Relations in Ireland* (Dublin, 2004), p. 149.

19   Hastings, Sheehan and Yeates, *Saving the Future*, pp. 49–50.

20   Martin Upchurch, 'Partnership: New Labour's "Third Way"?', in Gary Daniels and John McIlroy (eds), *Trade Unions in a Neoliberal World: British Trade Unions Under New Labour* (Abingdon, 2009), pp. 230–53.

21   Devine, *Organising History*, pp. 808, 822–4, 866, 881.

22   Hastings, Sheehan, and Yeates, *Saving the Future*, pp. 88–9.

397,000 between 1980 and 1984, and 237,000 between 1985 and 1989, so that strike activity fell under both free collective and centralised bargaining. This was too an international trend, and by international standards Ireland remained comparatively strike-prone.[23] Strikes are not necessarily a reflection of union power, but if they are taken as an indicator of union vigour, comparison with the UK suggests that unions in the Republic were relatively vibrant.

Table 11.1: **Strike days per 1,000 employees in Northern Ireland, Great Britain, and the Republic, 1997–2000**

	Northern Ireland	Great Britain	Republic of Ireland
1997	24	10	69
1998	7	12	31
1999	10	10	167
2000	33	20	72

Source: Department of Higher and Further Education, Training and Employment, Northern Ireland.

Union membership continued to decline under the PNR, and reached a low of 475,000 by 1990;[24] thereafter it rose steadily, as the numbers at work increased. The chief concern for unions was that the fall in density persisted, especially in the private sector, leaving them dangerously dependent on the public sector. Again, the position in the UK was more parlous.

Table 11.2: **Chief categories of ICTU membership, 2000**

Category of unions	Northern Ireland		Republic of Ireland	
	Number	Members	Number	Members
General	3	53,991	3	212,863
Public service	12	101,447	13	120,447
Professional/white collar	9	19,923	11	73,532
Total of all affiliates	36	215,478	48	543,882
Union density	37%		44%	

Source: ICTU; UCD data series on trade unions, Irish Times, *21 January 2010.*

23 Ó Gráda, *A Rocky Road*, p. 103; Wallace, Gunnigle, and McMahon, *Industrial Relations in Ireland*, p. 237.
24 Wallace, Gunnigle, and McMahon, *Industrial Relations in Ireland*, p. 146.

Union density for the UK as a whole in 2000 was about 29 per cent, roughly 60 per cent in the public sector and 20 per cent in the private sector.[25]

Internally, the social partnership process deepened and expanded, and involved a shift in values from a bargaining to a problem solving dynamic.[26] Externally, it consolidated the role of the ICTU, and strengthened the concept of social solidarity as a principle of trade unionism. In other respects, its impact is harder to gauge, for two reasons. First, as noted above, some change in industrial relations would have happened in any case. Secondly, the ideology of partnership was ambivalent. Corporatism is not normally associated with a dependent economy, a sectionalist, decentralised trade unionism, and a political system dominated by 'catch-all' parties. Ireland was unique in having a non-social democratic party initiate partnership, and the process did not lead to the ideological transformation of trade unionism that might have been expected had a Labour government led the process. The socio-economic values of partnership remained a mix of oil and water, of neo-liberalism and social solidarity. Despite the deepening of shared values in the method of partnership, the programmes were contingent on an acceptable pay deal rather than ideology.

THE LIBERAL BUBBLE

Spring had reached a nadir. The Labour Party was reduced to 12 seats in the 1987 general election, taking its lowest percentage vote since 1933. It could have been worse. Under the second FitzGerald government, Labour had been showing signs of disintegration. An unusual number of elected representatives – three senators, two TDs, and a sundry councillors – had pealed away for divers reasons. The anti-coalitionists were consolidating in Labour Left and in the Militant tendency, and found an efficient champion in the ambitious Kildare councillor, Emmet Stagg.[27] Fatigued by four gruelling years in government, Spring's management of the party was lax and coming under question. At Labour's 1987 annual conference, the left proposed that the leader be elected

25   John McIlroy and Gary Daniels, 'An anatomy of British trade unionism since 1997: strategies for revitalisation', in Daniels and McIlroy, *Trade Unions in a Neoliberal World*, p. 114. Their figures are based on workforce density, which includes the unemployed, and have been adjusted to compare with Irish figures for employment density, which exclude the unemployed.

26   O'Donnell and O'Reardon, 'Social partnership in Ireland's economic transformation', pp. 249–51.

27   Paul Bew, Ellen Hazelkorn, and Henry Patterson, *The Dynamics of Irish Politics* (London, 1989), p. 153; Ray Kavanagh, *Spring, Summer and Fall: The Rise and Fall of the Labour Party, 1986–99* (Dublin, 2001), pp. 9–10.

by the conference, and be nominated by at least two TDs, two constituency councils, and, to Spring's particular annoyance, two of the 17 affiliated unions. Spring saved his bacon with an amendment calling for the issue to be referred to a commission. It passed by 38 votes out of more than 1,000. Spring's fightback had started. Following the conference he assembled a team to crush the left and rebuild the Labour vote through more professional electioneering. A talent for picking, and working with, effective advisers was his forte, and created a new Labour right. The old right had been working class, conservative, timorous – of the clergy, of intellectuals, of socialism, of change itself – and would die in the Labour movement. The new right was more likely to be bourgeois–liberal, secular, and en route to careers in business, public relations, or consultancy. A shameless war ensued. The 1987 conference had appointed a trade union dominated Commission on Economic Policy. Its conclusions were simply shelved in favour of more populist and market-oriented recommendations from Spring's Economic Policy Group.[28] Right and left competed to pack the party conference and control the administrative council. As Spring put it: 'it was strictly the building of the armies. If they were going to bring 200 [to the conference], I'd bring 206'.[29] Spring banned smoking at administrative council meetings to unsettle the chain-smoking Stagg; in another notorious confrontation, he physically prevented Stagg from acquiring files with lists of party members. In 1989, at a conference held conveniently in Tralee, Spring finally stamped his authority on the party: the Militants were expelled, and Stagg was defeated for the post of party vice-chairman. The stage management reached excruciating heights in the novel format of Spring's leader's address, which was interwoven with renditions of poetry and songs from professional performers. Cynics sniggered; socialists squirmed; journalists, few of whom would know their Marx from their Engels, thought it fresh and slick.[30]

Spring had three strokes of luck. The Tallaght strategy and the PDs' affinity with government economic policy gifted Labour a breathing space and pole position against Haughey. Spring took up the slack. Haughey's minority government suffered an unprecedented six defeats in Dáil divisions, five of them engineered by Labour.[31] On the sixth defeat, in 1989, Haughey went to the country to win an overall majority. As the PDs tumbled to 5.5 per cent, the Labour vote recovered to 9.5 per cent, the WP won 5.0 per cent, and

---

28 Kavanagh, *Spring, Summer and Fall*, p. 47.

29 Quoted in Collins, *Spring and the Labour Story*, p. 161.

30 Tim Ryan, *Dick Spring: A Safe Pair of Hands* (Dublin, 1993), pp. 84–6, 96–9, 121–3; ibid., pp. 162–6.

31 Collins, *Spring and the Labour Story*, pp. 169–70.

the Greens tripled their vote to 1.5 per cent and elected their first TD. The Greens had been gestating since their foundation as the Ecology Party in 1981. Reorganised as Comhaontas Glas/The Green Alliance in 1983, they became the Green Party/Comhaontas Glas in 1988. In 1989 they claimed 600 members in 15 local groups. As yet, they abjured hierarchy, took decisions by consensus rather than majority, and declined to appoint a leader.[32] Haughey again failed to get a majority. Fine Gael refused to continue the 'Tallaght strategy', and Fianna Fáil was forced to enter its first coalition with the PDs. Now that the economy was back on track, the focus of politics shifted to Haughey's micro-management. There had long been speculation about how he financed his opulent lifestyle. It was rumoured that the 1989 general election had been called to enable his political cronies to raise funds. Harder information started to appear in the media, where Haughey was not popular, about shady practices to favour a 'golden circle' of businessmen. The most serious concerned allegations of malpractice and tax evasion in the Goodman beef-processing plants. A tribunal of enquiry was appointed on the insistence of Desmond O'Malley, leader of the PDs. For all his protests, O'Malley was in cabinet with Haughey, and Dukes never recovered from the Tallaght strategy. Spring became a steadily more effective opponent of Haughey and spearheaded the mounting popular antipathy to the culture of corruption and duplicity embedded in Fianna Fáil.

Spring's second stroke of luck came in the presidential election campaign of 1990. His nomination of Mary Robinson epitomised his professionalism. Robinson had offered legal counsel to Stagg in one of his battles with Spring, and resigned from Labour in protest at the Anglo-Irish Agreement.[33] She remained awkward, refusing to rejoin the party, and insisting that she was an independent candidate. Spring persevered. He didn't want Noel Browne, the preferred choice of the Labour left, and Robinson fitted his image of the party. The first ever female candidate for the presidency, she had made her name as a champion of the liberal agenda in the courts and in the Senate. She soon won the backing of the WP, the Greens, and women's groups, and stole a march on Fine Gael, where the hapless Dukes had difficulty in finding a runner. Robinson surmounted her stilted manner with a surprisingly personable canvass, but there were doubts as to whether she would match the hail-fellow-well-met charm of Brian Lenihan and the formidable Fianna Fáil machine. Then two events upturned the rancid underside of Fianna Fáil. Lenihan was tricked into giving conflicting accounts of a crisis in the GUBU days and the PDs

---

32   David Whiteman, 'The progress and potential of the Green Party in Ireland', *Irish Political Studies* 5 (1990), pp. 50–1; Nicole Bolleyer and Diana Panke, 'The Irish Green Party and Europe: an unhappy marriage?', *Irish Political Studies* 24: 4 (2009), p. 546.

33   Fergus Finlay, *Snakes and Ladders* (Dublin, 1998), p. 53.

forced Haughey to sack him from the cabinet, and another Fianna Fáil minister, Pádraig Flynn, blundered into what sounded like a misogynist attack on Robinson. With transfers from Austin Currie, the reluctant Fine Gael man, Robinson became the world's second woman to be elected head of state. For liberals, it was a hugely symbolic triumph, and Labour basked in its reflected glory. The subliminal message was that Labour could lead against Fianna Fáil, and win. Spring took the opportunity to move the party further to the right and strengthen links with businessmen and professional advisers. In 1991, the party adopted a constitution designed to facilitate leadership control, and the rose, first introduced for the Robinson campaign, replaced the starry plough as Labour's symbol.[34]

Spring's third stroke of luck was the implosion of the WP. Labour had been watching its flinty rival with obsessive concern and grudging respect.[35] The work rate of the average comrade in a cadre party far exceeded that of a member in an associational party, and the WP's membership – claimed to stand at 3,000 in 1987 – was less than Labour's but worth much more. The WP had overtaken Labour in Dublin. It won six seats on Dublin Corporation, to Labour's two, in the 1985 local elections, and outpolled Labour in Dublin in the 1987 and 1989 general elections. In 1988 the ageing and old-guard Tomás MacGiolla[36] handed over the leadership of the WP to Proinsias De Rossa.[37] Having earlier been 'dismissed as mere transfer fodder' for Labour, De Rossa near topped the poll in Dublin in the Euro elections of 1989, 14,000 votes ahead of Desmond.[38] Spring judged it politic to swap hostility for a more nuanced approach, and approved the creation of a Left Co-operation Group in the Dáil. The tactical shift carried risks. Fianna Fáil tried to make something of

34 Quinn, *Straight Left*, pp. 276–80; Kavanagh, *Spring, Summer and Fall*, pp. 86–9.

35 Kavanagh, *Spring, Summer and Fall*, p. 2.

36 Tomás MacGiolla (1924–2010), born in Nenagh, educated at UCD; an accountant with the ESB, 1947–77, when he became a full-time politician; interned during the IRA's border campaign; president of Sinn Féin from 1962 and pushed it to the left; leader of Official Sinn Féin after the 1969–70 split; elected to Dáil Éireann, November 1982; narrowly lost his Dáil seat in 1992; Lord Mayor of Dublin, 1993–4; took the WP to a more republican position after the split in 1992.

37 Proinsias De Rossa (1940–), born in Dublin; worked in the family shop and later as a postman and salesman; interned for IRA membership, 1956–9; elected TD for Dublin North West, February 1982; ardently revisionist on the national question and on the abandonment of Marxism–Leninism after 1989, and led the push for the reconstitution of the WP in 1991–2; Minister for Social Welfare, 1994–7; favoured DL's merger with Labour and was president of the Labour Party, 1999–2002; concentrated on his work as an MEP after 2004.

38 Michael Gallagher, 'A swing to the left: the European election in the Dublin constituency', in Paul Hainsworth (ed.), *Breaking and Preserving the Mould: The Third Direct Elections to the European Parliament (1989), the Irish Republic and Northern Ireland* (Belfast, 1992), p. 63.

Robinson's connections with 'Marxists' in the final days of the presidential elections, and signalled its intention to exploit the 'fall of the wall' against the Irish left. While the WP had welcomed 'perestroika', the ugly revelations about 'real existing socialism' came as a shock. To make matters worse, in the 1980s the Moscow press tried to counter western criticisms of the Soviet Union's human rights record by citing Northern republicanism as a symptom of oppression in the west, causing the WP to look further afield, to sclerotic North Korea, for foreign friends.[39] Further embarrassment was generated by media reports about the Official IRA, which continued to operate 'fund raising activities' for the WP, with and without the knowledge of party members. Internal demands for the abandonment of Marxism, the Leninist model of democratic centralism, and ties with the Official IRA – or Group B as it was code-named – gathered pace in 1990–1, culminating in a motion to 'reconstitute' the party at a special Árd Fheis in February 1992.[40] When the motion narrowly failed to win the required two-thirds majority, the revisionists decamped to form New Agenda. Of the WP's TDs, only MacGiolla stayed with the party; the other six, and about 1,000 members, joined New Agenda, led by De Rossa. In March, New Agenda became DL. DL sought to position itself as social democratic, but more robustly secular, 'post-nationalist', feminist, green, and class-based than Labour.[41] Instead, it became a more middle class and opportunist version of the WP. Its failure to siphon converts from the Labour left was an ominous start, and confirmed Spring's status. Coevally, Labour absorbed two micro groups: Jim Kemmy's Democratic Socialist Party in 1990 and Declan Bree's Sligo–Leitrim Independent Socialist Organisation in 1992.

Weeks before the split in the WP, Haughey was compelled to resign as Taoiseach following revelations about his involvement in tapping the phones of two journalists in 1982. Fianna Fáil's hopes that it could now dispel the whiff of corruption were short-lived. Haughey's successor, Albert Reynolds, was a key witness in the Beef Tribunal on the Goodman group, and while not accused of malpractice, there were questions as to why he had been so favourable to Goodman as Minister for Industry and Commerce. When Reynolds accused O'Malley of 'dishonesty' in evidence to the tribunal, the PDs resigned from the government. In the ensuant election, the media focused on the party leaders rather than policy. Reynolds seemed tired, and embarrassingly befuddled in a critical RTÉ interview. John Bruton, the latest Fine Gael leader, failed to

39   Chris Skillen, 'Pravda's Provos: Russian and Soviet manipulation of news from Ireland', *Irish Political Studies* 8 (1993), pp. 73–88.

40   Hanley and Millar, *The Lost Revolution*, pp. 468, 482, 492–3, 547, 561–87.

41   See Richard Dunphy, 'A group of individuals trying to do their best: the dilemmas of Democratic Left', *Irish Political Studies* 13 (1998), pp. 50–75.

make an impression. Spring opened the campaign with a resolute salvo: 'it must surely be considered amazing that any party would consider coalescing with [Fianna Fáil]'.[42] Lionised by the media as the nemesis of Fianna Fáil, his popularity soared. The election would be remembered for the 'Spring tide'. Labour doubled its vote to 19.3 per cent and won a peak 33 seats. An estimated 34 per cent of Labour voters had come from Fianna Fáil and 15 per cent from Fine Gael. Socially, Labour's biggest advance was in the middle class, where its support was reckoned to have risen from eight to 22 per cent. The professions predominated in its new parliamentary party.[43] Fianna Fáil slumped to its worst performance since 1927. Fine Gael and the PDs also lost ground. DL gleaned 2.8 per cent of the poll and four seats. The WP vote collapsed.

RAINBOW'S END: THE LIMITS OF LIBERALISM

The post-election permutations posed a dilemma for Spring and, trailing clouds of glory, it was his call. Clearly, people had turned to Labour to get rid of Fianna Fáil. But Spring had unhappy memories of Bruton in cabinet, the numbers did not allow for a non-Fianna Fáil government without the PDs, and Fine Gael and the PDs were against the inclusion of DL. By contrast, other than opposition to privatisation and an emphasis on moral rectitude, Labour's election manifesto – 'Put Justice back into Economics and Trust into Politics' – was broadly compatible with Fianna Fáil's, and if some Fianna Fáil people had deep reservations about Labour, others welcomed a return to the centre-leftism of 1930s vintage. Spring opted for Fianna Fáil. With the help of the billions promised by the EU to ease the adjustment to the Single European Market, and Reynolds's pragmatic acceptance of the 'liberal turn', Spring was able to secure a sound bargain. The programme for government agreed to boost social spending, adopt all of Labour's liberal agenda, and introduce an ethics bill and Dáil reform. Ministerial programme managers were to be appointed to ensure the implementation of the deal, Spring's office of Tánaiste was to be beefed up, and Labour would receive an unprecedented six cabinet portfolios.[44] In January 1993, a special Labour conference assembled in euphoric mood. Signifying the collapse of left opposition to coalition, Stagg seconded Spring's motion to coalesce with Fianna Fáil. Spring became Minister for Foreign Affairs, and appointed Ruairi Quinn to Employment and Enterprise, Brendan Howlin to Health, and Niamh Bhreathnach to Education. With

42 Quoted in Kavanagh, *Spring, Summer and Fall*, p. 120.

43 Collins, *Spring and the Labour Story*, p. 192.

44 Patterson, *Ireland since 1939*, pp. 300–1.

characteristic professionalism, Spring allotted posts to three former anti-coalitionists, awarding Arts, Culture, and the Gaeltacht to Michael D. Higgins, Equality and Law Reform to Mervyn Taylor, and a junior ministry to Stagg.

Holding the 'Spring tide' was always going to be a problem. Spring had become an accomplished manager and parliamentarian. He was not so good at relating to grass-roots politics or inspiring public opinion. The media had done that for him, and, unhappy with the results, they decided to cut Labour down to size. Nepotism in appointments by the incoming Labour ministers – trivial but always less acceptable from the left and insufferable from the self-righteous clique now controlling Labour – caused a furore. Labour incurred further charges of hypocrisy when, dazzled by the lure of a windfall for ministerial coffers, it tamely allowed Reynolds to introduce an amnesty – the second in five years – for tax evaders, and accepted a relaxation of tax regulations for expatriates. Tensions between Reynolds and Spring become the key problem. Oblivious to the fact that he had already destroyed one coalition, Reynolds prided himself on a bluff, go-it-alone, risk-taking style, and there seemed to an endless number of skeletons tumbling out of his closet. In June 1994 Spring's advisers were appalled to learn that Irish citizenship had been granted to two Arab businessmen who had invested in Reynolds's pet-food company. In July, contrary to a cabinet agreement, Reynolds issued a unilateral statement of self-vindication on the publication the Beef Tribunal report. Spring would have resigned had it not been a delicate moment in the Northern 'peace process'.[45] Reynolds's success in nursing the process and confronting British government foot-dragging while manoeuvring the IRA into a ceasefire, on 31 August, was his outstanding achievement.

A mortal crisis arose in November when Reynolds stubbornly appointed the attorney-general, Harry Whelehan, as president of the High Court, in the face of Spring's reservations. Whelehan was suspected of being a conservative Catholic and too close to Reynolds. In 1992 he had intervened in the 'X case' to prevent a 14-year-old victim of rape from leaving the state to obtain an abortion. Later that year he stopped the Beef Tribunal questioning a Fianna Fáil minister about cabinet discussions. When it emerged that Whelehan's office had been responsible for delays in extraditing paedophile priests, and that Reynolds had – inadvertently or otherwise – misled the Dáil on the extent of his knowledge of the cases, Labour withdrew from the government. Initially it seemed that the coalition would be restored under Reynolds's successor, Bertie Ahern. Then the *Irish Times* editor, former PD TD Geraldine Kennedy, announced that other Fianna Fáil ministers had known of the extradition

45   Finlay, *Snakes and Ladders*, pp. 164–73, 233–6; Patterson, *Ireland since 1939*, pp. 301–3.

cases. Whether this was new intelligence or an excuse to ditch Fianna Fáil remains a matter of controversy.[46]

Spring decided to coalesce with Fine Gael and DL. Three bye-elections, including two victories for DL at Labour's expense, had created the possibility of an alternative coalition. The abstruse reasons behind the switch in tack – even Quinn couldn't fathom Spring's thinking – and the fact that the transition took place without a general election, made Labour look more priggish and arrogant, and destroyed its defence of coalition with Fianna Fáil in the aftermath of the 1992 general election.[47] It was a defining moment of choice between Labourism and liberalism. Polls indicated that an Ahern–Spring government was the preference of 93 per cent of Fianna Fáil voters and 64 per cent of Labourites.[48] As Haughey's industrial relations troubleshooter and an architect of social partnership, Ahern was popular with union leaders, who saw the coalition as a guarantee of indefinite centre-left government, and were perplexed that Labour was flinging Fianna Fáil to the PDs. SIPTU's general president, Jack O'Connor, described it as 'one of the two worst decisions the Labour Party made in its history'.[49] The liberals, however, had never been comfortable with a party they reviled as the embodiment of gombeen Ireland.

Fortunately for Spring, Bruton was desperate for office, and the left got a good deal in the programme for government. The dreaded PDs were excluded, and Labour retained its six cabinet posts, DL too did well. De Rossa was appointed Minister for Social Welfare and DL secured three junior ministries, one a 'super junior', entitling Pat Rabbitte[50] to attend cabinet meetings. The cabinet functioned smoothly, aside from friction between Spring and De Rossa over the latter's hostility to Sinn Féin in the 'peace process'.

Spring now felt obliged to rule out another coalition with Fianna Fáil, and the rainbow fought the 1997 general election en bloc, asking the country to choose between centre-left and centre-right coalitions. With the acceleration of economic growth, and spectacular fall in unemployment from 1994, the

46   Finlay, *Snakes and Ladders*, pp. 251–74; Kavanagh, *Spring, Summer and Fall*, p. 165; Pat Leahy, *Showtime: The Inside Story of Fianna Fáil in Power* (Dublin, 2009), pp. 19–21.

47   Quinn, *Straight Left*, p. 318.

48   Brian Girvin, 'Political competition, 1992–1997', in Michael Marsh and Paul Mitchell (eds), *How Ireland voted 1997* (Boulder, Colorado, 1999), p. 17.

49   Hastings, Sheehan, and Yeates, *Saving the Future*, p. 177.

50   Pat Rabbitte (1949–), born near Claremorris, Co. Mayo; educated at University College Galway, where he became involved with the Union of Students in Ireland, serving as its national president, 1972–4; ITGWU official from 1974; elected TD for Dublin South West in 1989; prominent in efforts to move the WP towards the centre, and favoured the merger of DL with Labour in 1999; as leader of the Labour Party, 2002–7, he promoted the 'Mullingar accord', a pre-election pact with Fine Gael, which helped to revive Fine Gael at Labour's expense.

rainbow looked re-electable. Thanks in part to Spring's idea of having programme managers appointed to assist each minister, the Reynolds and Bruton governments delivered nearly all their election promises. But Ahern was a consummate populist, and the great schmoozoola was ahead in the polls on the big election issues such as tax cuts, crime, and repairing the Northern 'peace process' in the wake of the breakdown of the IRA ceasefire in 1996. Even on sustaining social partnership, the electorate had more confidence in Fianna Fáil. Labour was liberal, but so was every other major party since the divorce referendum. The top trump to play against Fianna Fáil – corruption – was reneged. If Fine Gael had the cleaner image, both of the main parties were inimicable to tackling its systemic roots. Ahern was allowed to present Fianna Fáil as having put its sleazy past behind it.

The election was a calamity for Labour; the Fine Gael tally rose substantially; DL's dipped a little. The Labour vote plummeted to 10.4 per cent. With much the same first preferences as in 1992, but extra seats from better vote manage-ment and Ahern's popularity, Fianna Fáil was able to form a government with the PDs and its pick of the plethora of independents. The outcome had major long-term consequences in leading to ten years of centre-right government. It also exposed the 'Spring tide' as a media-induced bubble. The *Irish Independent* declared in a front-page editorial two days before polling, 'It's payback time.' Fergus Finlay, Spring's closest adviser, recalled: 'we embarked on a campaign that was all about our 1992 voters taking revenge on us. We had known for a year that it would happen and we had known there was little we could do about it', a wretched admission of the limits of Labour's liberalism.[51] Quinn thought more might have been done to avoid alienating 'large sections of Fianna Fáil sup-porters and members of the trade union movement'.[52] The Spring era ended after the presidential election of October 1997. Adi Roche, selected by Labour and backed also by DL and the Greens, was widely admired for her integrity and work for victims of the Chernobyl nuclear accident. Her poor performance – winning 6.9 per cent of the vote – was another morale blow to Labour. Spring resigned, and Quinn defeated Brendan Howlin for the party leadership.

A NEW LEFT?

If the 1989 election was a watershed for the left, 1997 was a watershed within the left. The fall in the Labour and DL tally was offset by a rise of 3.1 percentage points in support for other radical groups. Joe Higgins[53] was elected for the

---

51   Finlay, *Snakes and Ladders*, p. 319.
52   Quinn, *Straight Left*, p. 367.
53   Joe Higgins (1949–), born in the Corca Dhuibhne Gaeltacht, Kerry, one of nine children of small

Socialist Party, as Militant had become in 1996. While his success relied on a personal vote in Dublin West, it encouraged the formation of another, relatively high profile, Trotskyist party in 2005, the People Before Profit Alliance. The Greens doubled their share of the poll to 2.8 per cent and took two seats in 1997. As the 'fundamentalists' lost out to the 'realists', a press officer and full-time national administrator were appointed, and, in 2001, a party leader, deputy leader, and general secretary, the top job going to Trevor Sargent.[54] The Green vote would increase to 3.8 per cent in 2002, and 4.7 per cent in 2007.[55] Following the campaign for H Blocks candidates in 1981, Sinn Féin had re-entered electoral politics in the Republic in February 1982. Despite dropping its policy of abstentionism in 1986, the Sinn Féin vote remained at under two per cent until 1997. Reaping the rewards of the 'peace process' and the Belfast Agreement proved to be more arduous in the Republic than in Northern Ireland, but the dynamic was essentially similar. Once republicans were perceived to have rejected violence, possibilities unfolded. In 1997, Sinn Féin won 2.6 per cent of the poll and its first Dáil seat since 1957. The Sinn Féin vote jumped to 6.5 per cent in 2002. Support came largely from working-class Dublin and more traditional republican constituencies like Monaghan, Donegal, and Kerry, and from former Fianna Fáil rather than former Labour electors.[56] Sinn Féin made plain its ambition to displace the bigger rather than the smaller party, and worried Ahern into going 'greener' after the European elections of 2004. Expectations of another leap forward received a setback in 2007, when Sinn Féin registered a modest advance, to 6.9 per cent. The party suffered from having a leadership indelibly associated with the Northern Troubles. Gerry Adams[57] on the 'peace process' sounded authentic; the Belfast MP on the Republic's health service

farming stock; trained for the priesthood in the US before becoming politicised by the Vietnam War and the US civil rights movement; completed his education at UCD and worked as a teacher in Dublin; a Militant in the Labour Party; expelled 1989; a TD, 1997–2007, when he lost his seat; elected to the European Parliament for the Socialist Party in 2009.

54 Trevor Sargent (1960–), born and raised in Dublin; educated at the exclusive and multi-denominational High School, Rathgar; teacher, Gaeilgeoir, Esperantist and organic gardener; joined the Greens in 1982; one of the first politically ambitious Greens; elected TD for Dublin North in 1992; resigned the leadership in 2007 after promising not to lead the Greens into government with Fianna Fáil, but commended the coalition and became Minister of State for Food and Horticulture.

55 Bolleyer and Panke, 'The Irish Green Party and Europe', pp. 546–7.

56 Patterson, *Ireland since 1939*, pp. 309–10.

57 Gerard Adams (1948–), born and raised in Belfast, of a republican family; left school after O levels to work as a barman; joined the republican movement in 1964; slow to go Provisional after the split, but was a leading figure in the movement when interned in 1971; MP for West Belfast, 1983–92, and 1997–2010; led the shifts in Sinn Féin strategy from the late 1970s, but always with caution to avoid splits; his support for the 'peace process' made him a more attractive figure in the Republic. See *Before the Dawn: An Autobiography* (Dingle, 2001).

sounded plastic. Labour floundered on about ten per cent of the poll in 2002 and 2007. Its share of the combined left vote declined steadily, from 75 per cent in 1992, to 55 per cent in 1997, 49 per cent in 2002, and 44 per cent in 2007.

In addition to Labour's assimilation into consensus politics, and the consolidation of a more ideologically tolerant society, the EU was an important factor in the emergence of the fringe left. European integration itself became another pillar of the political consensus, and was particularly significant in drawing the trade unions into social partnership. That the consensus ignored a substantial minority of the electorate was revealed after the Supreme Court's judgement in Raymond Crotty *v.* An Taoiseach in 1987 that EU treaties affecting competences of the Irish constitution required ratification in referendums. The decision created an unexpected platform for the fringe, as Ireland reflected a transnational pattern of widening divergence between Communautaire elites and Euro-sceptic masses. Another windfall was the McKenna judgement in 1998, arising out of a case taken by Green MEP Patricia McKenna, which obliged the state to allocate public money and airtime equally to both sides of the argument in referendums. Formally, Labour's position on the EU was one of 'scepticism and commitment'. In practice, the rank and file were sceptical – in 1984 the party's annual conference called for a debate on continued membership – and the leaders were committed.[58] Internally divided, Labour took no position on the Single European Act in 1987 and then, along with the ICTU, called for a 'yes' vote on the Maastricht Treaty in 1992, and in subsequent referendums. DL opposed Maastricht but supported the Amsterdam Treaty in 1998.[59] At least 30 per cent of the turnout in each of the seven referendums voted 'no', and opinion polls suggest that an even higher proportion of Labour Party supporters also voted 'no'.[60] Opposition to the treaties was led by the Greens, the WP, Sinn Féin, People First/Meitheal, and smaller parties; single-issue groups like the National Platform for Employment, Democracy, and Neutrality, the Irish Campaign for Nuclear Disarmament, and the Peace and Neutrality Alliance; and occasional alliances like the Campaign Against the EU Constitution. The referendums also mobilised the fringe right – Euro-sceptic over issues like abortion, secularism, and immigration – but before the powerful intervention of Declan Ganley's neo-liberal Libertas in the votes on Lisbon in 2008 and 2009, organised opposition to the treaties largely came

58   Tony Dermody, 'The EEC: cooperation or capitalism?', *Labour Left* 6 (Jan./Mar. 1985), pp. 13–14.
59   Michael Holmes, 'The Maastricht Treaty referendum of June 1992', *Irish Political Studies* 8 (1993), pp. 106–7; Lucy Mansergh, 'Two referendums and the Referendum Commission: the 1998 experience', *Irish Political Studies* 14 (1999), pp. 124–7.
60   Michael Holmes, 'The Irish Labour Party: the advantages, disadvantages and irrelevance of Europeanisation?', *Irish Political Studies* 24: 4 (2009), pp. 534–5.

from the left.[61] Direct elections to the European Parliament provided another avenue of advance. Invariably, the left fared better in the European elections. Assisted perhaps by the fact that they were not primordial and usually occurred in the mid-term of governments, people were likely to vote for personalities or anti-establishment parties. The aggregate left vote rose from a low of 18 per cent in 1979 to a high of 30 per cent in 2009, and the elections allowed the minor parties to score some high profile victories. De Rossa triumphed in Dublin in 1989, the Greens won two seats in 1994 and again in 1999, and Sinn Féin won a seat in Dublin in 2004, losing it to the Socialist Party in 2009. Labour enjoyed a recovery in the 2009 European elections, returning three MEPs, and in the short term benefited from the fact that the Greens were in government and Sinn Féin was shaped by the dynamics of another jurisdiction.

When Labour took 14.5 per cent of the vote in the European elections of 1979, it accounted for 82 per cent of the left-wing vote; its 13.9 per cent in 2009 amounted to less than 47 per cent. One could make a cognate point, on the basis of smaller aggregates, about general elections. That neo-liberal fetish, competition, was good for radical politics. The WP, the Trotskyists, the Greens, and Sinn Féin were able to mobilise people abandoned by Labour and get the vote out. Of course, once the votes were in, diversity became disunity, and, if the cabinet table beckoned, so too did the dilemma of squaring popular expectations with the limitations of office.

The financial crisis which emerged in 2008 has brought these, and all features of Irish politics, into sharper relief. Like the Emergency, it has made the chronic acute.

---

61 Jane O'Mahony, 'Ireland's EU referendum experience', *Irish Political Studies* 24:4 (2009), pp. 429–46.

TWELVE

UNITY OR RIGHTS?

Men make their own history, but not just as they please. They do not choose the
circumstances for themselves, but have to work upon circumstances as they find them,
have to fashion the material handed down by the past. The legacy of the dead
generations weighs like an alp upon the brains of the living.

Karl Marx, 1852[1]

—

In the mid 1960s the left was optimistic about a political realignment in Northern Ireland. Nationalism was looking passé. Republicans admitted their 1956–62 campaign had failed for want of popular support. Efforts to modernise their desiccated constitutional rivals, through National Unity in 1959, the National Political Front in 1964, and the National Democratic Party in 1965, gained little traction. With the gap in living standards between the North and the Republic reaching a peak of about 30 per cent in 1960, arguments against partition seemed weaker than ever. Even Unionism appeared to acknowledge that conditions were ripe for reform. Terence O'Neill was anxious to make the state less egregiously sectarian, creating the false impression that he was reform-minded. The civil rights movement was an idea whose time had come, but the oft-repeated claim that the unrest was generated by upwardly mobile children of the Education Act (1947) is misleading.[2] The campaign was orchestrated, largely by socialists, with the ulterior purpose of uniting workers in Northern Ireland, or in Ireland as a whole. And it was the return of a Labour government in London in 1964 that made civil rights the Achilles heel of Unionism. The expectations of political realignment were realised, up to a point. The civil

---

1   Karl Marx, *The Eighteenth Brumaire of Louis Bonapart* Unwin. edn (London, 1926), p. 23.
2   This interpretation was first offered in the Cameron enquiry into causes of unrest and conflict in 1968–9, *Disturbances in Northern Ireland: Report of the Commission Appointed by the Governor of Northern Ireland* (1969, Cmd.532), section 11, and is ubiquitous in the literature, but challenged in Henry Patterson, *Ireland since 1939: The Persistence of Conflict* (Dublin, 2006), pp. 199–200.

rights campaign dished the 'green Tories'. By the 1970s, almost all parties competing for the Catholic vote claimed to be socialist. But the project of effecting cross-confessional class unity did not succeed. Demands for reform evolved into a revolt against the state. Once the state was in the balance, socialist politics drained away.

Unlike the political left, trade unions were able to agree on a common interest. The new politics posed problems of dissent which they were practiced in neutralising. Unions also had an overarching unity in the NIC and had acquired a confidence and a solidarity from their unique tradition of progress in negotiating the North's anomalies since the 1940s. They were buttressed too by the novelty of state support, especially after the introduction of Direct Rule in 1972. Unions were tested in three areas: the prevention of workplace expulsions, the maintenance of organisational unity, and the assertion of human rights. They moved bravely to contain expulsions. Unity became the supreme concern and was often the excuse for procrastination on rights. In reality, disunity was never as big a threat as it seemed. The greatest challenge to union authority – the Ulster Workers' Council (UWC) strike – exposed the limits of Loyalism. Northern Ireland's peculiar trade union settlement survived, for much the same reasons as it had emerged: nationalist quietism, Loyalist inability to create alternatives, and the hegemony of officialdom.

FROM REFORM TO REVOLT

The demands – repeal of the Special Powers Acts, disbandment of the B Specials, one man one vote in local elections, and an end to gerrymandering and discrimination in housing allocation and employment – were not new. Neither were they won by the design of a powerful organisation. The groups that comprised the movement, the Campaign for Social Justice, the Campaign for Democracy in Ulster (CDU), the Northern Ireland Civil Rights Association (NICRA), and the Derry left – a network of activists in the local Housing Action Committee, Unemployed Action Committee, Republican Club, and NILP – were disparate and small in numbers before the watershed of 5 October 1968. What was new was the external environment. With its wafer-thin majority, the Labour government looked more critically at the Unionist Party, which usually gifted the North's 12 Westminster MPs to the Conservatives. Television brought America's Black civil rights movement and the wave of student protest in 1968 to Northern Ireland, and on 5 October 1968 it would bring Northern Ireland to the world. A second novelty was the emphasis on British Labour as the key to change, and on parity with Britain to the detriment of the national question. Unionists could defend the constitution.

They found it hard to argue against 'British rights for British citizens', with British people at any rate.[3] The Republic was sidelined. With individual exceptions, the still notionally 32-county IrLP stayed aloof from the North. The Irish government was advised by the Department of External Affairs in 1962 that pressing the British on discrimination was the obvious way forward in Northern policy, but Seán Lemass opted instead to improve relations with O'Neill.[4] It was illustrative of Fianna Fáil priorities that Jack Lynch would embarrass civil rights activists in 1968 by trying to replace Proportional Representation with the very electoral system they condemned in Northern Ireland.

The various left groups had differing means and ends. Within the NILP, addressing civil rights was seen as integral to transforming the party into a cross-community force. The NILP's failure to improve on its four Stormont seats in 1962 made it more receptive to courting the Catholic vote. At successive party conferences, the left won an 'uphill battle' to condemn the property franchise, the Special Powers Acts, gerrymandering, and discrimination.[5] Stormont MPs David Bleakley and Billy Boyd warned about the loss of Protestant working-class support to the emergent Ian Paisley. Notoriously, in 1964, three of the six NILP councillors on Belfast Corporation backed a motion to keep park swings closed on Sunday, in defiance of party policy. Yet O'Neillite Unionism also stole Labour's clothes, as it was intended to do, and compelled pursuit of the liberal agenda. Despite the loss of two Stormont seats in 1965, the NILP joined with the NIC in 1966 to underwrite a 'Joint Memorandum on Citizens' Rights', demanding electoral reform, representation for minority groups on public bodies, measures to 'diminish' discrimination in employment and housing allocation, an ombudsman, and repeal of the Trades Disputes Act (1927). After the government met an NILP–NIC deputation in January 1967 and denied the existence of discrimination, the matter was allowed to rest. The memorandum was a private challenge to O'Neill, not a platform for political action.[6] The intention was to act quietly, to avoid arousing Protestant fears.[7] Nonetheless, the NILP continued to attract progressives in the Catholic community, and not merely because they had nowhere else to go – the National

3 See Bob Purdie, *Politics in the Streets: The Origins of the Civil Rights Movement in Northern Ireland* (Belfast, 1990); Simon Prince, *Northern Ireland's '68: Civil Rights, Global Revolt and the Origins of the Troubles* (Dublin, 2007).

4 NA, DFA 305/14/303, Con Cremin to Molloy, 23 Mar. 1962. I am obliged to Edward Longwill for this reference.

5 C. E. B. Brett, *Long Shadows Cast Before: Nine Lives in Ulster, 1625–1977* (Edinburgh, 1978), p. 133; for the NILP at this time see Aaron Edwards, *A History of the Northern Ireland Labour Party: Democratic Socialism and Sectarianism* (Manchester, 2009), pp. 70ff.

6 Andrew Boyd, *Have the Trade Unions Failed the North?* (Cork, 1984), pp. 76–7.

7 Brett, *Long Shadows Cast Before*, p. 133.

Democratic Party was something of a forerunner of the SDLP: Labour seemed to be the coming thing. In 1968 the NILP would include many prominent civil rights activists, notably Paddy Devlin, Michael Farrell, Nell McCafferty, and Eamonn McCann.

British Labour engagement with the North escalated in 1965, when the Campaign for Social Justice inspired Manchester MP Paul Rose to form the CDU. The work received a huge boost with the sensational return of Gerry Fitt as Westminster MP for West Belfast in 1966.[8] Fitt and Harry Diamond had amalgamated their Dock and Falls machines as the Republican Labour Party in 1964. 'Republican' had other connotations before the Provisionals. For Fitt it meant rejection of NILP Unionism, and a pride in James Connolly – whom he was fond of invoking – as a Belfast workers' champion. An emotive man, Fitt also harboured an almost romantic feel for the great British Labour movement and its forward march to the new Jerusalem. Getting Labour to apply British standards to the North was foremost in his thinking, and Fitt was delighted to be supported by Connolly's children, Nora and Roddy, and the Connolly Association, which had long been advocating a similar approach. With his gregarious, demotic personality, street credibility, and disarming love of their party, Fitt 'galvanised' the CDU, to the point where it won the backing of some 100 MPs.[9]

The most important civil rights group, the NICRA, originated with Roy Johnston[10] of the Wolfe Tone Societies, which were created in 1964 to develop a new direction for republicanism. Johnston envisaged a united Ireland arising from 'stages' of struggle, stage one seeking to unite 'Catholic, Protestant, and dissenter' on reform in the North. To this end, the subsequent stages were not advanced at his point, and the NICRA executive was broadly based, with members of the NILP, the CPI, Republican Clubs, the Ulster Liberal Party, the Campaign for Social Justice, and, initially, a Unionist senator. Founded in 1967, the NICRA did not take to the streets until the first civil rights march, from Coalisland to Dungannon, on 24 August 1968. There were divided counsels in the NICRA on the wisdom of marching. The practice had connotations

8   For Fitt, see Michael A. Murphy, *Gerry Fitt: A Political Chameleon* (Cork, 2007), p. 49ff.

9   Paul Rose, *How The Troubles Came to Northern Ireland* (Basingstoke, 2000), p. 35.

10 Roy Johnston (1929–), born in Dublin, son of a Tyrone Presbyterian, Trinity don, and senator; studied physics at Trinity; active in the Irish Workers' League and the Connolly Association before joining Sinn Féin in 1963; edited the *United Irishman*, and was instrumental in pushing Sinn Féin to the left; supported the Officials before moving to the CPI, then the Labour Party, and, later, the Greens. His *Century of Endeavour: A Biographical and Autobiographical View of the Twentieth Century in Ireland* (Dublin, 2003) reflects his technocratic outlook, and includes some extraordinarily detailed account of political meetings and discussions.

of territorial ownership in the North, and many Protestants regarded the civil rights campaign as a republican stratagem and were finding a champion in Paisley. Sure enough, street protests produced a toxic chemistry of police and Loyalist collusion that would ultimately confound the NICRA's political project. When the NICRA was invited to a second march in Derry, the Apprentice Boys declared their intention to walk the same route at the same time, switching a traditional morning parade to the afternoon.[11] Both marches were banned. The NICRA proposed to back down, but the Derry activists insisted they should not accept the government's implication that civil rights marches were Catholic marches.

The 5 October march was planned as a socialist demonstration. McCann recalled:

> A glance at a photograph of the 5 October march, before it was batoned and booted into disarray, indicates the line of political cleavage which we envisaged. Labour Party placards – six of each slogan, and there were few others – proclaimed Tories are vermin! – Nye Bevan; Terence O'Neill, Two-Faced Tory Trickster; and Tories Out, North and South! Slogans from a Labour, and British Labour, not from an Irish nationalist tradition.[12]

Despite the presence of Fitt, Nationalist Party leader Eddie McAteer, and three British Labour MPs, under 500 assembled in Duke Street; thousands more were watching City pip Distillery in a five-goal thriller at the Brandywell.[13] Television footage of the RUC attacking the marchers, and batoning Fitt, MP, aroused massive indignation and changed everything. Civil rights became the central issue in politics. Riots and massive demonstrations followed. Under pressure from Harold Wilson, O'Neill announced a limited reform package on 22 November; crucially, he had not been able to persuade his party to have 'one man one vote' included. Moderates agreed to a one-month suspension of protests. The student-based PD, founded on 9 October, determined to push on towards revolution. On 1 January 1969, the PD set off from Belfast to Derry in imitation of Martin Luther King's Selma to Montgomery march. The marchers, swelling gradually from 40 to a few hundred, were harried by Loyalists and ambushed at Burntollet, while the RUC stood by. Riots followed in Derry. In the small hours of the following morning, RUC men rampaged through the Bogside. Barricades went up, a

---

11   Purdie, *Politics in the Streets*, p. 139.
12   Eamonn McCann, 'Socialism and 1968', in Pauline McClenaghan (ed.), *Spirit of '68: Beyond the Barricades* (Derry, 2009), pp. 148–9.
13   *Derry Journal*, 8 Oct. 1968.

Citizens' Defence Association was created, and the first 'no go area' was born.[14] The minority's agenda shifted from civil rights to regime change, or at least to getting the police and Loyalists off their neck. In February, O'Neill gambled on a general election to secure a mandate: good results for his Unionist critics further undermined his authority. April produced another turn of the wheel. Nationalists agreed to back the PD's Bernadette Devlin to win a Westminster bye-election in Mid-Ulster on the 17th. On the 19th, civil rights protests in Derry provoked a police riot and a fatal assault on Samuel Devenny in his own living room. O'Neill resigned on the 28th and was replaced by his more hardline cousin, Major James Chichester-Clark. When the Apprentice Boys parade on 12 August precipitated the 'Battle of the Bogside', nationalists were in revolt.

Revolt cracked the polity along the tribal fault-line. Could reform have consolidated progressive politics had the main Labour agencies thrown their weight behind the civil rights campaign? The NILP had liaised uneasily with the civil rights groups, wary of their style, and resentful of their growing contacts with British Labour. Most of the prominent NILP civil rights activists would forsake the party in 1969–70. They could understand their comrades frowning on street protest and illegality; they were less forgiving of covert attempts to undermine those who took civil rights seriously.[15] The IrLP was remarkably out of touch with the sea change in Northern politics, and, as ever, its approach was governed by the Republic's perceptions of the national question generally. When, in 1966, the NILP left mooted a Council of Labour in Ireland to strengthen the party's cross-community roots, Charles Brett[16] found Brendan Corish 'polite, reticent, and unenthusiastic', and the IrLP more concerned about being identified with the pro-Union NILP than with practical engagement with the North. Difficulties arose too with the NIC, as the NILP's trade union affiliates mirrored Corish's apprehensions.[17] The council finally convened in March 1968, after Dublin persuaded the NILP to accept the inclusion of the Republican Labour Party. Party officials did what

---

14   Eamonn McCann, *War and an Irish Town* (London, 1974), pp. 50–4.

15   Paddy Devlin *Straight Left: An Autobiography* (Belfast, 1993), pp. 109, 289–90.

16   Charles Brett (1928–2005), born in Holywood, Co. Down; educated at Rugby and Oxford; solicitor, journalist, and architectural historian; joined the NILP in 1950, an influential policy draughtsman in the 1960s, stood down from the executive in 1969 and resigned in 1974, describing the party as 'irrevocably' sectarian; on the board of the Northern Ireland Housing Executive, 1971–9; first chairman of the International Fund for Ireland, 1986; knighted in 1990. His *Long Shadows Cast Before* offers fascinating glimpses of the NILP.

17   Ibid., p. 136; see also Niamh Puirséil, *The Irish Labour Party, 1922–73* (Dublin, 2007), pp. 259, 290, and Matt Merrigan, *Eagle or Cuckoo? The Story of the ATGWU in Ireland* (Dublin, 1989), pp. 216–7.

they could to help people like Paddy Devlin and Fitt in the aftermath of 12 August 1969, but the IrLP as a whole remained chary of the North.

The trade unions were diffident. In theory, unions had an impeccable record of support for non-discrimination in the workplace. In practice, they rarely discussed the issue, and reflected the religious composition of employment. A survey of 53 unions in 1959 found that of 379 branch secretaries, 80 per cent were Protestant. Catholics accounted for 46 per cent of branch secretaries in the mainly unskilled ATGWU, 12 per cent in the Amalgamated Engineering Union, nine per cent in the Association of Supervisory Staffs, Executives, and Technicians, and zero per cent in the Boilermakers.[18] Initially, unions indicated a guarded willingness to address civil rights. Fifteen unions sent delegates to a conference on civil liberties in May 1965, organised by Belfast trades council, at the suggestion of Desmond Greaves. The trades council, from which Unionists had been alienated since 1910, had an involvement with the NICRA through its veteran Communist secretary, Betty Sinclair.[19] The NIC offered veiled support to the NILP in the 1965 Stormont elections, and co-sponsored the 'Joint Memorandum on Citizens' Rights' in 1966.[20] But as the perception grew that civil rights meant Catholic rights, unions recoiled. None affiliated to the NICRA, though four of the 13-person executive were trade unionists.[21] Even in Derry, the trades council distinguished between the principle of, and agitation for, civil rights, on which it was neutral for all but the immediate aftermath of 5 October 1968, when Billy Blease[22] intervened to stop a proposed political strike. Some spontaneous strike action in support of those arrested on 5 October occurred in Derry on 18–19 November.[23] Addressing the trades coun-

18 Denis P. Barritt and Charles F. Carter, *The Northern Ireland Problem: A Study in Group Relations* (Oxford, 1962), p. 141.

19 Betty Sinclair (1910–81), born in Belfast; daughter of a sawyer in the shipyards; began work in the linen mills aged 15; joined the RWG, 1931; attended the Lenin School, Moscow, 1933–5; secretary of Belfast trades council, 1947–75; served on the NIC, 1950–2; chair of the NICRA, 1967–9; opposed marches and resigned, claiming it had become dominated by ultra-leftists; worked in Prague for the *World Marxist Review*, 1976–7; 1978–9. See Hazel Morrissey, 'Betty Sinclair: a woman's fight for socialism, 1910–81', *Saothar* 9 (1983), pp. 121–32.

20 Boyd, *Have The Trade Unions Failed the North?*, p. 74.

21 Prince, *Northern Ireland's '68*, pp. 114–6.

22 William Blease (1914–2008), born in Belfast; left school at 14 to train as a chef, like his father; soon switched to the grocery trade; NILP candidate for Stormont, 1953 and 1965; Northern Ireland officer of the ICTU, 1959–75; collaborated with Paddy Devlin, with whom he shared an interest in boxing, in trying to revive Labour politics; opposed honours, and refused a knighthood, but accepted a peerage in 1978 to work at Westminster. See Terry Cradden, 'Billy Blease: from McClure Street to the House of Lords', *Saothar* 19 (1994), pp. 145–57.

23 *Derry Journal*, 19, 22 Nov. 1968; Fionnbarra Ó Dochartaigh, *Ulster's White Negroes: From Civil Rights to Insurrection* (Edinburgh, 1994), pp. 69–72.

cil's annual general meeting in April 1969, Blease urged unions to concentrate on the 'real issues'. 'Workers,' he warned, 'should be aware of those who seek to exploit their fears and legitimate grievances. Any alignment of the trade unions into sectarian camps would weaken the unity of the trade unions and their facility to improve wages and working conditions'.[24]

The critical player was, of course, the British government. The British Labour Party kept the North off its conference agendas until September 1969, when Home Secretary Jim Callaghan had some progress to report.[25] Wilson had resisted CDU pressure to review the relationship between the London and Belfast governments. Privately, as a gesture to Fitt, he urged O'Neill to introduce reforms in 1966, but did not insist on action until October 1968. The inability of the police to contain the violence of August 1969 prompted a decisive intervention, with the deployment of troops and the Downing Street Declaration on 19 August. The Declaration promised equal treatment for all 'irrespective of political or religious views', and Callaghan appointed enquiries into the North's security forces, the causes of disturbances, and accusations of discrimination by the Stormont regime, together with working parties on housing allocation, discrimination in employment, and community relations. The initiatives led to substantial reforms by 1971, which implicitly conceded the claims of the civil rights movement.[26] It was not too little, but it was too late. Policing was now at the core of the contention. It was a problem so intractable that it outlasted the Troubles themselves.

SWAPPING SOCIALISM FOR STATISM

The defining elements of the Troubles were created between 1969 and 1974. The British Army's collective punishment of 'no go' areas became both brutal and counterproductive in 1970. The IRA had 120 volunteers in Belfast in 1969, the Provisionals alone had 600 in mid 1970, and began their bombing offensive in 1971.[27] Two disastrous reactions, internment on 9 August 1971 and 'Bloody Sunday' on 30 January 1972, contributed to the replacement of Stormont with Direct Rule. When the Unionists imposed a veto on power sharing and an Irish dimension to a settlement in 1974, Northern politics settled into a stalemate. The Provisionals and the UWC strike did most to persuade the main

---

24   *Derry Journal*, 6 Apr. 1969.

25   Geoffrey Bell, *Troublesome Business: The Labour Party and the Irish Question* (London, 1982), p. 110.

26   James Loughlin, *The Ulster Question since 1945* (London, 2004), pp. 65–7.

27   Patterson, *Ireland since 1939*, p. 199; Thomas Hennessey, *The Evolution of the Troubles, 1970–72* (Dublin, 2007), p. ix.

Labour parties to adopt a statist response to the conflict. Within a few years, the same parties had lost confidence, not only in the idea of a socialist answer to the crisis, but in each other.

Republicans were the first to face the contradictions. Loyalist pogroms and British army intervention in August 1969 provoked a split in the IRA in December. Some blamed the drift towards Marxism for leaving the IRA unable to defend nationalists and causing them to ply their British protectors with tea and sandwiches. After an IRA convention voted to accelerate the left turn by forming a 'national liberation front' – with Sinn Féin and the Communists – and ending abstentionism, the traditionalists formed a Provisional army council. Echoing the split, Sinn Féin divided in January 1970 between Official and Provisional wings. In 1971 the Provisionals began a blitz on social and commercial targets in the expectation that they would make Northern Ireland ungovernable and persuade the British to withdraw within five years. By the late 1970s they had switched to a 'long war' scenario, envisaging a generation of struggle. The Provisionals rejected allegations that they were simply militarists or anti-socialist, and pointed to Sinn Féin's *Éire Nua* manifesto.[28] Yet Sinn Féin was primarily a propaganda and welfare auxiliary to the IRA before the 1981 hunger strikes. The Northern violence, and the Provisionals war in particular, became hugely divisive on the left. Sustaining the war in defiance of public opinion was perverse, the more so as IRA tactics entailed repeated atrocities.

After the failure of the IrLP in the 1950s, a second attempt to blend constitutional nationalism and social democracy was made in 1970 with the launch of the SDLP. The SDLP was put together by John Hume,[29] and built on the new wave of MPs thrown up by the civil rights movement.[30] Paddy Devlin and Fitt – who were chronically suspicious of Hume's agenda – regarded 'social democratic' as cant for neo-nationalism, and insisted the title include 'Labour'. Fitt became leader. As yet he was its best-known and best-connected MP. Through his and Devlin's contacts with the IrLP, the SDLP became the Northern Ireland affiliate of the Socialist International, giving it a European

28   Eoin Ó Broin, *Sinn Féin and the Politics of Left Republicanism* (London, 2009), pp. 225–7.

29   John Hume (1937–), born in Derry; teacher; came to prominence in the Credit Unions and the 'University for Derry' campaign; elected MP for Foyle in 1969; hugely influential in developing the concept of resolving the conflict through the 'three sets of relationships', and in the Anglo-Irish Agreement and the 'peace process'; criticised for neglecting SDLP organisation and thereby contributing to the rise of Sinn Féin; ardently pro-EU; internationally acclaimed as the 'statesman of the troubles', and awarded a Nobel Peace Prize in 1998. See Gerard Murray, *John Hume and the SDLP* (Dublin, 1998).

30   Loughlin, *The Ulster Question since 1945*, pp. 69–70.

dimension which appealed to Hume. The IrLP was supportive of the SDLP while southern opinion was still emotively nationalist. In August 1970, Corish and Fitt issued a joint statement, promising to work for power-sharing and Irish unity by consent. The IrLP also tried to bring the British Labour Party, the NILP, and the ICTU into the common front, but none wished to be identified with what they saw as a nationalist cause. Relations soured as Conor Cruise O'Brien pursued his tunnel-visioned mission to confront anti-partitionism. O'Brien's hostile response to the SDLP's 1972 manifesto *Towards a New Ireland* – which called for a condominium, pending unity by consent – was a tipping point.[31] In the wake of the UWC strike, O'Brien prepared an internal Labour Party paper arguing that the pursuit of nationalist demands would lead only to a 'doomsday situation' in the North. The SDLP believed the Irish government now favoured an internal settlement, for which it blamed O'Brien.[32]

How the SDLP would reconcile the search for a peaceful settlement with a socialist appeal to Protestants was never specified. Most party members were, like Hume, interested primarily in constitutional reform; 80 per cent of the SDLP's first 400 members came from the National Democratic Party.[33] The fall of the Sunningdale executive delivered a double blow: it ended the SDLP's best chance of showing how it might combine constitutional reform with the application of social policies, and compelled it to choose between them. Ostensibly, the UWC strike was directed against Sunningdale's provision for a Council of Ireland, and Devlin and Fitt believed an accommodation with Unionists was still possible if the party would accept an internal settlement. Most of their colleagues disagreed, convinced that the real target of Unionist ire was power-sharing. Devlin provoked his expulsion in 1977 by attacking the party for drifting away from social democracy.[34] Fitt resigned in 1979 when the SDLP rejected a Northern Ireland Office (NIO) initiative designed to achieve an internal settlement. His prestige had been slipping since the Sunningdale executive, which exposed him as essentially a stellar backbencher, while enhancing the reputation of Hume, as a thinker and negotiator. Hume, the obvious choice as successor, believed that the search for a settlement had to involve the British and Irish governments and be based on a frank recognition of the 'two traditions'.

The UWC strike was effective in changing British policy. Wilson had first developed a bipartisan position with the Conservatives, and then made dramatic personal initiatives while in opposition, calling in 1971 for a united

---

31 Puirséil, *The Irish Labour Party*, pp. 288–99; Devlin, *Straight Left*, p. 187.

32 Murray, *John Hume and the SDLP*, pp. 55–6.

33 Ibid., p. 4.

34 Devlin, *Straight Left*, p. 279.

Ireland within 15 years, and meeting the Provisionals leadership in a peace bid in 1972 at the request of Labour TD Dr John O'Connell. Corish was furious about the meeting and never forgave either Wilson or O'Connell.[35] Following the UWC strike the Irish government was sufficiently alarmed by rumours of a British withdrawal to lobby against it.[36] In reality, Wilson indulged the speculation to lull the IRA into a ceasefire and scare the Unionists into power-sharing. Bipartisanship continued, and on succeeding Wilson in 1976 Callaghan replaced the conciliatory Merlyn Rees with Roy Mason as Northern Secretary of State. The 'Stonemason' – as republicans called him – prioritised a security solution through smashing the Provisionals, and his pro-Union stance was complimented in London when the Labour government, which had now lost its majority, agreed to increase Northern Ireland's representation at Westminster in return for support from Ulster Unionist MPs. Even Fitt was disgusted. On 28 March 1979 the Labour government fell, losing a motion of confidence by one vote. Fitt had abstained. He explained sadly: 'When we look back in history, we see clearly that Labour governments are not the best governments to grapple with the Irish problem. That does not apply to Labour oppositions. When Labour is in opposition one sees the real conscience of the Labour Party'.[37] Indeed. Back in opposition, the hunger strikes encouraged Labour to move towards support for 'unity by consent', until Tony Blair brought Labour back to a pro-Union stance.[38]

The NILP meanwhile, was in terminal decay. The polarisation of Belfast after August 1969, a feeble response to escalating state repression in Catholic areas, and the emergence of alternatives, eviscerated the party. A wistfully re-membered 100,000 votes – 12.6 per cent of the poll – in the 1970 Westminster elections was a swansong. On all sides, it soon lost support: Catholics to the SDLP, Protestants to the Democratic Unionist Party, and liberals to the Alliance Party. It was symptomatic of its desperation that in 1970, while blaming its decline on the perception of Wilson as a united Irelander, it voted to become a region of the British Labour Party. With 'a handful of people present', the motion was carried by the card vote of 20,000 affiliated trade unionists.[39] London rejected the overture, and Callaghan had his party sever its ties with the NILP in 1974.[40] As in the 1950s, the NILP contracted to areas

35   John O'Connell, *Doctor John: Crusading Doctor and Politician* (Dublin, 1989), pp. 124–44.

36   Patterson, *Ireland since 1939*, p. 268.

37   Quoted in Bell, *Troublesome Business*, p. 135.

38   Martin O'Donnell, 'The impact of the 1981 H Block hunger strikes on the British Labour Party', *Irish Political Studies* 14 (1999), pp. 64–83.

39   Devlin, *Straight Left*, pp. 133–4.

40   Edwards, *A History of the Northern Ireland Labour Party*, pp. 206–7.

like Woodvale, Victoria, and Newtownabbey, but unlike the 1950s these districts were experiencing an upsurge of Loyalism which washed over the NILP and turned it into another esoteric socialist sect. Bleakley was its only victor in elections to the 1973 Assembly and 1975 Constitutional Convention. The NILP failed to contest the 1982 Assembly elections.

The ambivalent heritage of the NILP was claimed by two competing traditions, which each seized on one of its two lines of advance. The first virtually equated Labourism with a cross-community appeal, and found expression in the United Labour Party, formed by Paddy Devlin in 1978, the Labour Party of Northern Ireland, formed by Devlin and Blease in 1984, and Labour '87, which absorbed these groups along with the Newtownabbey Labour Party, the Ulster Liberal Party, and the remnant of the NILP, which dissolved formally in 1987. The second, initiated by the Campaign for Labour Representation in 1977 and continued by Labour in Northern Ireland, sought to persuade the British Labour Party to organise in the North, either as the best means of promoting pro-Union Labourism, or on the ground that 'normal politics' could flourish only by replicating the British party system in Northern Ireland.[41] Its efforts began to bear fruit in 2004 when the Labour Party took the first step in this direction.

TRADE UNIONS AND INDUSTRIAL RELATIONS

The outbreak of the Troubles coincided with major changes in the economy and employment, and added to the difficulty of attracting inward investment. An influx of external investment had underpinned economic growth in the 1960s. Government strategy was to continue the North's traditional specialisation in the UK economy, and it focused especially on synthetic fibres, which it regarded as an appropriate replacement for the withering textile and clothing sectors. By 1970, one quarter of the UK synthetic fibre industry was located in the North, in a small number of big plants. European synthetic fibres began to suffer from superior American products in 1971, and the energy-intensive industry was further hit by the oil crises of 1973 and 1979. Shipbuilding also suffered severely in the 1970s, and employment in Harland and Wolff had sunk to 7,400 by 1980. The problems of synthetic fibres and shipbuilding reflected more general weaknesses arising from dependence on a sluggish British economy for investments and markets, and a relatively high reliance on oil for energy. Difficulties intensified in the early 1980s when the Conservative

41   Ibid., pp. 220–4.

government kept sterling strong to combat inflation. Manufacturing employment fell from 172,000 in 1974 to 105,000 in 1986, the year unemployment
reached a peak of 18 per cent. The decline was partly offset by expansion of
public services. Seeing unemployment as a source of paramilitarism, both
Labour and Conservative governments treated Northern Ireland as a special
case, and public sector employment grew to a peak of 43 per cent of the labour
force in 1986. Thus, between 1971 and 1986, total employment fell slightly,
from 555,000 to 549,000, the percentage of workers in industry dropped from
42 to 27, and the percentage in services rose from 47 to 65 per cent. The
restructuring also entailed a rise in the female proportion of employees, from
42 per cent in 1977 to 47 per cent in 1986.[42]

The enemy of my enemy being my friend, Stormont took a kindlier view
of the NIC after the outbreak of the Troubles. A state subsidy of £10,000 per
annum was awarded to the NIC in 1970.[43] Unusually, the government did not
copy the Tories' controversial Industrial Relations Act (1971) onto the six-county
statute book, and instead appointed a Review Body on Industrial Relations.
By the time it reported, the Tories were back in opposition. Opportunities for
unions to influence public policy improved further with the introduction of
Direct Rule. Paradoxically, Direct Rule entailed a more regional approach to
governance, and a profusion of quangos to offset the 'democratic deficit'. By
2000, the NIC had representation on 40 of Northern Ireland's 144 public bodies,
dealing with human rights, industrial relations, the economy and society, education and training, and health and personal social services. Under the Wilson
and Callaghan governments, NIC officials enjoyed 'free and easy' access to NIO
ministers, and lobbied successfully for the extension of labour legislation to
Northern Ireland, notably provisions of the Trade Union and Labour Relations
Act (1974), the Employment Protection Act (1975), and the Trade Union and
Labour Relations (Amendment) Act (1976). When Mrs Thatcher put the boot
on the other foot, the employers' body, the Confederation of British Industry,
Northern Ireland (CBI–NI), did not forgive or forget. Whether the NIC might
have made more of its bargaining chips in fighting the Tories is a moot point.
As the propaganda war for the representation of the North as a normal society
plagued by a few terrorists persisted, so too did the NIO continue to cite
unions as evidence of 'normality'. Among others, NIO under-secretary Chris
Patten praised them as 'a civilising influence in this community throughout the
last fifteen years'. The annual subvention to the NIC grew fatter and fatter,
reaching £76,000 in 1984.[44]

42   Kieran A. Kennedy, Thomas Giblin, and Deirdre McHugh, *The Economic Development of Ireland
in the Twentieth Century* (London, 1988), pp. 107–9.

43   Boyd, *Have The Trade Unions Failed The North?*, pp. 49–51.

44   Ibid., p. 53.

Conservative industrial relations Acts were extended to Northern Ireland tardily and with some mitigation. The NIC, naturally, claimed credit, but it was standard practice for routine Westminster legislation to be applied selectively to the North after a two-year process of consultation with interested parties, and CBI–NI opinion usually carried more weight. The Employment Act (1980) was extended in 1982, though without the provision repealing union rights to seek assistance from the Labour Relations Agency (LRA) in recognition disputes. Norman Tebbit's contentious Employment Act (1982), outlawing secondary strike action, prompted the LRA to suggest that as an alternative to having the Act introduced to the North, the LRA, CBI–NI, and NIC form a standing conference which would distance the North from industrial disputes in Britain. Despite the fact that UK strikes rarely involved the North, and despite encouragement from the ICTU and BTUC, NIC affiliates rejected the proposal, and 'Tebbit's law' was extended to the North in 1987. A third Industrial Relations (Northern Ireland) Order followed in 1992, applying the Employment Acts of 1988, 1989, and 1990. Arguably, the delays in bringing in the 1987 and 1992 orders stemmed from the need to secure union support for the Fair Employment Act (1989).[45] Despite the delays, strike activity fell more rapidly in Northern Ireland than in the UK as a whole in the 1980s. Over the 1977–80 period, an annual average of 664 working days per 1,000 employees were lost in Northern Ireland, compared with an average of 587 in the UK. In the period 1987–90, the respective figures were 111 and 149.[46]

Some aspects of the pro-trade union tinge to NIO policy persisted into the 1990s, and the Industrial Development Board continued to take a broadly supportive position on union recognition in dealing with incoming companies.[47] However, a new challenge arose from the British government's ambition to promote regional pay differentials, and thereby undermine unions' traditional strategy of tracking British pay norms, and, ideally, incorporating the North in UK bargaining. Parity was largely attained in the public sector, where, for most, pay was negotiated on a UK basis, at regional level where employees came under the NIO, or under agreements providing for parity with analogous groups in Britain, so that public sector wages were only slightly below British norms. Private sector wage bargaining had also become more integrated with UK machinery, but local wage determination still applied to a large minority

45 Terry Cradden, 'The Tories and employment law in Northern Ireland: seeing unions in a different light?', *Industrial Relations Journal* 24: 1 (1993), pp. 59–70.

46 Brian Tipping and Patricia McCorry, *Industrial Relations in Northern Ireland: The LRA Survey* (Belfast, 1988), p. 174; Boyd Black, 'Industrial relations under competition', *Review of Employment Topics* 1 (1993), p. 28.

47 Black, 'Industrial relations under competition', p. 23.

and, on average, wages in Northern Ireland were the lowest of any UK region. In 1999, weekly earnings for men in Northern Ireland amounted to £344.90p, compared with a UK average of £398.70p; for women, the respective figures were £295.10p and £325.60p.[48]

In the three decades after 1969, economics and politics re-shaped trade unionism. In 1970, the unions had a very traditional profile, dominated by the 'three Ms' – male, manual, and manufacturing – with 83,200 members in the ATGWU and 27,300 in the Amalgamated Engineering Union.

Table 12.1: **Trade union membership in Northern Ireland, 1970**

Number of trade unions	77
Membership of general unions	103,400
Membership of white collar unions	71,600
Membership of other unions	88,000
Total membership	263,000
Men as a percentage of total membership	74%
Percentage of male employees in trade unions	66%
Women as a percentage of total membership	26%
Percentage of female employees in trade unions	36%

Source: *Charles McCarthy, Trade Unions in Ireland, 1894–1960, p. 597.*

Fifty-four per cent of employees were unionised, compared with 52 per cent in the Republic and 49 per cent in Britain. The decline of general and craft unions was offset, from the mid 1970s, by the growth of jobs in sectors of high union density. By 1983, union membership had peaked at 283,000, a density of 61 per cent of employees, compared with a UK average of 54 per cent.[49] Thereafter, membership began to fall. Economic recovery from the early 1990s brought some comfort: between 1988 and 2001, the number of employees grew from 517,210 to 597,000, and unemployment fell to 6.2%.[50] Union membership began to rise after 1997; and unions became more effective in recruiting women and clerical workers. By 2001, density was higher for non-manual (39 per cent),

48　Central Statistics Office, *Regional Trends* (London, 2000), p. 85.

49　Charles McCarthy, *Trade Unions in Ireland, 1894–1960* (Dublin, 1977), p. 597; John McIlroy, Nina Fishman, and Alan Campbell, *The High Tide of British Trade Unionism: Trade Unions and Industrial Politics, 1964–79* (Monmouth, 2007), p. 120.

50　See the reports of the Northern Ireland Labour Force Survey, conducted biennially, then annually, and quarterly, for the Department of Enterprise, Trade, and Investment.

than for manual workers (34 per cent), and about equal for men and women. Nonetheless, the fall in overall density continued.

It is likely that the strongest reason for the erosion of density was the restructuring of the workforce, especially the decline of manufacturing and public sector employment, and the growth of part-time employment. Workers in manufacture tended to be more pro-union. One survey in 1989 found that 52 per cent of all adults, 56 per cent of Protestants in manufacture and 78 per cent of Catholics in manufacture, agreed that 'workers need strong unions'.[51] Density remained higher in manufacture, and much higher in the public sector. By 2000, a yawning gap had opened between density in the public sector (65 per cent) and the private sector (22 per cent). Less surprisingly, there was a marked difference between density among full-time employees (41 per cent) and part-timers (22 per cent).[52] Public service unions accounted for almost half of the NIC's 215,000 members. Women comprised 50 per cent of the membership, compared with 46 per cent in 1997. There had also been a steep reduction in the number of unions. Of the NIC's 36 affiliates, three, with 44,000 members, were Northern Ireland based; the biggest being the Northern Ireland Public Service Alliance, a legacy of the North's separate administration under Stormont; four, with 20,000 members, were Dublin based; and the remainder were British based. Twenty unions operated on both sides of the border.[53]

SECTARIANISM STOPS AT THE FACTORY GATES?

For trade unions, the Troubles generated an overriding concern with unity and a nagging problem of how to respond to questions of human rights. The contrast between issues of unity and rights became apparent in August 1969 when the sluggish response to the civil rights campaign yielded to pro-activity. The immediate concern was to ensure that this round of conflict did not lead to expulsions, as had happened in crises from 1864 to 1939. The shipyard was the obvious place to start. On 15 August 1969, shop stewards and churchmen spoke to a meeting of 8,000 workers at Harland and Wolff to warn of the economic consequences of violence for a declining industry. A similar appeal was made later at Shorts aircraft factory.[54] Officially, shop-floor sectarianism

---

51   Black, 'Industrial relations under competition', p. 23.

52   Based on the Northern Ireland Labour Force Survey.

53   ICTU, http://www.ictu.ie

54   Edwards, *A History of the Northern Ireland Labour Party*, pp. 162–3; Robert Fisk, *The Point of No Return: The Strike Which Broke the British in Ulster* (London, 1975), pp. 116–7.

was nipped in the bud. The NIO would come to extol unions as havens of normality in a manner all the more curious for the vilification of militants in contemporary Britain: 'Members with all types of religious affiliation, as well as atheists and communists have played a full part in the development of trade unionism . . . with hardly an exception, sectarianism stops at the factory gates'.[55] Reality was more chequered. Groups of Catholics were evicted from the shipyard on four occasions between 1970 and 1972, reducing their numbers from 400 to 100 in the 10,000-strong workforce. Catholics were also run out of textile factories on Belfast's Donegall Road. And whereas the National Union of Tailors and Garment makers disciplined offending members, unions accepted that things were done differently in the shipyard.[56] There were innumerable lesser incidents of intimidation, and a 'chill factor' took root to deter both Catholics and Protestants from working in areas they deemed unfriendly. That there was no repeat of the horrors of 1920 reflected the weaker position of Unionists. Industrially, they were more dependent on external investment; politically and militarily, they were constrained by a Labour government in London.

In August 1969 the NIC rushed out 30,000 copies of its *Programme for Peace and Progress in Northern Ireland*; the first of a series of manifestos calling for the restoration of good order through stability, incremental reform, and economic improvement. The *Programme* also emphasised that the status of Northern Ireland within the UK could not be changed legally without the consent of the majority. On 9 September the NIC and Chichester–Clark issued a joint communiqué affirming the government's commitment to reform.[57] In 1972 the ICTU – with the backing of all affiliates – published its first statement of political policy on Northern Ireland. It began with an acknowledgement that 'political resolutions which went outside the scope of the Constitution of Congress' were routinely removed from its agenda; affirmed that it would not be 'appropriate' for the ICTU to comment on the constitutional status of Northern Ireland – though it would repeatedly endorse the status quo and later commend the 'peace process'; and suggested three bases for political dialogue: rejection of violence, acceptance of 'the principle of non-discrimination', and acceptance of the right to advocate peaceful political change.[58] While balanced and liberal in values, the unspoken rationale of Congress manifestos on the North was to discourage Labour Unionism in general, and shop-floor

55 Northern Ireland Information Service, 1979, cited in Liam O'Dowd, Bill Rolston, and Mike Tomlinson, *Northern Ireland: Between Civil Rights and Civil War* (London, 1980), p. 69.

56 Paddy Devlin, *The Fall of the NI Executive* (Belfast, 1975), pp. 74–7; Devlin, *Straight Left*, p. 173; Boyd, *Have the Trade Unions Failed the North?*, p. 76; Fisk, *The Point of No Return*, pp. 116–7.

57 Boyd, *Have the Trade Unions Failed the North?*, pp. 75–8.

58 ICTU, *Political Policy in Northern Ireland* (Dublin, 1972), p. 1.

Loyalism in particular. Aside from minor trouble in Derry in October and November 1968, nationalist workers were quiescent. Loyalists had a tradition.

Loyalist workers had organised soon after August 1969 with the formation of the Workers' Committee for the Defence of the Constitution by Billy Hull, a convener of engineering shop stewards in Harland and Wolff and former NILP member. In 1971 the Committee became the Loyalist Association of Workers (LAW). The LAW led a march of 4,000 shipyardmen in February 1971 to demand internment, protested against the prorogation of Stormont in 1972, and ran a two-day strike in 1973 against the internment of Loyalists. Hull hoped to turn the LAW into a working-class Protestant party, but was opposed by Bill Craig, leader of the Vanguard Unionist Progressive Party. Hull plumped for Vanguard instead, the LAW disintegrated, and most members backed the UWC on its establishment in 1973 and argued for industrial political action. The UWC included various trade union activists, notably Harry Murray, a shipyard shop steward, and Glen Barr, an Engineering Union branch president, but amounted to no more than a committee. Its strength lay in its connections with the Ulster Defence Association and workers in the power stations, under-pinned by the willingness of most Unionists to endure a struggle against the Sunningdale Agreement.

The general strike it called on Wednesday 15 May 1974 was poorly planned, and ignored by 90 per cent of employees until the barricades of the Ulster Defence Association started a snowball of genuine enthusiasm. Unwilling to fight a war on two fronts, the British Army did little to stop the intimidation. Power cuts were the UWC's trump card, and, unlike the 44-hour strike in 1919, the power stations were not brought under military control. Trade unions called for business as usual, and on Saturday 18th a meeting of 400 cadres of the Confederation of Shipbuilding and Engineering Unions and the Joint Industrial Council for the Electricity Supply Industry decided to organise two 'back to work marches', to the shipyard and to Castlereagh industrial estate. To counter jibes that unions answered to a 'foreign Congress', the Belfast march would be led by the BTUC general secretary, Len Murray. The NIO thought the marches might be a turning point. Blease claimed subsequently that he knew it was hopeless, but felt the NIC had to be seen to be giving a lead to its affiliates.[59] No attempt was made to mobilise the rank and file, and it all looked awfully perfunctory. On 21 May, about 200 turned up for the march in Belfast – many of them peace activists – and 19 in Castlereagh. On the 25th, Wilson broadcast to the nation, denouncing 'people who spend their lives sponging on Westminster' and signing off: 'We intend to see it through . . .'.

59   Cradden, 'Billy Blease', pp. 153–4; for the strike see Fisk, *The Point of No Return*, and Don Anderson, *Fourteen May Days: The Inside Story of the Loyalist Strike of 1974* (Dublin, 1994).

In reality, when anti-Sunningdale Unionists won 11 of the 12 Northern Ireland seats in the February 1974 Westminster election, the incoming Labour government concluded that Sunningdale was dead in the water. After the UWC called a 'total strike' on the 27 May, threatening a complete breakdown of power and control of sewage, the pro-Sunningdale Unionists pulled the plug on the power-sharing executive on 28 May. Normal service resumed on the shop floor. No attempt was made to challenge the unions. Union membership actually increased as workers sought to recoup money lost during the strike. Nothing came of talk about an 'Ulster TUC'.

The threat of further industrial political action prompted the NIC to escalate its response from programmes to campaigns involving public rallies against 'violence, sectarianism, intimidation, and discrimination' and for decent jobs, houses, education, and social security. Its first and best-known campaign – *A Better Life for All* – was launched in 1976, and followed by *Peace, Work, and Progress* in 1986. The pious policies which left everyone's politics intact caused bemusement about the point of it all. Joe Bowers, an official of the Engineers, a union with a strong base in east Belfast, gave the most revealing answer:

> We must continue to work to develop a campaign on the 'Better Life for All' Programme, because if we don't, trade unionists in Northern Ireland, in Britain, and in the Irish Republic will obviously flirt with one or other of the myriad constitutional solutions that will be presented to them on the media and will assume that we have lost faith in our own policy.[60]

In other words, the campaign was less about mobilising workers than sustaining the confidence of unions in the NIC. In the event, Loyalists were unable to repeat the triumph of 1974. The United Unionist Action Council, headed by Paisley, called a strike in May 1977 to demand tougher measures against the IRA and the implementation of the report of the 1975 Constitutional Convention. This time the NIO was prepared, and divisions within Unionism and a failure to secure power cuts rendered it less than effective. The strike was ended after two weeks.

Whereas the quest for unity was perceived as synonymous with moderation, defence, and common sense, human rights were seen as nationalist grievances and political, and they generated both internal dissent and international pressure. Under Michael Mullen, the ITGWU was the most feisty. The union collected 'very substantial' donations for Northern relief after August 1969 – almost £6,500 by December 1969 – Mullen toured the North, and his general officers

---

60 NLI, ICTU, *Report* (1978), p. 389.

lobbied the BTUC for a Bill of Rights.[61] The ITGWU's annual conference in June 1971 called for the release of 'political prisoners' in Britain and Northern Ireland, despite pleas from O'Brien and Corish.[62] Liberty Hall was targeted by one of two Loyalist bombs intended to speed the passage of the Offences Against the State (Amendment) Bill in December 1972. In 1975 the ITGWU called on Congress to demand repeal of the Offences Against the State Acts and deplore Section 31 of the Broadcasting Act.[63] Amalgamateds were more inclined to tender motions against violence, and those with no members in the Republic were most uncomfortable about dealing with civil liberties. The NIC's role was to discourage action and formulate balanced policy documents. Internment drew condemnation from the ITGWU and led the Irish National Teachers' Organisation to convene an anti-internment conference in Belfast. International federations and the Transport Workers of America protested to the British government. The NIC issued a non-committal statement on 10 August 1971 and said nothing further until its 1972 programme – *Peace, Employment, and Reconstruction* – slipped an end to internment into a list of demands which also included repeal of the Special Powers Act, a Bill of Rights, the return of troops to barracks, an end to the nationalist boycott of Stormont and inter-party talks, more jobs, and 200,000 houses.[64]

Trade union aphasia reached its nadir in the aftermath of 'Bloody Sunday'. Two days later, a joint ICTU–BTUC conference opened in Belfast to launch *Peace, Employment, and Reconstruction*. The only conference reference to Bloody Sunday was a remark by BTUC general secretary Vic Feather, deploring the 'condition of society which invited tragedies such as that at Derry'. Next day, Feather and Blease met Derry trade unionists to enlist their opposition to the blacking of British cargoes by American longshoremen. The aphasia ran deep. Derry trades council merely passed a vote of sympathy to relatives of the dead and hoped 'that those injured would soon be restored to health'.[65] The Northern response also illustrated how effectively the border had compartmentalised unions. Southern workers downed tools and marched en masse on the Republic's day of mourning on 2 February. Worried about a backlash against the amalgamateds, Matt Merrigan telegrammed a sharp denunciation of British policy in the North to his general secretary, Jack Jones, and circularised his

61   Barry Desmond, *Finally and in Conclusion: A Political Memoir* (Dublin, 2000), p. 136; Francis Devine, *Organising History: A Centenary of SIPTU, 1909–2009* (Dublin, 2009), pp. 517–18.

62   Michael Gallagher, *The Irish Labour Party in Transition, 1957–82* (Manchester, 1982), pp 138–9.

63   *Irish Times*, 4 Dec. 1972; ICTU, *Report* (1975), pp. 626–7.

64   Kieran Allen, *Fianna Fáil and Irish Labour: 1926 to the Present* (London, 1997), pp. 140–1; Boyd, *Have the Trade Unions Failed the North?*, pp. 79–82.

65   Paddy Logue, *Them and Us: A Socialist Response to 'Work is the Key'* (Dublin, 1994), pp. 91–2.

members with a mendacious apologia for British Labour.[66] Privately, Merrigan could be scathing about his UK brothers, and Jones had had a shadowy liaison with Irish republicans before joining the International Brigades in Spain. The Northern ATGWU remained pro-establishment just the same.

Unions gradually found a consensual voice on rights under Direct Rule. The establishment of quangos like the Standing Advisory Commission on Human Rights, the Office of Ombudsman, the Police Authority, and the Fair Employment Agency, encouraged the formulation of policies, and created acceptable outlets for policy implementation. It was too dilatory for some. The NIC was able to marginalise ginger groups like the west Belfast-based Trade Union Campaign Against Repression. International trade union pressure could not be ignored so easily, and it persuaded the NIC to adopt a *Memorandum on the Protection of Human Rights in Northern Ireland* in 1978.[67] Fair employment became a particularly thorny issue. Four trade union and four employer representatives were nominated to the Van Straubenzee committee in 1973, which laid the basis of the first legislation – the Fair Employment (Northern Ireland) Act (1976) – and established the Fair Employment Agency. Union satisfaction with the Act, despite an unemployment rate for Catholic men of over 35 per cent, compared with under 15 per cent for Protestant men, seemed to critics to be another example of foot-dragging.[68] Moreover, it was whispered that unions themselves engaged in discrimination and the Fair Employment Agency corroborated the allegation against one NIC affiliate, the General, Municipal, and Boilermakers.[69] The launch of the MacBride Principles, which called inter-alia for affirmative action for equality, by the Washington DC based Irish National Caucus in 1984, transformed the debate. The British were highly sensitive about their image in the US, and the NIO countered with a fierce propaganda war. Aghast at the willingness of Northern colleagues to be enlisted in the campaign, some senior officials in the Republic formed Trade Unionists for Irish Unity and Independence and canvassed for ICTU endorsement of the MacBride Principles.[70] To prevent a division of leading personalities between the NIO and the republican-backed MacBride Principles, the NIC's

---

66 Merrigan, *Eagle or Cuckoo?*, pp. 236–8.

67 O'Dowd, Rolston, and Tomlinson, *Northern Ireland*, pp. 82–3.

68 Vincent McCormack and Inez McCormack, 'Equalizing advantages: lessening discrimination': reviewing Northern Ireland's fair employment laws', *Review of Employment Topics* 2 (1994), p. 43.

69 Merrigan, *Eagle or Cuckoo?*, pp. 250–1; Terry Cradden, 'Trade unionism, social justice and religious discrimination in Northern Ireland', *Industrial and Labor Relations Review* 46: 3 (1993), p. 486.

70 Trade Unionists for Irish Unity and Independence, *Opposing Discrimination in Northern Ireland* (Dublin, 1988).

1985 conference adopted a stronger commitment to equality, and in 1986 the NIC appointed a permanent equality committee, adopted a *Charter for Equal Opportunities*, and launched a new campaign – *Peace, Work, and Progress* – to publicise its position. Thinking along the similar lines, the government decided to combat the MacBride Principles with the more effective Fair Employment Act (1989).[71] It was indicative of a greater confidence in addressing sectarianism that in 1990 the NIC appointed an anti-intimidation officer and launched an anti-intimidation programme, 'Counteract'.[72]

THE PEACE PROCESS

Like so many departures in republicanism, the 'peace process' originated in the politicisation of IRA prisoners. Politicisation and the 1981 hunger strikes emboldened Sinn Féin into contesting elections as part of an 'armalite and ballot box' strategy. But a promising ten per cent of the vote in the 1982 Northern Ireland Assembly elections turned out to be a plateau rather than a springboard. Hopes of a breakthrough in the Republic were disappointed, and support in the North began to fall as the SDLP was boosted by the Anglo-Irish Agreement in 1985 and public opinion hardened against IRA atrocities, which, in the 1980s, were less likely to be offset by British army blunders. It was evident, to Gerry Adams at least, that the armalite and ballot box were contradictory rather than complimentary, and one would have to go. Sinn Féin began reducing the price of peace, from a British declaration of intent to withdraw, to Britain becoming persuaders for Irish unity, to, in 1993, a British recognition of the right of the Irish people to self-determination. At that point, Hume broke a political taboo and opened talks with Adams, realising that everyone agreed with 'self-determination', depending on how the unit of self-determination was defined. The IRA declared a ceasefire in August 1994, and the Combined Loyalist Military Command followed suit in October.

In 1996 the government announced elections to a Northern Ireland Forum, which would serve also as the negotiation body for all-party talks. It was to be elected on the d'Hondt system – never used before in the UK – and representation would be given to the ten most popular contesting groups. One reason for the d'Hondt contrivance was to find a way of including the Progressive Unionist Party (PUP) and the Ulster Democratic Party (UDP), the political

71   Cradden, 'Trade unionism, social justice and religious discrimination in Northern Ireland', pp. 480–96.
72   Cradden, 'The trade union movement in Northern Ireland', in Donal Nevin (ed.), *Trade Union Century* (Cork, 1994), pp. 66–84.

wings of the Ulster Volunteer Force and the Ulster Defence Association/ Ulster Freedom Fighters, respectively. Both parties mixed militant Loyalism with a populist antagonism to the 'fur-coat' brigade and, in the 1990s, calls for an end to paramilitarism and a historic compromise. The PUP was avowedly left wing, with a constitution modelled on that of the British Labour Party. Though the PUP had been around since 1979 and the UDP since 1981, both popped out of obscurity early in the 'peace process', which was convenient for the NIO, making it easier for Stormont to engage with Loyalist paramilitaries and more difficult for mainstream Unionists to isolate Sinn Féin. Almost overnight, David Ervine[73] became a sensation; the sight of a fluent, progressive Loyalist bearing a passing resemblance to James Connolly caused many a double take. Secretary of State Mo Mowlam canvassed an incredulous IrLP on getting the PUP into the Socialist International.[74] The PUP and UDP secured representation in the peace talks negotiation body, though the latter was expelled in 1998 following the killing of three Catholics by the Ulster Freedom Fighters.[75] They subsequently suffered electoral decline, partly because of their support for the Belfast Agreement. In the 2001 local elections, one UDP councillor and four PUP councillors were returned. Divers left-wing groups also fought the Forum elections as the Labour Coalition. The Labour Coalition secured tenth place with 6,425 votes and was awarded two seats in the talks body. However, tensions within the Coalition led to its virtual disintegration within a year. Its impact on the talks was negligible. Three candidates associated with 'Labour' politics were returned in the 1997 District Council elections, and a similar number in 2001.

The 'peace process' drew Sinn Féin into the slipstream of the SDLP's strategy of prioritising cooperation with the three governments – the White House having become as integral to the process as Downing Street and Government Buildings – to find an accommodation between the 'two tradi-tions'. Indeed, the Americans turned the 'peace process' into a peace process. Republicans had envisaged a process for constitutional change. But the US political involvement was merely the spear point of an ideological intervention –

73   David Ervine (1953–2007), raised in east Belfast, left school aged 15 and joined the Ulster Volunteer Force at 18; arrested in 1974 for possession of explosives; directed towards politics and socialism by Loyalist guru Gusty Spence while imprisoned; released in 1980 and ran a newsagents; elected to Belfast City Council, 1997, and the Northern Ireland Assembly, 1998 and 2003; the second leader of the PUP from 2002, succeeding Hugh Smyth; died suddenly of a heart attack; widely admired as an advocate of new thinking and anti-sectarianism. See Ed Moloney, *Voices from the Grave: Two Men's War in Ireland* (London, 2010).

74   Ray Kavanagh, *Spring, Summer and Fall: The Rise and Fall of the Labour Party, 1986–99* (Dublin, 2001), p. 213.

75   Bertie Ahern, *Bertie Ahern: The Autobiography* (London, 2009), p. 216.

infused through politicians, foundations, peace groups, conferences, and junkets, and underpinned with public and private dollars – which moved the philosophy of the process 'from the bloodlines of ethnicity to the lifelines of human rights'.[76] The Irish government agreed to Unionist demands for concessions on strands two and three of the negotiations – dealing with North–south and east–west relations – in return for concessions on strand one – dealing with the governance of Northern Ireland. Concerned primarily with security issues, power-sharing, and policing, Sinn Féin left strands two and three to the SDLP. For traditional anti-partitionists, the Belfast Agreement was worse than Sunningdale, but Sinn Féin got enough on strand one to satisfy its Northern bailiwicks and the IRA. Electorally, it continued to gain ground. The IRA ceasefire removed both an encumbrance from Sinn Féin and a defining pillar of the SDLP. If Sinn Féin could be accused of tailing the SDLP, the choice was no longer war or peace, but 'stand-up' or 'roll-over' nationalism. In the 2001 District Council elections, Sinn Féin outpolled the SDLP for the first time.

The evolving consensus that peace, agreement within Northern Ireland, respect for human rights, and cross-border economic cooperation, were the fundaments of a constitutional settlement, and that the 'civic sector' had a role to play in fostering political convergence, encouraged the NIC to be more assertive. Congress was firmly behind the 'peace process' and adopted *Investing in Peace* as a priority programme in 1994. *Investing in Peace* sought to underpin reconciliation through an input from the civic sector into economic and social relations throughout Ireland. Its priorities were partnership between unions, employers, voluntary organisations, and both governments; European investment; social inclusion for the unemployed, women, people with disabilities, and peripheral regions; and social justice, human rights, and equality. The NIC further renewed its call for a Bill of Rights, for the parades problem to be resolved within the context of police reform, and made submissions on RUC reform, proposing changes in the accountability, complaints procedure, composition, recruitment, and training of the police. In response to the 1996 Drumcree disturbances, the NIC joined six business organisations in the 'Group of Seven' (G7) to encourage the politicians to reach an accommodation; and in the referendum on the Belfast Agreement it campaigned openly for a 'yes' vote. Mirroring the political architecture of the Agreement, the NIC appointed its own cross-border working group in 1999, which also liaised with the British and Scottish TUCs. To bolster the civic sector, a 60-member Civic Forum was established under the Belfast Agreement, with seven seats being allocated to

---

76 The quote is from Congressman Bruce Morrisson, and was cited in an invitation to a peace conference on 'Identities of choice', The Downings, Donegal, May 2006, itself an example of the level of US penetration.

trade unionists. The Agreement also provided for stronger equality measures. In reality, there was little to add to the Fair Employment Act (1989) other than cosmetic touches to flatter Sinn Féin, which had made much of   its 'equality agenda'. Existing legislation was consolidated under the Fair Employment and Treatment Order (1998), its scope was widened, and an Equality Commission was appointed, incorporating the Fair Employment Commission, and the three agencies dealing with gender, disability, and racial discrimination.

After 1969, working-class politics became more polarised than ever. Catholics found putting their community grievances first to be a more effective means of winning redress than pursuing 'bread and butter' politics; feeling threatened by the success of Catholic mobilisation, Protestants closed ranks behind the Unionist parties. The prospects for rebuilding the cross-community support garnered by the NILP before 1949 and again in the mid 1960s are remote. All of the constitutional agreements since 1973 have entrenched the concept of the 'two traditions'. Moreover, as the main political parties take a broadly neo-Keynesian approach to economic issues, a 'Labour' agenda has little of distinction to offer, other than a satisfying basis on which to canvass both sides of the house. Trade unions weathered the storm and succeeded in fostering a consensus on how they should address politics and, eventually, human rights. Given the history of the movement, it was always likely that unity would be sustained through membership detachment rather than participation.

The all-inclusive system of power-sharing established under the Belfast Agreement, and applied with effect under the St Andrews Agreement in 2007, has created a workable basis for devolved politics at the expense of institutionalising the confessional divide and making it more difficult to progress towards a secular party system. There is hope, however, in the fact that the contradiction is recognised and there is a growing desire to find some way of resolving it.

THIRTEEN

CONCLUSION

—

Reflections on Irish socialism invariably address its very un-European weakness. Liberal idealism and modernisation theory have provided intuitively appealing explanations in the historic weight of the Catholic Church, the land question, and nationalism, and the inordinate power of those three villains of socialist demonology, the priest, the peasant, and the patriot; explanations which are as old as socialism itself, and which were discovered afresh in the 'new labour history' and the more secular and anti-nationalist radicalism that developed in the 1970s. Yet the political weakness of Labour is odd. For most of the nineteenth century, trade unions were highly politicised. The century saw major popular campaigns, for Catholic emancipation, against tithes, for tenant right, for labourers' cottages, and for independence or self-government. In exile, the Irish sided naturally with the left. At home, they built a comparatively strong trade union movement in the twentieth century. Operating for the most part in conditions of chronic unemployment in a fragile economy, dependent on external investment from the 1960s, and invariably directed by governments of the right or centre-right, the unions fared surprisingly well. It took big blunders to ensure that the left was so spectacularly unsuccessful.

Within six years of the decriminalisation of trade unions in 1824, Labour politics in southern Ireland became determined by the need to protect native industry from foreign competition. The craft elite of the working class was badly hit by free trade with Britain's developing manufacture after 1826, and theirs was the premier call for Repeal of the Union. In Labour's first engagement with parliamentary politics, they supported Daniel O'Connell, realising that the constitutional question was a Labour question. One could not long defend wages, conditions, or employment levels in a declining economy; one could not reverse decline without tariff protection; one could not have tariffs without self-government. Whatever the deficiencies of national movements, whatever the prospects under a native regime might be – and workers were less naive about both than historians have given them credit for – trade unionists regarded economic sovereignty to be essential to the survival of their livelihoods and their unions. Popular sovereignty too was impossible without self-determination.

The alliance with the Repeal agitation in the 1830s set the pattern for Labour politics over the next 60 years. Workers supported the leading national movement of the day, be it constitutional or republican, though trade unions remained wary of formal association with revolutionists after the watershed of 1848. It was a strategy that, of its nature, militated against making class division the central question in politics and ingrained in Labour bodies a tendency to look to the national elite for leadership. However, it can hardly explain the weakness of forces for socialism or the marginalisation of Labour in the late nineteenth century: the reasons for these must be sought in de-industrialisation. One could scarcely speak credibly of a socialist future when capitalist colonisation was *un*making the working class. Irish Labour was therefore exceptional in nineteenth century Europe in two respects. First, it faced overwhelmingly a problem of de-industrialisation, long before most other countries had begun to industrialise. Secondly, self-determination was as much a Labour issue as a middle class one. Indeed, a nagging fear of the Dublin craft unions in the 1830s was that O'Connell would accept something short of Repeal. Nationalism provided a rallying point for trade unions and a platform for grievances. Invariably, it politicised Labour; occasionally, as in 1848 and 1916–23, it pushed workers to the far left.

With the growing coherence of interest group politics in the 1880s, the growth of trades councils, the extension of the franchise, and the stimulus of new unionism, the possibility of building a Labour Nationalist parliamentary lobby became real. However, just when it seemed that Labour might finally swap its diminishing share-hold in the national movement for a junior partnership, countervailing forces were to steer it in a completely different direction. Industrial and demographic decline had now reached the point where most Irish trade unions saw no future for themselves as independent societies. After decades of rearguard action against the encroachment of British trade unionism, they gave up the ghost. By 1900, Labour broadly regarded itself as a part of the British movement, adopting British principles of industrial and political strategy uncritically. Paradoxically, the splinter from the BTUC deepened this anglicisation. The ITUC was the last of four attempts to establish a congress between 1889 and 1894. Each of the previous three had envisaged a more political entity, in line with the vintage strategy of using the national movement as the channel of Labour goals. Dublin trades council directed a decisive breach with this tradition by seeking to copy the BTUC. The outcome was a nice, neat trade union forum which narrowed the definition of Labour from the working class to members of nice, neat trade unions, and which focused on industrial organisation, where Labour was weak, rather than politics, where it had some leverage. Political influence, if required, was to emanate from the ITUC's mythical industrial strength, and pursue industrial grievances only. Anything to do with the national question was no longer legitimate terrain. Because English, Scottish, and Welsh nationalism were seen as hostile to the cohesion of the emerging British Labour movement, so the ITUC blandly assumed that the same reasoning must hold true for Ireland too. From here on, with the notable exception of individuals like Michael Davitt, James Connolly, and Jim Larkin, Labour would see nationalism as a problem, not an opportunity. The result was depoliticisation. Whilst farmers, town tenants, and agricultural workers all pursued social interests through the IPP, trade unionists opted out.

It was not unusual that Labour should have been influenced by its nearest, and more successful, counterpart. The years from 1889 to 1923 were formative in the history of Labour movements worldwide. The German Social Democratic Party offered a model for kindred parties in Scandinavia; French ideas helped to shape Italian and Spanish socialism; Canadian workers looked to the US. British craftsmen built the most powerful trade unionism in the world after 1850, and exported it to most of the white English-speaking countries. But the vast gulf in political culture, economy, and employment structure between a highly advanced country and the undeveloping region on its western periphery, makes it impossible to understand how anyone could have thought of applying the British model to Ireland without an immersion in mental colonisation.

New unionism was the first of three great waves of agitation that revolutionised Labour between 1889 and 1923. If new unionism reinforced Irish reliance on British Labour, Larkinism – from 1907 to 1913 – challenged that dependency, and syndicalism – from 1917 to 1923 – sealed the making of the modern Irish Labour movement. Larkin came to Ireland an opponent of dividing unions along national lines. Within two years he had concluded that British-based unions could not build a bargaining power for the mass of Irish workers. The formation of the ITGWU in 1909 marked the beginning of a long and painful decolonisation that modernised the movement, and made it more relevant to native conditions. Why was the left unable to keep pace? After 1916, Congress modified its position of neutrality on the national question to one of acceptance of the prevailing consensus. It never shook off the sense that constitutional questions were foreign territory. This was far more effective in subordinating Labour to the conservative parties than a direct engagement with nationalism, as it invariably reduced it to tagging along behind the agenda of others. In particular, it prevented it from exploiting the political opportunities that arose from the national and international revolutions in the immediate post-war years, and from the division of nationalists over the 1921 Treaty.

Labour made four big blunders in the formative period of modern Irish politics, each of which intrigues for its sheer perversity. The foundation error was to spurn Davitt's advice – John Redmond's too – to build a Labour–Nationalist alliance with the IPP in the 1890s. The best-known opportunity missed was the decision to withdraw from the 1918 general election rather than do a deal with Sinn Féin. The third mistake was to offer uncritical support to the 1921 settlement. Blank cheques to the government are never politic for an opposition, the more so when a substantial minority, and soon a majority, favoured a peaceful revision of the Treaty. Instead of stealing a march on Fianna Fáil, Labour made a fourth mistake in helping its rival into Leinster House. Once Fianna Fáil accepted the rules of constitutional politics, Labour's minority status was sealed. One can cite other difficulties confronting the party in the 1920s: the industrial defeats of 1921–3; the Larkin split; an electoral system which encouraged Labour TDs to be consensual, clientelist, and mediocre; and two party leaders unfit for purpose. For all that, what distinguished Labour in the 1920s was a peculiar alienation from its own polity. It saw the Fianna Fáil and Cumann na nGaedheal/ Fine Gael divide as an extension of the Civil War rather than an expression too of conflicting class interests over economic dependency on Britain. Unable to make sense of the political culture in which it operated, Labour waited for nationalism to run its course, hoping that modernisation would eventually replicate British-type class politics in Ireland.

One might further contend that Labour missed the bus in disengaging from the North in the 1960s. Making common cause with civil rights groups, the NILP left, and British Labour backbenchers while Fianna Fáil Taoisigh took tea at Stormont would have been astute. It is also a fanciful counterfactual, suggesting a possibility which was never likely for a moderate, 26-county party. The four big blunders were of a different order; in each case the easier and natural thing would have been to do the opposite.

Another set of issues materialised in relation to the trade unions. The Labour Party didn't simply emerge in 1912: it was the product of an intellectual revolution in trade unionism, whipped up by Larkin's syndicalism and republicanism. In 1912 it was assumed that trade unionists would vote Labour. When that assumption unravelled after 1923, another intellectual revolution was required. Labour, quite sensibly, reorganised as a branch-based party, but without re-evaluating its role in the movement. Instead it adopted the British model of trade union affiliation, and persisted with an untenable scenario: the unions would concentrate on their industrial strength, and pursue bargaining power through wage militancy in free collective bargaining in a voluntary system of industrial relations, and their political agenda would be implemented by a Labour government. This laissez faire approach was all very well for a strong trade union movement in a strong economy, with a strong political wing. Yet, none of these conditions applied in Ireland before 1946. The scenario began to come unstuck when Fianna Fáil took office. Unlike Fine Gael, Fianna Fáil governments always had an agenda to reform industrial relations, their ambitions partly conflicted and partly converged with those of the unions, and Fianna Fáil in government could be of more use to the unions than Labour in opposition. Fortunately for Labour, the colonial legacy threw it a lifeline. The legacy had survived most egregiously in the sectionalist pattern of trade union organisation. In 1939, the bulk of Irish unions backed a plan to modernise Congress along industrial unionist lines. It was an opportunity to build a new type of Labour movement. In another act of perversity, William Norton sided with the British unions to defeat it. The effect was to drive the ITGWU and other private sector Irish unions towards Fianna Fáil, and induce a questioning of inherited assumptions about Labour–state relations which culminated in the 1945 split.

Superficially, the split was one between left-wing internationalists and right-wing nationalists. Structurally, it revealed a division between the better off unions who wished to preserve the status quo, and their weaker colleagues who were willing to accept a change in Labour–state relations, in the hope of augmenting their membership and bargaining power. That the ostensibly more radical ITUC was in practice the more conservative of the two Congresses, illustrates the degree to which Labour orthodoxy had become a disabling rather than an enabling ideology. The mistaken basis of that ideology is evident too from the fact that legislative intervention in industrial relations actually strengthened the movement. After all the huffing and puffing against the Trade Union Act (1941), the Act, or at least the amending Act of 1942, led to a modest wartime increase in union membership, and contributed to the fabulous and forgotten post-war expansion underpinned by the Industrial Relations Act (1946), the establishment of the Labour Court, and the wage rounds. Now for the first time, it became possible for all workers unable to win a bargaining power through wage militancy alone to become organised. The recruitment of over 100,000 additional trade unionists between 1945 and 1950 indicates the size of the constituency which the laissez faire approach had been incapable of reaching.

The 1940s was the pivotal decade in the history of industrial relations in independent Ireland. With the end of the Emergency, an equilibrium developed in the politics of industrial relations. Fianna Fáil's dependency on working-class votes gave the unions some leverage. The revolt against the Trade Union Act (1941) and the swing to the left in the 1943 general election were long-remembered shots across its bow. The party was careful to offer some accommodation to unions when ending statutory wage control in 1946, shifting to free-er trade and dependency on foreign investment after 1958, and tackling the economic crisis in 1987. Social partnership represented the culmination of the process. Displaying an admirably precise grasp of history, Jack O'Connor would describe the collapse of social partnership in December 2009 as the end of a contract between Fianna Fáil and the unions that began in 1942.

By the 1970s, the Labour Party had surrendered two strategic dynamics: it was no longer the party of last resort for trade union militancy or constitutional republicanism. The ITGWU and Fianna Fáil were the twin pillars of Labour–state relations, and the re-affiliation of the three major unions to the party in the 1960s scarcely affected that. On the national question, the party had withdrawn into reaction. The only remaining hope was modernisation. The splits in the 1940s had scuppered Labour's chances of benefiting from the Beveridge Report and the post-war swing to the left in Europe. Clann na Poblachta proved to be a false dawn. So too did the 'swinging sixties'. Coalitions with Fine Gael and deteriorating relations with the unions reduced Labour to the verge of oblivion in 1987. The 'Spring tide', five years later, turned out to be a bubble. Nonetheless, 1989 was a turning point for the left. The increasing difficulty of Fianna Fáil and Fine Gael in managing the deficit budgeting and auction politics embraced from 1972–3, led to a new electoral volatility. The WP, DL, Sinn Féin, the Socialist Party, and the Greens, took up the radical causes abandoned by the liberals of the Labour Party, and aggregate support for the left climbed to an unprecedented plateau of some 20 per cent in the 1990s and 2000s. From this springboard, Labour and the far left were able to capitalise on the agonies of Fianna Fáil in 2011. It remains to be seen whether Labour's decision not to become the main opposition party amounted to another wasted opportunity to twist those agonies into death-throes.

There were no magic bullets for northern Labour, which was beset by the primordial question of how to make a movement. Histories of northern Labour have focused mainly on politics, or looked at trade unionism for what it says about politics. Writing in the Connolly school targeted Orangeism as the problematic. Studies in the 'new labour history' have emphasised the importance of Ireland's uneven economic development in the nineteenth century, and treated Labour in pre-partition Belfast as an extension of British Labour and nationalism as the problematic. Neither approach is satisfactory in that they are more concerned with justifying republicanism or Unionism than explaining problems of Labour movement formation. Three problems of movement formation can be identified.

First, Ulster's two industrial revolutions produced two separate trade unionisms. The rise of the factory system of textile production smashed the old craft unions. Textiles remained the biggest employment sector by driving down wage costs, gradually becoming women's work. By 1914 only about ten per cent of its employees were organised in unions, which were local, small, and weak. The next wave of industrialisation – in engineering and shipbuilding – reproduced an approximation of British industrial relations in the metal trades, allowing for the growth of strong craft unions. Craft conscious, relatively well paid, Conservative in politics, and occasionally the self-appointed shock troops of Unionism, most workers in engineering and the shipyards wanted little to do with Belfast trades council, which they regarded as a vehicle for lower paid or unskilled workers, and politically suspect.

Secondly, there were the amalgamateds, who consolidated in Ulster during the First World War by extending to the textile sector. This had the positive outcome of bringing Catholic and Protestant workers into the same unions, and there was a logic to having Northern workers in British unions when their wage strategy was to track cross-channel pay rates. But provincialism had its negative consequences. The amalgamateds had no wish to address the oddities of Ulster or build a Labour movement in Ireland, north or south. To camouflage inaction, they fostered the myth that unions transcended working-class divisions, when in actuality the divisions were carefully contained through an oligarchy of officialdom. The result was a trade unionism built on pretence, which offered neither unity nor democracy. Such was the hegemony of British Labourism that few doubted that they should comply with its conceits, or challenged the bland treatment of Northern Ireland as just another part of the UK. Only the threat to the amalgamateds in Éire in the 1930s spurred their Northern branches into engaging with the ITUC, leading to the creation of the NIC. It took the outbreak of conflict in 1969 to prompt the ICTU and NIC into addressing the grittier realities of Northern Ireland. In fairness to the unions, they solved their problems better than the political left. The NIC was an imaginative response to the challenge of maintaining the outline unity of Congress and developing a public voice for unions in Northern Ireland – one which anticipated the post-1969 constitutional initiatives – and after 1969 it managed belatedly to devise an agenda on the North in difficult and dangerous circumstances.

Finally, there was the conundrum of how to mobilise politically. Before partition, the predominantly Protestant Belfast trades council's difficulties had less to do with sectarian divisions than the awkward fact that Labourism aligned it with parties that were pro-Home Rule, and Unionists would not tolerate any excuses on that score. Formally, the trades council avoided the questions of Home Rule and partition, though, like almost all Labour activists in Britain and Ireland, it was against partition on the ground that it would institutionalise sectarian politics. Given the Unionist Party's insistence on pan-Protestant solidarity, not to mention its forthright Toryism and seething hostility to Labour, it is hard to see how else the council could have responded. After partition, the NILP replaced Belfast trades council as the premier agency of Labour politics. Arguably, the NILP's best strategy would have been that eventually adopted by the ICTU and NIC: the construction of a pragmatic compromise on the constitutional question, with policies grounded on principles of democracy, non-violence, and rights. But unlike trade unionists that

had their wages and conditions to worry about, socialists were drawn to fundamental positions on the legitimacy, or otherwise, of partition. The NILP
made a cardinal mistake in taking a 'non-committal' stand on the constitution. It was a non-policy rather than a compromise policy, and without an
internal consensus-building process the NILP split on the national question
in 1949. The last chance to build a cross-community Labourism arose in the
1960s. It is possible that the NILP would have pressed publicly for civil rights
had the British Labour government done the same. What is certain is that the
reluctance of London to intervene before October 1968 proved fatal. In 1969 a
political struggle for civil rights was transformed into a violent clash between
nationalists and the state. After a period of ambivalence up to the UWC's
'constitutional stoppage', the British and Irish Labour parties put the state
first and foremost, and the very idea of a socialist answer to the problem
drained away to the political margins.

Why bother with Labour history? The grand misreading of southern
Labour's past through the delusion of modernisation theses and the implosion
of socialist thinking on the North are two reasons. No doubt, there are many
others.

Bibliography

Private papers
Public records
Newspapers
Books, articles, and pamphlets
Dissertations and websites

PRIVATE PAPERS

Lord French, Imperial War Museum, London
Seán MacEntee, UCDA
Seán McKeown, Linenhall Library, Belfast
Thomas Johnson, NLI
William O'Brien and Thomas Kennedy, NLI

PUBLIC RECORDS

National Archives of Ireland
Dáil Éireann Papers, DE 2/27, 2/52, 2/111, 2/333–34
Department of Justice, Larkin file, JUS 8/676
RIC District Inspectors' Crime Special reports on secret societies, DICS/3, 1891–4

National Library of Ireland
Census, 1926, 1936
Commission on Vocational Organisation, *Report*, 1944
Dáil Éireann debates, 1941, 1966
Dáil Éireann Proceedings, 1919–20
ICTU, *Annual Reports*, 1974–5, 1978
Irish Free State Statistical Abstract, 1931–6
ITGWU, *Annual Report*, 1942
ITUC, *Reports*, 1939
PUO, *A Trade Union Approach: Planning Full Employment* (Dublin, *n.d.* [1956])
Seanad Éireann debates, 1940
Statistical Abstract of Ireland, 1939–59

Irish Railway Record Society Archive, Dublin
Great Southern and Western Railway, files 1019, 1069

Public Record Office of Northern Ireland
Annual Report of the Ministry of Labour for Northern Ireland for the Year 1922 (Belfast) *Report of the Ministry of Labour for Northern Ireland for the Years 1923–4* (Belfast)
Ulster Year Book, 1938 (Belfast)

University of Ulster, Magee College
Belfast trades council balance sheets, 1899–1928, D/1050/6/F1
Belfast trades council, minutes, 1888–9, 1894, 1905, 1907, 1913
Dublin trades council, minutes, 1906
ILPTUC, *Reports*, 1918–20, 1922, 1925
ITUC, *Reports*, 1894–1914
ITUCLP, *Reports*, 1916–17

British Parliamentary Papers
First Report from the Select Committee to Inquire into the State of the Law regarding Artisans and Machinery (1824, V)
Third Report from the Commissioners for Inquiry into the Condition of the Poorer Classes in Ireland (1836, XXX)
First Report from the Select Committee on Combinations of Workmen: Minutes of Evidence (1837–8)
Second Report on Combinations of Workmen (1837–8)
Report of the Select Committee on Combinations of Workmen (1837–8, VIII)
Factory Inspectors' Reports for 1865–6 (1866, 3622, XXIV)
Reports from Poor-Law Inspectors on the Wages of Agricultural Labourers in Ireland (1870, C.35)
Report Upon Conditions of Work in Flax and Linen Mills (1893–4, C.7287)
Royal Commission on Labour: Third Report (1893–4, C.6894)
Board of Trade, *Reports on Strikes and Lock Outs* (1889, C.6176; 1890, C.6476; 1891, C.6890; 1892, C.7403; 1893, C.7566; 1894, C.7901; 1895, C.8231; 1896, C.8643; 1897, C.9012; 1898, C.9437; 1899, Cd.316; 1900, Cd.689; 1907, Cd.4254; 1908, Cd.4680; 1909, Cd.5325; 1910, Cd.5850; 1911, Cd.6472; 1912, Cd.7089; 1913, Cd.7658)
Board of Trade, *Reports on Trades Unions* (1897, C.8644; 1902, Cd.1348)
Board of Trade, *Fourteenth Abstract of Labour Statistics of the United Kingdom, 1908–9* (1911, Cd.5458)
Dublin Disturbances Commission, *Official Report on Riots, 30 August to 1 September 1913 and Minutes of Evidence of Enquiry* (1914, Cd.7269)
Disturbances in Northern Ireland: Report of the Commission Appointed by the Governor of Northern Ireland (1969, Cmd.532)

National Archives of the United Kingdom
Government Code and Cypher School decrypts of Comintern messages, 1930–45, HW 17/17
Ministry of Labour Reports on Strikes and Lockouts, 1901–21, LAB 34/1–20, LAB 34/24–39
Royal Irish Constabulary Intelligence notes, CO 903/2, 1887–92

Russian State Archive for Social and Political History, Moscow
John Pepper, 'Der Konflikt der Irish Workers [*sic*] League mit der Communist Party
    Gross-Britanniens', 27 Dec. 1924, 495/89/26–22
Memorandum by Big Jim or Peter Larkin, undated, 495/89/26–25/37
Memorandum to the CPI, 16 Sept. 1934, 495/89/96–46/47
To the secretariat CPI, 19 Sept. 1934, 495/14/334–24/27

NEWSPAPERS

Belfast Labour Chronicle, 1905
Belfast News Letter, 1834, 1920
Daily Herald, 1914
Derry Journal, 1968–9
Dublin Evening Mail, 1825
Freeman's Journal, 1849
Industrial Syndicalist, 1910
Irish Democrat, 1937
Irish Independent, 1911
Irish Independent: Trade and Labour Journal, 1873
Irish News, 1921
Irish People, 1864
Irish Times, 1918, 1972
Irish Worker, 1912–13
Irishman, 1928
Labour Left, 1985
Manchester Guardian, 1920
Munster Express, 1923
New Ireland, 1919
Northern Whig, 1914
Trade Union Information, 1949, 1951
Voice of Labour, 1923
Watchword of Labour, 1920
Waterford Mail, 1877
Waterford Mirror, 1817, 1826, 1828, 1842
Waterford News, 1884, 1931

BOOKS, ARTICLES, AND PAMPHLETS

On Labour and Radical Politics
Allen, Kieran, *Fianna Fáil and Irish Labour: 1926 to the Present* (London, 1997)
Beames, M. R., *Peasants and Power: The Whiteboy Movements and their Control in Pre-
    Famine Ireland* (Brighton, 1983)
Bell, Geoffrey, *Troublesome Business: The Labour Party and the Irish Question* (London, 1982)

Berger, Stefan and Hugh Compston (eds), *Policy Concertation and Social Partnership in Western Europe: Lessons for the 21st Century* (Oxford, 2002)

Bew, Paul, Ellen Hazelkorn, and Henry Patterson, *The Dynamics of Irish Politics* (London, 1989)

Bielenberg, Andy, 'Bandon weavers and the industrial revolution', *Labour History News* 3 (1987)

Black, Boyd, 'Against the trend; trade union growth in Northern Ireland', *Industrial Relations Journal* 17: 1 (1986)

——, 'Industrial relations', in R. I. D. Harris, C. W. Jefferson and J. E. Spencer (eds), *The Northern Ireland Economy: A Comparative Study in the Economic Development of a Peripheral Region* (London, 1990)

——, 'Industrial relations under competition', *Review of Employment Topics* 1 (1993)

——, 'Reassessing Irish industrial relations and labour history: the north-east of Ireland up to 1921', *Historical Studies in Industrial Relations* XIV (autumn, 2002)

Bleakley, D. W., 'The Northern Ireland trade union movement', *Journal of the Statistical and Social Inquiry Society of Ireland* (1954)

Bolleyer, Nicole and Diana Panke, 'The Irish Green Party and Europe: an unhappy marriage?', *Irish Political Studies* 24: 4 (2009)

Boyd, Andrew, *Have the Trade Unions Failed the North?* (Cork, 1984)

——, *The Rise of the Irish Trade Unions* (Tralee, 1985)

Boyle, Emily, 'The linen strike of 1872', *Saothar* 2 (1974)

Boyle, John W., 'A marginal figure: the Irish rural laborer', in Samuel Clark and James S. Donnelly Jr (eds), *Irish Peasants: Violence and Political Unrest, 1780–1914* (Dublin, 1983)

——, *The Irish Labor Movement in the Nineteenth Century* (Washington, DC, 1989)

Bradley, Dan, *Farm Labourers: Irish Struggle, 1900–1976* (Belfast, 1988)

Cahill, Liam, *Forgotten Revolution: Limerick Soviet, 1919, A Threat to British Power in Ireland* (Dublin, 1990)

Clark, Samuel and James S. Donnelly Jr (eds), *Irish Peasants: Violence and Political Unrest, 1780–1914* (Dublin, 1983)

Clarkson, J. Dunsmore, *Labour and Nationalism in Ireland* (New York, 1925)

Connolly, James, *The Axe to the Root and Old Wine in New Bottles* (Dublin, 1934)

——, *Labour in Irish History* (Dublin, 1956)

Cooke, Jim, *Technical Education and the Foundation of the Dublin United Trades Council* (Dublin, 1987)

Cork Workers' Club, *The Connolly–Walker Controversy: On Socialist Unity in Ireland* (Historical Reprints, no 9)

CPI, *Communist Party of Ireland: Outline History* (Dublin, 1975)

Cradden, Terry, 'The Tories and employment law in Northern Ireland: seeing unions in a different light?', *Industrial Relations Journal* 24: 1 (1993)

——, 'Trade unionism, social justice, and religious discrimination in Northern Ireland', *Industrial and Labor Relations Review* 46: 3 (1993)

——, 'The trade union movement in Northern Ireland', in Donal Nevin (ed.), *Trade Union Century* (Cork, 1994)

Cronin, Maura, *Country, Class or Craft? The Politicisation of the Skilled Artisan in Nineteenth Century Cork* (Cork, 1994)

Crossey, Ciarán and James Monaghan, 'The origins of Trotskyism in Ireland', in *Revolutionary History* 6: 2/3 (summer, 1996)

Cunningham, John, 'Popular protest and a "moral economy" in provincial Ireland in the early nineteenth century', in Francis Devine, Fintan Lane and Niamh Puirséil (eds), *Essays in Irish Labour History: A Festschrift for Elizabeth and John W. Boyle* (Dublin, 2008)

Curriculum Development Unit, *Dublin 1913: A Divided City* (Dublin, 1984)

Daly, Seán, *Cork, A City in Crisis: A History of Labour Conflict and Social Misery, 1870–1872, Vol. 1* (Cork 1978)

——, *Ireland and the First International* (Cork, 1984)

D'Arcy, F. A., 'The artisans of Dublin and Daniel O'Connell, 1830–47', *Irish Historical Studies*, 66 (1970)

——, 'The murder of Thomas Hanlon: an episode in nineteenth-century Dublin labour history', *Dublin Historical Record* 4 (1971)

——, 'The National Trades' Political Union and Daniel O'Connell, 1830–1848', *Éire-Ireland* XVII: 3 (1982)

——, and Ken Hannigan (eds), *Workers in Union: Documents and Commentaries on the History of Irish Labour* (Dublin, 1988)

Daniels, Gary and John McIlroy (eds), *Trade Unions in A Neoliberal World: British Trade Unions Under New Labour* (Abingdon, 2009)

Dermody, Tony, 'The EEC: Cooperation or Capitalism?', *Labour Left* 6 (Jan./Mar. 1985)

Devlin, Paddy, *Yes We Have No Bananas: Outdoor Relief in Belfast, 1920–39* (Belfast, 1981)

Donnelly, Edna, 'The struggle for Whitleyism in the Northern Ireland civil service', *Saothar* 10 (1984)

Donnelly, James S. Jr, 'Pastorini and Captain Rock: millenarianism and sectarianism in the Rockite movement of 1821–4', in Samuel Clark and James S. Donnelly Jr (eds), *Irish Peasants: Violence and Political Unrest, 1780–1914* (Dublin, 1983)

Dunphy, Richard, '"A group of individuals trying to do their best": the dilemmas of Democratic Left', *Irish Political Studies* 13 (1998)

Edwards, Aaron, *A History of the Northern Ireland Labour Party: Democratic Socialism and Sectarianism* (Manchester, 2009)

Enright, Michael, *Men of Iron: Wexford Foundry Disputes 1890 & 1911* (Wexford, 1987)

Evans, Bryce, 'The Construction Corps, 1940–48', *Saothar* 32 (2007)

Fajertag, Giuseppe and Philippe Pochet (eds), *Social Pacts in Europe: New Dynamics* (Brussels, 2000)

Finch, John, 'Ralahine: or human improvement and human happiness', *New Moral World*, 31 March to 29 September 1838

Fitzpatrick, David, 'The disappearance of the Irish agricultural labourer, 1841–1912', *Irish Economic and Social History* 7 (1980)

——, 'Strikes in Ireland, 1914–21', *Saothar* 6 (1980)

Fox, R. M., *The History of the Citizen Army* (Dublin, 1944)

Gallagher, Michael, *The Irish Labour Party in Transition, 1957–82* (Manchester, 1982)

Geary, Dick (ed.), *Labour and Socialist Movements in Europe Before 1914* (Oxford, 1989)

Girvin, Brian, 'Industrialisation and the Irish working class since 1922', *Saothar* 10 (1984)

Goodwillie, John, 'Lesser Marxist movements in Ireland: a bibliography, 1934–1984', *Saothar* 11 (1986)

Greiff, Mats, "'Marching through the streets singing and shouting'": industrial struggle and trade unions among female linen workers in Belfast and Lurgan, 1872–1910', *Saothar* 22 (1997)

——, "'Striking for the right to be late at work": workers' resistance to employers' time discipline in Lurgan power loom factories, 1899–1914', in Francis Devine, Fintan Lane, and Niamh Puirséil (eds), *Essays in Irish Labour History: A Festschrift for Elizabeth and John W. Boyle* (Dublin, 2008)

Hanley, Brian and Scott Millar, *The Lost Revolution: The Story of the Official IRA and the Workers' Party* (Dublin, 2009)

Hannigan, Ken, 'British-based unions in Ireland; building workers and the split in Congress', *Saothar* 7 (1981)

Hardiman, Niamh, *Pay, Politics and Economic Performance in Ireland, 1970–1987* (Oxford, 1988)

——, 'Pay bargaining: confrontation and consensus', in Donal Nevin (ed.), *Trade Union Century* (Cork, 1994)

Hastings, Tim, Brian Sheehan, and Padraig Yeates, *Saving the Future: How Social Partnership Shaped Ireland's Economic Success* (Dublin, 2007)

Henry, Brian, 'Combinations, the law and industrial violence in late eighteenth-century Dublin', *Saothar* 18 (1993)

Hepburn, A. C., 'Work, class, and religion in Belfast, 1871–1911', *Irish Economic and Social History* x (1983)

Hill, Jacqueline, 'The Protestant response to Repeal: the case of the Dublin working class', in F. S. L. Lyons and R. A. J. Hawkins (eds), *Ireland Under the Union: Varieties of Tension* (Oxford, 1980)

——, 'Artisans, sectarianism and politics in Dublin, 1829–48', *Saothar* 7 (1981)

Hillery, Brian J., 'An overview of the Irish industrial relations system', in UCD, *Industrial Relations in Ireland: Contemporary Issues and Developments* (Dublin, 1987)

Hirst, Catherine, 'Politics, sectarianism, and the working class in nineteenth-century Belfast', in Fintan Lane and Dónal Ó Drisceoil (eds), *Politics and the Irish Working Class, 1830–1945* (London, 2005)

Holmes, Michael, 'The Irish Labour Party: the advantages, disadvantages, and irrelevance of Europeanisation?', *Irish Political Studies* 24: 4 (2009)

Holton, Bob, *British Syndicalism, 1900–1914* (London, 1976)

Horgan, John, *Labour: The Price of Power* (Dublin, 1986)

Hutt, Allen, *British Trade Unionism: A Short History* (London, 1975)

ICTU, *Political Policy in Northern Ireland* (Dublin, 1972)

ITGWU, 'The facts about the Shannon dispute', *Liberty Magazine* (May, 1968)

Kelly, Aidan and Teresa Brannick, 'Strikes in Ireland: measurement, incidence, and trends', in UCD, *Industrial Relations in Ireland: Contemporary Issues and Developments* (Dublin, 1987)

Keogh, Dermot, *The Rise of the Irish Working Class: The Dublin Trade Union Movement and the Labour Leadership, 1890–1914* (Belfast, 1982)

Kilmurray, Evanne, *Fight, Starve or Emigrate* (Dublin, 1988)

Labour Party, *The New Republic: Complete Text of 'The New Republic' Address by Brendan Corish, TD, Leader of the Labour Party* (Dublin, 1968)

Lane, Fintan, *The Origins of Modern Irish Socialism, 1881–1896* (Cork, 1997)

——, 'Rural labourers, social change, and politics in late nineteenth-century Ireland', in Fintan Lane and Dónal Ó Drisceoil (eds), *Politics and the Irish Working Class, 1830–1945* (London, 2005)

Leckey, Joseph J., 'The railway servants' strike in Co. Cork, 1898', *Saothar* 2 (1976)

Lenin, V. I., *British Labour and British Imperialism* (London, 1969)

Lynch, David, *Radical Politics in Modern Ireland: The Irish Socialist Republican Party, 1896–1904* (Dublin, 2005)

MacDermott, Eithne, *Clann na Poblachta* (Cork, 1998)

Maguire, Martin, 'Civil service trade unionism in Ireland (part 1), 1801–1922', *Saothar* 33 (2008)

Marx, Karl, *Capital, Vol. 1* (Lawrence and Wishart edn, London, 1974)

McAteer, Shane, 'The "new Unionism" in Derry, 1889–1892; a demonstration of its inclusive nature', *Saothar* 16 (1991)

McCann, Eamonn, 'Socialism and 1968', in Pauline McClenaghan (ed.), *Spirit of '68: Beyond the Barricades* (Derry, 2009)

McCarthy, Charles, *The Decade of Upheaval: Irish Trade Unions in the Nineteen Sixties* (Dublin, 1973)

——, *Trade Unions in Ireland, 1894–1960* (Dublin, 1977)

——, 'Labour and the 1922 general election', *Saothar* 7 (1981)

McClenaghan, Pauline (ed.), *Spirit of '68: Beyond the Barricades* (Derry, 2009)

McConnel, James, 'The Irish Parliamentary Party, industrial relations and the 1913 lockout', *Saothar* 28 (2003)

McCormack, Vincent and Inez McCormack, '"Equalising advantages: lessening discrimination": reviewing Northern Ireland's fair employment laws', *Review of Employment Topics* 2 (1994)

McGarry, Fearghal, *Irish Politics and the Spanish Civil War* (Cork, 1999)

McIlroy, John, Nina Fishman, and Alan Campbell, *The High Tide of British Trade Unionism: Trade Unions and Industrial Politics, 1964–79* (Monmouth, 2007)

McIlroy, John and Gary Daniels, 'An anatomy of British trade unionism since 1997: strategies for revitalisation', in Gary Daniels and John McIlroy (eds), *Trade Unions in A Neoliberal World: British Trade Unions Under New Labour* (Abingdon, 2009)

McLaughlin, Eithne, 'Women and work in Derry City: a survey', *Saothar* 14 (1989)

Messenger, Betty, *Picking Up the Linen Threads: Life in Ulster's Mills* (Belfast, 1988)

Milotte, Mike, *Communism in Modern Ireland: The Pursuit of the Workers' Republic since 1916* (Dublin, 1984)

Mitchell, Arthur, *Labour in Irish Politics, 1890–1930: The Irish Labour Movement in an Age of Revolution* (Dublin, 1974)

Morgan, Austen, *Labour and Partition: The Belfast Working Class, 1905–23* (London, 1991)

Mortished, R. J. P., 'The Industrial Relations Act, 1946', *Journal of the Statistical and Social Inquiry Society of Ireland* 17 (1946–7)

Murphy, Gary and John Hogan, 'Fianna Fáil, the trade union movement and the politics of macroeconomic crises, 1970–82', *Irish Political Studies* 23: 4 (2008)

Murphy, Maura, 'The working classes of nineteenth-century Cork', *Journal of the Cork Historical and Archaeological Society* (1980)

Murphy, T. V. and W. K. Roche (eds), *Irish Industrial Relations in Practice* (Dublin, 1994)

Murray, Peter, 'Electoral politics and the Dublin working class before the First World War', *Saothar* 6 (1980)

Nevin, Donal (ed.), *Trade Unions and Change in Irish Society* (Cork, 1980)

——, *Trade Union Century* (Cork, 1994)

——, 'The *Irish Worker*, 1911–1914', in Donal Nevin (ed.), *James Larkin: Lion of the Fold* (Dublin, 1998)

——, 'The Irish Citizen Army, 1913–16', in Donal Nevin (ed.), *James Larkin: Lion of the Fold* (Dublin, 1998)

Newsinger, John, *Rebel City: Larkin, Connolly and the Dublin Labour Movement* (London, 2004)

Nolan, Sam, 'Labour and the unions: the rift widens', *Labour Left* 6 (Jan./Mar. 1985)

Norton, Christopher, 'The Irish Labour Party in Northern Ireland, 1949–58', *Saothar* 21 (1996)

O'Brien, William, 'Nineteen-thirteen: its significance', in ITGWU, *Fifty Years of Liberty Hall: The Golden Jubilee of the Irish Transport and General Workers' Union, 1909–59* (Dublin, 1959)

Ó Broin, Eoin, *Sinn Féin and the Politics of Left Republicanism* (London, 2009)

O'Connor, Emmet, *Syndicalism in Ireland, 1917–23* (Cork, 1988)

——, *A Labour History of Waterford* (Waterford, 1989)

——, *Reds and the Green: Ireland, Russia and the Communist Internationals, 1919–43* (Dublin, 2004)

——, '"True Bolsheviks?": The rise and fall of the Socialist Party of Ireland, 1917–21', in D. George Boyce and Alan O'Day (eds), *Ireland in Transition, 1867–1921* (London, 2004)

——, 'Problems of reform in the Irish Trades Union Congress, 1894–1914', *Historical Studies in Industrial Relations* 23–4 (2007)

——, 'Identity and self-representation in Irish communism: the Connolly Column and the Spanish Civil War', *Socialist History* 34 (2009)

O'Connor Lysaght, D. R. 'The Munster soviet creameries', *Saotharlann Staire Éireann* 1 (1981)

——, '"Labour must wait": the making of a myth', *Saothar* 26 (2001)

O'Donnell, Martin, 'The impact of the 1981 H Block hunger strikes on the British Labour Party', *Irish Political Studies* 14 (1999)

O'Donnell, Rory and Colm O'Reardon, 'Social partnership in Ireland's economic transformation', in Giuseppe Fajertag and Philippe Pochet (eds), *Social Pacts in Europe: New Dynamics* (Brussels, 2000)

O'Donnell, Rory and Damian Thomas, 'Ireland in the 1990s: policy concertation triumphant', in Stefan Berger and Hugh Compston (eds), *Policy Concertation and Social Partnership in Western Europe: Lessons for the 21st Century* (Oxford, 2002)

O'Higgins, Rachel, 'Irish trade unions and politics, 1830–50', *Historical Journal* 4 (1961)

Pare, William, *Co-operative Agriculture: A Solution to the Land Question as Exemplified in the History of the Ralahine Co-operative Association, County Clare, Ireland* (London, 1870)

Patterson, Henry, *Class Conflict and Sectarianism: The Protestant Working Class and the Belfast Labour Movement, 1868–1920* (Belfast, 1980)

——, 'Industrial labour and the labour movement, 1820–1914', in Liam Kennedy and Philip Ollerenshaw (eds), *An Economic History of Ulster, 1820–1939* (Manchester, 1985)

——, *The Politics of Illusion: Republicanism and Socialism in Modern Ireland* (London, 1989)

——, 'The decline of the collaborators: the Ulster Unionist Labour Association and post-war Unionist politics', in Francis Devine, Fintan Lane, and Niamh Puirséil (eds), *Essays in Labour History: A Festschrift for Elizabeth and John Boyle* (Dublin, 2008)

Pelling, Henry, *A History of British Trade Unionism* (London, 1974)

——, *A Short History of the Labour Party* (London, 1976)

Pender, Séamus, 'The gilds of Waterford, 1650–1700, parts I–V', *Journal of the Cork Historical and Archaeological Society* (1953–57)

Puirséil, Niamh, *The Irish Labour Party, 1922–73* (Dublin, 2007)

——, 'War, work, and labour', in John Horne (ed.), *Our War: Ireland and the Great War* (Dublin, 2008)

Purdie, Bob, 'The Friends of Ireland; British Labour and Irish nationalism, 1945–49', in Tom Gallagher and James O'Connell (eds), *Contemporary Irish Studies* (Manchester, 1983)

Quinn, Jim, 'Labouring on the margins; trade union activity in Enniskillen, 1917–23', *Saothar* 15 (1990)

Reaney, Bernard, 'Irish Chartists in Britain and Ireland: rescuing the rank and file', *Saothar* 10 (1984)

Rees, Russell, *Labour and the Northern Ireland Problem, 1945–51: The Missed Opportunity* (Dublin, 2009)

Renton, David, 'Class language or populism: revisiting the nineteenth-century history of the Norman Yoke myth', *Socialist History* 35 (2009)

Roberts, Paul E. W., 'Caravats and Shanavests: Whiteboyism and faction fighting in east Munster, 1802–11', in Samuel Clark and James S. Donnelly Jr (eds), *Irish Peasants: Violence and Political Unrest, 1780–1914* (Dublin, 1983)

Roberts, Ruaidhri, *The Story of the People's College* (Dublin, 1986)

Roche, W. K. and Joe Larragy, 'The trend of unionisation in the Irish Republic', in UCD, *Industrial Relations in Ireland: Contemporary Issues and Developments* (Dublin, 1987)

Roche, W. K., 'Pay determination and the politics of industrial relations', in T. V. Murphy and W. K. Roche (eds), *Irish Industrial Relations in Practice* (Dublin, 1994)

——, 'Industrial relations', in Donal Nevin (ed.), *Trade Union Century* (Cork, 1994)

Rumpf, E. and A. C. Hepburn, *Nationalism and Socialism in Twentieth Century Ireland* (Liverpool, 1977)

Ryan, W. P., 'The struggle of 1913', in Donal Nevin (ed.), *1913: Jim Larkin and the Dublin Lock-out* (Dublin, 1964)

Saville, John, *1848: The British State and the Chartist Movement* (Cambridge, 1987)

SFWP, *The Irish Industrial Revolution* (Dublin, 1977)

Skillen, Chris, 'Pravda's Provos: Russian and Soviet manipulation of news from Ireland', *Irish Political Studies* 8 (1993)

Thompson, E. P., 'The moral economy of the English crowd in the eighteenth century', *Past and Present* 50 (1971)

Tipping, Brian and Patricia McCorry, *Industrial Relations in Northern Ireland: The LRA Survey* (Belfast, 1988)

Townshend, Charles, 'The Irish railway strike of 1920; industrial action and civil resistance in the struggle for independence', *Irish Historical Studies* XXI: 83 (1979)

Trade Unionists for Irish Unity and Independence, *Opposing Discrimination in Northern Ireland* (Dublin, 1988)

Trench, Brian, 'Labour and the unions: one big movement?', *Labour Left* 6 (Jan./Mar. 1985)

UCD, *Industrial Relations in Ireland: Contemporary Issues and Developments* (Dublin, 1987)

Upchurch, Martin, 'Partnership: New Labour's "Third Way"?', in Gary Daniels and John McIlroy (eds), *Trade Unions in A Neoliberal World: British Trade Unions under New Labour* (Abingdon, 2009)

Walker, Graham, 'The Northern Ireland Labour Party in the 1920s', *Saothar* 10 (1984)

Wallace, Joseph, Patrick Gunnigle, and Gerard McMahon, *Industrial Relations in Ireland* (Dublin, 2004)

Webb, J. J., *The Guilds of Dublin* (Dublin, 1929)

Whiteman, David, 'The progress and potential of the Green Party in Ireland', *Irish Political Studies* 5 (1990)

Wright, Arnold, *Disturbed Dublin: The Story of the Great Strike of 1913–14, With a Description of the Industries of the Irish Capital* (London, 1914)

Yeates, Pádraig, *Lockout: Dublin 1913* (Dublin, 2000)

Labour and Radical Autobiographies, Memoirs, and Interviews

Adams, Gerard, *Before the Dawn: An Autobiography* (Dingle, 2001)

Bower, Fred, *Rolling Stonemason: An Autobiography* (London, 1936)

Brett, Charles, *Long Shadows Cast Before: Nine Lives in Ulster, 1625–1977* (Edinburgh, 1978)

Browne, Noel, *Against The Tide* (Dublin, 1986)

Connolly O'Brien, Nora, *We Shall Rise Again* (London, 1981)

Cradden, Terry, 'Billy Blease: from McClure Street to the House of Lords', *Saothar* 19 (1994)

Craig, E. T., *The Irish Land and Labour Question, Illustrated in the History of Ralahine and Cooperative Farming* (London, 1882)

Desmond, Barry, *Finally and in Conclusion: A Political Memoir* (Dublin, 2000)

——, *No Workers' Republic! Reflections on Labour and Ireland, 1913–1967* (Dublin, 2009)

Devlin, Paddy, *The Fall of the NI Executive* (Belfast, 1975)

——, *Straight Left: An Autobiography* (Belfast, 1993)

Finlay, Fergus, *Snakes and Ladders* (Dublin, 1998)

Gray, Malachy, 'A shop steward remembers: Malachy Gray', *Saothar* 11 (1986)

ILO, *Edward Phelan and the ILO: The Life and Views of an International Social Actor* (Geneva, 2009)

Johnston, Roy, *Century of Endeavour: A Biographical and Autobiographical View of the Twentieth Century in Ireland* (Dublin, 2003)

Kavanagh, Ray, *Spring, Summer and Fall: The Rise and Fall of the Labour Party, 1986–99* (Dublin, 2001)

Logue, Paddy, *Them and Us: A Socialist Response to 'Work is the Key'* (Dublin, 1994)

Macgougan, Jack, 'Letting Labour lead: Jack Macgougan and the pursuit of unity, 1913–58', *Saothar* 14 (1989)

Marx, Eleanor, 'Derry speech', *Labour History News* 8 (1992)

McCann, Eamonn, *War and an Irish Town* (London, 1974)

McGonagle, Stephen, 'Navigating a lone channel: Stephen McGonagle, trade unionism and Labour politics in Derry, 1914–97', *Saothar* 22 (1997)

Morrissey, Hazel, 'Betty Sinclair: a woman's fight for socialism, 1910–81', *Saothar* 9 (1983)

O'Brien, William, *Forth the Banners Go: Reminiscences of William O'Brien as told to Edward MacLysaght, D.Litt* (Dublin, 1969)

O'Connell, John, *Doctor John: Crusading Doctor and Politician* (Dublin, 1989)

Ó Dochartaigh, Fionnbarra, *Ulster's White Negroes: From Civil Rights to Insurrection* (Edinburgh, 1994)

Quinn, Ruairi, *Straight Left: A Journey in Politics* (Dublin, 2005)

Robbins, Frank, *Under the Starry Plough: Recollections of the Irish Citizen Army* (Dublin, 1977)

Labour and Radical Biographies

Bowman, Terence, *People's Champion: The Life of Alexander Bowman, Pioneer of Labour Politics in Ireland* (Belfast, 1997)

Buckley, David N., *James Fintan Lalor: Radical* (Cork, 1990)

Callan, Charles, 'Labour lives, no 9: Ronald J. P. Mortished', *Saothar* 32 (2007)

Callan, Charles, and Barry Desmond, *Irish Labour Lives: A Biographical Dictionary of Irish Labour Party Deputies, Senators, MPs and MEPs* (Dublin, 2010)

Cody, Séamus, 'The remarkable Patrick Daly', *Obair* 2 (1985)

Collins, Peter, 'Mary Galway', *Labour History News* 7 (summer 1991)

Collins, Stephen, *Spring and the Labour Story* (Dublin, 1993)

Coughlan, Anthony, *C. Desmond Greaves, 1913–1988: An Obituary Essay* (Dublin, 1994)

Cullen Owens, Rosemary, *Louie Bennett* (Cork, 2001)

Dixon R. (ed.), *Marx and Engels on Ireland* (Moscow, 1971)

Dooley, Thomas P., *Irishmen or English Soldiers? The Times and World of a Southern Catholic Irish man (1876–1916) Enlisting in the British Army during the First World War* (Liverpool, 1995)

Fox, R. M., *Jim Larkin: The Rise of the Underman* (London, 1957)

Gaughan, J., *Thomas Johnson, 1872–1963: The First Leader of the Labour Party in Dáil Éireann* (Dublin, 1980)

——, *Alfred O'Rahilly* (Dublin, 1986)

Geoghegan, Vincent, 'Robert Owen, cooperation and Ulster in the 1830s', in Fintan Lane and Dónal Ó Drisceoil (eds), *Politics and the Irish Working Class, 1830–1945* (London, 2005)

Gray, John, *City in Revolt: James Larkin and the Belfast Dock Strike of 1907* (Belfast, 1985)

Greaves, C. Desmond, *The Life and Times of James Connolly* (London, 1961)

Halligan, Brendan (ed.), *The Brendan Corish Seminar Proceedings* (Dublin, 2006)

Harrison, J. F. C., *Robert Owen and the Owenites in Britain and America* (London, 1969)

Henderson, James, *A Record Year in My Existence as Lord Mayor of Belfast, 1898* (Belfast, 1899)

Horgan, John, *Noel Browne: Passionate Outsider* (Dublin, 2000)

Hudelson, Richard, 'Jack Carney and the *Truth* in Duluth', *Saothar* 19 (1994)

Keogh, Dermot, 'Michael O'Lehane and the organisation of linen drapers assistants', *Saothar* 3 (1977)

Kirby, R. G. and A. E. Musson, *The Voice of the People: John Doherty, 1798–1854, Trade Unionist, Radical and Factory Reformer* (Manchester, 1975)

Kornbluh, Joyce L. (ed.), *Rebel Voices: An IWW Anthology* (Ann Arbor, 1964)

Koseki, Takashi, 'Patrick O'Higgins and Irish Chartism', Hosei University Ireland–Japan Papers 2 (Hosei, *n.d.*)

Lane, Fintan, *In Search of Thomas Sheahan: Radical Politics in Cork, 1824–1836* (Dublin, 2001)

Larkin, Emmet, *James Larkin, 1876–1947: Irish Labour Leader* (London, 1965)

Larkin, Jim, *In The Footsteps of Big Jim: A Family Biography* (Dublin, 1995)

Marley, Laurence, *Michael Davitt: Freelance Radical and Frondeur* (Dublin, 2007)

McGuire, Charlie, *Roddy Connolly and the Struggle for Socialism in Ireland* (Cork, 2008)

Morgan, Austen, *James Connolly: A Political Biography* (Manchester, 1988)

Moloney, Ed., *Voices from the Grave: Two Men's War in Ireland* (London, 2010).

Morrissey, Thomas J., *William Martin Murphy* (Dundalk, 1997)

——, *William O'Brien, 1881–1968: Socialist, Republican, Dáil Deputy, Editor and Trade Union Leader* (Dublin, 2007)

Murphy, Michael A., *Gerry Fitt: A Political Chameleon* (Cork, 2007)

Murray, Gerard, *John Hume and the SDLP* (Dublin, 1998)

Nevin, Donal (ed.), *James Larkin: Lion of the Fold* (Dublin, 1998)

——, *James Connolly: 'A Full Life'* (Dublin, 2006)

Newsinger, John, 'A lamp to guide your feet: Jim Larkin, the *Irish Worker* and the Dublin working class', *European History Quarterly* 20 (1990)

Norman, Diana, *Terrible Beauty: A Life of Constance Markievicz* (London, 1987)

Ó Cathasaigh, Aindrias, 'James Connolly and the writing of *Labour in Irish History* (1910)', *Saothar* 27 (2002)

O'Connor, Emmet, 'Seán Murray', *Dictionary of Labour Biography* XI (London, 2003)

——, *James Larkin* (Cork, 2003).

——, 'William Walker, Irish Labour and "Chinese slavery" in South Africa, 1904–6', *Irish Historical Studies*, XXXVII: 145 (May 2010)

O'Connor Lysaght, D. R., 'Labour lives, no 7: Thomas Foran', *Saothar* 30 (2005)

O'Riordan, Manus, 'James Larkin Junior and the forging of a thinking intelligent movement', *Saothar* 19 (1994)

——, *The Voice of a Thinking Intelligent Movement: James Larkin Junior and the Modernisation of Irish Trade Unionism* (Dublin, 1995)

Pankhurst, Richard, *William Thompson (1775–1833): Pioneer Socialist* (London, 1991)

Patterson, Henry, 'William Walker, labour, sectarianism and the Union, 1894–1912', in Fintan Lane and Dónal Ó Drisceoil (eds), *Politics and the Irish Working Class, 1830–1945* (London, 2005)

Pickering, Paul A., *Feargus O'Connor: A Political Life* (Exeter, 2006)

Plummer, Alfred, *Bronterre O'Brien: A Political Biography* (London, 1971)

Reid, J. F., *The Irish Party's Work Epitomised: Biography of William Field, MP* (Dublin, 1918)

Ripley, B. J. and J. McHugh, *John Maclean* (Manchester, 1989)

Ryan, Tim, *Dick Spring: A Safe Pair of Hands* (Dublin, 1993)

Walker, Graham, *The Politics of Frustration: Harry Midgley and the Failure of Labour in Northern Ireland* (Manchester, 1985)

Trade Union Monographs

Bagwell, Philip S., *The Railwaymen: The History of the National Union of Railwaymen* (London, 1963)

Brissenden, P. F., *The IWW: A Study of American Syndicalism* (New York, 1920)

Campbell, John, *'A Loosely Shackled Fellowship': the History of Comhaltas Cána* (Dublin, 1989)

Coates, Ken and Tony Topham, *The History of the Transport and General Workers' Union, Vol. 1, Part 1 and Part 2, The Making of the Transport and General Workers' Union: The Emergence of the Labour Movement, 1870–1922* (London, 1991)

Cody, Séamus, John O'Dowd, and Peter Rigney, *The Parliament of Labour: 100 Years of Dublin Council of Trade Unions* (Dublin, 1986)

Devine, Francis, *Organising History: A Centenary of SIPTU, 1909–2009* (Dublin, 2009)

Greaves, C. Desmond, *The Irish Transport and General Workers' Union: The Formative Years, 1909–1923* (Dublin, 1982)

Hogan, John and Gary Murphy, 'From guild to union: the evolution of the Dublin Bricklayers' Society, 1670–1888', *Saothar* 26 (2001)

Horn, Pamela L. R., 'The National Agricultural Labourers' Union in Ireland, 1873–9', *Irish Historical Studies* 17: 67 (1971)

ITGWU, *The Attempt to Smash The Irish Transport and General Workers' Union* (Dublin, 1924)

——, *Fifty Years of Liberty Hall: The Golden Jubilee of the Irish Transport and General Workers' Union, 1909–59* (Dublin, 1959)

Jones, Mary, *These Obstreperous Lassies: A History of the Irish Women Workers' Union* (Dublin, 1988)

Lane, Pádraig G., 'The Land and Labour Associations, 1894–1914', *Journal of the Cork Historical and Archaeological Society* 98 (1993)

Maguire, Martin, *Servants to the Public: A History of the Local Government and Public Services Union, 1901–1990* (Dublin, 1998)

Marsh, A. and V. Ryan, *The Seamen: A History of the National Union of Seamen, 1887–1987* (Oxford, 1989)

Merrigan, Matt, *Eagle or Cuckoo? The Story of the ATGWU in Ireland* (Dublin, 1989)

Pelling, Henry, 'The Knights of Labour in Britain, 1880–1901', *History Review* IX: 2 (1956)

Redmond, Seán, *The Irish Municipal Employees' Trade Union, 1883–1983* (Dublin, 1983)

Swift, John, *A History of the Dublin Bakers and Others* (Dublin 1948)

Taplin, Eric, *The Dockers' Union: A History of the National Union of Dock Labourers, 1889–1922* (Leicester, 1986)

Other

Ahern, Bertie, *Bertie Ahern: The Autobiography* (London, 2009)

Anderson, Don, *Fourteen May Days: The Inside Story of the Loyalist Strike of 1974* (Dublin, 1994)

Barritt, Denis P. and Charles F. Carter, *The Northern Ireland Problem: A Study in Group Relations,* (Oxford, 1962)

Barton, Brian, *The Blitz: Belfast and the War Years* (Belfast, 1989)

——, *From Behind a Closed Door: Secret Court Martial Records of the 1916 Easter Rising* (Belfast, 2002)

Beckett, J. C. and R. E. Glasscock (eds), *Belfast: The Origins and Growth of An Industrial City* (London, 1967)

Bew, Paul and Henry Patterson, *Seán Lemass and the Making of Modern Ireland, 1945–66* (Dublin, 1982)

Bielenberg, Andy, *Cork's Industrial Revolution, 1780–1880: Development or Decline* (Cork, 1991)

Black, W., 'Industrial change in the twentieth century', in J. C. Beckett and R. E. Glasscock (eds), *Belfast: The Origins and Growth of An Industrial City* (London, 1967)

Blake, John W., *Northern Ireland in the Second World War* (Belfast, 1956)

Boyd, Andrew, *Northern Ireland: Who is to Blame?* (Cork, 1984)

Breen, Anthony M., *The Cappoquin Rebellion, 1849* (Thurston, 1998)

Breen, Richard, Damian F. Hannan, David B. Rottman, and Christopher T. Whelan, *Understanding Contemporary Ireland: State, Class and Development in the Republic of Ireland* (Dublin, 1990)

Brunt, Barry, *The Republic of Ireland* (London, 1988)

Buckland, Patrick, *A History of Northern Ireland* (Dublin, 1981)

Buckley, Anthony D., '"On the club": Friendly societies in Ireland', *Irish Economic and Social History* 14 (1987)

Carey, Sophia, *Social Security in Ireland, 1939–1952: The Limits to Solidarity* (Dublin, 2007)

Central Statistics Office, *Regional Trends* (London, 2000)

Clarkson, L. A., 'Population change and urbanisation, 1821–1911', in Liam Kennedy and Philip Ollerenshaw (eds), *An Economic History of Ulster, 1820–1939* (Manchester, 1985)

Coe, W. E., *The Engineering Industry of the North of Ireland* (Belfast, 1969)

Cosgrove, Art and Donal McCartney (eds), *Studies in Irish History* (Dublin, 1979)

Crotty, Raymond, *Ireland in Crisis: A Study in Capitalist Colonial Underdevelopment* (Dingle, 1986)

——, *Farming Collapse: National Opportunity* (Dublin, 1990)

Cullen, L. M., *An Economic History of Ireland since 1660* (London, 1987)

Cunningham, John, *'A Town Tormented by the Sea': Galway, 1790–1914* (Dublin, 2004)

Curry, John, *The Irish Social Services* (Dublin, 1980)

Daly, Mary E., *A Social and Economic History of Ireland since 1800* (Dublin, 1981)

——, *Dublin, The Deposed Capital: A Social and Economic History, 1860–1914* (Cork, 1984)

——, 'The employment gains from industrial protection in the Irish Free State during the 1930s: A note', *Irish Economic and Social History* 15 (1988)

Davis, Richard, *The Young Ireland Movement* (Dublin, 1987)

Dignan, Most Revd J., *Social Security: Outlines of a Scheme for National Health Insurance* (Sligo, 1945)

Duggan, J. P., *A History of the Irish Army* (Dublin, 1991)

Farrell, Brian, *The Founding of Dáil Éireann: Parliament and Nation-Building* (Dublin, 1971)

Farrell, Michael, *Northern Ireland: The Orange State* (London, 1976)

Fisk, Robert, *The Point of No Return: The Strike Which Broke the British in Ulster* (London, 1975)

——, *In Time of War: Ireland, Ulster and the Price of Neutrality, 1939–45* (London, 1985)

FitzGerald, Garret, *All in A Life: An Autobiography* (Dublin, 1991)

Foster, R. F., *Modern Ireland, 1600–1972* (London, 1988)

Gallagher, Michael, *Political Parties in the Republic of Ireland* (Manchester, 1985)

——, 'A swing to the left: the European election in the Dublin constituency', in Paul Hainsworth (ed.), *Breaking and Preserving the Mould: The Third Direct Elections to the European Parliament (1989), the Irish Republic and Northern Ireland* (Belfast, 1992)

Gallagher, Tom and James O'Connell (eds), *Contemporary Irish Studies* (Manchester, 1983)

Girvin, Brian, *Between Two Worlds: Politics and Economy in Independent Ireland* (Dublin, 1989)

——, 'Political competition, 1992–1997', in Michael Marsh and Paul Mitchell (eds), *How Ireland Voted 1997* (Boulder, Co, 1999)

——, 'Contraception, moral panic and social change in Ireland, 1969–79', *Irish Political Studies* 23: 4 (2008)

Goldstrom, J. M. and L. A. Clarkson (eds), *Irish Population, Economy and Society: Essays in Honour of the Late K. H. Connell* (Oxford, 1981)

Harris, R. I. D., C. W. Jefferson, and J. E. Spencer (eds), *The Northern Ireland Economy: A Comparative Study in the Economic Development of a Peripheral Region* (London, 1990)

Hennessey, Thomas, *The Evolution of the Troubles, 1970–72* (Dublin, 2007)

Holmes, Michael, 'The Maastricht Treaty Referendum of June 1992', *Irish Political Studies* 8 (1993)

Hoppen, K. Theodore, *Ireland since 1800: Conflict and Conformity* (London, 1989 and 1999)

Horgan, John, *Seán Lemass: The Enigmatic Patriot* (Dublin, 1997)

Inglis, Brian, *The Freedom of the Press in Ireland* (London, 1954)

Isles, K. S. and Norman Cuthbert, *An Economic Survey of Northern Ireland* (Belfast, 1957)

Johnson, D. S., 'The Belfast Boycott, 1920–22', in J. M. Goldstrom and L. A. Clarkson (eds), *Irish Population, Economy and Society: Essays in Honour of the Late K. H. Connell* (Oxford, 1981)

——, 'The Northern Ireland economy, 1914–39', in Liam Kennedy and Philip Ollerenshaw (eds), *An Economic History of Ulster, 1820–1939* (Manchester, 1985)

——, *The Inter-War Economy in Ireland* (Dublin, 1985)

Joyce, James, *Ulysses* (Penguin edn, London, 1982)

Kane, Robert, *The Industrial Resources of Ireland* (Shannon, 1971, first edn Dublin, 1844)

Kennedy, Kieran A., Thomas Giblin, and Deirdre McHugh, *The Economic Development of Ireland in the Twentieth Century* (London, 1988)

Keogh, Dermot, *Jack Lynch: A Biography* (Dublin, 2008)

Leahy, Pat, *Showtime: The Inside Story of Fianna Fáil in Power* (Dublin, 2009)

Lee, Joseph, *The Modernisation of Irish Society, 1848–1918* (Dublin, 1973)

——, 'Aspects of corporatist thought in Ireland: the Commission on Vocational Organisation, 1939–43', in Art Cosgrove and Donal McCartney (eds), *Studies in Irish History* (Dublin, 1979)

——, *Ireland, 1912–1985: Politics and Society* (Cambridge, 1989)

Lewis, George Cornewall, *Local Disturbances in Ireland* (London, 1836)

Loughlin, James, *The Ulster Question since 1945* (London, 2004)

Mahon, Tom and James J. Gillogly, *Decoding the IRA* (Cork, 2008)

Mansergh, Lucy, 'Two referendums and the Referendum Commission: The 1998 experience', *Irish Political Studies* 14 (1999)

Marsh, Michael and Paul Mitchell (eds), *How Ireland Voted 1997* (Boulder, Colorado, 1999)

McCartney, Donal, *The Dawning of Democracy: Ireland, 1800–1870* (Dublin, 1987)

McCracken, Donal P., *Forgotten Protest: Ireland and the Anglo-Boer War* (Belfast, 2003)

McGee, Owen, '"God save Ireland": Manchester-Martyr demonstrations in Dublin, 1867–1916', *Éire-Ireland* (fall/winter 2001)

McKenna, G. B., *Facts and Figures: The Belfast Pogroms, 1920–22* (Dublin, 1922)

Meenan, James, *The Irish Economy since 1922* (Liverpool, 1971)

Mulholland, Marc, *Northern Ireland at the Crossroads: Ulster Unionism in the O'Neill Years, 1960–9* (London, 2000)

Murray, Peter, 'Irish cultural nationalism in the United Kingdom state: politics and the Gaelic League, 1900–18', *Irish Political Studies* 8 (1993)

O'Dowd, Liam, Bill Rolston, and Mike Tomlinson, *Northern Ireland: Between Civil Rights and Civil War* (London, 1980)

Ó Gráda, Cormac, *A Rocky Road: The Irish Economy since the 1920s* (Manchester, 1997)

O'Leary, Cornelius, *Irish Elections, 1918–1977: Parties, Voters and Proportional Representation* (Dublin, 1979)

Ollerenshaw, Philip, 'Industry, 1820–1914', in Liam Kennedy and Philip Ollerenshaw (eds), *An Economic History of Ulster, 1820–1939* (Manchester, 1985)

O'Mahony, Jane, 'Ireland's EU referendum experience', *Irish Political Studies* 24: 4 (2009)

Ó Tuathaigh, Gearóid, *Ireland Before the Famine, 1798–1848* (Dublin, 1972)

Patterson, Henry, *Ireland since 1939: The Persistence of Conflict* (Dublin, 2006)

Power, Con, *Metamorphosis: Lessons from the Formative Years of the Celtic Tiger* (Cork, 2009)

Prince, Simon, *Northern Ireland's '68: Civil Rights, Global Revolt and the Origins of the Troubles* (Dublin, 2007)

Purdie, Bob, *Politics in the Streets: The Origins of the Civil Rights Movement in Northern Ireland* (Belfast, 1990)

Rose, Paul, *How The Troubles Came to Northern Ireland* (Basingstoke, 2000)

Share, Bernard, *The Emergency: Neutral Ireland, 1939–45* (Dublin, 1978)

Sheehan, Daniel D., *Ireland since Parnell* (London, 1921)

Smith, Nicola Jo-Anne, *Showcasing Globalisation? The Political Economy of the Irish Republic* (Manchester, 2005)

Taylor FitzSimon, Betsey and James H. Murphy (eds), *The Irish Revival Reappraised* (Dublin, 2004)

Townshend, Charles, *Political Violence in Ireland: Government and Resistance since 1848* (Oxford, 1983)

Venn, J. A., *The Foundations of Agricultural Economics* (Cambridge, 1933)

Whyte, J. H., *Church and State in Modern Ireland, 1923–79* (Dublin, 1980)

Wichert, Sabine, *Northern Ireland since 1945* (London, 1991)

DISSERTATIONS AND WEBSITES

Banta, Mary M., 'The red scare in the Irish Free State, 1929–37' (MA, UCD, 1982)

Browne, Brendan Mark, 'Trade boards in Northern Ireland, 1909–45' (PhD, QUB, 1989)

Coe, W., 'The economic history of the engineering industry in the north of Ireland' (PhD, QUB, 1961)

Collins, Peter Gerard, 'Belfast trades council, 1881–1921' (D.Phil, University of Ulster, 1988)

Cradden, Terence Gerard, 'Trade unionism and socialism in Northern Ireland, 1939–53' (PhD, Queen's University, Belfast, 1988)

D'Arcy, Fergus A., 'Skilled tradesmen in Dublin, 1800–50: A study of their opinions, activities, and organisations' (MA, UCD, 1968)

Doyle, M. G., 'The development of industrial organisation amongst skilled artisans in Ireland, 1780–1838' (M.Phil, University of Southampton, 1973)

Doyle, Macdara, 'The Republican Congress (a study in Irish radicalism)' (MA, UCD, 1988)

Finlay, Andrew, 'Trade unionism and sectarianism among Derry shirt workers' (PhD, University of London, 1989)

Girvin, Brian, 'Protectionism, economic development and independent Ireland, 1922–60' (PhD, UCC, 1986)

Harbinson, John Fitzsimons, 'A history of the Northern Ireland Labour Party, 1891–1949' (M.Sc.Econ, QUB, 1966)

McCabe, Conor, 'The Amalgamated Society of Railway Servants and the National Union of Railwaymen in Ireland, 1911–1923' (PhD, University of Ulster, 2006)

Morgan, Austen, 'Politics, the labour movement and the working class in Belfast, 1905–23' (PhD, QUB, 1978)

Norton, Christopher, 'Unionist politics, the Belfast shipyards and the Labour movement in the inter-war period' (D.Phil, University of Ulster, 1987)

O'Higgins, Rachel, 'Ireland and Chartism: A study of the influence of Irishmen and the Irish question on the Chartist Movement' (PhD, TCD, 1959)

O'Shea, Finbarr Joseph, 'Government and trade unions in Ireland, 1939–46: the formulation of labour legislation' (MA, UCC, 1988)

Takagami, Shin-ichi, 'The Fenians in Dublin, 1858–79' (PhD, TCD, 1990)

Waters, Martin J., 'W. P. Ryan and the Irish Ireland movement' (PhD, University of Connecticut, 1970)

ICTU, www.ictu.ie

Northern Ireland Labour Force Survey, www.esds.ac.uk/government/nilfs

Spanish Civil War, www.irelandscw.com

Index

—

abstentionism, 110–12, 119, 124, 126, 139, 141, 272
Act of Union, 5, 23
Adams, Gerry, 261, 285
AE (George Russell), 93–5
agricultural labourers, 7, 9, 26, 32, 34–5, 41–4, 57–8, 64, 68, 105, 121–3, 143, 154–5, 180, 232, 291
  in Northern Ireland, 189, 194
Agricultural Wages Boards, 105, 121, 143, 155, 196
Ahern, Bertie, 246, 258–61
Amalgamated Engineering Union, 207, 209, 212, 270, 278, 280–1
Amalgamated Society of Carpenters and Joiners, 48, 61, 192
Amalgamated Society of Engineers (ASE), 35, 39–40, 47, 59
Amalgamated Society of Railway Servants (ASRS), 53–4, 84
Amalgamated Transport and General Workers' Union (ATGWU), 147, 149–50, 164, 182, 198, 205, 209–10, 214, 216, 227, 242, 270, 278, 283–4
amalgamateds, 48, 52, 63, 86, 107, 128, 131, 138, 147, 159, 176, 183, 186, 193, 210, 226, 248, 279, 283, 291, 293, 295
  and rationalisation, 117, 146, 149, 152, 158
  and Spain, 145
  membership, 166, 173
Ancient Order of Hibernians, 14
Andrews, J. M., 195, 203, 205
Anglo-Irish Agreement, 241, 254, 272, 285
Anglo-Irish Treaty, 118, 120, 123–6, 129, 291–2

Anti-Partition League, 181, 213, 216
arbitration, 15, 17, 86, 116, 120, 204
Arch, Joseph, 44–5
Argus, 20
Armagh, 4, 25, 55, 197, 215
Ashe, Thomas, 95
Askwith, George, 92
Associated Society of Locomotive Engineers and Firemen, 150
Associated Trades of Dublin, 12
Attlee, Clement, 213–14
Attley, William, 242
Austin, Michael, 62, 66
Australia, 110
Austria, 152

Baird, James, 191–3
bakers, 8, 13, 19–20, 33, 52, 55, 64, 148, 163, 168, 196
Barnsley, 30
Barry, Tadhg, 115
Beattie, Jack, 198, 201, 204–7, 215
Belfast, 7, 12–13, 16, 18, 20, 32, 39–41, 48, 53–4, 68–9, 195–7, 261, 267, 271, 280–1
  combinations in, 2–3
  merchant bodies, 17
  General Trade Union in, 19
  Chartists in, 26–7
  new unionism in, 53–6, 58, 60
  and ITUC, 65
  Larkinism in, 77–82, 91
  workplace expulsions, 96, 191–3, 203, 279–80
  soviet, 108
Belfast Agreement, 261, 286–8

and CIU, 179, 183
and social services, 180, 219, 246
and corruption, 223, 236, 254, 256, 258, 260
Field, William, 57, 62, 64, 67
Fine Gael, 139, 145, 151, 166, 184, 220, 228,
  230–3, 235–6, 238–40, 243, 246–7, 249,
  252, 254–7, 259–60, 292, 294
fisheries, 115, 228
Fitt, Gerry, 207, 215, 267–8, 270–4
FitzGerald, Garret, 232, 236–41, 247, 252
Flanagan, Fr Matthew, 19
flax roughers, 37, 39, 90
flaxdressers, 19, 39
Foran, Tom, 98, 101, 119
Forward, 89
France, 4, 11, 28–9, 46, 50, 76, 97, 291
Franco, General Francisco, 138, 145, 152–3,
  202
Freeman's Journal, 20, 62
friendly societies, 3, 10, 83, 85
Friends of Ireland, 213–15
Friends of Soviet Russia, 134
Fullam, Bernard, 30

Gaelic Athletic Association, 88
Gaelic League, 49, 87, 95, 112
Gallacher, Willie, 137
Gallaher, Thomas, 78
Galway, 8, 13, 23, 26, 34, 142, 259
Galway, Mary, 56
Galway Union of Trades, 13
Geddis, Hugh, 210
Germany, 11, 97–8, 111, 122, 125, 137, 158, 202,
  206, 291
Getgood, Bob, 166
gilds, 1–3, 10–11, 21–2
Glasgow, 14, 23, 30, 37, 74, 89
Graham, William, 54
Grand National Consolidated Trades
  Union, 13
Gray, Malachy, 203
Greaves, Desmond, 206
Greens, 220, 245–6, 254, 260–3, 267, 294
Gregory, Tony, 238–9, 242
Griffith, Arthur, 93, 100

Guardian and Tradesman's Advocate, 20
Guinness's, 8

H Blocks, 220, 236, 238, 261
Halley, Victor, 206
Halligan, Brendan, 227
Hanna, Frank, 215
Hanna, John, 193
Hardie, Keir, 66, 72
Harp, 87
hatters, 11
Haughey, Charles J., 230, 236–9, 242, 244,
  246–7, 249, 253–6, 259
health, 9, 31, 38, 67, 153, 162, 179–81, 219, 232,
  234, 238, 240–1, 243, 246, 257, 261
  in Northern Ireland, 195, 203, 208–9, 211,
  276
Henderson, Sir James, 37
Hibernian Excelsior Labour League, 47
Hibernian Philanthropic Society, 24
Higgins, Joe, 260–1
Higgins, Michael D., 239–40, 258
Home Rule, 38, 42, 47, 53, 68–9, 71–3, 88–9,
  96–7, 117–18, 295
housing, 31–2, 37–8, 43, 45–6, 64, 68, 78, 139,
  143–5, 147, 179, 181, 185, 219, 228, 232,
  234, 238, 245
  in Northern Ireland, 195, 201, 203, 208,
  216, 265–6, 271
Housing of the Working Classes Act, 31
Howlin, Brendan, 257, 260
Hoxha, Enver, 229
Hughes, Séamus, 113
Hull, Billy, 281
Hume, John, 272–3, 285
Hungary, 175
hunger strikes, 114, 185, 207, 236, 241, 272,
  274, 285
Hynes, Owen, 177

Independent Labour Party (ILP), 68–9, 73,
  90, 118, 141, 191, 199, 206
Independent Labour Party (of Ireland), 90
Industrial Development Authority (IDA),
  223, 225, 247, 249